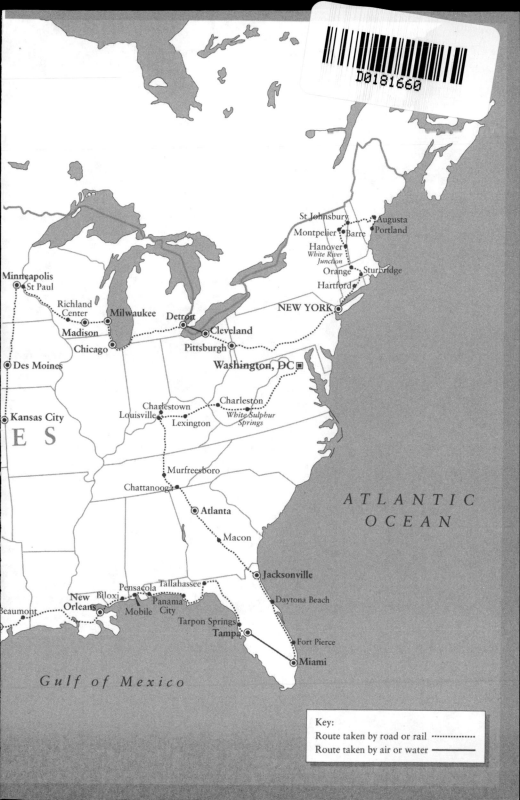

St Johnsbury

Augusta
Montpelier • Barre
Portland

Hanover
White River
Junction

Orange • Sturbridge

Hartford

NEW YORK

Minneapolis
St Paul

Richland
Center
Milwaukee Detroit
Madison

Cleveland

Chicago

Pittsburgh

Washington, DC

Des Moines

Charlestown Charleston

Louisville

Lexington White Sulphur
Springs

Kansas City

E S

Murfreesboro

Chattanooga

ATLANTIC

OCEAN

Atlanta

Macon

Jacksonville

Tallahassee

Pensacola Daytona Beach

New Biloxi Panama
Orleans City

Beaumont Mobile

Tarpon Springs

Tampa Fort Pierce

Miami

Gulf of Mexico

Key:
Route taken by road or rail ·············
Route taken by air or water ─────

Praise for *The American Home Front:*

"A remarkable record of his journey across America . . . Here are the antecedents of who we are now, grasped with a clarity and foresight that is all the more stunning for having been hidden away in a closet for nearly sixty years." Verlyn Klinkenburg, *Bookforum*

"This book sat forgotten in a closet in Cooke's Manhattan apartment until, shortly before his death, it was discovered by his secretary. . . . And if there's any decency left in this world, some grateful reader has sent that woman a couple dozen roses. . . . Cooke is clear-eyed, utterly free of cant, and with a healthy suspicion—if not contempt—about the tendency of journalists to issue sweeping proclamations. . . .Cooke captures a world brought to sudden stop, where every word, gesture, and action that does not take into account the immensity of collective grief seems obscene." —Charles Taylor, *Newsday*

"Cooke was one of our country's favorite Englishmen . . . In his time, probably the most widely read and heard chronicler of America . . . It is a story about the nation as a whole." —Art Chapman, *Fort Worth Star-Telegram*

"Reading his report is like unearthing a time capsule or finding a long-forgotten snapshot. At another level, his account is an interesting travelogue with perceptive commentary on practically the entire country." —Norman Rowlinson, *The Buffalo News*

"Even after all these years, and all those countless previous books about the wartime home front, Cooke has interesting things to tell us. . . . It is, in effect, a letter from the front lines, and the immediacy of it is real and valuable." —Jonathan Yardley, *The Washington Post*

"This is a work of admiration. It is hard to think of a better moment to remind a generation steeped in a facile anti-Americanism that without that country's gigantic moral and material support, Europe Britain included—might have found itself submerged for many a year under the Teutonic Taliban." —George Walden, *Bloomberg News*

"Revealing portrait . . . A vivid, endlessly interesting view of the home front." —*Kirkus Reviews*

"A deftly constructed time capsule." —*Library Journal*

"Something like reading a history and a historical document at the same time . . . Cooke's observation is keen. . . . The writing is, in the best sense of the word, polished—novelists should be as gifted as Cooke at capturing the beauties of nature—with striking, even elegant, metaphors and similes." —Roger K. Miller, *Pittsburgh Tribune-Review*

Alistair Cooke's American Journey 1942

Seattle
Tacoma
Spokane
Wallace
Missoula
Anaconda
Little Bighorn Battlefield National Monument
Sheridan
Casper
Cheyenne
Denver
Salina
Redding
Vallejo
San Francisco
Salinas
Monterey
Lone Pine — *Manzanar Japanese-American Internment Camp*
San Luis Obispo
Pasadena
Los Angeles
Santa Ana
San Diego
Phoenix
Tucson
Las Cruces
El Paso
Valentine
Alpine
Sanderson
Austin
San Antonio
Ho
UNITED STA

PACIFIC
OCEAN

The American
Home Front

The American
Home Front
1941–1942

Alistair Cooke

GROVE PRESS
New York

First published in 2006 in Great Britain by Allen Lane,
The Penguin Group, London

Frontispiece portrait of Alistair Cooke by
Ray Lee Jackson, early 1940s

All illustrations are copyright © the Estate of Alistair Cooke
except the frontispiece, where the copyright is untraced.

Printed in the United States of America

FIRST PAPERBACK EDITION

Library of Congress Cataloging-in-Publication Data

Cooke, Alistair, 1908–2005
    The American home front, 1941–1942 / Alistair Cooke.
      p. cm.
    Includes index.
    ISBN-10: 0-8021-4332-6
    ISBN-13: 978-0-8021-4332-7
    1. United States—Social life and customs—1918–1945. 2. United
States—Social conditions—1933–1945. 3. United States—History—1933–
1945. 4. World War, 1939–1945—United States. 5. Cooke, Alistair, 1908–
2005—Travel—United States. I. Title.

E169.C7495 2006
940.53'73—dc22   2005058860

Grove Press
an imprint of Grove/Atlantic, Inc.
841 Broadway
New York, NY 10003

Distributed by Publishers Group West

www.groveatlantic.com

07 08 09 10 11 12   10 9 8 7 6 5 4 3 2 1

Contents

Acknowledgements

The Estate of Alistair Cooke would like to thank those who have made the publication of this book possible.

Patti Yasek, who found the manuscript at the bottom of a crowded closet in Alistair Cooke's New York apartment, when clearing through other papers, just a few weeks before the author's death and was able, at the speed of light, to retype it ready for editing; Colin Webb, Mr Cooke's book editor and literary executor, who responded to his request to arrange this publication; George Perry, who provided the first assessment of the manuscript and recognized the considerable value of the content; Walton Rawls, who has edited, with distinction and understanding, the original manuscript ready for press; John Byrne Cooke, who has archived Mr Cooke's photographs and has expertly provided the images published in this volume together with notes that have informed the captions; Stuart Proffitt, publishing director of Penguin Press and Morgan Entrekin, the publisher, and Jamison Stoltz, the editor, at Grove Atlantic, who have enthusiastically encouraged us all.

Foreword

Wartime Britain, though few nowadays have a personal memory of those years, is fairly well etched into our collective imaginations: the silent blacked-out streets, the night skies lit by beams searching for bombers; the raucously cheerful Workers' Playtime lunch-hour concerts broadcast from a factory 'somewhere in the North'; the boxed gas masks on every scurrying shoulder; the nightly pip-pip-pip preceding BBC Radio bulletins, where the only consolation for the invariably bad news was that the unshaky baritone of the announcer Alvar Lidell suggested that somehow there would always be an England. There was a palpable sense of isolation, and then there was the marvellous moment when Mr Lidell at last had something good to relate. America had entered the war.

Nobody in Britain had much more than the foggiest notion then what the Americans might bring to the war, or indeed what Americans were really like: there was just a palimpsest of Franklin Roosevelt/Charlie Chaplin/John Steinbeck's Okies. Saul Steinberg's famous *New Yorker* cartoon was drawn years later but summed up the perspective then and now, the skyscrapers of Manhattan distended westwards to Hollywood and the Pacific, with something vague and dusty in between. The arrival in ration-book Britain of GIs armed with the temptations of nylon stockings and cartons of cigarettes excited more envy than curiosity; after all, they came in late last time, took the credit for whipping the Kaiser – didn't they? – and they were coming in late again.

What was happening in the vast mystery of America was, of course, of supreme importance and more than passing interest, as that new American citizen Alistair Cooke realized at the time. Having worked in London as the BBC's film critic, he had returned to America in 1937 in time to hear the drum rolls of war reaching Washington from the Far East; he was in the capital for Pearl Harbor on December 7, 1941; and then on the morning of February 27, 1942 he left the 'air of tobacco-choked energy that is the Washington odor of panic'. Forsaking the hot news from the capital, he set out on a prodigious journey to explore the country, south, west, north and east. On the first trip he drove much of the way in a car with five retreads, then in 1943 and 1944 he did the trip again by train and bus. Only a handful of Americans have seen the country like that, still less reflected on its diversities. There is nothing weird about the doctor he meets in St Louis who tells him, 'I never was west of Louisville nor east of Charleston, West Virginia.'

The reporter is long past deadline with his report, you may think. He did finish it in 1945, but everyone then wanted to forget and forge ahead with a brave new world, so he put his manuscript aside. A couple of weeks before he died, his secretary Patti Yasek was cleaning out a closet crammed with papers, and way at the back she came across two copies of a few hundred typed sheets headed *The Face of a Nation*. Cooke was thrilled at its rediscovery, and so will be his readers. Sixty years have enhanced its intrinsic interest, since it is at once a kaleidoscopic portrait of an America now vanished and a sketch of a 'fighting mad' nation spitting on its hands: very little has been written about that home front in comparison to the mountains of battlefront literature. Cooke was 33 when he began his journey, and while the manuscript lay unpublished for so many years what he learned clearly nourished the broadcasts about America he began in 1940, which became *Letter from America* in 1946 and continued until 2004.

In this book, so magically spirited from the past and into your hands, he is mostly concerned with a characterful people scattered on a panoramic landscape, emerging from one nightmare – the Great Depression – to enter another. He observes that a farm the size of Surrey is being transformed into a tank training ground, and that a lovely five-mile peach orchard in Georgia has been torn up for warplanes parked wingtip to wingtip like a plague of locusts, but he forbears to take us on exhausting excursions into factories. For that we can be grateful, but some perspective is necessary to appreciate what came out of all the encounters he records so well. We know now – and we have the word of Joe Stalin for it – that for all the sacrifices of our fighting men and women and the slog in our factories, the Allies would not have won the war in the West and the other war in the East without the way the American people, with amazing speed, created an arsenal no coalition of nations could come close to matching. Britain trebled its war output between 1940 and 1943, a ratio surpassing both Germany and Russia, who doubled theirs, though Japan excelled with a fourfold increase. And America? America stepped up its war output by a staggering twenty-five times. Instance: in 1942, a Liberty cargo ship of British design required 200 days to launch. Henry Kaiser, the dam builder from Spokane, had never before built a ship or airplane or handled steel, but he experimented with prefabrication and cut the time to 40 days. For his next trick he finished the *John Fitch* 24 hours after laying the keel. Without the fleets of Kaiser's ships carrying supplies, Britain would no doubt have starved.

Cooke once wrote that only by the wildest freak is a reporter actually present at a single accidental convulsion of history. This volume is not that. It is more of a pointillist painting than the flashbulb of a news report, but as it happens he was present at the convulsive opening moment of Japanese betrayal, and his writing throughout is informed by the qualities that drew so many millions to his current reporting. When he broadcast his account of the murder of Bobby Kennedy in 1968, for instance, we had read the news reports, heard the screams, had seen the fuzzy television pictures of Ethel Kennedy cradling her dying husband, but it was one of Cooke's most memorable *Letters from America*, for the same reasons that this volume emerges so vividly from the dust of sixty years. The detail was vivid but the language calm, as of someone struggling to keep hold of his sanity at the utter squalid futility of what he was seeing, the face of the bloodied Bobby Kennedy staring up from the kitchen floor 'like the stone face of a child's effigy on a cathedral tomb'.

Cooke's report moved us from contemplation of an external event to immersion in it. Because he is such a good observer, such a cool but evocative writer, and so schooled in the history of America and its personalities, he sees more than the camera or the casual onlooker, more even than those involved. On November 15, 1941, there landed at La

Guardia airport 'a small stocky man with spiky black hair, thick spectacles, and an excitable voice'. This was Saburo Kurusu, a Japanese diplomat and admirer of America who had married a girl from Chicago 'with the unthreatening name of Alice Little'. Now he was arriving to negotiate with America unknowingly in bad faith, unaware of the Pearl Harbor plot in which his masters had decided to 'act like a cunning dragon seemingly asleep'.

Kurusu had hardly unpacked in his Washington hotel before the Japanese battle fleet was ordered to sail for Hawaii, but Cooke records with characteristic honesty that he felt a touch ashamed at the rough questioning the press hounds gave the exhausted special envoy. Spiky Hair was so ragged from thirteen hours in the air he did not know whether he was standing or sitting: 'He would say one sentence up and the next one down.'

Cooke's deep affection for America and knowledge of its craggy cast of characters informs the sequel when Kurusu and the Japanese ambassador arrive late to deliver their terms to Secretary of State Cordell Hull, the silver-haired Tennessean, who knows what they do not – that the attack has begun. Hull's formal denunciation of Japan's 'infamous falsehoods and distortions' is on record; what Cooke adds, with a polite nod to the stenographer, is a surmise of what he really hissed – 'abusive idiom, deriving half from animal biology, half from the bible, of which the Tennessee mountaineers need never be ashamed . . . those who have seen and heard Mr Hull in indignation would hardly settle for a sentence from Gibbon.'

When Roosevelt arrived in Congress to indict the Japanese for their day of infamy, the world saw the lion-headed man standing strongly at the lectern. Thanks to a rare sense of delicacy in the press, and a patriotic scruple, the world did not see what Cooke records here. A weary, paralysed man enters the House of Representatives with infinite slowness, limping from side to side, holding the arm of his uniformed son. A gathering of people expecting to see the President of the United States 'see the Archangel Gabriel walk in instead. It is no less than the unexpected and dramatic revelation, very rarely made in public, of what a man can suffer and what he can grow to by reason of it.'

*

As late as the summer of 1940 you could drive across the American continent and never see a soldier. America's standing army was about the size of Sweden's. When the young reporter left Washington a few weeks after FDR's speech, the American leviathan was already beginning to stir. And not just with the manufacture of lethal instruments. Those dried eggs and powdered milk that the British fell on with grumbling appreciation came from Wisconsin's dairy farmers (so modern they had machines that recorded a cow's history and her horoscope). Before the war there were no egg-drying plants. In a jiffy, they had built a score. Within six months of Pearl Harbor they had shipped a hundred million cases of powdered milk, 600,000 of them to Britain. It is nice to read the dairy farmer's lament: 'The British take only the top grade of our dairy products, and the lesser grades are left on our hands.'

In West Virginia, Cooke sees women at work as hardwood carpenters, to the resentment of those few older men who have not been sucked into aviation and chemicals. He drives through the snow to the Greenbrier mountain resort hotel to find it is filled with 600 long-stay guests, German, Italian and Hungarian diplomats interned for the duration; the adjacent town is spooked by rumors of plots, murders and stabbings up there in the dark at the Greenbrier. In another town, 300 miles from the East Coast, 2,700 citizens have paid to learn how to look out for dive bombers in case Goering should ever find how to get them across the Atlantic in the first place. There are early warnings of more substantial threats to the American way of life. A small-town soda fountain carries the news: 'Regret. Out of Coca-Cola'. In Louisville he is reminded that 'in the interest of national defense' his morning coffee must be infused with no more than one spoon of sugar. The city swarms with men in uniform rehearsing manoeuvers for encircling the rouged and giggling teenage girls who have flooded in from the farmlands. In a café some soldiers from the North and West tease a Southern recruit about his distrust of Negroes.

Cooke is acutely aware that his patchwork experiences do not entitle him to make gravely definitive pronouncements on the state of race relations – or on wartime morale, profiteering, the emerging emancipation of women, the effects of mass migration, and the like. One of his agreeable traits as a reporter is candor. In the Kennedy shooting, he wrote: 'Everybody wanted to make space and air, but everybody also wanted to see the worst.' In this book, he discusses the dilemmas of the reporter/foreign correspondent who is expected to suggest omniscience on the basis of a conversation with a taxi driver from the train station and the barkeep at the hotel. 'We are a tribe of artful men who have learned over the years to stifle our doubts about our own capacity to observe.' So this writer of a foreword has to acknowledge that it is purely on the basis of random impressions of Alistair's random impressions that one notes his notes of pustules of anti-semitism. 'Gentile Clientele' says an engraved sign at a counter in a Miami Beach hotel. There can be no doubt, though, about the prevalence of prejudice against Blacks. In Kansas City the domestic helpers rushed into the small arms factories, their places in middle-class families taken by Negroes from the South. They would contrast the comfort of their new homes with the unyielding Jim Crow line down at the railroad station. There were showers for the white soldiers, none for their boys. The reporter records one terse comment: 'We're all right to shoot at, but not so good to keep clean.' Roaring Detroit, making jeeps, tanks, guns and bombers, was the scene of the worst hate riots in 1943, when the city tried to find somewhere to house the Negro labor from the South.

One stubs one's toe painfully from time to time on this long journey, but it remains exhilarating, sometimes inspiring. There are the Greek sponge divers of Tarpon Springs, Florida, who dive forty fathoms with a heavy stone, daily risking death from suffocation and sharks to fill an urgent war contract; few minorities in the country are so unprotestingly patriotic. There's the redoubtable 'Mr Higgins' in New Orleans, a big and profane lumber man disdained by the upper crust, who makes a point of hiring Negroes. He designed the first models of the PTs (patrol torpedo boats) snapped up by bootleggers of Prohibition days trying to escape the Coast Guard. Now under government contract, he's making the torpedo boats that will give the Japanese such trouble, tank lighters and landing barges. He turns out eight ships of one kind or another every ten days.

A striking feature of the reporter's journey across America and into its past is the anecdotal evidence of what men can achieve with security. A big cattle rancher in Wyoming tells him: 'Don't you forget it, son, folks around here are more dubious about Washington than the outcome of the war.' But throughout the journey, and especially in the wheatlands of the Western plains and the cotton country of the Deep South, it is clear that the framework of Franklin Roosevelt's New Deal gave America a running start. When the topsoil blew away in the early thirties and the Okies fled the darkened Dust Bowl in their jalopies for California, Roosevelt's Department of Agriculture nurtured a faith that grass could be made to grow again. Cooke reports that by 1941 the abandoned barren lands had grown enough grass for a whole new cattle industry: the Dust Bowl had become the Beef Bowl, a fact all too little known by the other industry of denouncing 'that man' in Washington. In the Deep South the Farm Security Administration kept alive at least a tenth of the nation's poorest farmers, and that paid dividends in the war. Cooke reports a conversation between a poor Negro sharecropper who thinks his land fit for nothing and a Mr McDowell, an FSA adviser. McDowell offers the sharecropper a loan if he will help to win the war by growing peanuts. The result is vintage Cooke:

'Peanuts!' he howls. 'The go'ment must sho' nuff be in te'ble shape.'

'Yes, we want peanuts for the fats and oils. And we need eggs, millions of 'em, to dry for the Army, and to send overseas. Can you raise some hens here, you think?' The Negro looks aghast. 'Mr McDowell, ef the go'ment wanna pay me for raisin' elephants, ah'll sho' make a powerful try!'

It is noticeable how much the war gets closer as the reporter moves west. He finds a subdued air when he arrives in Deming, New Mexico, ten days after the fall of Bataan and the surrender of all the Americans in the Philippines. The blinds are drawn, shops are closed. A hundred and fifty men from a town of only 2,000 were in an anti-tank unit of the New Mexico State Guard rushed into the battle zone as the Japanese smashed their way south. What can he say to the widows and mothers who come to see him, how shall he respond to their suspicions that there was something wrong with so many boys from one town dying 6,000 miles away for a place that some Senator, they read, had said should never have been defended anyway?

By the time he arrives in the booming port of San Diego the pace is

as frantic as the Klondike. He drops in on one of the busiest operators, a tattooist. The man testifies – what does one make of it? – that
in World War I, men came in and asked for a heart and their girl-
friend's name, but 'this time they seem to want . . . just the word
"mother"'. The backwater of Los Angeles throbs, proud of its trans-
formation into a war factory, 'endless worms of automobiles,
wriggling into the darkness, going into the night shift at Lockheed or
Vultee'. And going home, the reporter notes, to shacks, trailers, and
drab single rooms alien to the dream factory up the road.

Hollywood has its own problems. It is eager to make war movies
to boost home-front morale, but it's tricky in a strategic region very
jumpy about infiltration. It was all right to have Spanish loyalists and
Foreign Legionnaires fighting it out in the hills, but imaginary Japanese attacking a dummy airport near San Francisco would panic the
state. So the army tells the movie makers they have to stage their com-
bats miles away in Utah. It's their responsibility to alert the good
Mormons that the fleet of 'Japanese' bombers they will see being
destroyed by American fighters won't mean the war is over.

We can be grateful today that the young reporter was enterprising
and concerned enough to drive from Hollywood into the High Sierras. He wanted to assess a dark side of America at war. In March
1942, 70,000 American citizens in the West were cruelly removed
from their homes and businesses and shipped into ten desolate camps
in the High Sierras because they had Japanese mothers and fathers.
The day after Pearl Harbor, the FBI had swiftly arrested 2,000 male
Japanese 'bad risks'. This was a justified and entirely different process:
the 2,000 were entitled to review, the 70,000 citizens were not. When
they arrived at the camps in army trucks, bereft of their possessions,
they were dumped behind barbed wire and guards and had to make
do in windowless, heatless, tar-papered shacks.

Cooke is moved by the experience of visiting the Japanese-
Americans in a camp at Manzanar. They have put the ramshackle
place in order and run it themselves with elections, a newspaper of
their own and free speech. Somehow they have also kept their faith in
America. Driving away in a somber mood, he is 'none too proud' of
what his proudly adopted country has done: 'How slippery seemed

the solid abstractions we preach when you journey 6,000 miles and find democracy in a concentration camp.'

Alistair Cooke, sixty years on, retains his relevance: this is a time to reflect on the bad things that may be done in the name of a good cause.

Harold Evans
New York, November 2005

THE BRITISH BROADCASTING CORPORATION
International Building
630 Fifth Avenue
New York

TELEPHONE: CIRCLE 7-0656 CABLES: BROADCASTS, NEW YORK

To whom it may concern:

This is Mr. Alistair Cooke,
who has been travelling around
the United States on an official
commission from the British
Broadcasting Corporation in
London to collect material for
and write a series of pro-
grammes on the adaptation of
American life to the war, for
use in the Home and Empire
Services of the B.B.C.

This mission has the full knowledge and approval of
the War Department, the Navy Department and the F.B.I..
And this letter is to ask that on this final lap of
his tour, (namely through New England and through the
South), that he be shown all possible courtesy and
cooperation in his task of discovering and recording
material which will help him present to Britain the
part played in the war effort by the citizens of the
United States.

Lindsay Wellington.

Lindsay Wellington
North American Director.

October 5, 1942

Letter of introduction from the BBC used by Alistair Cooke during his travels in 1942

Alistair Cooke at the wheel of a Lincoln Zephyr he drove in the west in 1942

Alistair Cooke with two British flyers, Santa Monica, California, 1942

I

Introduction to a War

La Guardia Airport is more than just a place where New York-bound airplanes land. It is a City playground, and, as with all the best American games, it has a ritual to which everybody pays almost religious attention. At frequent intervals, a disembodied voice like God's or the *March of Time* recites from a loudspeaker and tells you what is coming in, and from where, and why, carrying how much tonnage of human flesh, after what storms and stresses, and how many miles. People who had gone out to the airport to smell the air, or to brood over the little red gasoline wagon that commutes among the bellies of every incoming plane, hear this voice begin to intone and bow their heads slightly. It is a custom as American as a Thanksgiving Day proclamation or the carols that are played in Grand Central Station at Christmas.

Lunch at the airport is paradise for children, who in the terrace restaurant are pacified with little paper airplanes and a special menu from which they may lisp their order to brusque but accommodating waiters, most of whom – just to scare up the proceedings a little more – sound and look like German spies masquerading as airport waiters in a Warner Brothers movie.

It is also a Parthenon of the living but anonymous great, of the tense little bureaucrats and correspondents in shabby overcoats, who may be seen at no cost to the visitors carrying their secrets and 'interpretations' in little black briefcases between the New World and Lisbon. Often you will see a little group of people waiting outside the immigration room who turn out to be practically a cheering squad for some arriving celebrity.

It was to this American place on Saturday, November 15, 1941, that a transcontinental plane brought into New York a small stocky man with spiky black hair, thick spectacles, and an excitable voice. As a special envoy from Japan, he was expected to know more than anybody else whether the situation in the Pacific was to come to a crisis or remain, in the diplomatic lingo, simply 'critical'. A month before, very few Americans even knew his name. It was Saburo Kurusu.

Pleasant news had flown on ahead of Mr Kurusu. He was said to be the most pro-American of all the close advisers of the Japanese government. A few years earlier he had been Japanese Consul in Chicago, and while there had married a girl with the unthreatening name of Alice Little. He had two daughters and a son. Mr Kurusu was very tired that Saturday, not only because he had flown 13,000 miles with hardly a break, but because he had had to miss his daughter's wedding and had left a brother on his deathbed. And because, as a national news magazine reflected, after flying 10,000 miles of ocean in a week, he had crossed the 'enormous room' of the American landscape and had looked down first on 'California's infinitely fertile farmlands, over forests of oil derricks', until by the time he reached New York 'he had glimpsed steel, oil, aircraft and other productive facilities that make pygmies of those which Japan possesses.'

Mr Kurusu was a few minutes too late for his plane connection to Washington, DC, and although most people at the airport seemed to know nothing about the visit from Japan, more newspapermen were on hand there than I'd ever seen before. We went after Mr Kurusu like a pack of Disney hounds and found him in a small, bare room containing one desk and one ashtray. He sat behind the small desk, and a very thin, sallow Japanese press attaché stood at his side looking tense and miserable, as if he already knew that Mr Kurusu was going to let the cat out of the bag – if that's what he had been carrying from Tokyo. Reporters sat or pressed on the edge of the desk, chiefly because the ones behind them were panting for air. All through the questioning that followed, the cameras were splashing light and puffs of smoke all over everybody, and Mr Kurusu was so ragged that he didn't know whether he was standing or sitting. He would say one sentence up and the next one down.

'What chances for peace?' somebody bellowed, and Mr Kurusu tried to make a wide gesture without hitting the two reporters who took his chair as he stood up. Still, the gesture collided with a waist-coat, and he grinned mechanically from ear to ear. The next instant he looked very gloomy and replied, 'A single man's effort is too small.' He looked around as if he were trying to memorize a slogan from a phrase-book. He said, with terrific pointlessness, 'We must all pull together.' He tried to sit down again, while the camera flashbulbs went off like rockets. His little secretary was wriggling at the back of the room saying something about 'rest'.

'Do the Japanese people feel that they want to fight?' Mr Kurusu was asked.

He blinked several times and looked down at the desk. He tried to answer, but he seemed to be so excruciatingly aware of his reputation for fluent English that he gave the impression of speaking the language in public for the first time. He panted, rephrased his reply, and managed to say, 'They feel just as your people feel, I suppose.' He fell back into the hurly-burly of notebooks, arms, legs, and smoldering cigarette butts.

Finally, his press attaché said aloud with a desperate smile, as if he were talking about the weather: 'I think Mr Kurusu very tired from long journey, yes?' He pronounced it as 'wrong journey', but nobody paid the slightest attention. The questions, the flashbulbs, the heavy breathing filled the air for another minute or so, and Mr Kurusu began to sigh and his hands were shaking. It was then that he scored his first touchdown. He pushed both hands out in an inadequate appeal and said, 'This country is the rland of rliberty, you call it. Please then, give me rliberty of silence.'

And we all mooched away, a touch ashamed.

It has become the habit of historical narrative in our day to assume that history is an inveterate believer in dramatic irony and throws out to sensitive people, and to journalists with a flair for the dramatic, hints and early symptoms of impending glory or disaster. By this tradition, which has been relentlessly cultivated by the movies, Washington, DC, on the evening of December 6, 1941, should have been a place of unexplained disquiet, or of almost criminal apathy. It was, of course, simply an evening like any other Saturday night in the early 1940s. Since the First World War, Saturday night has become the urgent festival of the Western World, the time when most people 'relax' into their favorite form of tension, whether it is the movies, or poker, or cut-rate shopping, or love, or alcohol, or, on a thousand neon-blinking Main Streets, a time to roam up and down and feel the pressure of other humans out for no harm and no good, and perhaps for a nightcap soda at the drugstore.

In Washington it was a raw, misty night, and poor weather for wandering abroad. At a Washington editor's home, half a dozen guests speculated on the pressing diplomatic topic of the moment: the imminent arrival of the new Soviet Ambassador, Maxim Litvinoff. As they sat around happy on highballs they wondered how the President would, on this delicate occasion, manage to synchronize his gifts for politics and drama. The tricky issue was how to reassure, among others, 20 million American Catholics who had been told continuously that Stalin was the Antichrist and would be, if Hitler fell, the succeeding overlord of the continent of Europe. We eventually settled for the prospect of Roosevelt's personal envoy to Russia, Harry Hopkins, standing at the prow of the welcoming Presidential yacht, the *Potomac*, bearing an icon or a fistful of candles from the Russian Orthodox Church. With just such pleasant whimsies could politically minded citizens of the United States reasonably beguile themselves on the evening before December 7th.

Similarly, the Sunday itself, which was later named 'a date which will live in infamy', was hardly recognizable as a December Sunday, and certainly not in Washington, where doing duty as a climate from November to April there's a clammy mist that covers the city like an unwrung dishcloth. This Sunday morning was balmy and crystal clear. It is conceivable that some Americans were thinking about Japan, for overnight the President had sent a personal note to Emperor Hirohito in hopes of learning that the Japanese troop concentrations in Indo-China were not aimed, as they clearly appeared to be, at Thailand. Yet the Japanese problem, if there was one, was still something to be left to editorial writers to balance on the one hand against the other hand. Some of them had other worries. Out in San Francisco, one of them was offering for the Sabbath meditations of his readers a prose sermon bearing the title, 'The Republican Party Must Save Itself'. Most of them, however, who only a few days earlier had been thrown

4

into verbal epilepsies over the cool remark of labor leader John L. Lewis that 'You can't mine coal with bayonets,' were now celebrating the success in the House of Representatives of a bill that outlawed all strikes on questions of union organization, banned all mass picketing, made a sixty-day cooling-off period compulsory before any sort of strike could be called, and further subjected the American labor movement to restraints unknown in its history.

Yet on such an impossibly sunny and tingling day Americans must have crawled out of bed and felt decently happy that the two news items carrying most space on the front pages were the romantic marriage of the King of the Belgians to a commoner and the timely reassurance of Secretary of the Navy Frank Knox that 'the American people may feel fully confident in their Navy. In my opinion, the loyalty, morale, and technical ability of the personnel are without superior. On any comparable basis, the United States Navy is second to none.' Any neurotic who might read these brave words with a twinge of doubt had only to thumb back to his Friday's copy of *Time* magazine and there read its first two printed sentences: 'Everything was ready. From Rangoon to Honolulu, every man was at battle stations.'

Isolated this way, these assurances suggest an anxiety that nobody – with the possible exception of the Japanese Ambassador and his stocky little guest, Mr Kurusu – had any reason to feel. The Vice-President of the United States was in New York. The Speaker of the House was out taking the air in his automobile. Washington correspondents were away for the weekend, abed, or like fathers everywhere throughout the land, were out in their preening Sunday innocence walking with their children. The psychological relation of the United States to Europe's war was still very much that of the charitable friend who leaves a hospital bouquet of lend-lease for the unhappy European psychopath having convulsions inside.

America was sleeping in after a week of work, or making dates for parties, climbing snow-laden fences in Minnesota and Vermont, flitting fruit flies in Florida, fishing in the mist off the rhododendron coast of Oregon, dishing up homemade ice cream and apple pie for the family dinner in Kansas, or pounding crab-cakes on the Eastern Shore of Maryland; chewing pecans on the high sidewalks of West

Texas, risking a newly earned pile of silver dollars on a high throw at faro in Nevada's saloons, taking grandmother to church in New Hampshire; slicking up for the Sunday whirl, away from horses and cattle in Cheyenne, away from oilfields in Houston, away from insurance in Hartford, Connecticut.

America was making arms and food for the British and feeling suddenly happy about Russia, but at home 130 million people were living their own lives, doing the American things: reading the football and hockey scores, taking out insurance, getting sinus trouble, sitting on the porch fanning themselves; thinking of turning in the old automobile for that 'snazzy' new model without the gear shift on the floor; thinking of having a baby, or getting a divorce, or going fishing, or staying home and listening to the Philharmonic; taking a nap; taking it easy, taking it easy everywhere.

The families who were privileged to feel the first sharp thrust of the awful event, the neat stab between the shoulder blades, were those who stayed in to listen to the Philharmonic, either because they are musical, or think it is a cultured thing to do, or who belong to the normal majority of families on this continent who use the radio as a background to living, a species of wallpaper, against which they eat and snore and quarrel. The Philharmonic was tuning up for the Shostakovich First Symphony when a flash was handed to a bewildered announcer. He read it, and at twenty-six minutes after two, a lot of people were left sitting in their homes not 'stunned' as the newspapers have it but fuzzily wondering where Pearl Harbor was. I remember sitting with my host in a living room in Washington. He was a man who knew a lot about the war fronts, and especially about how the battle lines that weave across oceans and continents come by their supplies. And as honestly as I can recall it, the moment the news came over, I tried to decide rapidly and guiltily if Pearl Harbor was where I thought it was. I don't know what my friend was thinking, for it took a half-minute or so for us to appreciate the miraculous impertinence of the Japanese in being – with or without aircraft carriers – anywhere so far from home. Possibly the most honest quoted reaction of a public man was the heartbreaking sentence of that same hellion John L. Lewis, who, caught at his home, asked, 'How the hell did they get there?' Isolationist Senator Gerald Nye had the misfortune to be addressing an America First meeting at Pittsburgh. Shortly before he started speaking he received a scribbled note about the Japanese attack. He fumbled and paused, said, 'I can't somehow believe this,' and then with a troubled brow continued warning his twitching audience against the American warmongers. For Isolationists especially, it must have been a lonely and terrifying day.

The moment the suspicion was confirmed that Pearl Harbor was indeed the main base of the Pacific fleet, yet where happily – as *Time* had reminded us – 'every man was at battle stations,' it was a matter of seconds before our minds began to move with reckless abandon. It was a minute or two later before the clammier thought struck us that this meant war. The bells on the news tickers in the National Press Club would be ringing like trotting deer, and things probably would be happening at the White House.

There was a discontinuous line of people staring through the White House railings. They were a handful of stragglers, families pausing, bums, and people who looked as if they had heard a noise and were not sure where it came from. As soon as a car swerved into the entrance, the police and Secret Service men swarmed around it with a zeal that was foreign to the White House custom. And whenever a car came out, the small gathering crowd craned as if the whole mystery was embodied in the somebody sitting in there.

The White House press room already had that air of tobacco-choked energy that is the Washington odor of panic. Reporters were passing notes to each other with the furtive haste of a bunch of bankers who have just heard their books are about to be subpoenaed. Very few people were writing but everybody was smoking, walking nervously around to see how they should adjust to their first world-shaking crisis. Two fat men were jammed into the only two telephone booths and would pass out a note to a waiting messenger or wave impatiently at the emergency electricians who were kneeling on coils of wire and plugging and unplugging attachments into the NBC microphone that Stephen Early, the President's press secretary, had let them set up. At agonizing intervals, Mr Early's secretary, a girl in a blue sweater, would tear into the press room like a nurse in a maternity ward where things are going badly. She would say, 'Mr Early will see you now.' We jostled into his room, and he announced that the

President was with the Secretary of War, the Secretary of the Navy, and the Army Chief of Staff, General George C. Marshall. There would be a Cabinet meeting at eight-thirty in the evening, and a half-hour later the Congressional leaders would meet with the President. The sudden summonses to the very bedside of the nation's woes came at such unpredictable intervals that after an hour or two, and even when the news was dull, it was too much for some people. After one such excursion a very pretty girl, correspondent for one of the news services, came into Mr Early's room when he was already half-way through reciting an announcement. She was ruddy and windblown and tugged at her trembling gloves. One glove wouldn't come off, and in frustration she pawed at her bag for a pencil and broke down. Coming after an hour or more of an emotional tension that hadn't yet resolved into any settled mood, it was one of those perfectly trite outbursts of emotion that have, like all good platitudes, to be felt to be understood. I bequeathed a newly sharpened press pencil to her and made for the door and my friend's car feeling inexplicably blithe. As we pulled into the driveway a long black limousine rolled down the center path and drove out ahead of us. It paused a second at the gateway, and there was a long glimpse of the single figure sitting in the back – the white hair, the aquiline composure, the glistening modest eye and the pink flushed neck of Secretary of State Cordell Hull. For once the crowd, which was now several hundred thick and blurred in the late-afternoon light, was not disappointed. Here was wise King Nestor himself, the people's spokesman, departing from a scene so classic in its staging that even the official reports cannot vulgarize it. It appeared that the Japanese envoys, having asked for an interview at two o'clock, had arrived twenty minutes late and thereupon were kept judiciously waiting by Mr Hull for exactly another twenty minutes. The moment they handed him their reply to the American proposals of November 26th, the news was flashed through to the White House of the attacks on Honolulu and Manila. Mr Hull is reported to have adjusted his black-ribboned pince-nez, read dispassionately through the document, and then turned on the two guests and replied: 'In all my fifty years of public service I have never seen a document that was more crowded with infamous falsehoods and distortions – infamous falsehoods and distortions on a scale so huge that I never imagined

until today that any government on this planet was capable of uttering them.'

This is magnificent, but I submit, with the greatest respect for the
State Department stenographer, that it is a pale, formal paraphrase of
the Secretary's words. Cordell Hull was bred in the mountains of
Tennessee, and there is nobody alive who in anger more nobly retraces
his spiritual ancestry. In spite of our acquaintance with the European
bloodbath, and even in the face of a decade of obscene persecutions,
ours is in some important ways a squeamish age. Mr Hull is capable
of an abusive idiom, deriving half from animal biology, half from the
Bible, of which the Tennessee mountaineers need never be ashamed.
Let us hope that Mr Kurusu, who is so adept at the American language, heard rolling periods that staggered him, and hissing, toothy
phrases he will never forget even if he may never know a place to
repeat them. This is no disparagement of the sentence that will go into
the historical record. But those who have seen and heard Mr Hull in
indignation would hardly settle for a sentence from Gibbon.

Monday was Franklin Roosevelt's day.

On the bridge leading to the Lincoln Memorial a single machine
gun had been mounted. Outside the State Department and the White
House were guards wearing tin hats. These little flourishes of the capital at war would have appeared pathetic to anybody who had lived
more than a day with Europe's war or seen anything of the uneasy
peace of the years that preceded it. But they were awesome signs to the
ordinary American civilian that the debates of the Interventionists and
the Isolationists had gone into history. For a decade before the war
began, even as late as the summer of 1940, it was the common experience to drive across the continent and never see a soldier. You had to
go out of your way in Texas or Kansas and look at an old fort from
the Indian wars to realize that the American people had had since
1865 no great cause to translate belligerent pride into the ubiquitous
symbols (in their own country) of uniforms, chevrons, and campaign
ribbons. The silent crowd at the Capitol, watching its breath smoke
up the winter sunlight, was as curious as any other crowd to recognize
arriving celebrities. But a European would remark how often people
nudged their neighbors to watch a sentry go by. They watched the

clockwork pacing of these few guards with a mild wonder, for it is a literal fact that few if any of them had ever seen a fixed bayonet. Seeing Americans stop to examine a soldier in drab Army overcoat and tin hat, it was not difficult to believe that when the German armies poured into Poland, the standing army of the United States was the size of the standing army of Sweden.

Shortly before noon a black limousine came out of the east gate of the White House and took its place in the middle of a convoy of protecting cars. The President was wearing a high silk hat and his voluminous naval cape. He looked oddly out of place in this magisterial costume, for what the small sober crowd saw whishing down Pennsylvania Avenue was a motorcade of squat little men in soft-brim hats, a load of cops, Secret Service men, G-men, special agents riding the running boards of the escorting automobiles and intently cocking riot guns. Somewhere in the middle was the big man in black, wanly saluting the crowd and creasing his coffee-colored face into a formal smile or two.

Up at the Capitol, it looked like a review of the Washington police department. They were three deep against the wire cable, put up at dawn to keep the crowd far away from the steps. Occasionally a photographer, a Congressman, or a reporter would approach the main entrance obliquely and get pounced on by every cop he tried to greet.

The main entrance of the Capitol had been barricaded. Every door had a soldier or a Marine, rigid with solemnity. As the Congressmen, clerks, reporters, diplomats, Army and Navy officials started to crowd the entrances, the guards clicked heels, rhythmically presented arms, and automatically blocked the way. It was another reminder that the ceremony of running a war was still an unfamiliar routine to the lucky generations of the United States.

Nobody's credentials were taken for granted. Every human who took off his hat and reached for his wallet was confronted by one of these flushed and solemn young soldiers, resolved to let no one pass who might possibly intend the most trivial harm to the Republic. There were compensations for the innocence of this bearing. Senators' wives and newly launched daughters, who had come up to the Capitol hoping to be whisked away under the old man's wing to a place of conspicuous comfort, were shooed aside and told that their word could not be honored. Of all misunderstood victims of the crisis, the most pathetic was a small man in black, with a cordial luminous face, stranded helplessly on the unfriendly side of a bayonet. He had failed to impress the guard and the Secret Service men that his credentials were genuine. They were taking no risks, after what happened yesterday, with anyone whose misfortune was an Oriental face. And not surprisingly this man had an Oriental face, for he was Dr Hu Shih, Ambassador from the nation that already had sustained four dragging years of war against the day-old enemy of the United States. Senator Tom Connally of Texas eventually swore to the guards that Dr Hu was Dr Hu, and the bayonet was lifted.

The floor of the House was very different from its usual appearance as a public auction on a slack day. The Congressmen who were on their feet were talking earnestly with friends, prodding waistcoats, sharing convictions for once instead of gossip. Many of them had on their best suits, and this seemed to drain away their local color, de-characterizing them and giving them an appearance of meek respectability, like mourners at a family funeral. The mood was heightened by the dozen or more little children wriggling happily on their fathers' laps, being shushed without any success into an awareness of dignity and right morals. While the Democrats sat magnanimously purring, a few of the Republican leaders consulted with each other across the floor, assenting warmly with anybody who had, at this late hour, a contribution to make to the party's stock, which it was easy to see was precariously low. Meanwhile the galleries, which had started to fill up after eleven o'clock, were taking on the astigmatic blur that radiates from a mob sitting in a hothouse. At five minutes after noon, Speaker of the House Sam Rayburn sounded the heavier of the two gavels he used and tried to bring the House to order. His bald dome swiveled uneasily from side to side as he took in the sight of the stewing galleries and the sound of protesting newspapermen who found their places taken by early risers and professional sightseers. 'Unauthorized persons' were ordered to leave; the less-hardened gatecrashers looked around uneasily and yielded their seats to newspapermen and a few Army and Navy officials sidling in late. We all composed ourselves, the floor was cleared, the coughers cleared their throats. At seventeen minutes after twelve, the door leading to the central aisle opened, and the Senate came in. First, walking slowly on the arm of Vice-President Henry Wallace, was the tiny, ancient Carter Glass of Virginia, who had come here many times unattended to demand a positive and independent American stand against the Third Reich and all its works. Not far behind was Senator Gerald Nye who overnight had evidently changed his mind about the sinister fiction of a Japanese attack. Arm-in-arm came Democratic and Republican leaders of the Senate and the House, a gesture that apparently embarrassed nobody. Once the Senate was seated, eight bright spotlights from the back of the Chamber shone suddenly at the Speaker's dais. The central door swung open again and the nine not so old men of the Supreme Court padded down in their black gowns. The Cabinet followed. With almost every known face in the United States on hand, it seemed inevitable and right that the House doors should close finally on the Secretary of State, the nation's sad grandfather, who took his seat on the middle aisle, crossed his long legs, composed his hands across them, and tilted his magnificent head toward the dais.

The Speaker gave a single stroke with his hammer and announced, 'The President of the United States!' There was a flurry of bodies and faces at the side door, the House rose and started to applaud, and then began one of the timeless ceremonies that belonged only to the public appearance of Franklin Roosevelt.

There was in the United States a tradition of silence about the physical affliction of President Roosevelt, an implication that it would be tasteless ever to mention the misfortune that galvanized his energies, transformed his personality and therefore the subsequent history of the United States. But this would be a prim chronicle indeed if it did not record the single most compelling fact about Roosevelt, wherever he appeared. Foreigners had heard, of course, one way or another that the President was paralyzed. But the knowledge was filed away, in the foreign and domestic imagination, as an incidental item of interest, not the first thing that springs to mind when the subject is brought up. Wherever the President went to pay a first visit, the energetic hosts overlooked nothing but the necessity, about which they always had to be reminded, of laying ramps in every public and private building where stairs have to be climbed. The heroes of this exercise in good manners would hardly be guessed by visiting Europeans, who discover curiosity and energy in the American press but assume that human delicacy must be looked for elsewhere. Yet I have never heard of a professional ethic so scrupulously observed as that of all American news and newsreel photographers never to show Roosevelt in motion or in any position before he was comfortably settled to be interviewed, or to make a speech or a journey. The image of Roosevelt that the world knows is therefore the fruit of this omission. It is the big-headed man with the enormous shoulders, the tolerant paternal smile, the confident hands grasping the lectern, the uninhibited laugh or grimace.

This was not the man who appeared at the side door leading directly into the House of Representatives. As the members came to their feet, they saw first James Roosevelt in the blue uniform of the Marines. He came in at a funeral pace, and on his arm was his father, a bulky man in morning clothes with a weary face. With infinite slowness, limping from side to side, Roosevelt came up the ramp to the dais, one arm locked in his son's, the other hand feeling every inch of the long sloping rail. At this moment, whenever and wherever it occurred, there was a suspension of the emotional mood that would normally receive so distinguished a man. Crowds cued to shriek and wave things were suddenly touched with something very like humility. Many times, at a university commencement, at party conventions, and at dinners when the President has appeared, I have seen the sudden frustration of all the easy joviality, the sentimental tear even of the willingness to do the decent thing by a gentleman and a scholar, which is a response of what we call breeding and you would think too deep to freeze. The faces of gentility, of innocence, and of corruption are equally exposed, and what you have is a gathering of people who, expecting the President of the United States, see the Archangel Gabriel walk in instead. It is no less than the unexpected and dramatic revelation, very rarely made public, of what a man can suffer and what he can grow to by reason of it.

But on the morning of the 8th of December, the tabloid cliché that he was a symbol of his country was a visible fact. All the fussy rhetoric about Japanese 'treachery' and 'the stab in the back' (which if they had been describing what our side had done would have been called 'superb military foresight' and a 'masterstroke of timing') came to life in the sight of the President coming gradually up the ramp.

Like all the most revealing passages in human relations, however, the emotion is of a moment's duration. The mere fact of perceiving it isolates it into an unreality that is outside its human context. By the time the President was on the dais, waving his arm, opening his loose-leaf notebook, and adjusting his eyeglasses – which he always did as if they were a new and clumsy invention – the vision had vanished. The House and galleries were seated again, were clearing their throats, were back to the formal view of a great occasion. Once he was at the dais, Roosevelt expanded again into the vivid unreality of the image the newsreels know. Yet for a moment we had seen him as the hurt psyche of a nation. Before we heard his confident tenor and listened to the sincere automatic applause, we saw him walk and thought of the wounded battleships slumped over in Pearl Harbor.

It was a short speech, just ten minutes, and it told the melancholy news as forcefully as it needed to be told: 'I regret to tell you that very many American lives have been lost . . . Yesterday the Japanese government also launched an attack against Malaya. Last night, Japanese forces attacked Hong Kong. Last night, Japanese forces attacked Guam. Last night, Japanese forces attacked the Philippine Islands. Last night, the Japanese attacked Wake Island. And this morning, the Japanese attacked Midway Island . . . I ask that the Congress declare that, since the unprovoked and dastardly attack by Japan on Sunday, December 7th, 1941, a state of war *has* existed between the United States and the Japanese Empire.'

Cordell Hull broke the trance, during which his stenciled fingers had been tilted motionless tip to tip. He uncrossed his lean legs, and the Speaker's gavel dropped again. The Joint Session was dissolved. Hull led out the Cabinet, then went the Supreme Court, the foreign diplomatic corps, the Army and Navy chiefs, with little Admiral Harold Stark pattering out last of all, his apple face crinkly and flushed behind his shining glasses. The long window panes of the Chamber streamed with perspiration. The eight great spotlights glowed for a second and went out. The House unbuttoned its collar. With a large audience of strangers still keeping their seats, it was up to the House to put on its own impressive ceremony. But the rest was tired anticlimax. You could see the Congressional leaders who would be called upon to have their say smoothing out sheets of typescript or moving their lips in a dogged rhythm as they tried to memorize from notes their own hopes for posterity. Before the routine was under way, one Representative stood up and suggested, 'This is the time for action,' evidently forgetting that in a democratic legislature every man is allowed his tongue, however inept or sentimental the things he may say with it. So this Congressional leader and that one came to his feet, jutted out his lower lip, and as the old original idiom had it, 'spoke for Buncombe'. The Democrats would wipe their mouths, or stick their thumbs in the armholes of their waistcoats, and moan impatiently, 'Vote! Vote!' From time to time in the back row a thin white-haired woman in a brown dress would stand up and press her nails together. Without any sign of energy or hope, this first female Representative, Jeanette Rankin, kept on trying to make an objection. Rayburn, whenever he looked her way, seemed to be staring through her. A Representative from Michigan turned his mouth over his shoulder and yelled, 'Sit down, sister.' She stayed up there, however, vainly waving her hand for recognition. But at three minutes after one o'clock, Speaker Rayburn suspended the rules and ordered the roll call. The clerk laid down the long list on his desk and prepared for his hour of triumph. And in a rolling baritone he called them, all the sons of the fleeing emigrants from Europe, who had turned their families' backs on war and now were being asked to make it, 'Allen of Illinois, Allen of Louisiana, Anderson of Minnesota, Anderson of California, Anderson of New Mexico, Andresen of Minnesota' – like an Old Testament prophet calling sinners to repentance. Their 'Ayes' hit the air at every pitch and tone from a squeak to a grunt, punctuated sternly by Rankin's lone 'Nay'. But always they were translated into the soothing grandeur of the clerk's baritone, with its falling cadence and its air of infinite sympathy and tenderness for the prodigals hotfooting it home: Sabath, Sacks, Sanders, Sasscer, Satterfield, Sauthoff, Scanlon, Schaefer of Michigan . . . Van Zandt, Vincent of Kentucky, Vinson of Georgia, Voorhis of California, Vorys of Ohio, Vreeland, Wadsworth, Walter, Ward, Wasielewski, Weaver, Weiss, Welch, Wene, West, Wheat . . . Young, Youngdahl, Zimmerman.

By the next day, most of America had had its baptism of the

strategy of terror. The first unbelievable warning was thumped out, to the accompaniment of insistent bells, on the AP tickers in Washington. An unknown plane had been sighted flying east toward Montauk Point, on Long Island, which rarely in its stormy history had seen anything fly through the air more threatening than a hooked swordfish. In the quiet Colonial towns of Eastern Long Island, the children were sent home from school. In New York, every plane was grounded at La Guardia field. The air wardens went on duty, and the police and fire sirens screamed down Manhattan's foolish canyons. Up in Boston the highways were cleared for thirty miles around and the hospitals were warned to stand by for an emergency. In Washington, black shades were going up at the White House. The floodlight on the Capitol dome was turned off for the duration. As the late-afternoon lights were dimmed, a low unrecognizable whine started up at the corner of Fourteenth Street and Pennsylvania Avenue. It climbed high, dithered a while, slid, and climbed again. To a million ears in Washington it could mean only one thing. It was, after all of the fury and spittle of the 1930s, the unbelievable voice of the devil who, the Isolationists always had said, simply could never be heard in America, because for one thing he spoke a European dialect and for another had no possible means of crossing the Atlantic.

In the offices of the British Supply Council, a secretary asked me, a visiting stranger, if there was anything she could do for me. There was nothing. We sat there listening to the universal song of the siren, thinking – as I suppose the native inhabitants of Madrid and London and Chungking had thought long before us – of our children and the few people we loved. 'Please God, don't let it happen to me and mine' is about the gist of the individual's prayer on such occasions, whether you are a storekeeper in Liverpool, a housewife in Boston, a brothel-keeper in Madrid, or – I imagine – a dictator in Berchtesgaden.

We turned to our inseparable daily drug, the radio. We twirled the dial and heard a sentence more bizarre than any that dramatist Orson Welles had used to terrorize a continent. It was an announcer smoothly saying, 'We now take you to news of the Far Eastern battle zone. Go ahead, San Francisco.' Even the West Coast had betrayed us, the traditional country for escape was blacking out too. There was suddenly no place to go to get away from it all. Only a few days earlier Barbara Hutton, the richest girl in the world, had been on the point of leaving for her dream palace in Hawaii, but the island that paunchy executives so longingly associated with pineapples and undulant maidens was smoking with Japanese bombs, and Sweet Leilani was just another air-raid warden. We heard too that the West Coast had had its second alert. Even Hollywood, the nonpolitical capital of the world, was putting blinkers on the klieg lights of its ivory tower.

The fact that no enemy planes were ever identified off either coast, and that the sirens in Washington sang for a regulation fire, did not come out till a few hours later. It made no difference to the way we felt. It was idle for Isolationists to assert days later, as they had positively computed long before, that no aerial attack on this continent would or could be made. Perhaps they were right. But we had gone through the emotions of the thing itself, and sitting there in Washington, on the Tuesday afternoon after Pearl Harbor, not many people hearing the whine outside could laugh with a light heart and refuse to believe it. The only man I saw whose spirit was cheered was an Englishman just arrived from London. He put his head in at a door and smiled. 'Sounds just like home,' he said. There was another man, a friend of mine who was a newspaperman and a fierce Isolationist. Only the previous Saturday he had been bemoaning to me the unnatural idiocy of an Administration that could believe there was any possible threat to the American continent either in the Atlantic or the Pacific. He walked over to the window and watched the traffic pulling over to the curb. All the fire had gone from his temper, and he looked unhappy and resentful. He came back and said, 'If I saw Marshal Goering going into the White House, goddamn it I'd believe my eyes.'

Although the news tickers told us an hour or two later there was no need to feel that way, we felt that way. It was as low a point as American morale could ever fear to touch.

2

A Passport to the People

During the next decade or so, much rousing stuff will be written about the way the Second World War came to Washington, DC, how its government drones came to regard their clerking chores as a holy office, how the War and Navy Departments, after three-quarters of a century of continental peace, miraculously assumed the cloak of Mars and ordered vast strategies with the dispatch of Julius Caesar. Mobilization Day was here, and it had been the point of M-Day to help the United States relive in a streamlined way the murderous calm of Prussian strategist Carl von Clausewitz, who being awakened to receive the news that the war was on, mumbled 'G2-file number 8375' and then turned over to catch the rest of his sleep. It may turn out in the long view that this is what America achieved. But as one who can enjoy only the distorted view of a victim is obliged to report, once the calamity of Pearl Harbor had registered, Washington most resembled that crisis in the old Keystone comedies when the resting firemen, grown amiable on undisturbed sessions of beer and games of pinochle, are electrified by the alarm and, diving headlong down the greasy pole, start to clomp importantly in every part of town. Washington suddenly became a capital city where everybody knew the grand strategy of the war but nobody knew whether his job on Monday would be the one he left on Saturday. Men who had worn a blue suit and were formerly known as secretaries or executive assistants appeared in a few weeks wearing 'checkroom tags' in their buttonholes and bearing the title of Coordinator. Whatever operating crew the engineers of the M-Day plan had figured on, they had possibly overlooked the huge staff of government hacks who had grown in a decade to be most of the resident population of Washington. In 1917, the city had 38,000 government workers. In February 1942, it had close to a quarter-million. And in spite of the pawky fun that has been made of this bureaucracy, it was the Secretariat of America's war and might be led or disciplined but could not be dissolved.

Perhaps in postwar memoirs, the legions of the unfooled, those Americans determined not to be taken in even by human nature, will read with admiration of the quiet and shrewd work of many a government department with a funny name. We shall marvel at the political and economic crises that were caught and strangled anonymously by the President's 'Kitchen Cabinet'. When all the play is over, we may know from the workings of Department of Agriculture economics why and how, after many a blunder, the American food crop of 1942 was to be the most abundant in history. Considering the tough infantile pride of both Americans and Britons whenever they are called on to compare each other's ways and institutions, we may learn how Americans as native as Carl Sandburg or Bing Crosby met several times a week with Britons as fundamentally British as Anthony Eden or J. B. Priestley and somehow managed Lend-Lease, or Combined Operations, with a success in equal responsibility unknown in the economic or military history of two modern nations.

But after the agony of Pearl Harbor, not many people in Washington, and fewer still outside, could know enough about these things to take courage from them. They were looking first for somebody to blame. And not since the return of crews from the defeated Armada to their native Spain have Navy men anywhere been so continuously under the scrutiny of the evil eye. At his press conference on the first Tuesday after Pearl Harbor, the President listened sympathetically while a reporter complained that the service departments were in such a tizzy of importance that it took four hours to release a communiqué of five or six sentences. The President asked for a little charity. After all, he said, those boys are in a spot. 'We're in a spot, too,' the newsman replied. 'I know it,' said the President, 'but you don't have somebody introduced to you every few minutes who looks at you and wonders – were *you* the leak?'

It was natural enough that visitors to Washington made bitter fun over the machinery of war administration as it creaked into high gear. In the first month or two, what Americans wanted, as would any people newly at war, was to feel some certain pride in their Army and Navy. But at the end of February, besides instances of individual bravery and the tireless stand on Midway and Bataan, there were not many places to go for a boast. The Japanese, whose audacity on the 7th of December had been diagnosed by most Americans as an itch for suicide, had in less than three months conquered Thailand and Malaya and were pouring through Burma. Hong Kong and Singapore had surrendered to them. They were masters of the Philippines, of Guam and Wake. They were entrenched in the Netherlands Indies in Sumatra and Sarawak and Celebes. They had captured Bali and isolated Allied reinforcements. They had submarines scouring the Indian Ocean from the newly captured base at Penang and were sustaining an aerial offensive over a 4,500-mile sweep between Southern Burma and the island of New Britain. If the cities of the Eastern Seaboard were too far from these disasters to feel their confidence shaken, there was a melancholy tune being picked up every night in the Navy Department from the wireless messages of oil tankers going down off the coasts of New Jersey, Delaware, and the Carolinas.

In the downpour of these humiliations, many publicists and politicians hastened to speak for the American people and reassure them that even if at the moment they looked bedraggled, they were really fighting mad and would stay so until the war was won. But this was a hangover from the literature of advertising, and especially from the sumptuous publicity that had been laid on to the American defense program like the fetching armor of a bride. For almost three years, ever since the first British and French orders had come in, and the first British investments in America had been used to build factories in the United States and Canada, the American people had been hypnotized by accounts of their own technical genius. They had been promised feats in the mass production of tanks, planes, and guns that would make the well-meaning craftsmen of Europe lay down their arms in shame. The plea of Premier Reynaud, on the eve of the Fall of France, for clouds of planes from America, which did not then even exist in blueprints, was only the most pitiful example of a misconception held everywhere, and not least by Americans. It was the disparity between American power, in terms of the tried weapons of modern war, and the American potential. It's true to say, I think, that not many people tried

– except from motives of fear – to falsify the picture of what American production could do. But when a powerful nation, proud of its technical skills and at all times susceptible to moral crusades, is told from the other side of the world that its machines and its moral support are being counted on, and when that nation is gallingly listed as a neutral, the temptation to win the war for the side you favor is as irresistible as the conviction of a cheerleader that the game is really won or lost by organized shouting. When the sympathies of the world's chief creditor nation are strongly felt, and when it is not spilling blood, then it must believe for its own self-respect that its machines are doing the trick. Long before the American declarations of war, it had become the habit of newspaper headline writers to comb through the day's news for any identification of an American plane, tank, or gun. Thus British raids on Germany were reported under the headline 'American Bombers Blast Ruhr', with nobody minding very much if the reader mistook the word 'bombers' to mean human beings. Once the American war was on, then the magazines bloomed with luscious three-color charts and graphs showing American production spiral, starting down with everybody else's but zooming by the end of the current year, at latest, into the stratosphere. Nobody heard much how the British and Russians felt about the weapons they'd had and how they stood up in mechanized warfare. We here in the United States studied our own production story and assumed the victory.

This frustration – pride in the so-bulging muscles of our arms and impatience that we somehow weren't landing any considerable blows – was the mood of most cities of the Eastern Seaboard in the late winter of 1941–42. Washington especially was a trying city to live out the war in because it was the capital of American activism, an activism that so far had seemed to pay off so little.

Even when you have once made this reflection, Washington is a government town first and last. It has no separate life as a city to lose yourself in. If, as somebody said, the new American frontier is government buildings, then the new pioneer is the the government worker, with an undramatic future. It was a boom-town based on a deep gusher of memoranda, and its prospectors, crowding the hotels and boardinghouses from every city across the continent, came panning for contracts.

To a correspondent who wanted faithfully to report what the war was doing to America, life in Washington in those days was an ecstasy of frustration. Here, everybody admitted, was the heart and hive of the war effort. All the hinging decisions of the war were supposed to be on file here, the confidential dope, the brainwaves that sent the correct impulses to a garrison in Iceland and to a Marine on Midway. But once you have recovered from the awe of this idea, you tend to pick up some pretty guileless assumptions. You assume that the Washington office of the junior Senator from New Mexico is the essence of New Mexico, bottled and sent to Washington for reference and tasting. Arguments about trucking tariffs over a state border you get to think of as a feud between two lobbies or two Congressmen from those states. You learned, without bothering to check firsthand, a sort of catechism of the American war effort and its issues. Only when you leave Washington do you begin to suspect that you already have picked up a patter as slick and monotonous as a vaudeville comedian's routine. In the bar of the Press Club you nod your head benevolently over what you all take to be one of the unsolved problems of government, namely how to bring the war home with equal force to 130 million Americans living, regrettably, faraway from Washington. If you ever think of these people, it is of stubborn provincials staring at a government form they do not want to sign. You listen to the President plead for 'equality of sacrifice' and you agree that clerks and storekeepers ought to match with war bonds the discomfort and loneliness of their sons in the Philippines. But only when you have an hour alone and recall the living map of America do you wonder how the word 'sacrifice' can be made to mean the same thing for a farmer in Iowa whose land is rolling and full of food, and a farmer in Vermont who before he could plant the seed of a decent meal must have spent days digging up rocks and glacial stones. Or how the farmers of Southwestern Kansas whose farms blew away in the dust-storms can feel that they have a stake in anything but a few blades of grass that will hold the soil. If these thoughts cross your mind, you then remember that you are sitting in the shadow of the Department of Agriculture, which, after all, has statistics on these distressing hardships. You dismiss your misgivings as sentimental fantasies and go down to the State Department, there to listen to news of statecraft that purges away, by the hypnosis of its own wondrous vocabulary, all gnawing concerns over men and women and four-letter words.

Yet to one who has known Ely, Nevada, or Alpine, Texas, better than Washington, DC, these thoughts will return. Perhaps, you dare to think, the war was changing the people and the landscape of America in ways that Washington undoubtedly knew, but only as the curve of a graph. There were things that those 130 million exiles from the nation's capital conceivably felt and knew about the war that no Washington correspondent could possibly read into a handout or throw-off from an imagination however lively.

It was with these misgivings, and with a little good hope springing from a hundred memories of the sights and sounds of the American landscape, that at the end of February, 1942, I set out to look for some of these things. I didn't know what I was going to look for, and was fairly untroubled by this aimlessness. When you go to look for something in a town you usually find it, and of all forms of pretentious journalism the hollowest is the feature story written by a man who knows beforehand the angle and the moral he is going to point out. Indeed, when I had doubts about my ignorance of America (and without wishing to be coy, I can honestly report that after the first three or four tours of the United States these doubts sometimes are overwhelming), I would read stories that undertook to tell you how Chicago 'felt' about the war, or what was the spirit of the population of the South or Midwest, or of the workers in the California aircraft plants. These assignments are innocently thought to contribute to popular morale. One is asked for color stories about places that perhaps have only the wrong sort of color to offer a nation at war: or for rousing accounts of the patriotism of people one had never known at peace. It seems there are few editors alive who will hesitate to point out to the departing reporter the significance of places and people neither he nor you have ever seen. It is one of the routine dishonesties of people with a popular cause.

The reading of this confident drivel, which is another of the whelps gotten by Publicity on journalism, restored me, however, to a trust in unaided observation. Since it is impossible for one person to know the enormous variety of scientific techniques that can alone describe industrial production for war, I thought such a report could safely be left to *Fortune* and the fifteenth edition of the *Encyclopedia Britannica*. I intended to see what the war had done to people, to the towns I might go through, to some jobs and crops, to stretches of landscape I loved and had seen at peace; and to let the significance fall where it might.

I had been warned that to see America at war, I would need a wad of credentials sufficient for a paper chase from coast to coast. I did not believe this, because one of the easy charms of America at peace has always been the accessibility of people and places you wanted to know about. If you came to a town bearing an odd name or plying an industry that interested you, all you had to do was go to the Chamber of Commerce or knock on the factory gate, and they would bring the town on over for you. At the War Department they told me darkly about some visiting British correspondents who had proceeded on this knowledge and been taken through bomber plants by the mere act of flashing a (borrowed) membership card in the National Press Club. Their tracks had been charted by the Public Relations bureau of the War Department as sedulously as those of any dinosaur. And anybody who came afterward was clearly a suspicious character. The disposition to regard visiting Britons as enemy aliens is, of course, a shrewd instinct, and much healthy American tradition lies back of it. As a correspondent for a British newspaper, I determined therefore to woo the War and Navy Departments.

On my first visit to the War Department, I was told by a junior officer the room number of the public relations officer I had to see. I followed the directions and soon found the door with that number. Unfortunately the forbidding word 'Women' was printed plainly on it, and I couldn't believe that even in our decadent plutodemocracy public relations would gain anything from being conducted so surprisingly.

This was getting me nowhere that I wanted to go. And it was later on this happy day that I had the luck to throw myself, at a friend's recommendation, on the mercy of one Captain Fox of the British Supply Mission. Having first told me that the War Department required eight copies of every application you filed to visit a war plant, he at once offered to do this chore for me. Several months later I figured he must have spent the better part of the spring doing the 'octupulating' for my casual visits. This tiny Newfoundlander, a dapper, mustachioed man with a skeptical blue eye and a chin against which transatlantic brusqueness broke as foolishly as the Pacific against the rocks of Monterey, simply had the knack of public relations, in the sense that he found out what you wanted to do, took the risk of your honesty, and would go to bat for you with the people who could help. Either from instinct or providential accident, he took me at once to the War Department and led me before a mild-eyed Colonel with an Irish prefix to his name. The Colonel duly recounted the now historic finagling of the visiting British correspondents, who it should be said in fairness were 'hot Britons'. A hot Briton may be defined as one sent over on a special mission to the United States chiefly because he has never visited the country before. The Colonel implied as tactfully as possible that he would do his best to try not to hold my breeding against me. But he couldn't promise that all the factories I approached would let me in, or that public relations officers would be willing to transmit to me what they call 'restricted information'. At an unarranged signal from the sitting Fox, I said as meekly as an aquiline face will allow that I would go only where the Army wanted me to go, write what they would permit, and that I could keep an Army secret at least as well as some officer friends with a buzz on. He seemed to accept this pleasantly and leaned forward to apologize for the restrictions. 'You see, we are instructed that every citizen of a foreign country – including British subjects . . .'

I told him they did right to treat the British that way, and that as an American I should expect the same trouble in England. His face opened up like a September oyster. I was an American citizen, then? *Alors*, I was an American citizen. The Colonel rose, gave rapid orders to two of his Lieutenants, who promptly opened drawers and walked around their desks twice in my honor. Excepting a slight brush with a Colonel in Pasadena, this was the last time I ever experienced a moment of tension with the Army. The Colonel asked me where I lived, thought kindly of New York, inquired if I was married and had propagated my kind. I did not have a picture of the little fellow but somewhere, somehow I had to mention his name for the record. No sooner had I got beyond the given names – 'John Byrne' – than the

Colonel flushed, and his eyes were hot with pride. 'His grandfather on my mother's side,' I explained. Perhaps at another time, and in another place, the Colonel would have embraced me. As it was, he called for papers, phoned for Majors and Captains and told them to get the United States ready for my tour. He was too happy and obviously too sensitive to apologize. He merely remarked that he'd been thinking how much accent I'd lost. I don't wish to convey that any member of the United States Army is subject to attacks of nepotism, even at one generation once removed. I was given no more than my legitimate right as a foreign correspondent anxious to report to an ally on the American people at war.

In the course of this same day I was presented with a general credential from the chief of the Overseas Liaison Branch of the Bureau of Public Relations. It was, I was later told, the last general credential to be issued by the War Department. All that remained, I was told, was to make application to the Office of Price Administration for the rubber I was going to need to roll on. All that remained, in fact, was to convince a board of fellow citizens that I had a better right than they to four new tires. It was a trick that would have fazed Hercules, though evidently it was child's play for a couple of ex-gangsters of my acquaintance (they bought their phonograph records where I bought mine) who, immediately after the order freezing rubber had gone out, started a snobbish game of seeing who could most frequently drive out in the morning with a new set of white-walled tires.

The ration board in New York was sympathetic but could find no privileged category to fit me in. I went on trying to get some tires by every legal means, but one day a friend of mine with one of the Supply Councils in Washington rang me up and told me I might as well forget all about them and go by train. In the end I managed to pick up some secondhand tires and, after a great deal of wrangling with a tire inspector, had them re-treaded.

There was no more to do now but visit Washington once more, confirm what there was of a schedule and pick up the necessary instructions from the Navy Department. Whereas it was almost impossible to visit an Army camp without direct posting from Washington, all that the Navy could do from there was to recommend me to the Commandant of a naval district, who had absolute authority over his own area. The morning before I left, I took a cab and gave the address, 'The Navy Department.' We eventually landed at an open yard, and I walked in at the first entrance I found. There were no guards at the door or anywhere in sight. I walked along a corridor and stopped a young woman to ask where I might find the Lieutenant Commander that Captain Fox had directed me to see. I found him and was made welcome in the modest, formal Navy fashion. The Navy men seemed to think it less than odd that a British correspondent should want to see something of the Navy. Our business was done briskly and without a hitch – without a hitch, that is, until I started to try to leave the building. I was walking along in amiable conversation with the Lieutenant Commander when at the end of the first corridor a guard lowered his rifle and barred the way. He was courteous but inflexible. He couldn't let me leave because I had no badge, button, or exit permit. The theory was that if you were not wearing a visitor's button, you never in the first place came in and were technically not present. This was reasonable but uncomfortable to anybody who hoped soon to resume his life in the world outside the Navy Department. It took an Admiral's permission and a personal escort of two Lieutenant Commanders to get me into the street.

It may appear from the foregoing that my experience with the armed forces was unhappy or whimsical. But it was nothing like so bad as I had been told to expect by civilian stuffed shirts whose chief claim to virtue was their daily thanks to God they were not brass hats. On the contrary, I came to the surprising conclusion that the Army and Navy were more reasonable to deal with than most government departments. If you knew what you wanted to do, and what you didn't want to do, you could quickly make good relations. And where there are good relations there is by definition no need of diplomacy. Everything was now ready. I had been sworn in, cleared, signed and sealed, and was to be allowed to observe almost anything from the functioning of a naval district to the operation of Link trainers, the upkeep of landing barges, and a thousand other privileges that would delight the heart of a graduate engineer. Unfortunately newspapers are seldom written by such men. I was a mere foreign correspondent, which is to say a man who is helped to report on mechanical processes he will never understand and to be entrusted with secrets he would never know enough to use. Of course I had a vain desire to be able sometime to step aboard a B-19 bomber, as long as it stayed aground, but I knew that my chief interest would be in people and that there would be much left untold, in any story I wrote, about mechanized warfare and practically nothing about the splendid courage of the nation's airplane riveters.

The reader ought to be warned, however, that I was not going out on any debunking expedition, for even though I was born at a time when it was compulsory to cut your literary teeth on debunking, I always had uncomfortable misgivings, which later became a conviction, that debunking was a slightly hysterical form of disappointed sentimentality. On the other hand, in the past year or two, we have swung to the opposite extreme, and in much public speaking and writing we tend to assume that war will endow people with a completely different and more elevated set of emotions to live their lives on. This overreaction has appealed especially to my own generation, which fretted away so much of the 20s and 30s in enjoying 'wide' experience, going places, doing things, looking for life anywhere but home, spreading its emotions wide and thin and hoping, a little pathetically, that a few deep loyalties would be delivered with the milk.

Consequently, in the first month or two of the American war, it was possible to hear, at least among so-called educated young Americans of the Eastern Seaboard – in their thirties and wondering whether to enlist – more surprising mawkishness about patriotism and the need to atone than from a convention of politicians or bishops in their best exhibitionist stride.

I left then with this single lingering prejudice: I was theoretically willing to be convinced that the war would improve the quality of human emotions, but like the man from Missouri, I wanted to be shown.

3

Through the Appalachians to
the Pioneers

So it was just before noon on the morning of February 27, 1942, that
I drove out of Washington with five re-treaded tires, the War Department's compliments 'to all Public Relations Officers', a rather daring
testimonial, from my paper's Washington correspondent, to my 'full
integrity and sense of responsibility', and an insurance policy cover-
ing one life and one color camera.

At the first traffic light, I hopped out to buy a newspaper, and
among the newsstand's groaning racks of westerns and love pulp I
noticed a newcomer whose cover pictured an idiot Mongol face
choking with teeth. The vendor said it wasn't selling very well so far,
'but I reckon they figure it's sort of timely'. It bore the terse title, 'Jap
Beast'. On the way out of town I saw a paper sign pasted across a
hardware store window. It was the first ominous symptom of America with its belt tightened. It said, 'Zippers repaired'.

After leaving US 50 and going west on 29-211, I drove almost a
dozen miles without seeing more than one truck and one private car
coming or going. It was a curious new feeling, like driving in Europe
– in England – on Monday morning. After Centerville the white
double highway narrows, and lines of cedars are planted along the
tops of little hills and branch off up dirt roads. Past historic Bull Run
and all through these small rolling hills and narrow runs, divided with
zigzag, split-rail fences, you realize how well this Civil War landscape
is known to millions of military students who have never seen
America. For it is the textbook tactician's 'classic' terrain, a checker-
board for infantry. Let us pray that the owners of pleasant Southern
voices at the War Department and the conscientious young soldiers at
Virginia Military Institute, which was soon coming up along the road,

would learn to overcome a natural pride in such country and study resolutely the Malaya jungle, the yawning swamps of Burma, and the rice fields of the Netherlands East Indies. It would do no harm if the War Department would assign some ornery brain to advertise the fighting possibilities in the conquered lands of the Pacific, where travelers had always said the climate and what it did to the mind made war there an impossible occupation.

West and always gradually south, you soon begin to know what part of the land you are in. The signs offer 'Virginia Ham, Fried Chicken, Hot Biscuits Ahead', and there is a lank young Negro with bare, tough feet walking the road miles from the nearest town. You climb the Blue Ridge. It is a cold, yellow, sunny day and the bare trees on the mountains run stiff and smooth as a comb from the peak to the winding valley. You descend into the Shenandoah Valley and stop for lunch at Luray. It is a small old town with a textile factory, a tannery, and nine denominations of churches. But in spring and summer it is a tourist center for its nearby caverns, and all the outward signs are advertisements of them, and in restaurant windows, souvenirs and rag-doll Mammies. The town is deserted. On the way out, you learn that yesterday they lost sixty boys to the draft. Through the afternoon the war begins to recede. The broad, tidy farms of the Shenandoah Valley are defined as always by handsome white fences. Here is a chinchilla farm and there some pretty stables, and nothing much to worry about on a board advertising 'thoroughbred hunters and steeplechase prospects'. But offsetting this graceful prosperity is the repeated reminder, in roadside signage, that fresh green vegetables will be something to hope and pray for, from here all through the Deep South, all the way to Florida. Signs are the hardy standbys of Southern highway advertising, which when they first appear seem to be milestones leading back into the difficult nineteenth century, faraway from the America of metropolitan Diaper Services and the sulfa drugs. They are the old familiar Southern ads for 'Black Draught – Family Laxative', and the dread '666, Colds, Fever'.

Suddenly you duck into a grimy industrial belt, from Longdale Furnace through Clifton Forge, a railroad terminal for coal and lumber export, and thence into Covington, a dark, cluttered industrial town, once an overnight stopping place for travelers on their way through to fashionable White Sulphur Springs, west across the state line. However dreary the prospects of the coal men in Covington, you reflect as you turn past Crow Tavern, an old frame-house with stone chimneys, that in their humble way they would probably resent the genteel restrictions that Crow Tavern insisted on, 100 years ago, that no more than five people should sleep in a bed.

In West Virginia snow flurries scud into the windshield, and soon it is snowing merrily though light and dry. In the darkening afternoon, I play tag with a Department of Justice car that is being driven by what looks like a forest ranger. There appears to be no sensible explanation of this, so I hang on his heels right into White Sulphur Springs, and before evening all is made plain. He comes to a stop, gives some secret Masonic sign, and swishes out of sight up the long driveway of the Greenbrier Hotel. This hotel is one of the finest of American pleasure gardens. It stands on rising ground overlooking a plain that has been elegantly converted into a polo field and a golf course. A hundred years ago, Southern plantation society and its aspirants came to take the waters by day and to carouse by night. There was even a quarter for bachelors that bore the oddly Hollywood name of Wolf Row. Today, the place is said in season to employ 1,500 natives, though the population of White Sulphur Springs is listed as something less than this. The hotel still can bed, however, a thousand of the rich, the old, the decrepit, and the fashionable.

A chain barred the entrance the mysterious car had been allowed to pass through. And at the gate was hung a sign, 'No entrance. Department of Justice'. It turned out that the guests were inmates who by no definition could be called legitimate seekers after health or sin. They were about 600 of the German, Italian, and Hungarian diplomatic internees. That evening, in town, over exquisite fried chicken and a melting lemon meringue pie, a very pretty and charming blonde girl spilled the gossip about 'them'. She had a bad attack of laryngitis that made the unwanted guests sound even more mysterious and cruel than you would patriotically assume. The town had threshed through every wild rumor and could find nothing very skulking to pin on the Hungarians and the harmless Italians. There was talk of loud quarreling at night, a hush-up stabbing was hinted at, and somebody invented the entirely plausible story that some of the Italians and the

Germans were not on speaking terms. It has become a point of principle with people in the town to insist that they never have liked Germans, Italians, Hungarians, and never will. The more heinous rumors are reserved for the Japanese, who are not here but forty miles away in Hot Springs, Virginia. I spent most of the evening padding through the quiet snow hoping to gather material for about a dozen workmanlike B films. But the most unmentionable crime the Japs were accused of was hissed at me by a vendor of pulp magazines. He said the foul sentence with a drawling contempt: 'They objected to the food. They oughta put em behind bars.' I remarked that they'd do the same to our captured diplomats but the man was unmoved. 'Twould make no diff'ence,' he replied. 'They oughta poison the whole breed. It's the diplomats that start the wars anyway.'

Next day, White Sulphur Springs looked as if it had been born in snow. The skies were leaden gray and cloudless. I start to drive, on well cindered roads, up into the Greenbrier Mountains. Ahead is White Rock Mountain, on which the snow, falling finely for the past three days, makes its timbered face look like a giant stone slab marked with graceful pencil strokes. In the mountains you come on little towns far apart but bustling. It is coal and lumber country. The lumber you might have guessed but along the highway there is no hint of the vast subterranean reach of the coal and iron mines, going thirty miles east to Lewisburg, almost seventy miles west, nearly to Charleston. High in the hills I stop at Rainelle, a lumber town, and inquire about the war.

West Virginia is one of the three main continental sources of hardwood. It supplies mainly white oak, poplar, hard maple, and birch. Business started to boom shortly after the defense program started, when wood was called for to replace steel and metal construction. The companies are busy supplying hardwood flooring for defense housing. But the more they were asked to do, the more demand there was for their skilled carpenters elsewhere. Since December 7th, you learn, 10 percent of the best local carpenters have gone to the chemical industries and airplane factories. Their most enterprising mechanics have moved to the shipyards on the coast at Norfolk. The companies have begun to take on women, especially in the wood heel shop: they make most of the wooden heels for the shoes that

American women wear. So already they have started to step up their usual forty-hour week to a fifty-four-hour week. You ask how the people feel about this. It's pretty obvious that a lot of men especially don't like it. Some people say 'most' don't like it. Between 'a lot of' and 'most' is the discrepancy between what the unions will grudgingly admit and what the employer wants to believe. A plant manager says 'We surely don't mind doin' the extra work, but we're sore at the delays in Washington. But mostly we're sore at the guys that strike for an ext'a ten dollars a week, when the men in the draft make thirty dollars a month.' You smell around the town for the always elusive odor of 'morale'. It is a meaningless scent. In the close embrace of the mountains, in which most of these men and women were born and will die, there is little call to know much about the war or any geography but your own. The group that appears to have responded most imaginatively to the idea of the war is the teen-age children, who have so far bought about 50 percent of the town's quota of War Savings stamps. A distrust has been building of homegrown fifth columnists, and the Italians who live in coal-mining camps are the special victims of local suspicion. On the surface, however, there is nothing to show a new situation in lumber. The workers would appear better-heeled if they had time to get to Charleston to buy the new clothes they can now afford. What you bring away is a memory of a town doing business a little brisker than it can comfortably manage. The sales clerks on the telephones are pressing their agents: 'If you can deliver it today, it'll suit us mighty good to get it.' It is the same all the way through the mountains. Only a politician or a cub reporter out on his first do-or-die assignment would burrow for 'a war situation'. The only situation to observe is the life situation that has been there for generations of men who dug for coal. For the next sixty miles you come on small, dirty, unincorporated coal towns with all the mean disorder of coal towns anywhere. The people live mostly on rocky banks by the highway in tarpaper or unpainted frame shanties. They are propped against the slope of the bank by wooden stilts of unbelievable frailty. Spring must be a longed-for season, when the Lombardy poplars can start to flash their leaves again and veil the squalor of these little towns with the memorable names that crouch by the Great Kanawha River: Boomer and London, Glasgow and Belle (alas), and little Plus. But even in these towns, which might be clinging to the Elbe or Mersey, there is an occasional native touch that you would not find in Germany or Britain, a casual assertion of 'the American way' that the inhabitants never seem to notice. At Glasgow I went past an irregular row of these shanties. They were all without a single dab of elegance, but docked between the stilts and the flooring of one was a shining 1940 Buick.

Down through the foothills the snow was melting into slush, and I leave the coal towns for a string of chemical towns, as grimy as the coal towns, only more pungent. I pass through piles of ore and silica at Alloy, ready to be made into ferrochrome alloy for toughening steels. At Belle a vast ammonia plant, making chemicals from salt brine. Outside the plant new wooden sentry towers have been built, thirty or forty feet high, and if you dawdle for a moment the soldiers on guard begin to get curious too.

As we come nearer to Charleston, the shanties break into every sort of architectural whimsy, as if they were hectically trying to prepare you for the fabulous crustacea of the State Capitol and its golden dome.

It is raining in Charleston, and the city is thick with shoppers from nearby towns. Out west of it a roadside billboard announces 'Wow, it's a sweet chew', and this is the cue for the approaching tobacco country. We see the first smokehouse and barns for drying. Then on through some more chemical towns, past a US Naval Ordnance plant built hastily in 1917, abandoned after the last war, and now puffing away furiously and guarded on all sides. By nightfall, we are on the outskirts of Huntington and noticing billboard incitements to enlist as an air-raid warden and defend your family. You recall with a shock the actual existence of Hermann Goering and wonder whose foresight has made this city, 300 miles from the East Coast, aware of dive-bombers. It turns out to be a 'Colonel' who is at home but prefers to explain over the telephone how his system works. I had written 'his system' not intending any guile, but it appeared it was nothing less. First he told me that 'civilian defense in our country' was made blessedly simple to organize because of the system of political districting. I threw in the obvious query here, but he came back with a resounding assurance that politics would not enter into it. They had, at least by March

1942, no appropriation from the state, so the 'Colonel' charged fifty cents to join his organization.

If a man was willing and looked able, even if he couldn't afford the fifty cents, they let him in anyway. He had already signed up 2,700 citizens, which by simple arithmetic should have brought in about 1,350 dollars. He was hoping for 3,000 air-raid wardens to graduate from a ten-hour course, based partly on literature put out by the Office of Civilian Defense and partly 'on local conditions'. Thousands of women, he said, were taking first-aid courses. 'You may say,' the 'Colonel' said, 'that most of us here are getting more war-conscious every day.' Whatever that means, there were probably thousands of patriotic citizens who felt it.

I met a sprightly youth in a drugstore who didn't feel the same way. He said, and he was evidently speaking for himself as forcibly as the 'Colonel', 'the defense set-up in this town don't amount to anything more than a joke, run by an old growler from last time who's packing the place with his cronies.' It is quite possible that this young man did the 'Colonel' and his town a disservice. His own interest in the war was a nonchalant one. He leaned across the pharmacy counter amiably and asked for 'a block o' rubbers'. He turned to me, gave me a blithe smile, and explained he was going in the Army next week. 'After that,' he said, 'I'll let them take care of me.' He slipped his purchase into his coat pocket, wished me goodnight. I went over to the soda fountain for a drink. The soda jerk, wiping some glasses, pointed silently with his towel at a sign over the orange-squeezer: 'Regret. Out of Coca-Cola'. To an Eskimo, this may seem a trivial anecdote. But I walked sadly back to the hotel, convinced that the war was beginning to – if not at last push us around with a velvet glove – administer a gentle nudge to the American way of life.

Fortified by a long sleep, I happened next morning to turn off the hot water faucet too rapidly, and the thing came to dust in my hands, stuffing fat deposits of porcelain under the skin of my second finger. At the hospital I sat waiting for a surgeon and held my right hand in a towel that took to my red corpuscles like an asp. It was not the best time to check on the war situation in hospitals, but the nurses drawled around complaining of the shortage of doctors. The young ones were going into the Army, and it took time to reorganize a staff of the old and the retired. There probably was much more that I mentally noted at the time but have lost forever in amnesia, for like even the mousiest creatures born on the tight little isle I felt it my duty at such a time to behave with ridiculous calm. As the sleepy surgeon held my finger and threaded wire through it that would have securely knotted a stallion's belly, I had the inner pleasure of hearing his aide gasping admiration at the patient's boredom.

When I came to, I had forgotten all about the plight of hospital staffs in West Virginia and lusted only for two eggs over easy. The sugar was rationed at breakfast, and there was a note on the menu requesting that you, 'in the interests of national defense', keep to one cup of coffee. The snow was far behind on this pleasant Sunday morning, and we were soon in small hilly country rolling with brown grass. Just beyond Kenova, so called because the Kentucky, Ohio, and Virginia rivers meet there, we pass over into Kentucky and were rolling through small hilly country with more unpainted barns and abandoned shacks than I had ever seen in the Dust Bowl. The US Department of Agriculture's map of 'rural cultural regions' describes it, in its unsentimental way, as containing 'a high percentage of low-income farms. Low level of living. Over one-third of farmers are tenants. Relief above average.' It doesn't much matter how you describe it – North–South Border, the agricultural Southeast, the Ohio Valley – it is the beginning of the American sadland, where there is plenty of good soil, a vast population of thrifty, willing workers but few good tools; where the livestock is underfed, where the tenant pays a third of his crop for the privilege of cultivating whatever land God and erosion see fit to leave him, and where he gives humble thanks when his meager crop is harvested by getting hungry mouths to eat his share.

We turn rolling corners and see small log cabins with individual wells out front – not far enough away from their outdoor privies. A material-minded man who lives in this ragged country of Appalachia must be grateful to grow a little corn, eat a fried squirrel on Sundays, and admit that his broken sod is so peppered with phosphates that at least he has no need of fertilizer. But these people are not material minded. They are Anglo-Celts, and in the midst of penury they think sternly of the life hereafter. The old 'Black Draught' and '666' signs come up as regular as proverbs. But you see every half-mile or so, nailed to posts and collapsing barns, the strong slogan of the South:

'Jesus Is Coming.' Near Olive Hill, we turn a hilly bend, and the commandments are printed out on drab wooden shields, like Burma Shave advertisements. The last one is left uncompleted. It just prints 'Thou Shalt Not Covet . . .' and leaves the rest of the hideous thought to perish. You pass a few farmers and think of saluting them as casually as may be. But there is something in their mild eyes and pitted, bony faces that makes you think better of it. You decide the tobacco story can wait till Lexington. All that America need ask of these sons by way of a war contribution is that they should try to stay fed, pay for their shoes at the general store, and keep their philosophy to themselves. One of them stands at a broken gate. He carries a pale infant, and by his side stands a soldier in a uniform new and stiff as cardboard. There is no need to ask him how he feels about the war. As we come by he narrows his eyes against the sun and smiles. The soldier, who is perhaps destined for the Southwest Pacific, suddenly sees the New York license plate and frantically tries to make the baby also appreciate the wonder of visitors from the never-never land.

There is a vertical line on the map a few miles east of Winchester, Kentucky, that marks precisely the beginning of the Bluegrass country. The region is shaded in so plainly that you cannot believe it until you get there. But exactly where the map marks X, and without any apparent rhyme or reason, the landscape suddenly grows spacious, the wide fields turn green, the tumbling fences tauten and come out in white paint, and the trees are high and delicate, carefully planted to hedge off the farms. The mules give way to horses, cows, and fat sheep. It is another world. If it were a touch more gracious and commanding, you might be in Maryland's exquisite Green Spring, Worthington, and Delaney Valleys. Though the Bluegrass is by no means as unique or breathtaking as its natives would have you believe, you can understand how it always must appear so to anybody driving west out of the drab sandy ridges of Appalachia. From now on there is every sign of a cared for, disciplined country. A sign says 'Advertising forbidden within right of way'. There is an excellent white two-lane highway, and you drive into Winchester ready to believe all the more ornamental legends of the Southern myth. We eat in a pleasant room that has warm paneling and racing prints tempered by a juke box. The menu offers 'escalloped salsify' and candied yams, and for dessert there is a mellow, incomparable chess pie. Behind the fountain there are three young girls, and they too make the Southern myth plausible by being uniformly pretty. The pie is good enough to ask about. But the girls can't say what it is, just chess pie. They don't know where it came from, how it's made, and when I offered the suggestion that maybe the kitchen knew, they laughed at the drollery, put a nickel in the juke box, and started jittering mildly to 'Why Don't We Do This More Often?' They didn't know why chess pie was spelled that way, or even if it was spelled right. It didn't seem worth asking them if they knew about the war.

From Winchester to Lexington there is no more call to brood over the Southern economy, and you think back to the scraping farmers of the eastern part of the state as characters from a comic strip in the morning's paper. Everywhere around you are hedges running trimly over hills, tidy carefree country, few evergreens, majestic stud farms, cocker spaniels for sale, all the charming nonchalance of a landscape made for the breeding of fine horses. It would be convenient to think that this is what all of the South might be like with a little more care and pride. But nothing could be falser. You think again of the Green Spring Valley north of Baltimore, and it strikes you painfully why the Bluegrass looks the same. It is estated country. It is not the easy best that any comfortable farmer could afford, it is the flaunted showpiece of fabulously wealthy people. The X on the map that marked the change from the rotting gullies of the Appalachians to the Bluegrass was not just the pretty idea of a mapmaker wishing to separate the poor from the rich. It is a geologist's signpost marking the dramatic beginning of limestone soil. And this limestone can be bought – by millionaires who want to breed bone in their show-ring horses. They hope to go on doing it, and among themselves they alternate between anxiety and reassurance, saying now that maybe the cavalry will want to buy their horses, the next minute reminding each other that this is a mechanized war and that, with no possible use for thoroughbreds, the government will certainly let the Kentucky Derby go on forever 'in the interests of morale'. You are now in the prosperous region of the Ohio Valley, and a score of billboards inciting the farmer to sell his crop in Lexington are a reminder that this town is the world's biggest loose-leaf tobacco market.

The tobacco beds are planted toward the end of March under canvas covers to protect them from frost and insects. In May and June the tobacco is transplanted to the open fields, in August and September cut from the stalk, in October and November stripped, prepared for market, and graded to be sold in December and January. The blow to the tobacco farmers came along before Pearl Harbor, in fact, in 1940 when Great Britain cut off all exchange for foreign buying. The government tried to provide exchange to companies that normally export by setting up a loan fund and buying the tobacco itself. The acreage of the 1941 crop was only two-thirds of normal and a whole new world away from the bumper crop of 1938–39, when 75 million pounds of loose-leaf Burley tobacco were sold in Lexington alone. But in March 1942, you hesitate to ask the small tobacco farmer about his interpretation of 'equality of sacrifice'. He is paid a dollar and a half a day and given a cabin on the farm. With such an endowment, he does not tend to meditate on the Founding Fathers, or ponder deeply what the radio commentators tell him about the war for democracy. His life is encompassed by the fear that next year the government's enforced smaller acreage will weaken his hold on a bare subsistence. Some of these farmers wished they could grow other crops that would help win the war and incidentally keep their faces fed. The young ones know that there is nothing much ahead for them but the draft. Everybody in the tobacco business knows that there is only one 'irreplaceable skill' in their trade, and it belongs to the man who does the grading.

Out west of the Bluegrass you pass into brown-grassed untidy country again, and so it stays through the rest of the Lower Ohio Valley, all the way into the Liverpool–Manchester–Cincinnati–East St Louis amalgam of cities known as Louisville.

It is Saturday night and the town is swarming with soldiers from Fort Knox, then the chief training ground of the US armored forces, and from nearby Bowman Field. It is the first town we have seen that looks as if it might be a city in a battle zone. The streets are rolling with dumpy broad-faced girls, sometimes pretty in a poorly rouged way, spanning the sidewalk six or seven of them arm in arm, breathing a kind of giggling defiance of the loitering soldiers. In this strolling swarm of humans, you notice the first wives on soldiers' arms. The husband wears his uniform gravely, aware of his responsibility, and the wives look resigned and modest, putting a gentle face on an essential sadness. They are what you would like to think are The People, yes. But the people are all about you, and they are a younger, more careless breed. They may grow up into these wives, conscious of having given something to their country. But now they are enjoying the new thrill of being able to pass up not one male but droves of them. You notice that it is by no means the trimmer ones who have the soldiers in tow.

There is a startling contrast between the complexions of the soldiers and the civilians. Maybe one should not judge the civilian youth of a town by scores of thousands of young men whose daily chores start at dawn and include the driving and maintenance of tanks, motorcycles, Diesel engines, and general field engineering, in hail, rain, and snow. But it is impossible to believe that the high-school kids crowding the drugstores will become these tanned and restless soldiers. They are gawky and lifeless and sit around with girls whose chalky faces, patched with careless rouge, are innocent of any flicker of intelligence. You talk to some of them and you are met with the same matter-of-fact listlessness and incuriosity that distinguished the girls in the restaurant in Lexington. Just as brashness is the abuse of the Northerner's liveliness, this looks like the dull, dark underside of Southern manners. The intelligent Southerner gives an impression you seldom meet elsewhere in America of having his own standards and of respecting you as a mature stranger while he keeps his own reserve. But when there is no intelligence, there seems to be, in the young people at least, only the tired motions of living and a glazed animal indifference to ideas, humor, the sight of new faces, even the presence of the roving soldiers. This is an atmosphere that no European need feel strange in. For it is the seeping seediness of English provincial towns. Yet this is an American town, and it has all the American fixtures, but it looks like a town in the English north or midlands trying to go American. In Texas, in Illinois, in Connecticut, in California, a drugstore, for instance, means the image of a complete American community – a shining fountain, the taste of lush syrups, an orgy of casual friendships and smart advertising, a halfway house between brisk comings and goings, the wayside first-aid station of American cleanliness and quick health. It should, and very often does, 'baffle the foreigner like an idiom'. But here it is what a drugstore might be in Bulgaria or Leeds – a sad imitation by a storekeeper who once read an American novel and was filled with immortal longings.

In the early evenings, the hotels are jumping with soldiers. The rooms were booked weeks ago, and this leads you to inquire about the price scale. None of the hotel managers you talk to will even tolerate the notion that he is exploiting the soldiers. But you later have ways of checking on this. You sit in the lobby and watch the soldiers come in to make their reservations. Time and again they confront a smooth clerk, ask for a room for such a date, put their hand in their inside pocket, then catch their breath and ask the clerk to repeat the price again. Sometimes they shake their heads and go away. Most of the time they sigh and say it will have to do. The point was seldom lost on the buck private. It was one way of assuring that only officers should be accommodated.

That same night, I decided to stay up and see what happened to the thousands of ordinary soldiers who had no room, no hotel, no girl. It was a dreary experience, but nothing much happened to them that would choke a social worker's notebook. They walk round and round the block in twos and threes, arguing where to go, what to do, whether or not to pick up some girls. They end up in the railroad station or an all-night café, their heads between their arms on the table, grabbing an hour or two's sleep before they catch the bus and chase back to camp at 4 a.m. Sitting up in one drugstore, I overheard a conversation, at 3 a.m., between two soldiers and their girls. One boy sat bending the straw of his soda between his thumb and first finger and making monosyllabic conversation with his girl. But the other couple was deep in some sort of emotional crisis. The boy stared at her and she looked downward at an empty plate. Then suddenly she started to cry. She climbed down from her stool and walked quickly out of the store. Her friend casually came to her feet, said goodnight to anybody who cared to hear, and followed her. The soldier with the straw looked down at the counter. Without lifting his eyes he said, 'You bum, what'd you say a thing like that for.' The victim hotly defended himself, 'I didn't say anything. What did I say?' They both fell silent. And then the hurt one turned the other way round, saw me, and held out both hands. He looked at me in utter bewilderment. 'Tell me,' he said, 'what makes a woman cry?' I looked foolish, mumbled something about that being quite a question, and we ordered some eggs and meditated in the doubtless naïve male fashion on the wonder and mystery of women. 'All you ask for,' protested the blunderer, 'is a good time. Just an evening. A little fun.'

'Yeah,' the friend commented, 'but you gotta watch a thing like that. A nice girl you know. She don't figure it the way you do.'

This was the last word, as it will be for the duration, on many a changed relationship between soldiers and wives, rookies and pick-ups, hostesses at USO socials and an evening's acquaintance. The other soldier breathed a sincere melodramatic sigh, 'Jesus Christ,' he said sadly, 'I give up,' with an inflection that implied he, like most other men, would never give up and would never know quite why. We talked about camp life and the feeling of being a new soldier, of KP and getting up early and what it did to your weight, of laying off hard liquor and what it did to your health, of officers ('not one real officer in a camp-load, not among the college boys'), of rates of pay, then about girls again, and about camp entertainment. I looked around the drugstore. There was hardly a soldier awake. A Negro boy was mopping the floor round the legs of sleeping men. On most tables where they hadn't already started to pile chairs before they locked up were a pair of sprawled khaki arms and an oblivious resting head. You wondered why men chose to leave camp just for this, for a few beers, an aimless walk around the centre of Louisville, and a sandwich and an hour's collapse over a café table. The soldier with the straw, which by this time he had taken to careful shreds, had the answer. He was talking about the efforts of the Army to recreate and distract its young. He said, 'You can bring over all the movie stars and radio comedians, as many as you want. You can entertain soldiers all you like, but you can't entertain them out of homesickness.'

There is another alien population in Louisville that wanders round the town one or two nights a week. It is made up of humble people who speak every dialect of the American language but do not claim any stake in the city or indeed in Kentucky. They only sleep in Louisville. And early every morning, you will see their cars, like a re-incarnated junk pile, file in thousands across the toll bridge over the Ohio River, meet another convoy of cars in Jeffersonville, and go on north up Route 62. Their destination is the place they work, the world's biggest smokeless powder plant, in Charlestown, Indiana, twelve miles across the state line.

Charlestown is an old town that history abandoned. In the 1820s the first Governor of Indiana lived there, soon after the Shawnee Indians had given up all hope of retaining, and the British of annexing, this section of the Northwest Territory. Indiana had been a state only four or five years, and as settlers from Virginia and the Carolinas poured across the Ohio in horse ferries, Charlestown played host to the land-office customers of Jeffersonville. There was a famous tavern for wealthy travelers going north, and there is a record of a dashing inaugural ball for Governor Jennings. But from the 1820s on nothing much was heard of the town. By 1940, it had a hundred and something houses. A steak house. A café. A couple of poolrooms. A general store and a hardware store. A small Baptist church and a Catholic church. There were exactly 939 people living there. It was the sort of town that is too small to get on anything bigger than a state map, and when it does they spell it wrong. Thousands who came in later were to go on calling it 'Charleston' as long as they stayed there.

For a reason that nobody in the town has ever agreed on, Charlestown was chosen in July 1940 as the site of a smokeless powder plant. The government contract was stated to be for 25 million dollars. However, the news soon got around that the Army expected to employ maybe as many as 5,000 men there. Nobody knew who these 5,000 people would be. If you had stopped anybody in Indiana in the summer of 1940, they would have been as vague about it as Miss Turner, a wispy, middle-aged schoolteacher who began to wonder before most of the others how the town would take care of five times as many people as lived there. Talking with the first employment service men who came into Charlestown, she was told to expect – while the construction was under way – lumber men from the Appalachians, men from the Southern mill towns. Then probably there would be steel workers from the Calumet region. Then later there would be seasonal farm labor, tomato pickers, disappointed farmers from the Ohio Valley and the Deep South. 'After the place is built, you can expect anybody.'

In the language of Washington, Charlestown might expect a

'defense migration'. What that would mean to the life of Charlestown, nobody could reasonably imagine, because Charlestown was to become the focus of many sorts of interest that in 1940 were thousands of miles apart. The synthesis of them would be, and without much warning *was*, suddenly, the Charlestown of late 1941. But in 1940, Charlestown had little say in its own alarming future. From faraway industrial cities the telephone wires hummed with talk of solvents and brine and ether mix. In Chicago, and in Philadelphia, there were board meetings about a freight train service linking the big cities with – what's the name again? – Charlestown.

The human cargo that was to float into town during the following twelve months would provide an American saga that Mark Twain alone could accurately relate, for it would require nothing less than his easy mastery of a score of dialects, an eye for American river life, and a nostril as delicate as his for the pungency of people whose home is not in this or that town but who inhabit most comfortably a continent. However, it is remarkable that not even Hollywood has mined this bottomless pit.

Since nothing travels in the direction of hungry men like news of work, they started to roll in, on foot and in old Model Ts, as soon as the contract was announced in the newspapers. I asked some of them to recall how they first got to Indiana. Most of them had no trouble at all remembering. A man from a small town in North Carolina said, 'I seen this paper lyin' there on top of a bag o' potatoes. Well, since the cotton mill shet down, I ain't seen no kind of decent job. My wife was always takin' sick, an' then we had a cyclone come into town. Blowed some families all to pieces, geese, bedstead, fences, ev'theng. We was just skeered near 'bout to death. That was in '36 or '37, understan'. So when I seen this thing in the paper I said, Ma, I'm takin' th'automobile 'n goin' no'th to git me a job in that dee-fense factory. Next day I was on my way.'

About the same time, 700 or more miles to the north was a Vermont man, a French-Canadian born seventy-five miles from the Canadian line. 'I been a house painter mostly, on the Eastern Shore o' Maryland. My son married, got a job down here in Louisville, and took to keepin' home down here. Well, he told me about the factory goin' up, and my wife and I started down right away.'

There was a scrawny, cheerful-looking little man from the Lakeland country of Florida. He said, 'I laift Geo'gia when I was a li'll fella. N'ever since I been scrapin' around, tendin' limes, pickin' or'nges. Nothin' ever happens in Flo'da. Twas on the radio I first heered it, ah reckon. N'ah says to my old lady, Sue, ah says, we're headin' fo' Charlestown. She says where's that? I says ah doan' know, but we're headin' theyre. We're leavin' Flo'da f'good 'n all.'

A huge clean-shaven blond man with faint blue eyes smiled when I asked him if he could remember. 'Do I remember? Yes, sir. I was in Detroit an' 'n a heap o' trouble, what with being laid off at the automobile factory and my wife pregnant. So a man was through Detroit from my hometown, Hutchinson, Kansas. And he told me they wanted millwrights. When I went back an' told my wife, I said what you gonna do? An' she said, "Any place you can live I can live too." We had seventeen dollars an' a tire with a bad hole. Anyway, we took off for Charlestown.'

To the original 900 inhabitants of the place, it seemed that the whole world had had the impulse to take off for Charlestown. The expected 5,000 came and stayed and were joined by another 5,000. Highway commissioners were called in to do something about a transportation crisis that threatened to stall the whole project in a murderous jam of automobiles outside the factory gate. There had been an ordinary two-lane oiled road. By the time there were 14,000 employees, it took them fifty minutes to get in and park their cars from the moment they hit the main entrance. On the other side of the road the trains arrived while the automobiles were still going in. The commuters started to come across the tracks, the two streams met and, according to the plant manager, 'you'd hear nothing but honking horns and train whistles for the next thirty minutes.'

So they had to stagger the train schedules and construct a divided four-lane highway over which they built three overpasses to pour commuters into the plant area so they wouldn't tangle with the cars coming in. The railroads had to put in more spurs connecting branch lines as far away as six miles from the vast plain that was the factory area. The Police Commissioner appointed three police posts more than they ever allowed for, added a dozen patrolmen, a flock of parking officers, a half-dozen more sentry towers. By this time, the original contract figure of 25 million dollars had been trebled. By this time too, at the peak of construction, there were 26,000 men working there.

You go along to the administration building and enter the employment office, or what they call 'the bull pen'. The office was designed neatly, as a reception room for prospective employees. But it looks more like a stockyard. Hundreds of men are milling round the receptionist's desk and squatting down in the adjoining corridors. They are leaning, standing, pushing – one young Negro is lying fast asleep, washed up against the far wall of the office. They are dressed in every sort of shirt and pants known to the mail-order catalogues. The early settlers would recognize themselves in all of them. All that is missing is a man in a coonskin cap with a rifle. The noise is suffocating. The ones nearest the receptionist's desk shuffle nervously, waiting for application blanks. Through the din of conversation they throw single sentences at the harassed girl.

'I'm from Ohio, how do I get to see . . . ?'

'I wanna see the transportation foreman.'

'I come to look for a fitter's job. I'm from Chicago.'

'I was steered here by a gauge grinder.'

The girl bangs a rubber stamp in monotonous two-four time and shouts, 'Fill out this application form, bring it in here tomorrow. Fill out this application form, bring . . .'

A man's voice from one of the corridors yells for 'Riefer! Jacob Riefer!', consults a sheet of paper and tries, 'McCoy – Timothy McCoy!' The men in the corridors hold their application forms in their hands and wait to be called for their interview. The interviewer looks down at his paper again and shouts, 'Heissman, Alvin Heissman! Oh, there you are. You got your separation papers? Okay, come with me.'

Once they're hired, they go through a series of rooms for a vision test, X-ray, and finger prints. Thus they are signed, sealed, and delivered to the manufacture of smokeless powder. Many thousands in 1941 came out of this office to a wife parked on a muddy field in an automobile and brought the glad news of a steady high wage for the duration. Then they looked around for a place to sleep. But very early in the game Charlestown and Jeffersonville had filled and rented every room in stores and houses that could hold a bed or trestle.

Hundreds came in trailers till every muddy patch of brown ground was black with them, like beetles on a dung heap

A Texan and his wife had tried, in sequence, sleeping in a drugstore cellar, a firehouse, a barn with a patched roof, a trailer, and for a time had parted, to share a bed with somebody of their own sex. The man from Hutchinson, Kansas, who came down from Detroit, agreed that it was no place to be having babies, 'When we got to Charlestown from Detroit, we had eight dollars left, and they wanted fifteen dollars a week for one end of a trailer with an old sheet dividing it half-way. So we bought a small tent on time, Sears and Roebuck, and pitched it down near the river. When summer came, my wife hitched a ride back home to her folks to have the baby. It was quite an experience.' There were many mothers in Charlestown who undoubtedly looked on this man's wife as being much too fastidious. Most of them stayed and had their babies with the help of Miss Turner and the grace of God. By the late winter of 1941–42, Miss Turner had delivered, or assisted at the birth of, something like a couple of hundred young Hoosiers.

Through a winter and a spring and a steaming, rancid summer they came and settled and somehow stayed fed and alive. By the fall of 1941, the construction gang was almost gone. And it was a memorable day when on one side of a trailer there was painted the unbelievable words: 'For Sale'. Somebody was making room! But 15,000 stayed; of every shape, name, and heft under the American sun. Vermonters and couples from Oregon and Colorado full of disdain for anybody who said the grass was green in Indiana; Californians who sat around in the evenings and described to a skeptical audience the smell of orange groves and the grace of pepper trees. Kansans who affected to feel cramped for the sight of wheat again, 'stretching from your toes clear to the horizon'. There were New Englanders who fussed over the chowder and sighed for soft-shell crabs. There was a girl who wanted to go back to Texas because she missed 'the Neiman-Marcus dress ads in the *Dallas News*'. You ask them if they will go home when the war's over. And ironically it is only the New Englanders, the original pioneers, who are determined they will go back home. A quiet, stooped lad with glasses, listening to some of this proud talk, stamped on a cigarette and said, 'Go home? Why didn't they stay where they came from anyway? This is a nat'chl thing. Where would Ame'ica be if a hund'ed years ago ev'body had stayed home?' It was the only sentence I heard from anybody there that showed an instant historical sense of the Charlestown boom. An old man in his eighties had said, 'There never was a thing around here to give a man a day's work but what went blooey.' In the evening, you read the bitter truth of this remark in the history of Southern Indiana. A hundred years ago, they came in similar droves, with equally high hopes. They did not suffer from trailer troubles, and they died by nothing they knew of as a streptococcus. But they had Indians and cholera.

You have only to go into an Indiana graveyard to realize that they came young to Indiana and most of them died young, unredeemed by bloodletting, whiskey, and the incantation of local proverbs. Especially will you notice the graves of young girls buried with the babies they were too ill to bear. On one of these is the inscription:

> Thirteen years I was a virgin,
> Two years I was a wife,
> One year I was a mother,
> The next year took my life.

French Jesuits and Welshmen sleep side by side with Presbyterians and Quakers, Virginians and Irishmen.

They say that as far up the river as Cincinnati, you could look south from the bluffs on a clear night and see, over 100 miles away, a glowing arc against the horizon. It was the Charlestown smokeless powder plant, with its sweating, joking, cursing mess of humans with license plates from every state of the Union. A lot of people in Louisville and across the river deplore the boom and the invasion by strange people far from the ways they were born to. But you think of those tombstones again and have to admit that the boy with the glasses and the stoop had the word for it: 'this is a nat'chl thing.' Though they came in jalopies and worked on smokeless powder, it was an American migration in the classic tradition. Many of the natives said contemptibly that these invaders weren't Hoosiers and never would be. But it required only the ministrations of a midwife to change all that. For who is a Hoosier or a Missourian? The French and the Kentuckians went into Missouri, and Missourians made Oregon.

4

Deep Down South

Starting south out of Louisville on US 31W on a mild, sunny afternoon, we drove through more rich, horse-breeding country and at
Kosmosdale entered into the typical landscape of central Kentucky:
little rolling sandstone hills with narrow gullies running down them.
'The summer's longer than in the Corn belt, and the rain goes on fo'
ever' is what a farmer says. The land, it seems, could be as fertile as
Iowa, but torrential rains monotonously wash the topsoil away and
leave the farmer looking ruefully at hills scarred by trenches of erosion or little plains of good corn standing up to their ears in rain. Here
is a natural enemy as unremitting as the Japs.

Near Fort Knox there is a bustling increase of traffic, but it is of
jeeps and dull, khaki-colored automobiles whisking by. And as
evening closes in there are few signs of peace or war. Your headlights
hit frequent reminders that you are only fifty, and forty, then thirty
miles away from Mammoth Cave. And occasionally Burma Shave
signs flick a warning: 'Car was whizz'n/ fault was her'n/ funeral his'n'
– apparently they save wood by reducing their verses from five to
three, which at any rate puts a premium on pithiness.

Night closes in, extinguishes Kentucky, and pushes the war reeling
away into memory, leaving you with the special timeless intimacy of
driving at night. You have no goal, only a plowing shaft of light on
white cement, and to remind you happily of your own warmth, you
hear faraway the lonely call of a train. The little dead towns tick by
like tombstones of a pioneer's past – Munfordville, Rowletts, Horse
Cave, Bear Wallow, Good Night – and then you see a string of lights
coming up above your headlights. It is Glasgow, and as good a place
as any to stay the night.

In the morning you are back to a country that is much like the poor farming ridges of the Appalachians. Still, undulating land, spiked everywhere with dried cornstalks; it is not so much barren as rusty land. The farmers have been urged by the state Commissioner of Agriculture to solve the sugar shortage by growing an acre of sorghum on every farm. Made into syrup, they are told, it will serve for sugar in ice cream, waffles, pies, cookies, doughnuts, and there is the further incentive to get more calcium and phosphorus into your diet. This prospect does not greatly excite the farmers. They don't honestly believe that America will have to go short of sugar. The papers this morning report that the Japs are now in Rangoon, but still a long way away from Jamaica and Cuba. Also, the farmers are from bitter experience allergic to the promise of paradise via a new crop. The sting of the Commissioner's appeal is in the warning that there is no visible market for Kentucky sorghum syrup, and it would be catastrophic for anybody to look forward to a Kentucky 'sugar bowl'. All he is asking is for each farmer to provide his own sugar. It is good advice and maybe next year they will take it. 'But hell,' they say, 'they's plenty of good syrup in the drugstores, and if they's one thing America at war don't need to start it's rationing. Then again, it costs money to buy a mill to crush the juice from the cane, and anyway sorghum is murder on good soil.'

Pigs and black cattle are ranging over brown grass. Then the landscape grows barer and more stubbly, barns and houses are unpainted again, and mules and goats nibble at the foot of red cedars. We leave Kentucky at Adolphus, and in Tennessee the grass looks greener. With little warning we are in backcountry, a cramped little wilderness in which apparently there are still people hopeful enough, or poor enough, to try and drag out a living. It is like a bad caricature of a backdrop for the play *Tobacco Road*. The sky is clear, and faraway birds are mocking the thin goats and the pigs that snivel for garbage in small wallows. The uneven fields on both sides of you are swollen with jutting rocks and stones. There are many Tennessees – yet this is one of them. And you recall, not without some pride, that from this gnarled, unlovely country came Secretary of State Cordell Hull.

We get back again on to the main highway, and in Murfreesboro there is a cloudless sky. Spring has soared in from nowhere. And you are a thousand miles away from the backcountry of an hour ago. Trim cedar forests give way to fertile, well-cultivated land. The streams are flashing and rippling in the sunshine and a warm breeze fans the hides of fat Jersey cattle. We duck over rolling hills prim with fine stands of cedar and start to climb toward the Cumberland Mountains on our left. The spring plowing is starting. There is a sign advertising 'walking horses'. At Hillsboro I ask a garage mechanic about the few young men around. An old man in an open shirt standing by says, 'They're takin' the boys away, truckloads ev'y day.' He looks out on the good fields and shakes his head: 'Gotta have a crop though; they can't fight on empty stomachs much.' He chuckled and added, 'They said ah was too old for the last war. Reckon I ain't too old for this one.'

We go on climbing up to Monteagle, a cool, green place as clean and stirring as somewhere in the Colorado Rockies. From here all the way to Chattanooga, through sweeping mountain valleys, it is impossible to think of Pearl Harbor. I suppose Corregidor is as beautiful, and to General Douglas MacArthur it is the natural and fearful terrain of war. But after Virginia, one's imagination is bound by the old-fashioned memories of Bull Run and Appomattox, by lines of infantry running up little hills, by pride that Capt. Oliver Wendell Holmes received a musket ball through the breast, the ankle, the neck, and survived to become a Supreme Court Justice. This is the kind of landscape God planned for a civilization that had emerged out of war. It is by a disturbing coincidence the same kind of landscape that He gave so richly to Germany. Perhaps that is why the Germans, who can fight so ruthlessly, weep and give in when their own border is threatened.

Alas for these ideals, you soon learn that where the Indian could fight, there the white man had to fight too. And, when the time came, he fought his own kind. Southwest of the city of Chattanooga, Lookout Mountain rises 1,400 feet, and there is no further translation needed of the Indian word, Chat-to-to-noog-gee, meaning 'rock rising to a point'. The ascent is so sheer that you are reminded of the drive through the control road at Yosemite, where before you flatten out into Tuolumne Meadows, you have the terrifying experience of driving continuously over your right shoulder. Up at the top of Lookout you expect to find a bare clearing. But at the top of the mountain is a most elaborate park from which you look down on the Tennessee River and on the smoky network of Chattanooga's railroad tracks. There is the sight of moving freight cars and busy transportation but no noise at all; it is like a movie without a soundtrack. All around you are gorgeous memorials, cannon preserved inside iron chains, innumerable plaques and tablets recording not alone the 'Battle Above the Clouds' but every day-long engagement of the small Confederate force that was stationed here in the fall of 1863. You look down at the silent bustle of Chattanooga and wonder if 'the war' can ever mean anything to the South but the most romantic, the best described, and, alas, the most elaborately remembered war in history. It is possible to honor the dead enshrined here and yet, weaving through the smooth slabs of marble and granite and reading the eloquent inscriptions, to wonder how the vast, unsentimental scope of the Second World War can banish from the Southern mind the memory of a period and a type of war that has gone forever. The young Southern boys who come back will know the difference, the ones who probably went off to Guadalcanal and North Africa because they wished, in a youthful way, to be worthy of a grandfather who waited and breathed in the mist on that November night almost eighty years ago. But the civilians left behind, the ones down there making iron and steel and the 1,500 other things that Chattanooga makes, how will they humbly judge America's just share of the peace? How, treading reverently through the memorial park on Lookout Mountain, will they understand the monstrous casual courage of hundreds of thousands of Russian foot soldiers, of the ones who strapped grenades to their waist and hurled themselves before a fleet of Nazi tanks. Or how measure our 'contribution', as we civilians unironically call it, against the incomprehensible valor of the millions of common people of China who throw away a few-score-thousand lives any day they're needed, and who gave no marble urns, no statues, no turnstiles to commemorate their sacrifice?

These are ticklish times to question any man's understanding of the war, and it was natural that driving down into Chattanooga as the evening lights came on, I should fall to examining my own trade and its awful pretensions. The description 'foreign correspondent' covers a multitude of sins. The name has been glorified by a few observers, De Tocqueville above everybody, then Bryce, and Lawrence of Arabia; their greatness consists, I think, in their ability to practice the scientific method, which I take to be the capacity to deduce good generalizations from all the known facts. These are alone in their genius to absorb the infinite detail of a foreign country's life and digest it into great objectivity. Below them are the disguised crusaders – the idealists, who in asserting a personal need to reform the world, smell out the trend of the times, sometimes before their readers are willing to hear it: of these are Edgar Mowrer reporting prewar Germany, Ed Murrow in London, and the man who without fuss refused to compromise the day-to-day truth as he saw it, who died in England in wretchedness of mind and body, unsyndicated and unsung – the noble exemplar of our trade, Norman Ebuts. The rest is a fine, confusing gallery of energy, talent, disappointed novelists, commentators, and graphic reporters. I thought of these men as I prepared to spend an evening wandering around the town to see if there is any intelligent method of reporting 'attitudes' and 'feelings' toward the war. For this is the glibbest pretension of the roving correspondent, who lands up in strange places with little humility and reports his findings with less misgivings.

At the end of the evening, I had learned a few sobering things. The people I talked with admittedly did not constitute anything so scientific and foolproof as a 'sample' in the Gallup sense. But they were as various as any handful of humans you could expect to meet in a week in any town. Whether they talked about the railroads, the draft, girls, steel equipment, or the Pacific, they talked about the things that were closest to their interest and anxieties, and so can tell you much more, by implication, of their feeling about the war than if you had prodded them into answering specific questions about it. If you want to know how the war is affecting a family, a man and woman, or even a community, there is a simple but forgotten fallacy in asking them directly how they stand on the war. They are at once startled into self-consciousness, they grow grave and weigh their opinions. And since many of them have never had to weigh an opinion since they left school, the answers they tend to give are perfectly sincere and perfectly dishonest. It is like asking a man if he thinks he's neurotic and if he thinks he's adjusted. Faced by what he can only regard as a challenge, he will give an answer unconsciously designed to banish the fear that you have aroused in him. He will understandably reply in a way to assert, or to reassert to himself, his decent standing in his community. When you can recognize the motive in a man's reply, the reply is likely to be useless as a record of anything more than the way he resolved a psychological dilemma you suddenly put him in. This is why reams of conscientious 'reporting' of civilian attitudes, by reporters who are quite sincerely eager to know, is a brave waste of curiosity. It is possible to gauge the functional effect of the war on an industry or a crop, because industries and crops are selfish abstractions that have no opinions about war but react with admirable selfishness in the direction of protecting themselves. But when you ask a human being how he feels about the Japs, or whether his town is prepared for air raids, or if he thinks we'll win, or whether his neighbors know what the war's all about, you are putting forth nothing but leading questions, enclitic invitations to answer Yes, sir, or No, sir. It is for this sad reason that most roving reporters, and indeed all foreign correspondents whenever they desert statistics for judgments of opinion and 'morale', become models of self-deception. They may call themselves, with proper gravity, 'reporters'. But anytime after the youth of Sigmund Freud, they are nothing but quack psychiatrists who do not even know that this is the field they practice.

High-school and college boys who wish they had been born twenty years sooner, so that they could have covered the Wall Street wail, Abyssinia, or Munich, can take comfort from the naked and terrifying fact that there is yet no such profession worthy of the cool, scientific name of foreign correspondent. We are a tribe of artful men who have learned over the years to stifle our doubts about our own capacity to observe. We soon renounce the human beings we deal and live with for a context of 'public affairs'. This means usually the society of other journalists, diplomats, businessmen, civil servants, and the minor functionaries of State Departments and governments recently dethroned. Within this convenient frame of reference, you can find an approximation to the 'truth' that will glibly describe any current crisis in the political life of any country you care to name. If any ambitious sophomore doubts this thesis, let him pore over the files of correspondence in the newspapers of the mid-30s and he will be grateful that a merciful fate saved him from being the author of so much chimerical and ponderous speculation while it preserved him featly as a bright gleam in his father's eye. He may protestingly note that a handful of American correspondents in Europe managed to call the turn on the future of the Third Reich. But these were men with hunches better than the society they kept. There has never been anything to prevent even a minor poet from stumbling on an emotional truth that is a daily truism of an analyst's parlor. The only difference is that the 'foreign correspondent' solemnly believes his 'conclusions' are 'reached', when in fact his best and worst sophistries, and predictions, and reports of group attitudes, are wholly disorganized plunges in the dark. So the field is still wide open, and the envious sophomore might wish he had been born in 1960, so that by the year AD 2000 he would have a prospect of being one of the responsible pioneers in a profession that in the early 1900s was the unclaimed land of psychological squatters, some witless, some fortuitously inspired.

Shaky from these meditations I started out after dinner on my experiment. It entailed rousing a business man, an editor, a doctor, and roving in a planless way through some bars, the railroad station, a movie, and finally an all-night café.

Whenever people expressed themselves consciously about the war, they sounded trite though oftentimes full of conviction. They had a defiant faith in General MacArthur and very little knowledge of Pacific geography. Most of them thought Bataan could be held for the duration. Most of them were disgusted at the fate of the liner *Normandie*, now slumped on her side in New York harbor. They inclined to think it was sabotage, but one man said, 'It's what you'd expect of smart-aleck New Yorkers.'

But when they talked about their own affairs, they were more revealing. Most of them seemed to worry little about air raids, except a man whose wife was learning first aid. But I noticed an attitude that is strong in every city – they wish to believe that their city is important enough, in some unique way, to invite sabotage. They do not say, 'Who'd ever think of flying in beyond the Smokies, five or six hundred miles from the coast.' They say, 'After all, you know, we're an important railroad center.'

Some of them were raging democrats, some of them easygoing appeasers, those with no relatives in the war zone didn't pretend to know what the war was all about. Some of them were confident, some were anxious. Few of them would have recognized themselves under these labels. They obviously thought of themselves first as Americans, and one or two of them were above everything else Southern Democrats. There was a doctor who distrusted Roosevelt because 'He listens too much to the Jews.' I asked him rudely, which Jews? He took the bandage he was about to tie around my same hurt finger and cut it slowly with a penknife that left a faint rim of rust. He said, 'Oh, they're all over the place. I'm from Louisville. If you look into any of the businesses around town, you'll find a Jewish syndicate took it over.' This was possibly a hazardous time to argue with him. But a Jewish syndicate was something, like a total eclipse of the sun, I had been promising myself for years. He couldn't name any but said if I knew Louisville like he knew Louisville, well, I'd be able to see it for myself. Then he sailed off on his next tack. 'Roosevelt's obsessed with all this social reform. The unions have come into the South here and caused more misery than the War Between the States.' We agreed that the chronic headache of the South is to meet the budget, to pay off the annual expenses. He talked bitterly of speculators who, if it hadn't been for the federal benefits, wouldn't have looked twice at an offer of poor land that 'grew a little corn an' cotton and kept the niggers and the poor whites happy enough, happy as they're ever able to be.' But once the government steps in to take land humanely 'out of production', the speculators are happy to 'outbid honest money' and pay a ridiculous price so as to be able to sit back and collect the federal benefits. There was another man, a disappointed Democrat, who said that 'maybe the Department of Agriculture quotas are fair enough if you're looking at the whole picture of the Southern economy, but nobody's farming the whole picture.' They talked in a melancholy way about the 'new type of labor' that had come into Chattanooga since the Tennessee Valley Authority instituted its prodigious payroll, and since 'the make-work WPA started hornin' in.' They admitted that the new population had stimulated retail business, especially in furniture and hosiery, in which Chattanooga leads the South. 'After all, if the government'll pay these people to leave their farms and take to wearin' stockings, I reckon the clothing stores don't complain. And then these people don't know how to live in cities, they come here and take sick right away. So the patent medicine boys like it too.' But they both had friends who were considerable landowners, and the argument comes full circle when you realize, but do not say, that few landowners are virtuous enough to watch the birth rate rising on a vast labor market and relish the Works Progress Administration's paying out regular money to deprive them of the golden chance to employ more and more people at lower and lower wages.

The doctor made a gesture of friendship and said, with a strained, faraway look in his eyes, as if honestly trying to envision what would be best for all the people all the time, 'I can see that in some countries they needed this social reform. Countries like England, where they lived under a class system. Naturally, a man wants to make his own way, and if's denied, well he's likely to wind up in the slums. If there's no place fo' an ambitious man to go, he's gonna get dangerous if you don't give him some sort of insurance, I reckon. But this country was founded on an entahly different i-dea.' It was hopelessly clear that the doctor, who was an extremely mild and amiable man, had not observed too closely the ways of life in his own part of the country, so I asked him if he'd ever seen Pittsburgh, or East St Louis, or downtown Los Angeles, or Baltimore, or Mobile, or New Orleans, where there are slums as offensively European as Marseilles or Paris or Sheffield. The inhospitable sarcasm was lost on him. He replied with candid pride: 'I never was west of Louisville nor east of Charleston, West Virginia. Ah don't think I'd ever want to live anyplace else.'

I wandered off through the town and paused before a Sears, Roebuck window, where there was a flaming advertisement draped with the flag and captioned, 'Remember Pearl Harbor'. In a café some soldiers and sailors, from the North and West, were kidding a Southern boy about his distrust of Negroes. 'You jest don't know them, that's all there's to it,' he insisted. 'They're a mean race o' people.' A big-boned Westerner, with humorous gray eyes, went on drumming the table with his fingers and saying, 'They're okay.'

Chattanooga goes to bed early, and before I turned in I noticed two sailors talking the erotic preliminaries to two squat little girls, fifteen or sixteen at most. In spite of the lavatory legends about sailors, there was much decent embarrassment on both sides, and, by the time they left, the girls were more subdued, and the sailors more shyly courteous than prep school boys at their first dancing class.

South again, to Atlanta, you follow Sherman's predatory route, through a fine valley with the mountains on your left, and soon the highway cuts clean between rolling red clay hills. It is at about this point that it becomes hard to recall the picture of the Northern landscape. All around you are the trees of the Deep South – hickory, short-leaf pine, gum, and spacious oaks. And crowning them, as a reminder that Florida is ahead, are bulging piles of cumulus clouds. The air is moist and warm. You go through fields of cotton and corn, and much spare land is being turned over to the growing of peanuts. In the Georgia backcountry many a county agent is going out to sell a poor farmer on the new idea that growing peanuts is a privilege, and a service to one's country. 'These few acres of yours are gonna be mighty useful to the government,' says an agent to the poor Negro.

'Mr McDowell,' the Negro replies, his thumbs locked in his suspenders, 'the go'ment can have 'em. This ain't nothin' but bad old cotton land.' He is informed that the government will give him a loan if he'll put his land into peanuts.

'Peanuts!' he howls. 'The go'ment must sho' nuff be in te'ble shape.'

'Yes, we want peanuts for the fats and oils. And we need eggs, millions of 'em, to dry for the Army, and to send overseas. Can you raise some hens here, you think?' The Negro looks aghast. 'Mr McDowell, ef the go'ment wanna pay me for raisin' elephants, ah'll sho' make a powerful try!'

A single incident like this illustrates a native modesty, or indifference, in the Southern farmer that will deprive him, in the record, of much of his due credit in the war program. The poorer ones, especially, have accepted a dependence on the Department of Agriculture, and a rather bewildered trust in its recommendations, which would undoubtedly strike our Louisville doctor as a sign of the decay of American individualism. But the Farm Security Administration has kept alive at the smallest reckoning a tenth of the nation's poorest farmers, and it would be fastidious to ask where they are to be found. They are mostly in the South. As the large combines rushed for the available steel equipment after Pearl Harbor, the poor farmer waited for a loan and was helped to buy feed and fertilizer, which are his only capital. In Virginia, West Virginia, North Carolina, Tennessee, and Kentucky, over 50,000 farm families accepted food-production loans for cows, sows, and hens. They managed, in their undemonstrative way, to market 2 million cockerels. All through the Deep South, they are being offered loans to grow peanuts and soybean, in a region whose small farmers still cling with pathetic stubbornness to the unchanging single crop – cotton. Among the qualities that the South shares with Britain, one of them is undoubtedly the total inability, or indifference, to advertise its skills. You could drive 1,000 miles through the South today and not hear much about the vast and subtle changes that are transforming its landscape. To a Northerner or a Westerner, it is a monotonous landscape, growing cotton and corn all the way to a horizon fringed with inevitable pine. But it is deeply known to its own people, and I do not think it an accident that the most indigenous descriptions of American life, and food, and growing things are written not by the more flamboyant Midwestern and Western talents, strenuously aware of their unique American context, but by Southerners who take for granted the land that reared them. William March is a brilliant example of a writer who hardly seems to be aware of himself as an intensely American writer. His novels and stories happen to be set against the background he knows, and the dialect is merely what he best recalls. But seen from the outside, the background is the infinitely known landscape of the Deep South, and the language, in all its delicacy and rightness, could be heard nowhere else.

Similarly, the poor Negro stumbling off to grow peanuts because 'the go'ment man' says to plant peanuts, cannot think of his work as 'a vital contribution to the war effort'. He does not read as much advertising copy as other Americans, and Southern newspapers are composed in a more sober idiom than the *Bridgeport Herald* or the *Los Angeles Examiner*. So, clear down to the Gulf, thousands of Southern farmers are growing peanuts and soybean, and they may tell you in a shambling, uncertain way that they understand the government needs them. They do not know, or seem to care much, that they will be planting most of the nation's million extra acres of peanuts, and 3 million extra acres of soybean. Very few of them, I suspect, could tell you that their humble peanuts will make up for the loss of coconut oil that we imported from the captured Philippines and the Netherlands East Indies, and their soybean for the palm oils that, when labor and transport were cheap, we took easily from Latin America.

Down through this pleasant country you pass little cabins with pelts strung under the porch and a sign out: 'Hand-made furs'. Running alongside cabins that stand on grassless soil are rows of beautiful jonquils. You pause by a field, an automobile junk heap, and notice the grim indication of a war in which the United States was cut off at the start from its main source of rubber. There are hundreds of rusty and decrepit automobiles, looking as usual like an anthology of old accidents, like a rusty memorial to the hip-flask era of American culture. But you notice that not one of them has an inch of rubber. Every other part of a car is frozen in its rotting state. But every single car is naked of its tires.

At a gas station you ask the attendant casually for a road map of Georgia. He goes inside his office, is gone a long time, and comes out wearing a smiling frown. He blows the dust off and hands it over. He says, 'They're hard to get a hold to. Can't hardly get.' This detail registers as alarmingly as the shortage of Coca-Cola in Huntington, West Virginia.

From Dalton to Marietta is the chenille counterpane belt. All the way along the highway you see bathmats and bright rugs and bedspreads hung on clotheslines. Some of the farmers, who help their wives with the 'tufting' of the bedspreads, hope in a nervous way that the Army will like their designs and place an enormous order – a hope that, when you consider the riotous designs the Georgia wives like to indulge in, seems doomed to defeat.

You pass on to a fine divided highway, and in a sunless haze ahead of you is the town of Scarlett O'Hara, the town of rearing smokestacks, clanging railroad shops, hustling fruit markets; of textiles, Coca-Cola, and sidewalk rabbis; of factories going up and going down; of clattering streetcars, paper mills, refrigerator plants; the home of bakers, printers, soft drink executives, railroad men, and garment workers; the brash, noisy, smoky city that stands as a healthy enigma to any visiting debutante from the North come to look for Peachtree Street and Clark Gable. Atlanta.

Atlanta always looks as if it's being made over, but now there is more riveting than ever, more construction, more wrecking, more seeming haste and preparations for booming business, and air raids, and for a war to be lived, in the ways that the teeming cities of the Eastern Seaboard know. If it is true, as a fair-minded Southerner has said, that Sherman's occupation hurt the South less than the tariff, and that the economic occupation hurt the South less than the tariff, and that the economic occupation of the South by the North had hardly ended in 1938, Atlanta is surely the town to prove it. A Southerner may call it a symbol of 'the New South' and keep his head up when he says it before strangers. But I doubt it is the kind of symbol he would have chosen. The investing capital comes from the East. It is Chicago grafted on to Charleston or Savannah. What is most Southern about it is the guaranteed presence of an inexhaustible source of cheap labor. But you do not look here for wartime changes in Southern folkways. All the signs are the signs of a metropolis at war. The bookshops have stacked piles of first-aid books. A best-seller, widely advertised, is a book called, *How Your Business Can Win the War*. The hardware stores are advertising 'luminous paint for civilian blackouts', and the hotel requests that you never leave a room with its lights on: 'the saving of electric current is necessary in the production of aluminum for fighter planes.' There seems everywhere a more nervous alertness to the prospect of air raids than in any town you've seen, and it seems strange that a visiting English lecturer (they are still around) should choose to tell the people of this awakened industrial city that 'war may have to be burned into the minds of American women before they'll know it's a life and death affair.' You go back to your hotel room, and on the door is a prominent notice saying, 'Before a blackout, all lights in this hotel will blink three times at intervals of five seconds, then again after five minutes. Draw shades, lock the door, stay away from the window. There will be no transportation during actual raids.'

You ask who makes up this alert crew of civilian defenders. And your answerer lowers his head, smiles with his eyes, and asks a strange riddle: 'If you live in Atlanta, what's the first thing you ask of anybody?' I ask to be told. He says quietly, 'Are you an air-raid warden or a Gentile?' It tells you more about an attitude to bombing than all the first-aid books, hotel notices, and public handbills. It tells you also that Atlanta must be either like New York or Kansas City – it must have a lot of Jews or almost none, for these seem to be the first conditions of anti-Semitism. The answer is that Atlanta is, in this respect, more like New York. You notice in the newspapers, and in general conversation, a kind of easygoing acquiescence to the British view of the war. This is not to say that the Deep South is particularly pro-British or anti-British. It merely does not seem to react, as some parts of the country traditionally do, against the war interpretations that come from London.

But Georgia has problems of its own that are debated more urgently than the war. And the sorest of these is the 'cracker' regime of Governor Eugene Talmadge. Like most Southern cities, Atlanta has better than its share of determined liberals, in a region where being a liberal is as hard on individual endurance as being a conscientious objector in a city at war. The ambition of these people in Georgia had been to have the state Constitution revised, no revolutionary itch in this, a revision every ten years is promised in the Constitution itself, but as the years go by it gets harder and harder to loosen a vested interest away from its foundations, if only to give it more breathing space elsewhere. In Atlanta, the cry is for 'redistricting' and sweet release from the county unit system, whereby the electoral system is figured on antique population figures, which consequently allow two representatives in the state legislature to the smallest county – with a population of a few hundred – and only six representatives to Atlanta, which has a population of nearly half a million. Northerners politely but condescendingly bemoan the superstitious ignorance of Georgia in allowing a man like Talmadge to have and hold such high elective office. But there are Democrats in Atlanta as enlightened and cour-ageous as any in New York or Cleveland. They happen to be the angry victims of a system that is a total failure as an index of the effective intelligence of its citizens. Thousands of liberals in Atlanta can meet and parade and spout floods of good passion against the dominance of Talmadge. But all he needs to do, if he feels his throne wobbling, is to climb in an old roadster, drive out into two or three surrounding counties, say 'hiya' to a friendly farmer or two, and ride back to Atlanta secure in the knowledge that he has assured himself of six supporting votes, which is as much as Atlanta can muster if every man, woman, and child there turns against him.

You drive out of Atlanta on the road to Macon and pass through some of these rolling counties of the Piedmont that swear allegiance to old 'Gene'. The barns are unpainted but well stored. There are plenty of vegetables. These farmers are not prosperous. But neither are they poor enough to be leery of folksy promises. To have the land support them in this malleable state has been the lucky experience of Gene Talmadge.

The slopes of the hills swim up and away from you, and careful contour plowing curves over the hills like waves of surf. Every other roadside sign is an advertisement for pecans. This little drive to Macon superficially reflects the war less than any landscape you have seen. If you go into the Georgia Experimental Station, just before Griffin, you will learn that they are doing laboratory experiments on pecan parasites, planning to teach the surrounding farmers simple ways of putting their fruits and vegetables into cold storage. You learn there is intense excitement, in a laboratory kind of way, over the wartime possibilities of Georgia's muscadine grape. Perhaps a variety can be found that the Army will want to use. According to the scientists, the Army is looking for a favorite fruit with a high vitamin content that can be packed into the mysterious and precious 'K' ration. But aside from these minor excitements, there is nothing in the emerging spring around you to tell of war. The drive into Macon and all the natural symbols are of an easy, spacious town of the Deep South – the even spacing of palmettos along broad streets, the crape myrtles, boxwood hedges, and in the air the smell of warm blossom.

Strolling in a speculative sort of way down the main street is a boy in the gray-blue uniform of a Royal Air Force Cadet. He is less shy to approach than most young Englishmen, which is understandable enough since he turns out to be a Scot, and weighs everything he says with a kind of judicial gravity. Now does he like the country? He likes the country, and the people have been more than friendly. But he speaks for more of the cadets than himself when he says that he doesn't like the training. It seems, at least in this stage of the transatlantic training of the RAF boys, that they haven't yet managed to work out a form of discipline that is acceptable to training Britons and yet would not suggest to nearby American soldiers the personal advantages of anarchy. The Scot thinks that Americans have not heard how different and new to British military traditions is the Royal Air Force, and how much further away than a quarter-century are its customs from those of the Royal Flying Corps of the last war. His observations are pointed sharply by the sudden appearance of half a dozen other British trainees. They join in the conversation shyly but easily, and in a moment you recognize the accents of the ordinary people of London, Lancashire, the Midlands, and Scotland. These boys, whether they know it or not, are the first rough hew of a new generation of English democrats. However aware of social and class differences, they don't show the old characteristic servility of an enlisted man before an officer who sprang from a family life, an education, and a code of manners as foreign to the working-class habits of England as the blubber-feeding ceremonies of an Eskimo wife and her mate. These boys were not recruited out of a theory of social democracy. They were Britons, seventeen years of age, who were available, deceptively apt, and in a galumphing way responsible and personally courageous. They all agreed that the training here, demanding 210 flying hours for their Wings instead of 150 at home, was a great advantage, and they were grateful for the daily practise on the ground, inside Link trainers, in which they can be fed any kind of atmosphere or navigational hazard that they will know on top of the clouds. But they came back all the time to solemn headshaking over petty punishments that, in the hard-working, unsentimental grind of the RAF, they had never known at home. They were aghast at the sight of American soldiers doing penance for some casual crime or impudence by walking up and down a yard in full kit in steaming heat. They also were bewildered by being required to salute officers of a land army. They all felt that this obligation to respect an alien and to them old-fashioned military etiquette was a daily irritation. But when they seemed to be pressing the point, one of them would mention the people and what they had learned from the South. With great seriousness the Scot said, 'I have two or three homes here, and it's the same, I think, with all of us.' They each tried out on the others their own highly unconvincing performance of Southern idiom. They had evidently dredged up from the sea of strange language all about them several pearls they meant to hold on to. A small boy from a London suburb threw his head back like a man about to imitate a coyote and said, 'I betcha' with a rare expression of pride. As we drove away from Macon, the RAF boys waved to us. The bony Scot flashed his even teeth; 'Bye, y'all,' he moaned.

Down through Macon and Cochran we drive through prosperous, rolling farmland, and the road shoots through fine forests of long leaf pine. Near Cochran the red earth turns sandy and you know that you have pulled out of the Piedmont and will soon be heading across the Coastal Plain. There are cheerful roadside invitations to 'come and see us', and soon it's made clear that these refer to a 'Free Zoo Ahead – Performing Coon, Rattles Snake'. The war does not seem to have affected snake life so far, but raccoons have other uses than performing for Southern tourists and are hard to come by.

We're now heading due southeast on US 341, and on both sides of the road is cotton land. Near Helena the pink blossoms of peach orchards pepper the countryside and a cryptic advertisement appears for 'Bees and Queens, Italians and Caucasians'. Tall pines flash by and more and more of them show the sharp white gash that tells of nearby turpentine stills. This is flat, sandy country, and you might think that all the prosperous farmers were behind you in the Piedmont. But this flat section of central Georgia has the perfect cotton climate, and even if there were no fresh fields to clear there is enough fertilizer to go on sucking cotton from soil that long ago produced its best. Today the county agents have better arguments than usual to urge a wider diversity of crops, and with the export cotton market practically frozen, farmers who had made it a principle never to grow anything but cotton are turning to dairying, peaches, and poultry raising. Outside Waycross you see an elaborate layout of motor courts, but not a tourist or automobile in sight. After Waycross the highway bridges the first small stagnant swamps, and where there are oaks tufts of moss are hanging from them. You are now on the edge of the great Okefenokee Swamp, and you wonder if the war can have any interest in conquering this wilderness of 600 square miles of scummy water and ghostly timber. We drive up a dirt road to Camp Cornelia, and in the brooding heat of the afternoon two big black buzzards flap away from a mess of unrecognizable carrion in the middle of the road. A turtle ambles out of a swamp shadow, and as you hear only the very distant cawing of an owl and curious low throb of the swamp's wildlife, you seem to be geological ages away from any war or civilized peace. But the sharp reminder comes again when you try to get a boat and a guide through the swamp. There are no guides. And the man who employed them has gone off to Jacksonville to get a defense job. You think of bargaining with his wife for a while but there's no hope for it; the Great Okefenokee is something you will have to forgo until Mr Harold Ickes and the Interior Department can get the guides and rangers back again and restore the National parks and monuments to the old easy accessibility of the 1930s.

We cross the St Mary's River and the Florida line shortly after Folkston and see pink dogwood out and peachtrees in blossom. There is no doubt about the principal crop ahead, for all the highway signs start appealing to it – the Northern tourist. A broken airplane is merely a restaurant and an invitation to dinner. Every shape and size of trick advertising is planted by the highway and forms almost a separate species of Florida scrub pine. A few of the signs are simple advertisements for hotels, motels, tourist courts. Most of them magnanimously share a confidence with the Southbound tourist, warning him against those who may be more indifferent to his welfare: 'Don't be misled by cut-rate hotel folders'. The slash pines flick by like roadside markers, and soon the tourist camps form a wide fringe of petticoats all the way into Jacksonville.

As you drive into Jacksonville, you will notice that its proudest beacon has been blacked out, the high electric sign over the municipally owned light plant that preached the slogan, 'Do It Electrically'. The retail stores are doing a roaring business, and though the women's dresses in the store windows are as carefree as ever, there are more uniforms behind glass than you have seen before. Some of the 100 passenger trains, which Jacksonville boasted was the regular daily flow during the winter tourist season, are being unceremoniously sidetracked for troop trains rolling in and out. There are barricades of freshly cut lumber piled up in the warehouses and along the wharves down by the river. But to Jacksonville the war has made most demands on two of its most ancient industries: turpentine and prostitution.

Jacksonville is the Atlantic capital of the 'naval stores' industry. The name needs printing in quotes because ever since the New World shipped its first load of turpentine and rosin to England, in 1608, 'naval stores' has meant the turpentine industry. The mainstay of the industry is a tribe that is cute to the literary tourist, contemptible to the resident white, and essential to the Navy. They are the 'turpentine niggers', who have been as typical inhabitants of the Florida peninsula for the past forty years as an oleander or a Seminole. The chipping of the pine for its gum, which is then distilled into turpentine and rosin, is a Negro monopoly for the commonest and most wearisome reason: it is work thought unfit for whites. If the weather stays fine, a Negro worker in a turpentine camp may expect to make a dollar, even as much as a dollar fifty, a day. He lives in a pine camp with his spouse and together they produce offspring who would need little schooling, even if they could get it, before they learn to toddle off and tap the pines. You do not see these miserable families in Jacksonville or anywhere in towns, and nobody misses them much. They are, however, one of those subterranean populations of essential American workers who bear the same relation to what we call 'our American society' as H. G. Wells's brutish slaves, who supplied the intelligent people aboveground with most of their essential needs. In 1942, they will produce half as much turpentine again as Florida normally supplies, because Washington has insisted that a 50 percent increase in naval stores is essential for 'the successful promotion of the war'. It is only fair to say that the Negroes have been helped in this lucky patriotic assignment by a discovery, of the Russians, that if you spray a sulfuric acid solution on slash pine, it will yield exactly the increase of gum that Washington is after.

The other troublesome trade is one that no reasonably adult citizen of Jacksonville will try to belittle. It is what our solemn forefathers called the traffic in human souls. The soldiers who invade the town at weekends have a more relaxed, and perhaps grimmer, name for it. They call it 'recreation'. By the spring of 1942, there were 130,000 soldiers to whom Jacksonville was home, playground, and metropolis. With two swelling camps nearby, there will be many more of them, and Jacksonville and the Surgeon General have good cause to worry. In the First World War, Florida could boast a higher percentage of draftees with venereal disease than any state in the Union. From the figures of the Surgeon General's office, the record has been maintained at this time. The red-light district has been closed to servicemen, and it is patrolled by the military and shore police. This, you hear, satisfied the Jacksonville natives for a time, but a US Public Health officer concludes that the main difference the military patrol has made was that 'now they draw the shades.' Whether or not the residents knew this, they started to make complaints as hordes of the ousted ladies moved into apartment houses, hotels, and bungalows whose morals had never been formerly called in question.

We start out of Jacksonville and begin the long drive south, down into the never-never land of the Florida peninsula. You drive through the cutover pineland, past rambling ditches thick with fern, the road fringed with dusty cabbage palms. A wooden post shows a hand pointing to heaven and bears the threat, 'Prepare to Meet Thy God'. This is no subtlety of advertising, just a reminder that grim and godly men have come through here and stuck up their signs along a highway of winter tourists.

We see blue iris shining out of cypress swamps. Through St Augustine and south across salt marshes, down through small turpentine towns, through Korona, a potato town populated, needless to say, by Poles. Past Daytona, orange groves appear fenced with pine windbreaks. This is the beginning of the winter resort belt. Fronting on the highway is a trailer camp. In front of a newly painted trailer three men in late middle-age, wearing seersucker pants and polo shirts of blue and green, are merrily pitching horseshoes. They are by their accent farm people from the Corn Belt, and their wives sit contentedly on the trailer steps knitting and making cracks about the comparative senility of their mates. Just along the road is a fruit-stand boasting 'Orange Juice, 10 cents, All you can Drink'. One of the horseshoes pitchers, a raddled old man with silver hair and an enormous grin, calls out, 'and they mean it, too.' The wives go back to watching the game. You think, perhaps impertinently, of the wasting children of Europe. It seems the wrong time and place to ask about the war.

In the evening you sit around outside a beach hotel and listen to the talk of a baseball team owned by a soft-drink firm. Many of them are young and husky enough to begin worrying about the draft, but aside from these personal fears, which they pretend to kid into thin air, the only war talk is the sort you will hear along all the beaches from here to Miami. There is lurid speculation and dramatic rumor about the chances of Jacksonville being shelled. You hear the story many times, with many attractive variations, about a pocket submarine being washed up somewhere off the coast, well stocked with loaves of bread bearing the unnecessary label – 'Baked in Miami'. The bartender recalls that in the last war the Germans sank oil tankers at precise locations in the Atlantic from which submarines could refuel, and there is much cynical agreement that the Nazis hold the whip hand in the Battle of the Atlantic. Since the submarines' first appearance off the Atlantic Coast in the middle of January, seventy-two American ships have gone down, seventy-two merchantmen. And everybody is mad, but the only retaliation reported came from a crew of a freighter. Somebody has an editorial from a Tampa newspaper that chalks up the score for the Nazis at seventy-two to nothing and indignantly asks the Secretary of the Navy to search for the operating base for these submarines and 'do something about it – and now!'

After the swift twilight falls, you stroll barefoot along the warm sands and watch steel black clouds loom over the horizon. A palm tree rustles uneasily, and far off to the south the sky winks with sheet lightning. Then suddenly out of nowhere comes an electric storm that leaves you standing on the terrace blinded by the stutter of blue lightning. Just as you're saying a little private prayer for those in peril on the sea, the bartender, who was on a merchantman in the last war, reckons 'the men on the tankers will be grateful for a little rest.' It seems impossible that anybody out there could stay afloat in the plunging foam. But the bartender is a Florida native – that is to say he's a man from Chicago who's been here twenty years – and we soon take the breathless spectacle for granted and fall into a close discussion on the relative hazards of two trades: whether men on tankers or submarines rate the heavier pay. And once again it occurs to you, what had first struck you in the lumber towns of West Virginia, that ordinary people talk very little about the strategy of the war, or indeed about the battles lost and won, but think first and always about the way the war affects their work.

The work of Florida is in outline almost brutally simple to describe. It is the sale of its climate, either directly to a couple of million people it can lure down each winter from the North, or indirectly in cans and boxes in the shape of oranges and grapefruit or citrus juices. Way behind these two products is the frantic cultivation of vegetables to be shipped north before Georgia and the Carolinas can get enough sunlight to grow a sizable competition. The moment you start to go inland from Daytona the sand ridges turn into luxurious citrus groves, and from Deland all the way across the peninsula to Tampa you will see and smell vineyards and truck gardens that make Florida's second crop. But from here, on the coast road, all ways point to the first crop, over grassy marshlands, sand flats tunneling through little jungles and pine woods, over salt marshes splotched with sunflowers, through small citrus ports whose streets are lined with coconut and date palms. Then after Fort Pierce the tropical seascape merges into Coney Island, and the roadside signs plead and beg and shriek at you, offering everything for a winter escapist, from trailer camps to patent medicines and guava jelly. After Jupiter you drive for many miles between rising inland dunes covered with palmettos, and on your left the ocean, a light translucent green, is breaking gently on a sloping yellow beach. This is what Florida means to millions of Americans, and Florida knows it. You pick up a copy of a Miami Beach newspaper, the *Miami Beach Daily Tropics*, and a banner headline proclaims, 'Record Snow Blankets East'. Underneath is a single headline, a third the size – 'Japs Report Capture of Toungoo'. It is the second headline that makes you look out across the smooth, wide beach and suggests what a good place this would be for the drilling of soldiers. By the time you get to Miami Beach you learn that the Army has had the same idea.

Army procurement officers have been down here and taken options on a half-dozen small hotels. The Army says that they are thinking of Miami Beach as an ideal place to establish the Air Corps Replacement and Training Center and the Air Corps Officer Candidate School. But the big hotel-keepers are unalarmed. They feel that although the Army shows excellent judgment in drafting the climate, they will undoubtedly cooperate with maximum patriotism and arrange to win the war, and yet not intrude on the healthful capers of their million winter visitors. It is a curious fact you have noticed in other places that the last people to believe in the possibility of total war are those whose living is made out of total pleasure. The old order may change, giving place to communes, European federations, a self-governing India, and a liberated China, but as one hotel operator says, 'All joking aside, there doesn't really seem to be any urgent reason why Miami Beach shouldn't go on next year and the year after as it has done in the past. After all, this place is a sort of sanctuary of American morale.' You spend a day and a night looking at what morale can mean to rich widows, spry old executives in white caps and golf shoes, to upper-class families with bouncing children, to tanning debs, to the theatre people and unattached playboys and other such, who from the restless tension of their appearance would certainly seem to be in need of a winter's course in morale. The visible shell of this community has been twice made over, and in the late 1930s, during the period of Miami's second boom, it became an architects' playground. Some of the big, newer hotels on the beach are working models of most of the resources of modern design, using a beautiful range of cement, glass, steel, light metals, and the widest use of plastics. By contrast the ritzy spots of the 1920s are very sad and crumbly, being in the main cocky little essays in MGM rococo, in tiled roofs and pebble façades. There is no denying the melancholy fact that the only clubs that lay any claim to age and exclusiveness unfortunately lay claim as well to the architectural styles of the period, namely to various sorts of California bungalows, sometimes dignified with the name of Spanish Patio style, combined with vague aspirations toward Morocco. The apotheosis of this contrast between the refined but crummy, and the upstart but good design, is made vivid by comparing the ultra Surf Club, so exclusive that the only regular inhabitants are the staff, with a small, cleanly designed nightclub that mimics the friendly craze for Latin America by calling itself 'El Dumpo' and greets the visitor with the unexclusive sign: 'Bums! This is one place where you're welcome.'

At 11:00 in the morning the streamlined pleasure forts come to life. The bald, the glamorous, the lobster-faced new arrivals line up at the hotel desk and cash checks at a window over which hangs a handsome metal sign with inlaid letters – 'Gentile Clientele'. Handsome matrons emerge on the terrace overlooking the ocean. A couple of blondes, wearing terry-cloth robes over a coal-black tan, go into a conference with their escorts. They're trying to decide whether to swim in the tiled swimming pool at their feet or in the green, green ocean just fifty yards away. They settle for another drink and a needed rest on the beach under a large striped umbrella. All around you are other couples, trios, handsome families, everybody dressed easily and exquisitely. Whatever else has been said about these people – and it has been practically everything – they are the handsomest, best dressed, and best behaved of the very rich anywhere. They also look extremely healthy in a careless, natural way, although it is conceivable that before nightfall the life of a troubled oilman may finally expire for all its beautiful mask of tan and Waikiki shorts. In the late afternoon they will go into the shadow of their suites again to rest or dress for an evening in the Peacock Room, the Flamingo Bar, or any of a score of modern nightclubs sprouting metal blinds and fine pastel greens and blues. Apparently there is little cliquishness in this town. There are no places where movie stars or businessmen or writers may expect to meet only their kind. Everybody here is presumably rich and wanting to play, and the only variety at the clubs is in the type of entertainment. You sit up at a bar and watch the archetypes of Miami manhood: the playboys in their late thirties or early forties wearing polo shirts, slacks, wristwatches – all are tanned, all slightly weary. They are either talking about somebody's love affair with a woman in her middle thirties or foxily eyeing the showgirls who, after each performance, come up to the bar to seize their contract drinks.

This is the status quo. And while you're there, the Army sets it rocking. It seems that in the first conference between the hotel operators and the Army's procurement men, a price had been agreed on that was thought fair enough by several attending Miami bankers and real-estate men. While the contracts were on their way to Washington for signature, five or six of the hotels reneged on the deal and tried to double the original figure. The Army suspended its plans, and the hotel men sat back and confidently expected that the Army would be unable or unwilling to hold out against the unique attractions they had to offer. At this point the editorial writers of the Gulf Coast papers suddenly felt a juicy story falling into their laps. They began to write little homilies about patriotism and human acquisitiveness that, considering the way the Gulf Coast feels about Miami, were master-pieces of understatement. The Army one day boldly declared that it had pulled out of the Miami Beach area and was looking elsewhere for a location for its training center. The West Coast began to hint modestly at its own advantages and suggested that Bellaire, St Petersburg, Tampa, and Clearwater were only a few of the places that had hotels only too willing to house an Air Corps in the interests of national defense. Nothing could have been better calculated to give Miami Beach an acute case of raging patriotism. It became known that the Officer Candidate School, which then included only about 500 men and another 500 administrators, would in all likelihood be expanded to a revolving personnel base of about 5,000 men. Before the war is over, an Army officer predicted, the Replacement Center would have a permanent population of not less than 45,000 men. Instantly about 175 members of the Miami Beach Hotel Association passed a resolution, unanimously agreeing to do business on the Army's terms. The Army officials called another meeting, and this time faced a more pliable though apprehensive body. Out of this tense conference came an official statement from General Ralph H. Wooten, Commanding Officer of the Air Corps Technical Training Command in that area. He said in effect that all was forgiven and that the Army and the hotel men had agreed to locate the school and the center there on the Army's terms. Immediately the publicity hounds of Miami Beach grabbed a camera and an expression of good will and started mailing back to the homes of the boys already here glossy 8 x 10s of sons posing in rude health on Miami's coral strand. The hotel-keeper who had hoped for a continuation into eternity of Miami's civilian pleasures now explained that Miami Beach had everything to gain from an arrangement whereby half the hotels would be filled with soldiers and the other half with parents visiting them. You take a look at one of the hotels that the Army has moved into. A couple of weary trainees are stretched out on the satin coverlets of twin maple beds. Another is sitting at a modern unit desk and bureau, tilting the metal Venetian blinds to adjust the strong light to the taste of his reclining friends. Downstairs the Flamingo Bar has been converted into a projection theatre for slide lectures on ballistics.

You hear afterwards that the crux of the negotiations was reached on a sunny afternoon when the Army acquainted the hotel operators with its normal basic rate. The hotel-keepers started to expound the woes of their business. They pointed out that most of the big hotels had been built at a cost of anything up to half a million dollars. Through the winter season they asked and got anything from $20.00 to $35.00 a room a day. The Army repeated the grievous news that its basic rate was $10.00 a man a month. It would be hard to imagine a more exquisite opportunity for use of the word 'compromise'. But the deadlock was resolved by a young Lieutenant who remarked that the Army does not theoretically engage rooms, it rents cubic feet. After a moment's silence, the perspiration rolled happily down the foreheads of the hotel men. The only problem now was how many men you could pack into a room, 16 x 20. A little hasty arithmetic was figured on scratch pads, and the conference was amicably ended. The only headache they had to wrestle with was how to store or dispose of the furniture and furnishings, for again the Army likes its cubic feet to be uninhibited by four-poster beds and Jacobean trestles.

It is true to say that most of the hotel-owners were frankly enthusiastic about the prospect of the Beach's contribution to the war effort. The alternative, they now clearly saw, was between a three months' season at $25 a day a room and an unending season at the rate of 60, 80, 100 or even more dollars a room a month. The happiest of the innkeepers was one whose hostelry had been built in 1938 at a cost of $800,000. He was carrying a $400,000 mortgage, and he figured that with the help of the Army he could start paying it off. The authentic Miami touch was added by one glowing real-estate man who described the Air Corps invasion of Miami Beach as a simple switch from a normal winter season to a 'twelve-month Army season'.

5

The Gulf Coast

The airplane rises in the twilight and heads north and west to the Gulf Coast. Behind us is the glassy ocean, with the lights of Miami Beach frothing to its edge like scummy bubbles. As we gain altitude the twinkling coast fades into memory, and we look down on the inky, drowned plain of the Everglades.

For the first time on this trip I pass through a landscape that suggests no connection with the war or even with human society. For the first time I can feel the eerie emotional privacy that is the special quality of certain regions of the West. The map tells us that we are in fact still east of Raleigh, North Carolina, of Roanoke, Virginia, even east of Rochester, New York. But the Everglades are akin to Zion, and the Grand Canyon, and the Black Hills at night. A geographer may maintain that these are measurable parcels of marsh or limestone. But to a traveler born in a temperate zone, they are kingdoms of the imagination, vast fantasies in the mind of God that a man may analyze at his peril. You reflect that a Navajo or a Seminole probably feels quite different, and that to him they are the cozy habitation of hearth and home and a warm supper. You wrestle with this mystery a little longer and decide that all you are saying to yourself is that to an Anglo-Saxon a deciduous tree is the anchor of reality, and when it is no longer there the rest is chaos and black night. Comforted to have analyzed something that seemed poetic, and to have watched it turn into a prejudice, I can look down again and bear to admit that there is a perfectly scientific recipe for the concoction of a swamp as awful as Milton's Hell. Down there somewhere in the stinking ocean of weed and mud are slender egrets standing near honeysuckle, alligators sloshing through a wilderness of cypress, and, rising from purest muck, orchid trees that bear a thousand blossoms. But from the plane, all you can see round to the purple rim of the horizon is a sedgy lake floating with lily pads. We are low enough to scan through glasses what look like islands of matchsticks. They are the houses of Seminole Indians, on stilts, high above the water. The pilot reports that because of their traditional mastery of sky signs, and the happy accident of their domestic architecture, the Seminoles have been signed up as airplane spotters. It is a pleasing thought that while you are peering down through binoculars at these tamed inmates of the swamp, they are also skeptically focusing on you, with the full encouragement and authority of the Office of Civilian Defense.

A fellow passenger looks down gloomily and says he never did understand why the federal government or anybody else should want to enclose the Everglades into a National Park. 'Park!' he exclaims. 'Just look at it. Just a mess of muck and sand.' A small, wiry man, a Texan, remarks that on the contrary there's good sugar cane and wild rice down there. 'They raise an av'rage of nahnteen thousand acres. This year the gov'ment is askin' 'em for more.' I was cheered by the thought that somebody in Washington keeps a careful file on this ocean of dirt and works from nine to five arranging for a poor white, or an Indian, or a fugitive from his draft board, to reclaim an acre of mud for Uncle Sam. The first man is not so easily comforted.

'Y'ever driven through it?' asks the Texan. 'No, sir,' he replies, 'and I never hope to. Ev'y time I fly over here, I just pray to God the pilot knows which way he's going.' After a while, he rubs his cheek restlessly with the palm of his hand and sighs, 'Oh I don't know. Maybe when I retah, I'll feel diff'ent.' He confesses that since the war began he has been a chronic insomniac, waking with a start and wondering 'how many boats I lost last night'. He operates a small fleet of tankers round the Gulf and up to New Jersey. The Texan asks him, how many boats does he run? He says, with a long face, 'Well, I have twelve. Least, this morning I had twelve. By the time I git to New Orleans, I reckon I'll have eight or nine maybe. I had twenty, three months ago.' He says if the government doesn't do something about that pipeline up from Texas to New York and Pennsylvania, 'I'll settle for a little Caribbean trade, and dump the cargo – of coffee or whatever – at Key West. And the hell with oil.' We ask him about signing up a crew for his tankers, and he says sorely, 'Might just as well advertise for suicides. Fifty percent of a crew you pick up in Galveston or New Orleans either quit when they reach New Jersey, and take a train home, or they finish the round trip and go look for a job in a shipyard. Can you blame 'em? Ev'y night I wait for a phone call f'om New Jersey. They don't stand a chance. These submarine commanders know the Atlantic Coast better than we do. Two weeks ago, one o' my boats was hit. And inside a few minutes the sub comes up to the surface. The Commander shouts across if any o' my men are hurt. In English? Sure in English. Well, there was one fella with his leg pretty badly smashed. They rowed him over to the sub, and the Nazis picked him up and went to work on him. Operated on him, dressed him, and ev'thing. 'Bout an hour later, they lifted him back up, and our fellas took him back into the rowboat. The tanker was almost sunk by this time, and the crew that was still alive was in two rowboats. Just before the Nazis submerged again, the Commander yells out, "Any o' you boys from Brooklyn?" Well, nat'chily, they said nothin'. Then the Commander shouts, "Maybe I worked with some o' you guys. I was twelve years in the Brooklyn Navy Yard. So long," he says. Can you tie that?' We had passed over Charlotte Harbor, and though it was dark down below the sparse lights of small towns were dotted at familiar intervals. Ahead on our left we saw St Petersburg, and the oilman breathed a happy sigh as we droned over Tampa Bay and came down at Tampa.

Between here and the East Coast is citrus country, the core of any stable prosperity that Florida has ever known. Waking the next morning in Clearwater, and driving along a waterfront brilliant with flowers, the oilman's anecdote of the night before seemed like a guilty dream and submarines a dirty European joke. In Dunedin, the dense scent of oranges wafted into oblivion any further preoccupation with sinking tankers. Near a small factory you wonder why this smell should be so powerful and finally appreciate that it comes from a plant working to concentrate orange juice for shipment to Britain and Russia. If there were no submarines, there might have been no pressing reason to concentrate the juice of oranges that in the last war would have been shipped whole. And once again you are made to recognize that a war economy is not a separate study of generals and munitions-makers and economists in Washington and London working on supply. It is the whole economy of a nation at war. My trip so far had demonstrated in bewildering detail that if you look carefully enough into any part of the nation's economy, into the manufacture of gloves or the marketing of camellias, you will learn about profound changes that only the war could make.

This plant that carries the important title Citrus Concentrates, Inc., is a ramshackle assortment of low buildings throbbing in a series of Joe Cook rhythms, and held together by rusty screws, worn rubber tubing, and the fanatic ingenuity of its research director, Dr Robert James. He is a gawky, raw redhead, a small, determined chemist who sports a toothbrush mustache, a perpetual wry frown, and a deputy sheriff's badge at his belt. To the shopkeepers and waiters in the taverns of Dunedin and Clearwater he is known reverentially as 'the Professor'. To the orange growers he is a humorous, alarming, reformer and the most puzzling of the wartime gifts from Washington. The fact that he is a Republican and an active agent of the Department of Agriculture alternately cheers and depresses them. For when he came down here, not many months ago, he told a meeting of the Citrus Commission, to begin with, that 'the economics of the citrus industry is crazy, and you know it. You have to gather the fruit crop as cheaply as possible, because you have to figure in the cost of packing, shipping, and distributing. You are jittering on the verge of bankruptcy, because all you know is the worth of an orange as salable orange juice up north. Most of you are well aware that 97 percent of the oranges you ship north are used only for their juices. I'm simply here to tell you that we're bringing this industry into the state not to crowd you out but to make orange-growing a profitable undertaking. All I'm here to prove is that the part of the orange you throw away – the pulp, the peel, the seeds, the rag – is worth many times the value of the juice. If you won't see it on your own initiative, then the war and the government are going to have to make you realize it. Some of you who've been in the citrus game for thirty years or more may have the notion that all we do is concentrate the juices. But that's only the beginning. If it isn't too painful to recall what it costs you to pack and ship your fruit, you may be interested to know that we could take the entire citrus crop of Florida, concentrate the juices, and store it in a single warehouse in the Port of Newark – and for one-tenth of what it costs you to get it up there. Orange juice is almost a minor by-product of what we do with your spoilage. If you think I'm down here to tell you how to run your business, you're right.'

Dr James approaches the reformation of the citrus industry with all the bigotry of a convert. He had been a research director for Parke Davis, and then for DuPont, when he was won over to the exciting and far-reaching work that the Department of Agriculture was doing in a hundred fields. 'My God,' he cries, 'if only they'd advertise. If only they'd tell people what they are doing. They simply don't know how to publicize the tremendous work they're doing.'

Thoroughly agitated by the prospect of citrus concentration, Dr James came down to Florida and found a humble factor working with three lab assistants and practically no equipment. He got a small appropriation to run the place as a government project. And ever since, while steel plants and airplane factories and ordnance plants have been constructed of beautiful and durable materials denied for the duration to civilians, Dr James has had to bum an old Bunsen burner here, a length of copper wire or low-grade lumber there, has had to make distillation units out of rubber bands and old bottles, but he got Citrus Concentrates, Inc., booming into sizable production of all the things he had promised the Citrus Commission. Above all, his job was to help meet the British demand for orange juice, which they needed, as the children of the occupied countries are going to need it, as a vital protection against scurvy. The British wanted the juice but did not have the shipping space for whole oranges. Nor did the United States. So under Lend Lease, the US government ships, say, 10,000 gallons of the concentrated orange juice, the British receive it and add seven parts of water, and thus have 80,000 gallons of orange juice that is not exactly whole but close enough to the original to be very welcome. But this is, to Dr James, only the routine 'by-product'. Once the juice is out, Dr James and his staff are left with the peel, pulp, rag, and seeds. With alcohol and acetone they extract from the seeds a dye mordant that will fix any known color in artificial silk. The only other known oil that will do this is tea-seed oil, and Dr James adds waggishly that 'it's a Japanese monopoly, and you may have heard that we are not doing the same type of business with them that we used to.' In these seeds too are some residual fats from which they extract oleo-margarine and some vegetable fats for cooking. After the juice is expressed, the peel is left with a pigmented layer and some white pulp. By continuous distillation processes, they recover from the colored layer terpenes and carotene. The Navy uses the terpenes for marine paints, for a paint hard enough to use on battleships. Carotene is the start of Vitamin A, and from the process used at Dunedin Dr James gets an annual production running into trillions of units. From the remaining white pulp, they treat the albido to get pectin, a superlative jelling agent now being used by every modern army in the early treatment of deep wounds. What is left over is largely cellulose and sugar, from which they extract ethyl alcohol for making smokeless powder; the Vitamin B complex; feed yeast for cattle. And when all these are removed there is left an activated carbon, which can be used in war for gas masks, in peace for absorbing unpleasant smells; and an extract available for dried milk and dried eggs. 'There remains,' says the undefeatable Dr James, 'alpha cellulose, which we mix with some of the other products to give us cellophane, a very tough cellophane. In other words, we make the orange provide its own jelling agent, in the pectin, and its own container, moreover a container that's water-proof, and gas-proof, that'll carry the juices better than any tin can ever did.'

You leave this tumbledown house of magic prepared to believe that Florida belies its mystical setting and superstitious history and is the laboratory of the new hygienic world. But as we drive away, the sput-tering motor of a loaded truck is the bridge passage between the heavy silence of the groves, where the humble orange ripens unconscious of its reincarnation in the distillations of Dr James. From the end product to the beginning is only 100 yards or less, and as the truck rumbles away into the distance another sound drifts up over the veg-etable palms. It is a handful of Negroes trudging with their sacks up and down the orange groves, singing with a wistful monotony:

> Bread of Heav-en, Bread of Heaven,
> Feed me till I
> Want no more.

We are restored to the intervening norm, to the well-meaning amateur hopes of middle-class human beings, by a lunch in Clearwater. On the café tables are camellias sparkling with dew. An old lady with silver hair dips her spoon into a fragrant mess of fresh peaches, grapefruit, orange, and melon and remarks, 'They say the famine in Poland is worse than the last war.'

'No?' her companion retorts with well-bred incredulity. And they step out delicately into a garden of azaleas. Here, and elsewhere going north on Route 19, you hear murmurs of admiration for brave General MacArthur, whose colored picture is displayed in store windows, parlors, and the lobbies of hotels.

Up past Palm Harbor, the orange and grapefruit groves are protected from the wind by high, stiff rows of Australian pine. We come into the outskirts of a small seaport town whose streets are paved with bricks. And suddenly on our left the sky is penciled with a long cluster of sail-less masts. It is the sponge-fishing fleet of Tarpon Springs. The bows of a hundred boats of many colors are tied to the docks, and Greek fishermen are busy painting and mending them. They bear names like *Andros, Amarkos, Fannie C. Angeli,* and *Franklin Roosevelt.* Half-way along the dock there are a wooden hut and a board barring entrance to the boatyards. In the name of the US government, unauthorized persons are forbidden to enter. The sponge fleet is now working on a government contract, and the Greeks standing around and chatting quietly are courteously uninformative about what goes on in there. Only the youngest of them talk American, but there are few minorities in the country so unprotestingly patriotic as the Greeks. They insist on making their own living and running their own stores, with a minimum of interference from town or state government. But they are obviously very impressed by the honor of working on a war contract. Of all professions, the sponge-fishermen have most right to dramatize their work. But their traditions do not run the advertising copywriters, and while the war is on, and afterwards, few Americans are likely to know what a thing it is to ask them for an extra effort. The fleets, however, have been told by the government that most of their perilous haul will go to the armed forces and that what is expected of them is 'a record harvest for the duration'. C. P. Rodocanachi, in *Forever Ulysses,* has memorably described the daily round of a sponge-fisherman's life, and it will serve as a hint of the measure of their war contribution:

Their life is an endless struggle with death. On the surface they fight against the waves, and in the depths against sharks, against suffocation, and against the paralysis brought on by the terrible pressures they endure when, weighted with a heavy stone, they descend ever further and further down, even to forty fathoms deep. The sponge once plucked, they leave their stone and rebound to the surface. Such is the pressure with which they remount to the boat, that they are flung several yards into the air, to fall into the water again like bleeding phantoms, drawn on board almost inanimate, sweating blood through all their pores, convulsed and panting. This is the cost of the soft sponge that we use so thoughtlessly, and the sanguinary price is always paid by the miserable Greeks who have the sad monopoly of this accursed trade.

This, it has to be admitted, describes the trade as it has been practiced for several thousand years. It is typical that Tarpon Springs, the American capital of the industry, should have devised a trick or two to moderate the traditional suffering. The colony here was established in 1905, soon after the equipment for deep-sea divers had been perfected. And the present generation feels at once superior to the European practitioners and grateful to their new country for reducing the hazards of their work. But the game still calls for stubborn courage and grueling physical endurance. And every time the fleet goes out a priest of the Orthodox Church blesses each boat, and when the fleets turn homeward at Easter the thanksgiving services are held. The invention of diving equipment has not pacified the Gulf storms or made the prayers of wives and mothers less devout.

We went out on a new road through semi-tropical brush, with slender blue flowers growing out of the parallel bayous. Wherever the country widened into cutover pine, black hogs and cattle roamed everywhere. We drove through cypress ponds and in the late afternoon watched Negroes standing up to their knees in swamp and cat-fishing with long poles. We were going up across the narrow neck of the peninsula where, according to lobbying Southerners in Congress, there is angry agitation for a Florida barge canal. But as the twilight descended, the countryside buzzed only with the eerie music of all the swamp flies and frogs. Nameless birds wheeled and squawked against the orange rim of the horizon. Till, at dusk, we climbed up to Tallahassee.

Tallahassee is a state capital, and like most state capitals its first interest is in the continuing promise of a pork-barrel. Its index of health or 'normalcy' is the number of its citizens on the state or federal payroll. And it is more likely to become agitated in an election year in peacetime than in an 'off year' in wartime. Consequently, the local problems of the war tend to get thought of as exercises in political science. I talked with a citizen or two who held, or had held, city appointments. They considered the possibility of an air raid entirely as a prospective test case between federal and state administrations. They were suspicious of the Office of Civilian Defense. They thought very little of Mr La Guardia's plan to organize civilian defense municipally through a congress of Mayors. They modestly drew attention to 'the forthrightness' of Southerners and admitted they couldn't think of a better plan than the one Florida had evolved, which gave the supreme authority to the Governor to appoint statutory officers, who would summon county authorities, Red Cross officials, and the local chapters of the American Legion, 'to work in harmony' if by chance the Nazis' touted long-range bombers should descend on Tallahassee. Under direct questioning, they confessed that if by chance a bomb should drop on the high sidewalks of Park Avenue and then bounce into the gutter, it would provoke a state crisis of protocol. For it seemed that both the Mayor and the Governor could legally claim authority over the sidewalks, but once the bomb lay simmering on the public (i.e., US) highway, both the sheriff and the Office of Civilian Defense might want to establish their authority. I suggested that the London Blitz had presumably simplified a good many problems in etiquette for the administration of the London County Council. But the point was ignored as a light-minded irrelevance. The conversation then turned to Negroes, irritating as it must be to a native Southerner when a Yankee or other alien is around. And one man, who was affable, thoughtful, and politically wise was ready to quiet my outlander's fears. 'The Nigras,' he said, 'are doing all right. In spite of what you read, they always have done. Since the war came, the Nigras aroun' here have taken care of most of the construction, of cantonments and the like. If any of 'em thought they were doing badly, they just had to get a taste of a war boom and find themselves paying out to the American Federation of Labor. I've had Nigras I know, and like, come to me in great distress. They were carpenters, bricklayers, and so on and they just nat'chlly took it for granted when the call came they'd be used to build the camps. When they went to sign on, they got in line and found themselves up against AF of L union leaders, asking 'em two, three, four hund'ed dollars initiation fees before they could start in working. Well, for some of 'em it was their first taste of being treated like a white man. And they didn't like it. But, I'm telling you, a lot of 'em paid up. That goes to show you. Now, you notice the way they came to me, a white man, for help.'

He went on, in measured and even uncomplaining tones. But I was not listening any longer. I recalled the almost psychic change that comes over you when you go south across the Virginia border and thence for 1,000 miles, and round the arc of the Gulf, through a region rich in resources and in unkempt, disillusioned, but able labor. It is not hard or cynical to see why the South hugs the Democratic Party like a sickly child at the only breast it knows. It wants many more things from President Roosevelt, but with his help it can just about keep its head above water and gasp a little gratitude for the Farm Security Administration, the Home Owners Loan Corporation, and the other federal admissions that the incomes of the South are barbarously low. Because its incomes are low, no Southern state can raise enough funds to match the federal grants. The South is the richest potential agricultural region of the continent. It cries for money to save itself from long abuses and make the potential a rich fact. It cries for materials on a fair exchange for its own manufactured goods, to develop its industries, to equip its ring of ports. Not many Southerners I talked with were deceived by the superficial boom of the war industries. They knew that the great shipyards and the new factories of the South would be, to the postwar hungry, mocking memorials if, while the war is on, the fair principles of an equitable peacetime economy, and permanent federal support for an industrial South, were not guaranteed. As I thought of these things, I realized with a shock that all through the South, ever since the day I left Washington, I had never heard any election talk.

I walked out cheerlessly into the warm night past giant magnolias and live oaks that, like the South itself, look so grand and haunting from a distance, until you come close and see that Spanish moss is much like the dead fuzz that gathers under beds. I walked up the main street for the human signs of war. Along a couple of city blocks, where the neon lights were, there was human material for a whole committee of sociologists, and short-story writers, to say nothing of irate parents and magistrates from the juvenile courts. There were hundreds of soldiers in the saloons, hanging around newsstands, soda fountains, backed up against walls laughing and brawling with girls. It was the most casual sort of crowd. And on the surface taking its innocent ease. But something strikes you that you have not noticed before; the girls are not professional houris, nor are they girls in their twenties coupling off with the soldiers they like. They were fifteen-year-olds, mostly squat or thin or otherwise unattractive. They were girls whose favors, however childish, would never be competed for by the boys in their schools. They stood in twos and threes, surrounded by dozens of big, raw, joshing soldiers. They were getting the first tumble they ever had in their lives. And they were loving it. The new and grisly idea dawns on me that the fifteen-year-old unattractive girl might well be the debauchee of the Second World War.

The next morning was fresh and springlike, and driving west past fields of pursuit planes shining in the sun, I thought the native soldiery seemed more innocent and purposive than they had the night before. We hummed along on an asphalt road past hogs burrowing their snouts in the delicate blossom of cypress ponds. We ran parallel with old railroad tracks being reconditioned by Negro work-gangs and so came eventually to Panama City and turned south to the sea. Across the Bay Harbor, the sight of a fringe of flowers along the dunes touched off one of those casual fantasies that spring up without warning when you are driving silently across a strange landscape. The flower was rosemary, the flower of fidelity. And I thought again of last night's fifteen-year-olds, whose forebears must surely have been offered the first rosemary by English soldiers who introduced it from their native land as the rarest exotic. In the intervening 179 years, it has had time to become as common as dandelion, and for 100 miles, from here to Pensacola, it carpets the dunes and flats. All the way at our side was an incomparable beach, smooth as sugar, of the finest gypsum sand, sheering off into an aquamarine sea. It was a lonely beach, so empty of any objects suggesting time or place that when we reached Santa Rosa Island I stood by the water and, with a foreground of two Coke bottles and a dead shark, confronted a Dali landscape of the finest Renaissance clarity. The reverie was disturbed the moment we entered Pensacola, which is no longer the red-snapper capital of the country, but a town for tourists to explore the origins of Spanish America. Its name has been restored to the news tickers, as it was a quarter-century ago, by the swarming activity of the Naval Air Station. There are no more tourist trips to Fort Barrancas, for this is now part of the naval area. There were about 1,500 men training here, and 700 Britons doing their primary, basic, and advanced flight training. It seemed a good place to observe the early relations between Britons and Americans, but I found it hard to make much contact with the young Britons, chiefly because, by late afternoon, the weather had reduced them to coma. They lay prostrate in their clubroom and in time ventured a guarded remark or two. They got along well enough with Americans. But they couldn't take the food. One said it was 'too spiced', another 'too fancy', another 'very hot and too many sauces', another felt for an adjective and dropped his hands in despair. Evidently the whole experience was baffling in the extreme. Each of these boys had had his own private vision, inspired by the movies, of what America was to be like. And each of them had probably hoped to live it out. But none of these visions contained cabbage palm, bayous, hominy grits, garlic, and North Falafox Street, all stewing hazily in a summer noonday temperature of 98 degrees. The Americans were equally discreet, perhaps by official advice, for there is no place where a civilian is less likely to hear uninhibited opinion than inside an Army or Navy camp. A young ensign summed up the general feeling: 'You could find most anything you wanted round here, I guess. Sure, maybe once in a while a Britisher and an American quarrel in a bar. And that's news. But the fact that 700 of 'em get along okay with us, well, nobody's interested. That's not news.' The boys from the air station had more or less taken the town over, and in the lobby of the Hotel San Carlos was a new sign, every seat was taken by a waiting Navy wife.

So far, the revival of the naval station and subsidiary shipyards had not produced a great invasion of workers from faraway, but there was an appreciable influx of strangers from the North and the Midwest to have an interesting effect on the town's racial mores, which for a Southern town have always been peculiar and for all I know unique. There is in Pensacola hardly such a thing as a Negro colony. There are sections where the inhabitants are predominantly white or Negro. But you may never be sure that the house next door is lived in by people of the same color as the inhabitants of the rest of the block. White families live alongside Negro families with apparently no more racial consciousness than an everyday over-the-fence pride. The reason usually given is that the leading society of Pensacola has always been of Spanish blood, and that to this nation these fastidious distinctions of color are about as unimportant as the recognition of Jewish blood in the family is, or was, to an Italian. But the Pensacolans, like the Italians, have suffered from the influx of civilizing outlanders. And however humble the Midwestern and Northern families that had come down to work in the shipyards, few of them wished to be denied the mild pleasure of race superiority that they had heard was a compensation for living in the South. Accordingly, city officials and renting agents were beginning to try to coax white families marooned in a street of Negroes back into wholly white sections of the town. And Negroes were being asked if they wouldn't find it cozier to live exclusively among their own race.

We turned on to US 90 and drove past many flying fields and out across cutover pineland into Mobile. The bay was dense with smoke from stacks by the shipyards, but the sense of what we vaguely call 'a city at war' was everywhere camouflaged by spring blossoms pouring over every wall, bursting from every fence and cranny, thousands of azaleas making gracious all the grimy streets. This luxuriance was so overwhelming as to make Mobile seem like a well-ordered garden, blooming the war to shame. And the senses were so drugged by it that I was prepared to give the town the benefit of any doubts about its contribution to the war and push on west along the coast road to New Orleans. If the reader is abashed by this nonchalance let him sometime drive inch by inch around a continent and discover what mild excuses fatigue or impatience will provide for him, when he wishes to pass up something that undoubtedly he should investigate. After Louisville,

Atlanta, Jacksonville, Miami, Tallahassee, and Pensacola, the blossom of Mobile was like a camellia growing in a steel mill. I felt grateful for it and unwilling to know that behind each petal lay merchant vessels, destroyers, an aluminum plant, and the Southeast Air Depot of the Army Air Corps. It sounds irresponsible enough. But it seems absurd not to confess it.

Down from Mobile the landscape grows handsome enough for a time to discourage further concern over the grubbing farmers of what, for 1,000 miles, we had thought of as 'the typical South'. A white cement road is always a buttress against depression. Fringing it was sifting spring foliage, well-kept fields, pecan trees, and once again fine stands of unhacked pine. But there is always something to beckon you away from an escape into the natural scene. At Kreole, half-hidden by these same handsome pines, was a 'defense' plant. At Pascagoula, a small but clattering shipyard, streams of workers' jalopies jammed the highway on the outskirts of the town. The magnificent live oaks fronting the Gulf at Biloxi form a natural arch against the sky, but they cannot shut out the sight of trainer planes shuttling in and out of the Air Corps Technical Training School here. When the evening comes on again, the war shrinks to the width of the highway and your own thoughts. And I hardly noticed when we crossed the sluggish Mississippi and soon saw the dark water of Lake Pontchartrain to the west, and so came at night into New Orleans.

I do not know if any psychologist or traveler has ever published a study of the differences that affect the human mind when a city enjoyed as a tourist spot has turned into a place to live in. This would not be a study of fancy hardening into fact; for there is some truth in most guide book clichés, and there are fancies about any town that it is more comfortable not to expose. A roving journalist has for his own physical safety to become familiar with certain universal points of pride that may never be brought up to the native. The weather is obviously one. There is not, so far as I have heard, a town or city in the United States whose inhabitants do not, in their bleakest moments of despair, thank their Maker that they were born or live where they do. I have been regarded with genuine Christian pity by the natives of Memphis, Boston, Des Moines, Louisville, Duluth, Bakersfield, Montclair and all Californians, because I had the misfortune to be born elsewhere and so suffer from a dearth of the good vitamins, the beneficent ultra-violet rays, the gobs of penicillin that pour from their sunshine, rain, fog, humidity, or blizzards. I have, however, the advantage here, because the good people of Manchester, England, saw long ago that they were getting nowhere by not admitting to the hellish misfortune of their gray and utterly unproductive climate; so that some time far back in the nineteenth century they agreed, in public conclave, that it would be better for everybody if visitors were greeted with thoughtful commiseration and seen to their trains with the friendly hope that they had not contracted viral pneumonia or bubonic plague. By this time, the custom has passed into the manners of the Mancunians and is pleasantly commented on by all recent visitors. It is an expedient worth commending to several American cities I could name. The inhabitants of Baltimore (sometimes known as the Manchester of America) profess themselves astounded every time they are called on to endure the July heat and the March cold. Yet the rancid agony of the first, and the brass-monkey blight of the second, come up every year with unfailing regularity. I remember once the awful experience of driving across the Imperial Valley in late July. For three days our thermometer had not fallen below 120 degrees in the shade, anytime after nine in the morning and before four in the afternoon. We came to El Centro, and it was a foretaste of Hell. But the inhabitants warned us not to go north by way of Indio. 'It really is hot there, a terrible place.' And even the federal states guides, supposedly written with ladylike objectivity, invariably begin the chapter on climate with a sentence, 'The state of Maine (or Arkansas, or Wyoming, or Oklahoma) is peculiarly fortunate in that . . ,' These reflections grew out of an item of town pride that is peculiar to the war. I think it was in Charleston, West Virginia, that I was first told the sober fact that the number of enlistments into the armed forces immediately after Pearl Harbor was the highest in proportion to the population of any town or city in the United States. The same information was vouchsafed to me again in Atlanta, Nashville, and St Petersburg. I was told the same thing in New Orleans. Next to ideal weather, it is to be expected nowadays that a city will assume it has subscribed to more War Bonds, given more men to the forces, and that its peacetime crop or industry is more vital to the war program than any other town in the land. You do not ask about these things. It is better to take them as said and then go off and see what effects are the ones you notice.

Superficially, New Orleans had changed little. Stout little women emerged promptly from the Hotel Monteleone three times a day for a conducted tour of the city. The wrought-iron balconies of the French Quarter apparently had not been needed for the nationwide scrap-iron and metal drives. Most of the people walking along Canal Street were civilians. The hotels were doing a booming business, and there was evidence that soldiers were being unscrupulously rooked for a night's lodging. A few imaginative businessmen had offered free to weary soldiers and sailors their stores and offices, and I even ran into one or two walking the street for the purpose. Storyville, the crummy cradle of the blues and of every vice but babies, had been at last done away with and was replaced by a handsome, low-rent federal housing project for Negroes.

But what was most different was what people talked about. Most conversations that started with the affairs of New Orleans seemed willing to shelve the affairs of city government for the duration. If war calls for responsibilities, it also offers easy escapes from those nearest home. The corruption in local politics was something that most people expected to do nothing about. 'It's impossible,' sighed one editor, 'to interest people now in a strong reform movement. It could only be done by the independents. And the independents are just the people who are busy on war work, British relief, Red Cross, and so on.' This editor put his head in his hands and moaned when he was asked about the women taking nurse's aid courses. At this stage of the war, it appeared that there were too many amateur nurses around for public safety. A hospital ambulance driver was given patriotic instructions to drive like mad whenever he was answering an accident alarm. As a jittery intern explained, 'There are so many first-aid mavericks around, that by the time we get to a fella fainted on the sidewalk, we have to use a flit gun to shoo off the debs who are looking after him.' The social snobbisms that had grown up around war-work distressed one editor sufficiently to make him issue a written order to the staff of his society page. It read as follows: 'You will henceforth stop printing the pictures of debutantes just because they are sponsoring a Red Cross tea or doing nurse's aid. From now on, they will rate a picture for the same reason as other mortals: if they get killed or if they are in a scandal.'

The topics I heard most talked about were the campaign for a Florida barge canal, the shortage of sugar, and the work of Andrew Jackson Higgins and his assembly-line methods at his boatyards.

The agitation for a Florida barge canal cutting across the neck of the peninsula, and the alternative agitation for a ninety-mile pipeline across the same route, seemed to be based in motives of sound patriotism. Over the winter, about fifty American tankers had been torpedoed off the coast south of New Jersey. The proposed canal would simply provide the missing link in the Intracoastal Waterway system. It was argued that oil going this way, either by tanker or pipeline, would save about 400 miles of ship travel for each cargo. But chiefly it would provide a protected route for oil shipments all the way from Corpus Christi to Trenton, New Jersey. The value of the torpedoed tankers was figured, by the enthusiastic chairman (a Texan) of the House Rivers and Harbors Committee, at about four times the cost of the construction of the canal. New Orleans had its own interest in the suggestion of diverted shipping. 'The Gulf and Caribbean are precisely the areas under the Navy's most constant vigilance,' declared a New Orleans editorial. The inference was that most of the Latin American trade (coffee and bauxite especially) should be shipped into New Orleans instead of to the Atlantic ports. The Under Secretary of Commerce proposed 'a foreign trade zone at some Gulf port'. And New Orleans, in common with St Petersburg, Mobile, Port Arthur, Galveston, and Corpus Christi, thought it heard its name being called. Great respect was belatedly paid for the opinion of a chief Army engineer who ten years before had surveyed the possibility of protecting the Atlantic coastline for shipping and said it couldn't be done.

But there was plenty of internecine strife among shippers and port authorities west and south of the proposed canal routes. The ports south of the neck became panicky lest a canal would quarantine their traffic for the duration and leave them afterward with no trade at all. The more vocal residents of Northern Florida, and of the Gulf Coast, were eager enough for the canal not to heed the dry report of a group of oilmen that the Intracoastal Waterway draws only about nine feet and that you need at least thirty for an oil tanker. The sugar shortage was a more obvious puzzle, at the nation's largest sugar port. It seemed odd to be rationed down here, with sugar stacked high all around the countryside. But the strongest local complaint, through all the sugar country west of New Orleans, was that there was not enough rolling stock to get it to a ship or station.

Mr Andrew Jackson Higgins is what I mean by the stone of reality that refuses to be digested into a romantic legend. New Orleans citizens by and large, whatever their daily business, have been content to let New Orleans be known as a town of what the ads call 'gracious living', as the home of historic squares, graceful houses by the levee, fine indigenous food, the whole giving off a mellow odor of magnolia blossom and chicory. The New Orleanais have been lately insulted by the appearance of visiting Englishmen and Frenchmen and members of the staff of the music archives of the Library of Congress, to whom New Orleans meant only one thing – the source of America's truest native music, the blues. The blues are, however, still close enough to their origins to be raffish and thoroughly uncultural. And when these eager musicologists asked questions about the old sporting houses of Storyville, and worse, went sleuthing there among the filthy cribs, their presence was sometimes loudly resented. These days the old and leisurely citizens have another indignity to swallow. It is Mr Higgins. Although he was born in Nebraska, Higgins is undoubtedly a genuine product of New Orleans, for he has been sailing lumber out of the Mississippi for a third of a century. So long as he remained a lumber shipper his fame was humble enough to do nothing to blur the tourist legend of New Orleans. Nowadays the first thing the visitor is likely to ask to see is one of the shipyards of Higgins Industries, Inc. You can hear a good deal of resentment about Mr Higgins that would be inexplicable if you did not bear in mind the picture of the city that most natives like to hold up. Higgins is big business in person. He is aggressive, appallingly successful, has a vocabulary richer than a Marine, and makes a point of hiring Negroes. He is what Southerners have always liked to associate, condescendingly, with Chicago, a type they have successfully overlooked for years when it bore a Southern accent and operated in Chattanooga, Nashville, or Atlanta.

The non-local fame of Mr Higgins was clearly indicated one day in 1915, when a strange-looking boat sailed into New Orleans and Mr Higgins, looking out of his office window, saw it and was curious about it. It looked like a huge mushroom floating upside down. It was British, was called a turret ship, and had been built that way to defeat the toll charges on the Suez Canal. Higgins at once meditated on all the space on each side of the turret that was going a-begging under-water. So he asked permission to put up stanchions on each side, so that lumber could be loaded to the width of the whole ship. The British were willing. And he went to work and used acetylene welders. Sixteen years later he developed the technique of welding on steel river tugs and, during the era of the Noble Experiment, designed the first models of the PT (patrol torpedo) boats that have given the Japs such murderous trouble in this war. Back in the 20s, many of them were bought by bootleggers and used effectively against the pursuing Coast Guard. But in 1939, Mr Higgins, whose name was known the world over to foreign importers of long-leaf pine (what the British call pitch-pine), was a comparatively unhonored name in American business, signifying an annual sale of about a half-million dollars' worth of his product. With the orders he had on hand for 1942, he expected at the end of that year to have raised this figure to $100,000,000.

His first claim on the attention of the US Navy was, considering his slow and rather humdrum background, untypically dramatic. The Navy knew that he had built barges for some of the trickiest of the world's rivers. They knew his boast that he had designed barges able to operate in nine inches of water. They hinted darkly, in a special communication to him, that they would like him to design a barge for an unnamed river with so much draw, such and such undertow, so many wriggling currents. The problem was put up to Higgins as an abstraction, because the Navy was anxious not to say where its barges were going to operate. They wanted the design urgently, within the month. Higgins spotted the 'river' at once and had the plans flown to Washington the same evening. Since this incident, he has taken over the manufacture of practically all the landing barges, PT boats, and tank lighters that are being used, and will be used, by the United Nations forces. His first torpedo boats were used in this war by Fin-land and next by the British. When the war broke out in Europe,

Higgins had bought up vast quantities of lumber and started construction on shipyards that he had no right (or government contract) to think he could work at anything like capacity. But today, this large, red-faced man with the slant eyes and the double-breasted gabardine suits, purrs like a well-dined Jove over the shops and yards that turn out eight ships, of one kind and another, every ten days.

We drove out of New Orleans in the late afternoon on the Jefferson Highway over the Huey Long Bridge ('Do Not Photograph Bridge') and through winding pleasant bayous, across endless sugar fields, deep into the Teche country. So far the sugar doesn't know the war is on. It came about a month too late to affect the 1942 crop. Fourteen months intervene between the planting of the stalk and the harvest. And December 7th came in the middle of this period. The sugar farmers were sad about this and about the fact that they had been working on a low production quota. Between 1922 and '32 there was a mosaic disease that played havoc with the crop, and the AAA had distributed production quotas based on this very unproductive decade. 'Now,' says a farmer, 'they swoop down on us and say "Grow all y'can," ' – as if the stalk ripened in a week.'

The whole drive across Louisiana is a deceptive experience. You brush under swaying limbs of live oaks, skirt high levees, stretch out across long sugar fields, observe a little rice-planting, and the details that natives are willing to give are wholly about rice and sugar and lumber. At one place we are told that Louisiana has a new industry in the Easter lily, a Creole lily that they hope will replace the popular and profitable Japanese lily. But you need to remind yourself all the time, without any visible evidence, that Louisiana's oil reserves are third only to those of Texas and California; that it has the largest sulfur deposits of any state in the Union and the largest natural gas fields in the world. Thinking of industry, you look out on the innocent sugar fields and, because this is wartime, think of the one-quarter of the nation's industrial alcohol that will come from it.

In the early Sunday evening we watched small families, clothed in shabby black, sitting near the bayou shacks along Bayou Lafourche and drove through a fine racial sequence of American towns: Thibodaux, Schriever, Chacahoula, Donner, and Gibson. We took on some gas at a station run by a Cajun family. An old unshaven man was sitting out under the porch whittling on a stick of wood and occasionally lifting a gnarled throat and singing a high plaintive Cajun song. He had three boys, of whom he said, 'They speak English best.' One of them, a slim, relaxed boy of fifteen or thereabouts, leaned over a fence and swatted a dying wasp. 'Yeah, the old man knows the song all right. Of course, he's American too. We're all American. None of us here ever saw or knew anybody from Nova Scotia. But it's been two hund'ed years.' He moved over into the shade and leaned against a wooden wall on which was carefully stuck a highly flattering photograph of Huey Long. 'But the people up the road here call us the Frenchies. Ah reckon we're Americans at that, but they forget about us.' He shouted to his brother and spread the magic word that Gene Autry was in a movie at the theater twelve miles away. They made a date to drive there. As it grew dark, we came into New Iberia and ate a gorgeous meal of crayfish bisque among families dressed in Sunday blue or black, any one of whom could have been seen, at the same hour, eating similar seafood piled up on a table laid with newspaper all along the Mediterranean coast, from Barcelona to Marseilles. The fathers were small, modest-looking men tenderly feeding bits of crab to craning children. At the next table was a huge-bellied man with a handlebar mustache. He peered round a craggy mountain of crayfish and tendered jocular compliments in French to his wife, a sweet, shapeless, enormous woman that Rubens might have painted with his foot. All around us were the facial types of Southern France and Spain. And it is here, as it was also among the Greek fishermen at Tarpon, that you realize how dumb, tasteless, and mischievous is our present insistence on the Anglo-American war effort as an Anglo-Saxon crusade. Easterners think of such communities, if they ever imagine them, as decorative eccentricities stemming from a daily American scene all too short of such 'color'. Sociologists examine them relentlessly as end products of old cultures. Politicians more wisely use them. But they are the core of the American idea. They keep their food habits, and their manners are their own, but in the evening their sons meet up at the dingy showboat, lying like an expiring shark against the dark bank of the Teche, and drop nickels in a juke box. And it is Bing who is their troubadour.

The next morning we crossed the border of Louisiana and came dramatically, as always, into Texas. The Sabine River is almost a continental divide, separating sharply two ways of life, the life of the South and the life of what is at once familiar America. The moment you enter Orange, there is an emotional lift on to a higher, and possibly more superficial, plane of life. The sidewalks are high and handsome. The roads are smooth. The people are confident in the riches of their colossal state. At the first gas station, a tall, bony man with a thick grinning under-lip hailed us like forgotten brothers and sped us on our way with 'Was good to see yuh; come right back now,' a greeting and a human as far removed from the natives of the Deep South as Frank Capra is from Dostoevsky. A shipyard is in full steam on the Sabine. Hundreds of shining automobiles line the streets of Orange. A large sign triumphantly announces, 'From here on, this highway (US 90) is known as MacArthur Drive. By Order, A. Sikolski, Mayor'. We drove past a man on horseback, a tract of land being cleared 'For Defense Workers Only', a boy working a tractor on the edge of it, and stopped to wait for an endless train of tank cars to pass.

Beaumont, for all its noisy shipyard and its impressive piles of lumber, is suddenly a Western town, with its wide streets, false fronts, brick buildings, and the sense it gives of fronting on to a boundless plain. As we drove on, the landscape widened, approximating more and more to the scale of tautness and flatness it would have from here on. We whisk past an enormous billboard on which two-foot-high letters admonish, 'This is God's Country, Don't Drive Thru It Like Hell'. At noon we are already in Houston, admiring its elegant stores, its modern suburbs, its air of sparkling and easy prosperity. I am sidetracked from finding the first name I look up in the telephone book (a name beginning with U) by the cocky competitiveness of two stores. One is called the 'U Tote 'Em Grocery'. The line above lists the competitor, 'U Toot We Tote Grocery'.

A hundred years ago Houston was a bayou town. As late as 1900, it had only 50,000 residents. Now it has over 400,000. It is probably the most prosperous inland port in the United States, made by cotton and oil. The cotton men feel bad about the war, for Germany, Japan, and Italy were the chief buyers of Texas cotton. Says one of them, 'Our shipping's shot to hell. It fell off in '39, fell to nothing in 1940. Go down to the port and you'll see hardly a single boat. Ah mean, you won't see any loading cotton. The port's comatose till the war's over.' But there is lots of shipbuilding going on. And with an ordnance plant going up nearby, Houston is glad that the Federal Housing Authority put up 10,000 units in one year: they feel this provision will easily absorb a serious immigration of war workers. Everywhere around the town you notice brisk acceptance of the war as a healthy sort of challenge to show what you've got. Nine thousand air-raid wardens had signed up, having the imagination to picture what Houston might be like in a good-sized oil fire. With the CIO union entrenched in the oil business, and the AF of L union as much in control as ever of the building trades, Houston regards itself as, for better or worse, a strong union town. It is also strongly Democratic, had long shared Roosevelt's concern for the European war, and likes to remind you that the state legislature petitioned for a bill introducing a declaration of war some time before Pearl Harbor.

But the blood in its veins is oil. One-quarter of the world's oil is drilled in Texas. And East Texas is the gas-tank of the nation. The war has made vital demands on this gas-tank, demands that unfortunately recompensed the big refineries at the expense of the small. The oilmen were plunged into depression at the start, when they recognized that the war would force them to abandon a principle of distribution that had taken many bitter years to establish. It is the principle of what they call 'equitable rating', whereby the resources of each field are fairly matched with its competitors. The state railroad commissioner, who administers oil transportation, allots to each field a maximum number of barrels that may be shipped each day. One pipeline must take equally from many distributors in a single field. This system had maintained a more or less even flow from each field, and each distributor, of the motor-fuel gasoline that since the first days of the family automobile has been the chief product and chief source of revenue of the oil industry. But today the rationing of rubber for civilians has greatly cut the amount of gasoline that the nation can fairly use. What the government demands from the industry is certain refined products, especially toluene for aviation gasoline and butadiene for synthetic rubber. These were formerly minor special products. None of them calls for much crude oil, thus the total expected production of synthetic rubber for 1942, 400,000 tons, would use only 150,000 barrels a day. Yet by an unfortunate irony more crudes than ever have to be poured through. For these special products come from the gases produced in normal distillation processes, and to secure them you have to refine ordinary crude oil. So the government's needs incidentally call for even more motor-fuel gasoline than usual, which the normal consumer is to be denied. Consequently the oil tanks are full to overflowing. And the small refiner, who does not have the equipment to refine these special products, is having to close down. Neither the consumer nor the bewildered gas-station operator can quite understand the connection between this abundance and this rationing. He picks up his newspaper and reads that an official in Washington is promising oceans of oil for the armed forces and urging Texas to give its all. In a parallel column he reads that yesterday twenty-two small refineries closed down outside Dallas. A gas-station attendant, on the verge of quitting his job for almost anything that will pay, harangues his sympathetic customer: 'Y'only have to turn on a faucet down heah in Texas and oil pours out like water. Yet they talk about gas rationing in the East. It don't make sense. There's more oil than there ever was.' But oil gushing up in Texas is not the same as oil at the ports of the Northeastern Seaboard. The problem is how to drain off the flowing Texas supply to the places that need it most, how to get the oil north and east, in the direction of the war. The oil distributors think of a Florida pipeline as a hopeless makeshift. They grumble that the government won't release enough steel for pipelines. While I was there, the problem was unsolved. The most effective single step had been the compulsory elimination of one stage in the normal transportation process. Normally, gasoline goes in tank cars to bulk stations, then to gas stations by truck. Now, all refineries must send trucks direct to the bulk stations and thus free the tank cars for more frequent trips over shorter journeys up north.

One social effect of rubber rationing that I noticed first in Houston, and afterwards everywhere, was the sudden overcrowding of buses. This is uncomfortable anywhere, but in the South means an irritating crowding of the Jim Crow customs. There was not yet any organized, or Klannish, objection to the apparent gain in the Negro's social status. But I overheard plenty of grumbling comments on the emerging fact that 'these damn Nigras are gettin' underfoot. They don't know their place anymore.' Up in Austin, the young editor of the University daily had the impertinence to write an editorial about racial discrimination and go so far as to suggest the equal admission of Negroes to the University. The older generation of Texans sat by and waited for the heavens to open. This editorial was very likely only an expression of a nineteen-year-old's opinion. And group opinion is perilous stuff to discover, let alone interpret. But the boy was a Texan, and there were others who felt like him. There were other Texans, not all young ones, who, like reformed rakes counting their sins, began to talk with a touch of shame about the White Primary. Here one got the first hint that after the war a new liberal party, or a revivified Republican party, might crusade to some purpose to abolish the weapon that gives the Southern white the assured right to fix the election his way months ahead of election day. It was here also, in the gracious town of Austin, that you could hear about other racial suspicions that, while they do not disturb the narcissistic unity of Texans, at least suggest the possibility of future conflicts. Not far from here, for instance, is a compact German population, not politically strong enough to affect elections, but the Governor likes to respect its wishes. According to some observant natives who have known them a lifetime, they have considerably more admiration for Hitler than their fathers had for the Kaiser. In 1938, a boatload of them was taken over, at ridiculously low cost, to see and admire the Fatherland. Which they accordingly did. It may be that their enthusiasm was simply a reaction against the fact that, after all, the Interior Department had never given them a free trip to Yellowstone or the Grand Canyon. But since the 7th of December, they have tactfully concentrated their patriotism against the Japs. Those who live by the Guadalupe River still look down proudly on other American strains running to amiable rack and ruin. And they still, as they did in the last war, call the river 'the Hindenburg Line'. Just to even up this condescension, the surrounding Poles make a habit of driving out, over the period of a decade or two, the second-generation Germans. The Germans take (in time) to radios, refrigerators, automobiles, and other American beguilements. The Poles save everything (for a wedding) and prosper in their own hard way.

I did not get up to Dallas, which knows as much as the Industrial

East and Midwest about the problems of labor in an industrial democracy. But over most of Texas it is striking how unreal and irrelevant labor problems seem to most people. It is no epigram to say that Texas is an American world apart. Most Texans would move the state elsewhere if it were not so. When you say 'American history', they think at once of the history of Texas. The first dinner party I attended, I came in when a seventy-year-old man was panting hard in argument with a younger man over some question of military treachery. From the pitch of their emotion, and the vocabulary they used, I judged they were talking about the German spring offensive in Russia. But the old man's ire was aroused over a small group of conservatives who deserted Sam Houston after the Battle of San Jacinto. It seemed almost precious to bring up Bataan, which had fallen overnight. And academic to ask about the labor problems of Texas at war. The main point is that when you say 'a Texan' you can talk more sense in regarding him as a separate national, inside the American federation, than about any other native of any other state. You notice that the young men of Texas of all classes talk in a matter of fact way about pursuits that anywhere else in the country could only be affectations. Their work and play, and the succession of the seasons, is closely linked with hunting, trapping, horses, javelins. They inhabit an agricultural region, and a playground, of immense spaciousness. In such a landscape, the individual acquires a subjective dignity that industrial cities long ago destroyed. The individual can therefore romanticize his relation to the Good Society. So that when you try to discuss labor problems, people tend to think of human charity as the nostrum. They believe in the idea of the Good Man, kindly, resourceful, the physical protector of his family making its living between earth and sky. You ask about Governor W. Lee O'Daniel and appreciate that a man who carries a Bible, smiles, and sings to a guitar has acquired a foolproof formula for convincing his constituents that he is a good guy, a regular fellow. They are used to personal independent relations, as between a planter and slave, a rancher and cowhands. They have not had to face the unsentimentally collective relationships that an industrial society, in any part of the globe, forces on its citizens. But there is a little dawning apprehension. War factories are going up in places that the Texan secured from the Indian with nothing but a horse and a six-shooter. There are magnesium deposits near Bastrop. And a chemical dye plant on the Brazos River.

South of Austin, you have the feeling of driving a line between the East and the approaching West. On your left is rich cotton land dotted with willows and pine. On your right is the long sweep of brush country disappearing at the far horizon in barely perceptible foothills. All along the seventy-mile drive from Austin to San Antonio, the land was drenched with the scarlet smear of Indian paintbrush, and for miles at a time the highway was banked with verbena and bluebonnet.

It was an unexpected and charming mask for the land that Eastern-ers think of as a shuddering plain, whose only virtue is that it is an American reservoir of oil, beef, textiles, cotton, wool, and mohair. As we came near to San Antonio we heard the high, intensifying roar of planes that were rising in formation from somewhere beyond the Indian paintbrush and the bluebonnets and soared across the tumb-ling white clouds like a wave of locusts. On our left, it was not hard to figure, was Randolph Field.

The war to San Antonio is like a bugle call to a soldier on leave, a summons to return to normal. For the tradition that San Antonio is most conscious of is its long history as an outpost and a fort. The reason is obvious enough, for in the thick of the business district you turn a corner and there is the narrow, winding river, which has pro-vided an inexhaustible water supply to people who live on the edge of the West, where water is the constant threatening need. San Antonio was an outpost against the French. Here the Catholic Church pitched tent with the Army and made a trading post. Here was the funnel of minerals brought north by Mexicans. Here through the 70s and 80s the cattlemen hired their crews and did all their banking. Here, the oasis in a surrounding brush country of 200 miles, the Army long ago established its Southwest purchasing center. Since the Eighth Corps Area is the greatest supply center in the United States, San Antonians logically explain that San Antonio is therefore the biggest retail trading town in the country. At any rate, it is surprising to run into an Ameri-can city whose chief source of income has often been military income. In peacetime it has a normal military population of between 12–15,000 men, most of whom are active purchasing staffs, and the rest retired officers who find the living cheap, the atmosphere congenial, and a fetching supply of widows to whom Army customs are the breath of normal life. San Antonio therefore looked much as usual, except for the incoming swarms of Air Corps men on weekend leave from Randolph. The construction crews on airfields and cantonments hereabouts have caused the usual housing shortage. And the Army has abolished the red-light district and intelligently converted San Antonio's old licensing system for prostitutes into an experimental course for 'rehabilitating' the profession. You hear that this works well enough with the regulars, the confessed ladies of joy, but as in the last war – and for that matter the ensuing peace – the trade is sabotaged by amateurs and by the countless thousands of respectable, teen-age girls to whom technically unconsummated sex is the ultimate amenity of a pleasant evening. To their families they are often known as high-spirited daughters full of the joy of life. To the soldiers they are known as broilers, dishes, bed-bunnies, popovers, free-wheelers, touchables, Susies, teasers, free-lances, and those who are frankly promiscuous for the duration are called Liberty or Victory girls. There is a unique group of determined brides who make a profession of marrying young officers just before they are about to be transferred or sent overseas. This gives them the right to draw dependency pay. Once the recent husband has gone to glory, they register under another name, receive another Post Office box number, and proceed to seek another mate whose shining qualification is the certainty that he will not be long at this present station. The trade in overseas caps has been briskly improved by the presence of so many fliers, whose training is limited in length and whose future is promisingly hazardous. There was one lusty girl, just thirty years of age, who was making a handsome living on the receipts of seven separate dependencies before the Army and the Post Office authorities caught up with her. But she bore no malice, and from the safe side of her prison bars declared that in a time of national emergency she retained feelings only of the warmest affection and most unswerving loyalty to the Army of the United States.

6

The Southwest

Where the West begins is a question that has greatly disturbed English mystics, pulp writers, and Republican National Chairmen. It still worries travelers, who usually recognize only the demarcations they already know. 'The West' is one of those names like 'Yankee' or 'Creole' that even people anxious to find out what it means already presuppose what it should define. So they accept the definition that most closely describes their own preconception. It is not surprising that the word should have been made to bear almost every meaning that anybody ever wanted to invest it with. For myself, I always feel that the East is behind me a few hours west of San Antonio. It seems that at this point, crossing the Pecos River, a preconception has been satisfied that dates back to an early acquaintance with this part of the country.

I had been driving hesitantly for days, it seemed, along the Gulf Coast, through Texas, and on the fourth day drove out of San Antonio. After passing through Count Castro's peculiar Alsatian town, the highway soon became a ribbon of civilization running across the wide earth. Wooded hills gave way to sprinkled mesquite and greasewood. You then saw part of the brush apparently on the move – which turned out to be sheep. We drove all day across alkaline plains and around low treeless hills. Toward sunset, we turned sharply round a little knoll just before Sanderson, and there suddenly below us was an ocean of plain, and far to the east and south range after range of mountains stacked against the horizon in a violet haze. It was absolutely silent and untouched by human sign or movement. It had the untricky, straightforward grandeur of Bach. This was the West – a circle of earth, something of vast, clear distance, balmy heat, high still mountains, light sharp as a sword. Its impact makes a European aware for the first time of the spiritual quality of size. And the introduction to this is the Edwards Plateau, where it raises the curtain on the Trans-Pecos Highlands.

In this context, it is hard to keep in mind the realities of war. Here Nature itself imposes the fundamentals of staying alive: water, shade, a sense of direction, a regular supply of food. And up against these, the problems of equipment, of war factories, of the draft, of rationing, of what is called 'civilian sacrifice' seem picayune and the war itself a bad habit, a fuss of scratchy humans far from home. In the towns of this brush country, there is not a visible sign of war. The young men who are missing have 'gone off to the war'. But the war does not come to them, as it has to every city of Europe since September 1939. You have been passing all day through a land of scrub and greasewood. The cows standing silently beside the railroad tracks look big as boxcars. Cows of the same herd in the middle distance could be sheep or horses. Farther off still they could be low cactus plants. And at the horizon they are as indistinguishable as grains of pepper.

'The war, huh?' muses an old cattleman. 'Of course, the cows don't know the war's on. Don't know even the big prices they're gonna bring. The war won't change much the way they eat or the way they're handled. But maybe they already noticed they ain't seein' the same faces around. The worst effect's on the men on the ranches. There's going to be an awful scarcity of labor and trucks and ranching equipment. Still, it can hardly be as bad as it was right after the Civil War. They didn't have enough hands around then to brand the cattle, and after the war there were millions of mavericks. It couldn't ever be as bad as that again. All we can see ahead is more higher-priced cattle 'n we've ever seen. Was a man through here who'd been from Florida clear to Colorado and back. He said there was more cattle in the Southwest than ever before.'

I mentioned irrelevantly that the best beef I'd ever eaten was in a yacht club in Clearwater, Florida. The cattleman was properly suspicious and then admitted, 'Sure, some of the Florida herds are gettin' better all the time. They've been importin' a better grade of cattle lately, mostly from Texas. Some from Kentucky, too, they say. But as for this state, what you're gonna see from here on west is young boys learnin' how to finish baby beef. Thirteen- to fifteen-month beef. That's what the government say they want. Take a father. Buys his son a beast right after weaning. Then he trains 'im to go into competition with another kid to learn feedin' methods, step up the whole process, and produce these fat babies.

'And after cattle, they want condensed milk. The price is goin' up to the farmer – 40 percent. Some of these farmers are makin' money for the first time in their lives. So, that's the picture. The cattle country at war; yes, sir.' He lifted his eyebrows in a mock-guilty chuckle. 'Yes, sir, it's makin' our fortunes.'

There was nothing obscure about what the Department of Agriculture demanded of the cattlemen. 'America at war needs meat, more and more of it, and we need it now.' By the end of 1941, the average American was eating more meat than ever before. In the 20s and 30s he had eaten a little over sixty pounds of beef and veal a year. In 1940, it was seventy pounds. To meet the extra needs of the armed forces, the government asked for the slaughter of about another 8 percent more cattle than in 1941, but wanted to keep as many cattle and calves on the range as before. Hence the campaign for the intensified production of baby beef. The fear was that either there would be too enthusiastic a slaughter in 1942, and a serious shortage of cattle later on, or that the campaign for increased production would be too successful and the ranges would once again become the victim of overgrazing. But in the spring of 1942, as long as there was a normal supply of feed, not many cattlemen appeared to worry much about this threat. They were too busy being elated over the prospect of their highest cash income in twenty years.

At Sanderson, a little group of men and girls stood watching a naval cadet take the train for San Francisco. It was a strange sight – the first uniform I had seen outside a big city or an Army camp. And seen against the background of deserted prairie, hard sun, and no sound anywhere but the humming bees around flowering mesquite, he was a surrealist figure. The girls had on blue and red dresses. They went up to him in turn, and none of them seemed shy, nor was there any crying. They said, 'Well, look after yourself, Bob,' and 'Don't get your feet wet,' and 'Come back now, Bob,' to which he smilingly answered with a regular 'Sure will' and 'You bet.' As the conductor yelled 'board' and the train started to move, one girl moved toward it and said, 'We'll be thinking of you, Bob,' and he nodded. The train gained its rhythm, and the cadet leaned out and waved at the retreating blobs of red and blue, took a last look at the faded railroad shops and a bum and a Mexican in their shirtsleeves squatting almost invisibly in the dark shade of a storefront. The train hooted twice, we rattled up toward a wide mesa, and started the long, imperceptible climb up the plateau.

Perhaps it is because we recall the Southwest in terms of vast distance and daylong travel that we think back to it as being more arid than it is. Easterners gape out into the hard pink haze of sunlight and soon tire of the slow-shifting pattern of rock and scrub. They wonder what in the world the natives can see in it and would applaud the Englishman who thought the Texans should insist on another war with the Mexicans so as to lose it back to them. Yet in a unit of this land not much bigger than his own back garden, the suburban Easterner could discover more wild plants and flowers than he could ever grow at home. It must be the scale of the landscape that humbles into oblivion all its exquisite detail. All through the day we were going up through spinning pools of bluebonnets, brilliant mustard, yucca in flower, prickly pear, and verbena. As the bare Davis Mountains rose up, a buzzard wheeled over the highway ahead of us like a seagull sighting land. And we stopped at Alpine.

The cattlemen in this region of West Texas obviously like you to marvel at the size of their ranches. It is little enough to ask of any stranger, for the boast hides the central anxiety of anybody who makes his life in this part of the country. It may sound good to remark, in a small country, that in West Texas most ranches are about ten square miles, with many up to 100 square miles. If this suggests bountiful pastures, it is only another way of saying that the land is so desolate and barren that only twenty-two cattle can stay alive in a section, or square mile. This fact is a sufficient rebuke for one's pleasure in the brush flowers, for even a cow with the most aesthetic sensibilities might look out on miles of verbena and phlox and Indian paintbrush and see nowhere to go for a square meal. It is no accident that this is the goat center of the United States. A goat can go for weeks, and may have to go for months, without water and can feed happily on the most miserable scrub. Of this necessity the goat – and sheep – farmers have made a profitable virtue: the Army's demand for mohair is insatiable, and the breeder looked forward to the richest future, just as long as the Army needs men and uniforms. With all the ranches losing skilled hands, the value of a Mexican hired-hand has gone up. This naturally brings up, at least to the Mexican, his value as a human being and irritates susceptibilities that from long habit have been comfortably repressed. Alpine is a good place to observe the regular set-up, among a settled and modestly prosperous South-western community that certainly does not have, has never needed to have, much active 'race' feeling.

Alpine has a little less than 4,000 people. Fine rows of juniper and cedar run up to the state agricultural college and down to the pleasant main street, with its modern shops, hotel, parked cars, and lounging sheep-farmers and cattlemen. Across the Southern Pacific railroad tracks is the Mexican part of town, and you might have stepped back a couple of centuries. All the streets are unpaved, the houses made of sun-dried brick and unfloored. You do not see any sign of sewers. Children play around in the square of dirt – the floor of the one room – which is living room, bedroom, and bathroom. The Mexicans do not work in drugstores, nor do you see them at the movie theater, because as one frank resident of Alpine puts it, 'they are dirty and might spread disease.' A young photographer admits, when the subject is put up to him (and it is a subject that does not come up in the everyday life of the white town), that 'sure, they get no sort of an even break.' While I was there the only figure who seemed to flit regularly between both parts of town was a young priest. He was a Spaniard who came here in 1938, and nobody knew or cared much whether he was a missionary or a refugee Loyalist. He arrived and looked around him at the stony earth and the cowed, resigned life of the Mexicans. He told them that he realized their material condition was about as low as it could be. He did not promise them any improvement in it. He simply suggested that with all these rocks and boulders jutting out of the sandy soil, there was the raw material to build monuments to the glory of God. He told them they'd start with a new church. And in no time at all they were digging and carrying the stones around. It was an occupational therapy that, for the time being at least, had magic results. The photographer said, 'There's no comparison in the way those people look and act. They have something to live for all of a sudden.' Of course, this rousing evangelism is no solution. The whites in most Southwestern towns might say that only a Communist, a crackpot, or an editorial writer would even find a problem there to solve. But when you reflect that most of these 'Mexicans' are Americans, you are forced to conclude that it will take only a couple of generations of breeding to produce enough of them to constitute a problem.

West of Alpine we snaked through the mountains toward El Paso. After Marfa, the tawny gramma grass went by in waves, and the track's edge was scratched by cat's-claw. Soon after Valentine you go through beautiful ranching country where the fat Herefords trundle happily away from the oncoming train. Past the bare Sierra Blanca range we go into more desolate and eroded country and over wide, waterless riverbeds. The trenches of erosion trickle down the mountainsides like running wounds. You notice how the mountains slope away to the east from a vertical western ridge. After Sierra Blanca there is more rough mesquite country, by this time so familiar to westbound travelers that it seems devoid of all wartime interest. But swallowed up by the blinding distance and the sage are countless airfields and training schools that the Army Air Corps has established all the way across Texas.

Forty miles before El Paso there is a break in the mountains, and across the level valley of brown soil you see much careful farming. This is not due to any appreciably heavier rainfall. The broad fields of alfalfa and cotton that slide by are nursed by the rectangular channels of stored water that you see dividing every field. You are now meeting another Western phenomenon – mass irrigation. A hundred and twenty-five miles north of El Paso is the Elephant Butte Dam, a commendable undertaking imperiled by the over-pasturing of the uplands. The washes grew wider over washed-out land and the dikes went up higher and higher to hold the water, which is now above the level of the valley floor. So El Paso prosperously irrigates its parched earth but confronts a future threatened by floods and no water at all for irrigation. The biggest demand the war has made has been for El Paso's long staple cotton, which is needed for airplanes and parachutes and tire fabrics. Before the war, the price was seven cents a pound. Now it is thirty-five cents a pound. This is easily the most important wartime fact about El Paso. Since El Paso has the largest cavalry post in the United States, and since it is the biggest city between San Antonio and Los Angeles, it is a newly awakened supply center. It is the main railroad junction of the Southwest, and in wartime this means it will become a troop center, and the main channel of Mexican labor into the United States. It is the source of many rumors about Mexican–American relations. In a café in Juarez, I heard two El Paso residents speculating on the probable feelings of Montana and Colorado beet farmers at having to pay a dollar fifty a day for Mexican workers, 'who'd be lucky to earn that much a week in their own country'.

Once again, the border relations between Americans and Mexicans is the topic that everywhere catches your attention. The Mexicans, and Mexican-Americans, are full of talk about discrimination against Mexican workers in the copper mines and smelters hereabouts (and in New Mexico and Arizona). They say that they do the same work for lower wages; skilled Mexican furnace men and burners often get a little more than half of what is paid the white American novices. Morale writers have been through here to show that the Mexicans north of the border are happily joining hands with their American comrades and letting bygones be bygones till the dawn of the Four Freedoms. But when I was through El Paso, the Mexicans kept their pride in public, and in private looked to the Mexican Labor Department and to the CIO (through the International Union of Mine, Mill, and Smelter Workers) to right a wrong they regarded as insufferable and characteristic of their long and feeble battle to work on equal terms with the Anglo-Americans.

To a West Texan, the Mexicans who settled on the American side have always been of two kinds: the upper and the lower. The upper went to school with him, used the same washrooms and toilets, and theaters, and became officials, merchants, secretaries. (From the striking brown eyes and swarthy dignity of the daughters of many of El Paso's most authentic families, I should say that there has been in the past plenty of unlamented intermarriage, if not some lively miscegenation.) The lower, the *criado*, were the poor, the peasants, the feckless, who have no more identity than their ability to provide a labor pool. An El Paso merchant defined them as people you think of 'for whatever they might be used for'.

Mexico has never had in modern times the wealth or prestige to protest this comfortable American classification and has had to make the most of such firm revenges as the oilfields' expropriation. But you have only to talk to a few Mexicans to feel their long and well-controlled resentment at the condescension of American manners and the exploitation of Mexicans who cross the border and become Americans. The war has unloosed their pride, so that they do not go around in quite the same sullen and apologetic way. Juarez, the border capital, is a gaudy symbol of this change. Ten years ago it was a raffish tourist town of a few dusty streets that had its own civic pride, to be sure, but at night it gave itself over to presenting obscene entertainment in cribs and dim-lit nightclubs for the delectation of well-oiled Americans slumming from El Paso. Juarez accepted its fate and built a brewery, several small factories for the manufacture of the wooden mules, straw hats, gourds, salad bowls, and crucifixes that American tourists feel obliged to take away. Now on the basis of its brewing and souvenir industries, it has paved streets, a bustling population of 60,000, a self-respecting administration (that did not hesitate to arrest and jail drunken American soldiers until the American Army intervened and settled to have these indignities handled by the Mexican military police). It has a wide-awake Mayor, who, some time since the war started, reminded the residents of El Paso in a public speech that 'Mexico is the back door of the United States. It will be protected.' The Americans obediently applauded this hint, remarking simply that 'a year or two ago, no Mayor of Juarez would have dared utter any such syllables. But I reckon he's right. We'd look pretty foolish if we didn't protect it.' The Mayor also reversed the usual flow of condescension by permitting the Juarez Philharmonic to go across to El Paso and regale the Texans with a free symphony concert in the interests of Mexican–American solidarity.

I took a bus out of El Paso going west in the early afternoon. We dropped a passenger or two at Las Cruces and turned west on US 70–80, into the full pinkish glare of the afternoon sun. It soon got very hot inside the bus as we streaked across the scrub desert and as people started using hats and newspapers to fan themselves. The atmosphere took on a not-unpleasant pungency, that compound of the smell of sage from the desert and of sour apples from too many hot humans together, which you get in all trains going through the semi-arid West.

After the sun went down, we stopped at Deming in the brief twilight. We all got out, and the passengers who were going on to Lordsburg and beyond grabbed a clattering meal in a café. Then the driver stopped flirting with the girl behind the soda fountain, hitched up his trousers, and called time. The diners swallowed their coffee, and soon the bus snorted and went west in a cloud of blue smoke. I phoned my hotel for a taxi and presently along came an old man in a jalopy with no door on his side and on mine a tattered one that I had to hold on to for fear of falling out. We came to a small hotel, and I went out to have dinner and roam the town.

Deming is a thousand small Western towns. The kind of town that makes the East seem as far away as Surrey or Normandy. It is like a child's blocks on a nursery floor, a few rectangles of streets interrupting the desert. A few wide streets, some lining cottonwoods, a spatter of neon lights, all making a pigmy human protest against the enveloping circle of dark sky. At the movies, they were showing a British film, *Target for Tonight*, and though the audience couldn't follow much of the dialogue they were strangely attentive and, on the way out, audibly impressed. This curious reaction was explained the next morning, when I saw the shades drawn in some houses and several stores inexplicably closed. On one of them, a butcher's, was a scribbled note hung on the inside of the glass door. It said: 'Open again tomorrow. Sorry'. As I moved around the town I couldn't fail to notice a sort of gentleness in the way people treated each other. There was little enough backslapping and joviality to cause curiosity in any stranger. The hotel manager made it clear to me that this was no subjective impression of mine. Deming has about 2,000 inhabitants – aside from boys in the Air Corps at a nearby field who drift in and out. A few months before Pearl Harbor, the New Mexico State Guard had supplied engineers for an anti-tank unit that went at once to the Philippines. Deming had well over 100 men out there. And I was visiting it about ten days after the fall of Bataan and the final surrender of the Philippines. It was eerie to see a whole American town, however small, in mourning. I realized there was probably not a town or village in Great Britain that could afford to be superior to it on the count of personal sacrifice. A hundred and fifty men from a population of 2,000 is a crushing percentage of casualties. And after talking to some of the wives and parents, the only consolation I felt was one that you cannot give to people who have to bear this routine grief of war. I thought of the Pilgrims' brave hymn, 'He that is down need fear no fall, He that is low, no Pride.' Deming was about as low as it is possible to go. I went back to my hotel, and the manager alarmed me by saying that a deputation of mothers and wives of the lost men were coming to see me. Somehow the rumor had spread that a newspaperman, from an English paper, was in town. I did not relish the prospect, for I knew at once they would assume I had come direct from Dunkirk and would have understanding sympathy to offer them. I had nothing to offer them, and when they appeared, as meek and mannerly as if I were doing them a favor, I felt as pretentious as you do before a dead man. We sat in a small parlor that the manager hastily crammed with chairs. In our talk there was probably little consolation for the women, except the foolish assurance of warmth that you get from any stranger who, you assume, has been through this thing and can speak the same uneasy language. But there are several politicians and Congressmen I know that I wish could have been present. They would have had an object lesson in reality, a reminder that patriotism speaks the conventional rhetoric of Congress and the newspapers only when it is untouched by personal frustration. None of these women was there to exhibit a stiff upper lip, or to pay tribute to MacArthur, or to champion America. They were not quite resigned to their own loss. They were puzzled and suspicious. They clung to many of the mischievous rumors that columnists chew on who are short of a subject. Why were the boys sent out there? Why were there so many from New Mexico? And from Deming? Some Senator had said that the Philippines ought never to have been defended anyway. Why did we have to fight 6,000 miles from home? They were quite simply looking for a scapegoat. The shock of the war's most intimate cruelty had come too soon for them to feel that a philosophical calm was natural or right. Only one woman, with bright eyes and a humorous crooked mouth, was ready to allow that it was sheer unpolitical bad luck and that all you could do was to make the best of it. But before we broke up, they relaxed their belligerence, and as they walked off down the street in twos and threes it was plain to see that they were sick of sympathizing with each other and had come to a stranger not to blame or make a protest but just to break the hard pretense of resignation.

I caught the noonday train and was glad to pull out of Deming. But the mood of the place stayed with me. The landscape could not distract me. Rather, it intensified my mood. For the Western landscape, being so empty of trivialities, and enclosed only by the eternities of shade and horizon and silence, acts as an echo chamber to the small sadness of persons and sends their feelings back to them magnified into a grandeur of despondency they had not felt indoors. This may be the West's peculiar variation of the pathetic fallacy, for I have noticed that it has the same effect on feelings of cheerfulness. You project a joke and a smile into the sky, and the very earth seems to be struck dumb by the rightness of your most casual feelings, and the thunder of its silence gives back a godlike approval to a good humor that may derive from nothing more jovial than a healthy movement of the bowels. This phenomenon may explain the expansiveness of many Western characters and also their honest conviction that they are God's chosen people, in a place that He chooses so obviously to share only with them. However this may be, there was nothing small or prosaic enough in the afternoon's journey to take my mind for long off the memory of the Deming mothers traipsing quietly back from the hotel.

After crossing the Continental Divide we went through the San Simon Valley, whose gullies are now eroded to 100 feet in barren width, where not so long ago a covered wagon could roll through grass up to its axles. Then across alkali flats, above which the distant mountains seemed to float, baseless, in mid-air. When the landscape wasn't desolate, it was eerie and haunting.

But Tucson was another world. Getting off the train and stepping from the long milky shadows into the golden sunlight, I thought still of Deming. It was like leaving a morgue and coming out again into the untroubled, haphazard land of plenty. Tucson was in fact as bright and painful a contrast as I could have found in so short a time. In peacetime, the advertising booklet looks innocent enough, tempting the rich and the tired with patio homes, swimming, riding, golf, fishing, hunting, guest ranches, 336 days of sunshine every year, and the Fiesta de Los Vaqueros in February. But at a time when Burma was falling, and the RAF was pouring high explosives on Rostock, Tucson looked like a deliberate sanctuary from Armageddon. I realized that this too was a mood conditioned by the misfortune of Deming, and after a night's sleep and a walk around the pleasant wide streets it vanished and was replaced by simple curiosity, which probably produces less stirring prose but better truth.

This curious town, which has quintupled its population in forty years, and not long before that was a trading center for surrounding forts in Apache country, has in the past twenty years struck it rich with the well-advertised discovery that the surrounding landscape is as different as possible from the landscape its visitors work or live in. So the winter residents tend to be, if anything, a little more neurotic than most. There are the genuine sick, especially the tubercular who have not heard of the thirty-year-old discovery that climate has little to do with the fundamental cure of the disease. But these you do not see. They are in sanatoriums and rest homes. What you see mostly are retired Midwestern couples, and 10,000 very comfortable Americans who have arthritis, or wheezing bronchi (or who think they have), or who have lately suffered from too much work, or too much money, or too much love. These people play and walk in gingerly comfort in a town with wide streets and high sidewalks that is still a prairie town. High-hipped ranchers walk into the Santa Rita Hotel on Saturdays and push their Stetsons off their brows to write an occasional check for 10,000 dollars – payment for some high-spirited bet – to be left at the hotel desk till called for by Tim or Steve or Donald so-and-so, 'a little square, runty guy'. And the rancher makes the appropriate descriptive gestures and ambles away.

The Tucson season was almost over, but there were still plenty of coal-black blondes, spry ranchers, and persecuted Republicans staying on to catch the desert in its marvelous bloom. The Sunshine Club was happy in the recollection of a full tourist season. There were disquieting rumors that twenty-eight miles west of here the Army Air Corps was to build the largest training field in the nation. But so far there was only one small training field. And the copper miners were far enough away not to seek a bed in Tucson.

As long as you stay inside the town you can enjoy a cozy escape from the war. But outside of it in all directions it is the bare earth that knows the changes. Here in Southern Arizona was proof to me, more dramatic than in other places I had been, that the resources of a nation cannot be defined, in spite of the fashionable Puritanism of our time, in the character of the people. The natural resources of the land itself may be overwhelming. This is an unpleasant truism to the natives of small, highly civilized countries whose earth does not have enough natural loot to attract powerful neighbors. Everybody but the State Department judged the war contribution of a Greek, a Dane, or a member of the European underground, by the moral fervor and ingenuity of his personal stand against Fascism. But in the end, the total American contribution to the defeat of the Nazis must be judged by the resources this country was able to enlist, even when they were being used by men more skilled than politically aroused. Ideally, the best nation would be the one that made the most of its natural resources for a noble end. But I doubt if history has ever recorded this Platonic coincidence. These are sum qualities of persons not of nations. And we dissipate our morality in using it to justify wants and needs that are at least as naturally active in all men as the impulse to virtue.

Tucson, Arizona, was a good place to consider this sober fact. It is easy, and sometimes profitable, to stir bad blood between Allies by reporting, from the standpoint of morality, what they call 'the spirit of the people'. And I suppose it would have been almost irresistible for a Briton, fresh from Coventry, or Libya, to watch the resort population of Tucson at play and go away with scorn for what the 'people' of Arizona were doing for the war. The 'people' themselves are hardly to be pitied, for they anticipate this reaction by elaborating to you their own vigilance in the matter of such things as Civilian Defense and the collection of scrap metal.

But this was irrelevant to the awesome contribution of Southern Arizona. 'The people' who live there also happen to include mining engineers and Papago Indians. And what they were doing in their daily work – mining one-third of the nation's copper – reduced to insignificance the playful shenanigans of a few thousand businessmen, debs, and playboys.

The earth in which Tucson nestles is hard as iron. To the vacation-ist its only value is as a background to horse-riding and, in the violet nightfall, to romance. To the botanist it is a bare and ungracious table-land that once a year blossoms into breathless flower, to the incredible number of over 400 separate kinds of blossom. But this same earth has been a godsend to the Allies. By night in all the surrounding mountains, which for two decades have been known only to hikers and moonlight riders from dude ranches, newly trained surveyors are going out looking for and finding unsuspected deposits of the strategic minerals. Formerly, you had to have a long and tedious training to learn how to recognize them in their common bed of scrub and under-lying rock. Nowadays a field officer rounds up new surveyors and, under the auspices of the United States Bureau of Mines, located here on the campus of the University of Arizona, instructs them in the use of a new lamp. It is an ultra-violet lamp, and all a prospector has to do is to memorize or carry a color chart, go out in the mountains at night, and flash his lamp on any lump of gray rock. If he is lucky he will see smears of color embedded there, like tropical fish frozen in the earth, some yellow or purple or red or green. He consults his chart and knows at once that there, according to the color, he is seeing tungsten, antimony, chrome, manganese, and, less likely, mercury, tin, or nickel.

Just over 100 miles west of here on the reservation of the Papago Indians is one of the three biggest copper pits in America. There is always a lot of inconclusive argument between the natives of Arizona, Nevada, and Utah about the relative size of their great copper pits. Maybe I should report the official description of the United States Bureau of Mines that the one at Bingham, Utah, is biggest in area, the one at Ruth, Nevada, is deepest, and this one here at Ajo is widest. Before 1936, the Ajo mine, which had been worked as long ago as the 1850s, was closed up, and the permanent miners thereabouts were on relief. However, it went into operation again soon after we started shipping a lot of copper to the Japanese. By 1940 it was going at nearly full blast, and surveyors were scouring the earth for more copper. Until 1939, indeed, mining engineers complained about a surplus of metals above ground, and their problem was to keep pro-duction down. After 1940, the surplus vanished. In 1942, the best sign of healthy mining was the fact that, as one engineer put it, 'these miners work seven days a week. That's something new. This ain't ten-day mining.'

The Papago Reservation, where the pit is, is a corner of the earth that only an incurable desert man would love. The surrounding land, topped though it is by ironwood and prickly pear, looks like a part of the desert that God had abandoned and petrified into sterility. The man who thought of Arizona as the land given to the Devil for his own special sway must have been recently through Ajo when he wrote the classic song:

> He fixed the heat on one hundred and seven
> And banished forever the moisture from Heaven
> But remembered as he heard his furnace roar
> That the heat might reach five hundred or more;
> And after he fixed things so horny and well,
> He said, 'I'll be damned if this don't beat hell.'

Driving through this frightening reservation, on which the Papagos manage somehow to raise enough beans to keep their bodies together and to drink enough agave juice to pacify their souls, you can imagine no growing thing that would help anybody in war or peace – till suddenly you come on Ajo and stagger up to the rim of the enormous hole itself. It is a mile long, half a mile wide, and nearly 500 feet deep. Down along its baking bottom tiny trains back and fill, load with slabs of blasted rock, disappear into the bank and emerge on the surface of the rock about an hour later as copper ore. What started out as dusty rock down below enlists the combined processes of electric shoveling, filter plants, crushing plants, railroads, trucks, and a million-dollar well, and emerges on top as 17 percent of all the copper in the country, or slightly more than Hitler can scratch together throughout the Reich. The town, which lies off from the pit, is another and a different shock. It is not the camp of cribs and saloons that the miners knew before the last war. It is a neat community of three divisions, housing whites, Mexicans, and Papagos. It is a company town, owned exclusively by the Phelps Dodge Corporation. It is a sort of model American town, in the *Saturday Evening Post* style. And your first thought is wonder at the benevolence of corporation democracy. Here in a landscape where Indians lived in caves for

20,000 years, caves that still house Papagos when they harvest the cacti fruits, here where a Harvard geologist recently stumbled over the undisturbed bones of dogs dead for 7,000 years, is a town baking inconspicuously in a temperature of 110 degrees and cheerily advertising to the 'intending resident' a community 'where water is pure and soft as rain, where there is never any fog, where there is a modern aviation field, fresh fruits, vegetables, and eggs brought to your door, a cooperative department store, handsomely paid schoolteachers, a municipal target range, golf, tennis, horses, a public park, and – a mere ninety miles away – the greatest horde of game fish in the Western Hemisphere'. You do not stop to ask the natives if they feel secure in the freedom to speak their mind in public, to crusade for a free press, to use their vote as they choose. These issues are as irrelevant as they would be to convalescents in a sanatorium. The corporation provides. Even the federal government and the state of Arizona itself seem like distant abstractions recorded in books. If all corporations created such model communities, American democracy could confidently cease to exist. You reflect nervously that if all corporations were as omnipotent in their own neck of the woods, it probably would anyway.

These unpredictable reflections are the liveliest pleasure of a long tour through different types of country. The unsung variety of the United States could stimulate boredom only in people who are the unconscious victims of a preconception that America is a standardized country. Unhappily, most Europeans and Eastern Seaboard Americans were bred in this warming belief, and, most sadly, the Americans who have it may travel thousands of miles in their own country and never lose it. But here was I, traveling west to Ajo, or Little Garlic as it is sturdily called, hoping at best for a glimpse of a bone of a 7,000-year-old dog. And, by the courtesy of Phelps Dodge, I ran into an American variant of the town of tomorrow.

Coming at night into Phoenix, whose inhabitants would doubtless think of Ajo, if at all, as a hell-hole in the desert, I thought I had gone back into an old grimy town of the Deep South, if it had not been for the bare mountains that appear at the end of every street. This impression was due simply to the railroad station, and the streetcar tracks, along which the trolleys rattle as deafeningly as the streetcars of New

Haven, Connecticut. But coming out of the station, you have only to ask your way of a native and you know at once that you are in a Western town: 'four blocks south, one block east', they say. For all its pretended 'progress', it is a typical town of the Southwest. That is to say, a town where the men are older than the buildings and the earth is older than Europe. They take city values lightly and know the points of the compass better than the Ten Commandments. Stand anywhere in open country, or for that matter in open town, west of San Antonio, and the visible stake in life is you, the earth, the sun, and sky. There are no alleys, or winding streets, or directions that can be described in the twisting geometry of old towns and villages. A foreigner or a stranger from the East visiting Phoenix notices the chic women (and for the record, I had better say I have never seen so many pretty American girls in one place who also looked thoroughly healthy); he notices the men wearing polo shirts or their shirt collar turned in; and he is liable to accept the tourist view of Phoenix as a carefree, young, upstart place made by the natural advantage of automatic sunshine. A stranger in the West, whose early education was not American, cannot fail to marvel at this thoughtless superiority of educated Easterners. That they should visit the West only for its dramatic scenery and its sunshine is proof of the woeful failure of American education, and the best American education, in grounding its children in the elements of American culture. Of all the casual snobbism that one encounters in Eastern visitors to the West, the hollowest is their deprecation of the West's rude youth. Irrigation farming is usually picked on as a regrettable sacrifice of get-rich-quick farmers who would settle for quick, big crops of fruits that might be grown better with long and loving care elsewhere. Yet you have only to go a few miles outside Phoenix to see the ruins of irrigation canals used centuries ago by the Indians, whose agriculture was watered then – as the Salt River Valley is now – by a controlled flow from the Gila-Salt River, the fickle source that sometimes is a mere trickle and at other times carries more water from a single 'shower' than all the rain of the previous year. Before Christ, Indians were raising fine crops of cotton and corn on the same principle as the Salt River Valley Water Users Association. In fact, there is probably no single region of America whose farming is more traditional than that of the brisk farmers who grow cotton, citrus fruits, the second-biggest crop of United States lettuce, and who harvest six or eight crops of alfalfa a year, from the stored water of the Roosevelt Dam and its subsidiaries north of Phoenix. Of course, there is nothing marvelous in this. But it is odd that Americans, and 'educated' Americans especially, should so deplore their lack of 'tradition' and 'background' when they are surrounded by traditions that antedate Europe. It must be that the schools and universities have been, from God knows what deep sense of shame, only too eager to confuse the words 'culture' and 'civilization' and surrender too meekly to Santayana's wildly fallacious taunt that 'America is the only country that achieved a civilization without passing through a culture.' It would be truer to say that America is unique in having achieved a modern civilization without being aware of its culture. For though American civilization is something that the average American glories in or apologetically accepts, American culture is something that he has rarely learned about.

Because of the strong traditionalism in the way it lives and works, Phoenix is reacting to the Second World War very much as it did to the first. Once again the most valuable crop it can offer is long staple cotton, which in the last war was found essential to the making of tire and balloon fabrics, and fetched dreamlike prices – prices that seduced dairy farmers into dumping their cattle on the market and putting in long staple cotton instead of alfalfa. But Phoenix well remembers the unexpected slump in the demand for long staple cotton the moment the war was over. And although it has since become popular in the manufacture of shirts and women's clothes, it is today being planted guardedly by veteran farmers of the last war, frantically by youngsters who know that they had better gather the long staple while they may. It is, compared with lettuce or citrus fruits, a bothersome crop, hard to pick and handle. There is only 70 percent of the needed farm labor, and much of the seasonal labor that is the standby of irrigation farmers has vanished into the Army or war factories. Consequently, there is a lively agitation for Mexicans – from California or Texas – to pick and chop the crop at a wage that the farmers have been used to paying. The government, worried over the nation's needs for meat, is urging the dairy farmers not to abandon their herds, as they did last time. And so you hear the now utterly familiar grumbling against the Office of Price Administration as a Washington institution designed to provide farmers with less labor at higher wages.

The people you talk with have a sense of alertness that springs from something more than the new call for long staple cotton. It is the sense of living on a possible frontline. This may seem merely jittery to citizens of the Atlantic Seaboard, whose newspapers play up the threat of a Japanese invasion more or less as a necessary wartime slogan. But here in the Southwest, there seems to be an active fear of what might be done through the back door of Mexico. Many people tell you that for a decade before Pearl Harbor the only people who seemed to know much about the tactical possibilities of the Lower California coastline were Japanese fishermen who – according to Southwesterners – spent most of their time taking soundings in little-known bays and coves. At any rate, the taxi-driver who takes you to the station boasts about the number of airfields around Phoenix not as breeding grounds of the men who will bomb Germany but as the first line of defense against 'them sneaky Japs'. He repeats – in case I happen to be a Japanese agent – fearful rumors of 'hundreds, yeah thousands of our planes patrolling the Mexican border', and adds that in an air raid most of the towns of the Southwest could be plunged into instant darkness because the lighting is on unit switches.

The train out of Phoenix was very late, and by one in the morning the life of the station had slowed to a characteristic calm of American wartime life. At the end of the platform, a huge silhouetted cotton-wood was lapped by a warm breeze. Not a bird or plane or smear of smoke against the wide purple sky. The yellow cabs, like enormous wasps, dozed in formation. Redcaps sat propped against the stanchions of empty express trucks. Their arms were folded and their caps tilted over their eyes. There was no movement anywhere except for the winking reflection of an unseen neon sign. A Mexican in a blue coat padded by and went off somewhere to the end of the world. The long tracks glistening in the moonlight seemed to bisect the earth.

Inside the station the waiting passengers sat or straddled numbly on long wooden benches. Soldiers, their collars unbuttoned, lay prostrate, a few of them exhaling wispy snores through their teeth. A young soldier sat next to me engrossed in *True Stories* and turned avidly from 'The Lure of Courtship' to a piece called 'Rattlesnakes Are My Playmates'. Another lay almost asleep with his head on a girl's lap. She was not a pretty girl, but as she sat upright there, her legs out at a wide angle to leave a friendly lap for the head and shoulders of the soldier, she was a Madonna, exquisitely self-contained, smoking a cigarette – his wife, mother, mistress, guardian angel. Two MPs strolled in and out with nothing to do, no friction to ease anywhere. It was such a tired and inoffensive world that the gleaming ash of the girl's cigarette was almost an aggression.

This in American town life is the rare beauty of stasis, the period when all the turbulence and grinning, competitive frenzy of the day is spent, when the brash and the bold are truly relaxed. The night and the silence beamed on them. A soldier would occasionally switch his elbow from one knee to the other. Never are Americans so still as when waiting for a train late at night, and never more attractive, their good and various features composed in the ultimate humility of tiredness.

I do not know if this idyll of the soldier and the guardian angel was shattered or heightened by the fact that when the train-whistle blew far off, and the baggage clerk came to life again, the soldier roused himself, straightened his cap, and with a slight nod murmured, 'Okay, babe', and went off alone in the direction of the tracks. She rose, dusted the ash off her skirt with the back of her hand, and said, 'You're welcome, soldier.'

7

Westward the Course of Empire

Early in the morning, we awoke with a jolt as the train chugged out of Yuma, Arizona. Dusty and heavily skirted Indian women sat against the platform fence, fingering little piles of beads, charm bags, and turquoise jewelry they had laid out on the platform. A feathery palo verde tree drifted by the window, and where a road turned away into the desert there was a reminder of many a Hollywood infatuation that had broken the front pages in London and Vienna: 'Drive-In Marriage Guide Station. Licenses Secured'.

We crossed the Colorado River, noticed a highway sign marking the entrance to California, and passed over into the Golden State without any appreciable feeling of entering Heaven. Instead, as we flattened out across the rolling sand dunes of the Yuma Desert, we saw a wooden board stuck forlornly in the sand, advertising 'Triple A Artesian Water – Free from all Alkali'.

It may have been that the early sun, throwing long horizontal shadows, gave an unreal body and life to the scattered scrub and the brown tips of buried mesquite. Or it may have been the knowledge, picked from the memory of a fruit cooperative's ad, that soon we should be coming near the All-American Canal, pouring its 15,000 cubic feet of water a second into the Imperial Valley. But anyway, the Colorado Desert did not look as horrendous as always described. I sat next to a young Californian soldier whose gaze as he stared out the window had acquired an expression of affectionate pride that was shared by none of his yawning companions. But you have only to drive across this desert, or try to isolate your memory from the steady comfort of the train, to wonder again at the crazy resolution of some of the men who walked or muled it; Coronado 400 years ago; the incomparable Captain Juan Bautista de Anza, organizing a second expedition after thirst killed some of his best men and Apaches stole his best horses. Or the priests, Father Kino and seventy years later Father Garces. Turning back to the reassurance of an omelet and the waiters' shiny white coats, you decide that a Jesuit is just about the last and only man who would still walk it. I kidded the soldier with a reminder that the first explorers into his beloved state had gone this way and named it Devil's Highway and the Journey of Death. He said with absolute sincerity, 'Well, they certainly couldn't have known much about California.' I mentally tiptoed away from him and spoke no more, not wishing to assault his simple faith in a timeless California that, if the dumb Coronado had just taken the right turn in the summer of 1540, was waiting there to offer him Lana Turner, a jumbo cheeseburger, all the orange juice he could drink for ten cents, and a Thursday luncheon reception from the Sons and Daughters of the Golden West.

It was during this final stretch of train journey, edging the Great American Desert and then plunging into the sudden luxuriance of the irrigated Imperial Valley, that I began to realize the hopeless superficiality of traveling the rest of the continent by train. Whole types of country and ways of life slide by the window of your train and deposit you in cities, a very necessary custom since most people live in them. But it is a false analogy to suppose that cities focus what the American landscape is doing for the war. To report only on cities at 300-mile intervals is, for a roving correspondent, like learning to breathe in an oxygen tent. I had driven from Washington, DC, to San Antonio, but my companion, whose car it was, was called back to New York. So from San Antonio west I had taken the train, and at one or two places here and there acquaintances had been kind enough to lend me their cars to mooch around the surrounding country. But it is no way to see, let alone report on, the rest of the country. And the long day's train journey from Yuma to Los Angeles showed me nothing of what the war had done and, worse, tended to support the train-traveler's notion that California is hunks of desert and mountain with intervening valleys artificially watered to produce oranges and avocados.

I therefore decided to forget anything I had seen west of Yuma, to buy a car in Los Angeles, drive back to the edge of the desert, and take up the account from there. A few mornings later I had bought my car in Pasadena and was shipping southeast by the dawn's early light. A European may be shocked at the crude nonchalance of this automobile purchase in wartime, and I should explain that it was not quite as casual as that. The salesman who finally sold me was in a state of high excitement for forty-eight hours after hearing that a visitor wanted to buy a car for no other reason than to drive around the country. Throughout the subsequent negotiations, he regarded me as an amiable madman. His storeroom was a funeral parlor, the cars lined up there like so many coffins. He admitted stoically that he saw no future for himself unless he went into the Army. About once a month somebody would come in on the pretense of wanting to buy a car and then sneak around prodding the tires and not even bother to look at the engine. These were pestiferous middlemen looking for cars with good rubber and making heavy profits on the immediate resale. I was obliged to share this obsession for 'good rubber', and in the end settled for a make I did not want that had four solid retreaded tires with about 15,000 miles of rubber still left on them.

The skies were pouring torrential rain when I stopped very early in the morning at Banning, for breakfast. But fifteen minutes later I was streaking under cloudless blue across the dry desert before Palm Springs, with the lofty white peak of San Jacinto topping the mountains that brood over this highway through a violet haze.

In Palm Springs, the swank clothing stores and the masseurs' parlors were empty, and I looked in vain for elegant playboys with an Esquire tan. This restraint was doubtless not due to a general feeling of shame or respect for the Americans fighting abroad. But the chief hotel, a huge sanctuary of oleanders, lawns, tamarisks, and 200-dollar a weekend bungalows, had an Army guard posted outside. I asked if I might see the manager and was taken to see a Colonel and a Major, the only visible residents of the place. It had been taken over very suddenly by the Army to be prepared as a convalescent hospital. The lease was signed abruptly one weekend. The movie stars were told to pack their bags and leave. By midweek, it was as hallowed as a monastery garden. The proceedings had all happened rather violently for the manager, who had difficulty adjusting to the coming new regime. As we walked through blazing flowerbeds and stood looking into the still, green swimming pool, I said all that was missing was Hedy Lamarr. 'Want a picture?' asked the manager, nostalgically.

The highway from Palm Springs to Indio is bordered with cottonwoods and tamarisks. Narrow irrigation canals duck under the highway, and as you come near to Indio roadside billboards challenge you to taste the incomparable dates of Shields' Desert Date Garden. I went by a deserted Bedouin tent that had formerly housed a date stand. Then Mr Shields' billboards grew larger and beseeched you to stop at the best, the rarest, the most luscious of all American date gardens. A dark grove of date palms loomed up west of the highway, and some smaller billboards suggested that the date gardens of Dr Sniff would also be worth a visit. I went first to Mr Shields, a small, stocky man who sat down on a bench in the shade and after a pause, in which he evidently waited for an invisible audience to collect, launched, without ever looking at me, into a fifteen-minute spiel about the miracle of the date and the marvels of the Shields Date Gardens. His voice rose and fell with a well-practiced tune as he discoursed on the plant imported from Algeria, the size of his garden, the breeding habits of the palm ('One good male pollen will pollinate forty-eight females'). Without any change of tone he would reel off figures, bemoan the shortage of pickers, and get off such lyrics as 'the date palm requires its feet in water, its palms in the fires of Heaven.' He was obviously not used to interruptions and regarded any discussion of the war as an irrelevance. 'The war,' he flatly declared, 'hasn't done a thing to the date business. Forty thousand mail-order customers. That's my business. And people ain't gonna give up eating dates whatever the government says about freight shortage.' Dr Sniff, a little farther along the road, had other opinions. He was a tall, rather distinguished looking man, and when I asked him how many varieties of dates he grew, mentioning that Mr Shields confessed to 119 varieties, he smiled and allowed there were four kinds he was particularly proud of. He said the rubber shortage had caused a terrible drop in highway travel and that 'road business is down about 40 percent.' The Mexicans who did the packing had gone off into the Army. 'The picking's the problem. You can get old men, but they won't work in the high trees.'

Later, in Los Angeles, I heard that the great disappointment of the date-growers and packers of Riverside County was that the Army had been cold to suggestions that dates might provide an essential ingredient of the K ration, the concentrated meal for combat use that Army chemists were then working on. It seemed that every fruit-grower in California was hoping, if not lobbying, for an outright choice of his product for the ration. One date-grower hired a chemist and begged him to discover in the date some vitamin, or laxative ingredient that had never previously been known. Unfortunately, he was a good chemist and his findings confirmed only the melancholy conclusions of other chemists that dates have a lot of sugar and a luscious taste. The Army went ahead trying out grapes, figs, raisins, pears, peaches, and practically everything else.

I started for the coast west from Indio on the cement highway that runs like toothpaste across the desert plain straight into the Santa Rosa Mountains. It is a celebrated drive and is known as the Palms-to-Pines highway. It is none the less magnificent because a thousand travelers have found it so. This drive alone will reveal to a skeptical Easterner the lovely and audacious variety that Californians boast for the landscape. You start at noon in the shade of clustering palms. In a few minutes you are skimming across gaping desert. You wind slowly up the jagged face of mountains on which only sage and cactus grow. The low piñon trees are everywhere around. You slide under the shadows of enormous slabs of rock. You are beneath rock and sky, an eternity away from anything that goes into a twentieth-century kitchen. The land is so bare and terrifying that you do not wonder it was turned over to two tribes of Indians. The word 'reservation' takes on an awful cynicism. Then you top the mountains and might be in Alaska. Stiff pines brush the elbow of your steering arm. Slowly you start the long, winding drop to the coast thirty miles away. And you traverse the astounding and typical pattern of the bountiful agriculture of Southern California. Once over the rim of the mountains, sheep line the slopes like boulders in Vermont. Then you dip into green mountain valleys where fat cows trundle, leg-less in the high pasture. You drop through wide fields of swaying barley, and with every descending mile the rainfall loss may be as high as eight or ten inches a year. Soon the irrigation pipes start, dividing the mountain green from the brown irrigated valleys below. You tumble through lemon and avocado orchards on the highest slopes, farthest from the fatal frost. Then orange groves ripple over little hills and merge into orchards of peaches and grapes. By mid-afternoon, you are taking all this for granted, driving contentedly along highways laced with euca- lyptus trees, weaving without surprise through fields of tomatoes or peaches or poultry farms. I left Rancho Santa Fe as the sun was drop- ping down, hummed along smooth highways drenched with pepper trees, wound and curved through all the warm scent of orange groves, and suddenly tasted a sharp salt breeze from the ocean. Climbing up to a bluff stiff with the spreading branches of Torrey pines I was shocked by the wild sight of a gun emplacement in the cliffs. I looked down on the Pacific and suddenly remembered Tokyo.

The evening lights were gleaming around the cove at La Jolla, and then all the bedraggled petticoats of a city spread along the ocean highway – the billboards, undesigned auto camps, gas stations, and flocks of trailers. I came into San Diego, and fronting the ocean was the low, vast plant of Consolidated Aircraft, the ominous flat roofs stretching a mile or more down to the sea, with only a dull glow coming from the blackened windows and at the fence gates high, hooded sodium lights. Tramping in the semi-darkness all around were groups of men and women in overalls, banging the frame-doors of diners and lunch-counters. From inside the buildings and mingling with the gentle wash of the waves was a low sort of roar. It was an actual effort to recall the day's ride, the mountain background to this throbbing industrialism. The memory of the landscape came back in unreal flashes. It was as if I had been idling on a brightly lit stage-set of a country garden, ripe with every sort of pastoral fancy, and then had turned a flat and come on the stagehands and the wings, the propped sets, the men working in the flies – all the dark mechanics that produced the pretty picture the audience saw.

When the sun goes up on San Diego, you see a war city so swollen and distracted with its new problems that natives of long standing can only give out a dry, bitter laugh at the soothing description of their town written in the federal guide just a year or two earlier: 'The city has much of the easygoing spirit of Spanish days, and people live and dress for comfort.' You cannot get near the waterfront, no matter how fat your credentials. It is wired off and patrolled by tough-looking Marines and sailors. If you ask an innocent question about the clanging noise coming from the docks, where presumably the wreckage of Pacific battles is being beaten into shape again, you are liable to suspicious questioning from sentries.

It looks as if there had been a revolution and, although some sort of order had been restored, the barricades were still up and strangers were expected to keep moving. The streets are crowded with sallow families, or rather with mothers and small children trotting from office to office, and agency to agency, trying to find a place to lay their heads. The prewar population of 200,000 has gone up by 100,000, a frightful load on a city that has planned no community housing and never dreamed of itself as an industrial frontier. It is like no Western town you've ever seen. Back in the fruit valleys and the mountains are millions of acres where, you would think, a man could build any size home he chose and breathe quantities of fresh air. But here in a mesh of paved streets are thousands of families, with husbands in the aircraft plant, to whom suddenly the most breathtaking ideal that America could offer would be an ordinary, decent daily routine of sleep, food, work, and a school for the children. They have set up all sorts of harried emergency services, staffed by that fine and tireless type of American who yearns to shoulder the humdrum worries of a community. These people flash news to the line of waiting mothers of a vacant trailer, or a room over a cigar store, and the cry goes up as jubilant as the day Prohibition ended. There is no organization, but only brave individuals who fish all over town for families, schools, churches, institutions that will take part-time care of children, or adopt a child whose parents both work in the city and cannot find a spare room or crib or watcher for the baby. I heard of many frantic devices for what they call 'the care and management of children', but in wartime America in the twentieth century this means keeping a baby in the land of the living. The resource and ingenuity shown by a few local citizens (who trade on the idea of Colonial neighborliness in helping war workers with the nursing and cleaning) would be a stirring thing if it were not pathetic. But installed as it is in the shell of what we call 'the American standard of living' – surrounded by steel and concrete buildings, zooming elevators, tiled bathrooms, aluminum kitchens, Rotarians and Elks, and the rest – it only shows the pretty pass that private enterprise, or self-help, can bring us to in any social crisis not foreseen and arranged for by our grandfathers. We talk nauseously about the 'spirit' of America, the pioneers, individualism, and what have you. But here in one town, nearly half of whose new inhabitants are fighting to satisfy the ordinary appetites we believe to be the exclusive property of ignorant Chinese peasants, many of the pillars of society look stonily on, resourceless to do more than deplore the uncouthness of the invading 'foreigners'. The solid citizens look glum and quote an 80 percent increase in juvenile delinquency. But in the evening, roaming the bars and saloons, you see, alongside much healthy ribaldry among sailors and Marines fresh from the Pacific, plenty of saddening adult delinquency – husbands high on airplane wages toasting newfound chippies, fifteen- and sixteen-year-olds sitting up at chromium bars starting out with Cokes and going on to Cuba Libres and highballs just for the hell of it. A hotel owner, who had been in the Alaska Gold Rush, called it 'the greatest boom-town since the Klondike'.

The town is swarming with sailors and Marines, and an unexplained impulse took me in the afternoon along Fourth and Fifth Avenues to eye the bluejackets banging away in the shooting galleries and lining their pockets from close deals in the pawnshops. I stopped at a window containing a very elegant framed sample of several score types of tattooing. I went inside to wonder what the war had done to tattooing. Sitting at a small machine like some sort of printing press was a sleek, foxy-looking character in his early fifties, wearing a bow tie, his shirtsleeves rolled up baring arms blue with wriggling cooch dancers, hearts pierced with arrows, patterns of lacework, and assorted nicknames. Unlike Mr Shields, the Indio date man, he was very willing to open up about his business, and indeed the very fact that somebody could suggest to him the idea that the war had affected his trade spurred him at once to maintain that no craft or business 'in these United States' had been more profoundly affected.

'It's a very different picture, mister, from the last war. There's no trouble getting dyes. But, I mean the mental attitude, you know what I mean? Last time, the sailors used to come in here and ask for hearts, and their girls' names. And, sure, Coochie-woochies – they're always in demand. But this time they seem to want their mothers, just the word "mother", and maybe the insignia of the outfit they belong to. Then, you know, it's not as simple as it was. I mean from the medical angle. I never had a customer yet get blood-poisoning. But in the last twenty years, the doctors started hornin' in and setting up what they call "standards". Today, tattooing is – well, you might call it a scientific, surgical operation. Sterile needles and all that stuff. That sorta thing makes you pretty leery. The docs don't encourage tattooing on some parts of the body I could name. So I'm not takin' any risks. I tell you, I seen the time when two dozen sailors and a pile of horny women'd come in here and ask for the goddamndest things. But in thirty years of tattooing there've always been some things I don't do. Drunks, for one thing. And girls who don't give a damn what you tattoo on 'em, just so long as you give 'em the needle. Hell, I'm broad-minded. I'm not too old to take care of a woman if I have a mind to, but I don't use a needle. They just want it to hurt. Get it? It's a queer business. Most guys who get tattooed do it on a dare, just to show they're tough. Sure it hurts. That's the psychology of it. If it didn't hurt, I'da been out of business thirty-five years ago.'

He started cleaning his needles, and as I moved to the door he said, 'Another thing. There's ethics in this game. I don't want to harm anybody. I charge five dollars a square inch on the forearm, ten dollars on the upper arm. But I wouldn't touch a chest for fifty bucks.'

At night I went on a saloon crawl. Civilian men were hardly to be seen anywhere. It was leathernecks and bluejackets all over the place, and the prevailing spirit among those sitting at the bars was expressed by one hefty sailor who longingly eyed a pretty, plump girl dancing with his friend: 'Gotta grab me a hunka meat before I sail if it's the last thing I do. God knows what kinda shape I'll be in after a run-in with the Nippers.' He had to be back to the ship before midnight, but his eyes followed the plump girl with infinite desire. He ordered another drink and shouted to his pal, 'How's to stand my watch tonight, Mac?' His pal, swooning cheek to cheek, turned his head and gave a short sharp laugh through his teeth.

I drove out of San Diego past Consolidated again, with thousands of workers sitting out in the grilling noonday sun listening to the news from loudspeakers. They sat inside the plant enclosure, eating their lunches, thousands of lunches, sitting in line on wooden benches that started here as benches and ended as sparkling points on the horizon. Going north I passed a housing project going up, bearing on a huge billboard the sign, 'Homes For OUR Defenders'.

The busy disorganization of San Diego died away as I drove up to the coast and the fine green and gray curve of La Jolla Bay came in sight. The surf was lapping quietly against mossy rocks, and a pelican flew low toward the cliffs. Occasionally quails stepped importantly across the highway. It was all very calm and pleasant. But almost anybody who had ever driven before on Route 101 would have wondered about the sudden clumps of trees and littered foliage covered over with nets, and occasional Coast Guardsmen or soldiers patrolling the highway wherever it dipped down to the sea. There were rumors of long-range guns back in the hills. However that may be, there were enough evidences of shore batteries and emplacements nestling in bean fields to give you the idea that the Japanese islands lay not many miles offshore. I had been promised that California was more alert to the war than any other part of the country, but it was a Californian in Washington who said so, and it sounded at the time like routine local pride. Anyway, there is not much to say for the intelligence of anybody who will offer to name the 'feeling' of any place. It may be that I am allergic to the idea of regional 'feeling', but all I had been able to sense so far were preoccupations, and sometimes the grievances, of people who do the same work, or face the same community problems. I wasn't disposed to credit that the laws of individual psychology do not apply to California. But without generalizing about what the signs meant, they were the same signs you would see on a coast that was close to actual fighting. Driving up this highway, you were rarely allowed to forget that Japan is the special American enemy. And from the alarmist talk of residents of the coast, and the irregular fortification I spotted, I recognized too an aroused respect for the Japanese fighting ability that would have seemed panicky if it had appeared on the East Coast, only half as far from Hitler.

The usual amusements of this highway used to be diners built in the shape of puppies or overflowing ice-cream cones, one-story funeral parlors, and billboard invitations to be 'saved' by some weird religion homegrown by the more paranoid natives of the state. There were odd reminders of this immortal Californian trend, but a billboard to build a beautiful home and stay blissful for life would be followed by signs warning 'Oil is Ammunition: Use it Wisely' or 'Keep Faith With the Wives of the Men of the Merchant Marine'. Right up against an 'Open Air Wedding Chapel' was a detachment of Marines working in a field of tomatoes. Up beyond San Luis Rey was a one-room office building carrying the mysterious sign, 'I Am Sanctuary'. And then you would see scores of Mexicans, and even a few women, busily weeding in vast fields of lima beans that stretched all the way along the ocean-side, on the left of the highway.

At Balboa, and the resort towns north, the real-estate men were with some skepticism getting accustomed to a wholly new population of tenants. They assumed that 'the summer trade is shot', chiefly because of 'the general scare about the Japs (you'd be surprised how many people are renting shacks in the mountains, figuring the Japs are going to land right here at Balboa)'. But also because yachts had been forbidden to go out to the ocean. Only commercial fishermen were allowed out, on Coast Guard permits. During the winter and early spring the real-estate boys usually expect about half their houses to be vacant. This time, there were only about one-fifth of them unoccupied. But instead of retired couples and vacationing families, the occupants were foremen from airplane plants at San Diego and Los Angeles; war workers; and the wives of officers at nearby camps.

If you turn inland off the coast highway at Balboa, you will join US 101 again just below Santa Ana. From there the run up into Los Angeles is a wriggle through a patchwork of fruit orchards, bungalow communities, oil wells, and palm-lined streets. It is not the loveliest trip in the state, but within these forty miles most of the paying resources of Southern California may be seen in the microcosm of a string of suburbs.

Starting from Santa Ana, with its sugar-beet refinery and chili pepper-canning plants, you whisk through walnut orchards, orange groves protected by borders of eucalyptus trees, main streets flashing neon invitations to movies, ice-cream parlors, and salvation through spiritualism or real estate (one illuminated sign says 'You Can Still Be Happy In Wartime' on a two-acre 'ranch' away from it all). At Fullerton, the scent of oranges seeps through the heavy smell of oil wells.

Victorian houses stand on the corner of small lettuce fields, then a ripple of tiled Spanish bungalows goes by and you are trundling through small hills past unbroken fields of avocado, walnut, and persimmons, past truck gardens, busier main streets, and oil derricks marching through garish flower gardens. It is not the scale of this productivity that impresses but its confident variety. The whole stretch looks like a small-town agricultural fair, the successive orchards being the tables on which the local housewives lay out all the crazy and ambitious things they have managed to grow in their backyards. Only at Orange, with its surrounding groves of Valencias and navels, do you get any idea that this county, and the adjacent Los Angeles County, produce more (and more valuable) farm produce than any other counties in the United States. Stop anywhere along this highway and drive slowly toward the foothills and the word 'intensive' takes on a new meaning. Back of the main streets are refrigeration plants, or canning factories, packing sheds, office buildings given over entirely to men whose days and nights and files are absorbed with the growing and harvesting and marketing of lemons or oranges. On the edge of town, fields of cauliflower or lettuce change at once into fields of walnuts. And all along the highway nearer the hills you will see wells, or small reservoirs, or men working on canals or digging back into the hills for the water, water, water that makes the prosperous wheels go round, all over this state.

The main problem of fruit-marketing in wartime seems to be the alarming reassessment of the value of any single crop. What the Army needs has had to be the first of the war's demands on the nation's farmers. In the Midwest, this has been simply a problem of growing more with less labor and transporting bumper harvests in fewer freight cars. But in a region of intensive, and greatly varied, fruits and vegetables, the whole hierarchy of food values is liable to be upset by government decree. In peacetime, a date presumably gets the same marketing consideration as an apricot or a cauliflower. But comes the war, and the government, adjusting the nation's agriculture to the Army's demands, can at once make new and devastating distinctions between 'necessary' and 'luxury' crops. The War Production Board, acting on the shortage of base metal for cans, is able to invent two categories of foodstuffs: primary and secondary. It will release materials for the canning of the primary foods – for vegetables, some fruits, beets. But it orders that the canning of secondary foods must cease at once. And so the grouching you hear, against Washington, the WPB, 'bureaucrats', and the President himself, comes naturally enough from people who have the bad luck to be in the second class – the canners of vegetable juices, plums, beer, and dog food.

The tin shortage means, according to the shrewdest packers, a major change in the buying habits of American housewives, 'away from canned fruits to packed dehydrated fruits'. Dehydration seems to be the answer to many more related problems. The Army found that whole milk often rancified long before it reached its destination. But a method of spray-drying whole milk has been very successful. A California milk company sent a shipment from San Francisco, through the Panama Canal, to a European country that was invaded before the ship was due to arrive. The ship turned around and came back via South Africa and eventually docked at Baltimore. The shippers and insurance companies were disgruntled over an undelivered cargo, but Army chemists at once examined samples of the cargo and found the milk quite unspoiled. This accidental experiment was a brilliant confirmation of the spray-drying process, and it has been used for all subsequent Lend-Lease shipments to our Allies.

Then there was another loss of time over the lack of wood for the trays on which apricots are dried in the sun. Dehydration was a quick solution but it changed the color of the apricots, and the farmers protested that until people had lost their lifetime preconceptions about the 'natural' color of a fruit, a discolored apricot would get a bad grade.

Grading is the fruit farmer's preoccupation even more in wartime than in peace. For again the Army's insatiable need lifts his hope that he will be able to get a high price for off-grade fruit, that is for the poor-quality product he often had to scrap or sell in bulk for incidental use in, for instance, the manufacture of candy. The Army takes the first-grade grapes for the tables of its camps, and for the making of its famous fruit-bar rations. So the wine-growers agitate to have second-grade grapes approved as first-grade. Pears in the Santa Clara Valley don't dry well, but inferior or not they constitute a crop that cannot be ignored in wartime. So again there is a lowering in the quality of civilian food. The grading of sugar, though hardly affecting this region, is another pretty example. The government rations cane and beet sugar. Whereupon farmers who raise corn for corn sugar start an agitation to have corn sugar recognized as standard. Corn syrup becomes the regular thing for sweetening fruits and candy. And in no time at all the candy advertisers make a virtue of this necessity and the highways blossom with billboards flatly stating, 'Corn Sugar is Better for You'.

A newspaper may simply report that civilians will have to make the best of what the Army leaves them. But this confession would be bad for business. The fruit-grower, if he is successful in his campaign to get off-grade prunes or apricots marked up at first-grade prices, has to pretend that they are, if anything, an improvement on the prewar product.

The Army desire for vast quantities of food in a hurry, like the War Petroleum Board's demand for special products that only elaborate refineries could produce, spells the temporary eclipse of the small grower, as of the small refiner. For its K ration, the Army did not have a prejudice in favor of any special fruit. It wanted quantity. So apricots, prunes, and a raisin mix won out, while the small luxury date industry lost out. Told about the date cooperative's desperate expedient to prove that a date was Southern California's gift to a lost patrol, an Army chemist smiled wryly. 'The vitamin content was never the issue. The date-men lost out because their industry's too small. They talk about thousands of pounds, instead of thousands of tons.'

Wherever you go, in the citrus- and fruit-farming country of California, these are the kinds of problems and arguments you will hear. Undoubtedly, fruit-growers too have sons in training in 'some God-forsaken swamp' (this is a Californian's description of such vaguely imagined states as Georgia, Tennessee, Alabama, and Louisiana), or fighting in the Pacific, but anxiety over them is the private anxiety of all families, whatever their occupation. In public, and during the working day, an enormous number of people in Southern California are worried all the time over the grading of fruit, the ceiling price on their product, the difficulties of getting enough shipping space and freight cars to take all the fruit the government has asked them to grow. All the way into Los Angeles, I saw and heard men whose instant reaction to a general query about 'the effect of the war' was a complaint over the shortage of trays for drying, over the price of avocados, of lemons, and, everywhere, over the sudden shortage of Mexican and Japanese farm labor.

You hear this last complaint so often that you would think California was helpless without them. But the apparent pain of losing them is out of all proportion to their numbers. A little persistent inquiry reveals, however, that the Mexicans and Filipinos and Japanese are the staple population of 'stoop labor'. They are the pickers. The special California affection for them is due to the fact that they get the crops in, at very low wages. There is, obviously, reasonable concern that the crops will rot, with the government demanding 20 percent more produce, and with the draft and the aircraft plants beckoning packers and pickers alike. But it will not be easy to replace these virtual serfs who traditionally harvest bumper crops for a few dollars a day, and who are not white.

This local obsession, like any other, is swallowed up by the swarming suburbs of Los Angeles. Whatever may be said against big cities, it becomes very clear on a continental trip that their noise, samenesses, and the press of hurrying humans constitute a comforting blanket of insulation against urgent problems of regional life. Without doubt, cities have their own problems, but they rarely engross the whole community.

The 'whole community' is indeed a deceptive misnomer. For big cities in our time are not integrated units, except in the most superficial ways – they draw on the same water supply, have a common transportation system, and standardize the folkways of comfort. But their tragedies are buried in the swarm of more or less healthy humans, who derive psychological protection and reassurance from the mere fact of belonging to a herd. The reader may have noticed, as the chronicle has gone along, how much easier it is to discover what makes a small town tick. Small towns usually depend for their upkeep on a single trade or crop, the welfare of which usually has an immediate impact on the daily lives of their citizens. But it is possible to live in Los Angeles and know nothing and care less about the fruit canning, movie production, furniture making, oil refining, by which Los Angeles commercially lives and has its being. The citizens of Los

Angeles have more in common with the citizens of Chicago, New Orleans, or New York than a native of Orange, California, could ever have in common with a native of New Iberia, Louisiana. The similarities of big-city life also seem to drug the curiosity of its natives about how their city works and lives, and is different from other cities. You can drop into a small town in Texas or Wyoming, look up the city or night editor of the local paper, and he will tell you unerringly in five minutes what the town lives by and how its work has been affected by the war. You do the same in a big city, I discovered, and you can sometimes spend hours with imposing editors and hear nothing but wishful abstractions about 'prosperity' or 'morale', about the activities of the Red Cross, the USO, or scrap metal drives, and some rough generalizations about the state of retail trade. I think therefore it is safer for a roving reporter to renounce any idea of picturing the skeleton of life in big cities, except where he is lucky in his sources. In Los Angeles, I was fed mostly group prejudices, and lurid accounts of booms and oppressions unfailingly described by their victims as 'the most vital single issue' in Los Angeles. The manic prosperity of real-estate men, the men with an interest in synthetic rubber, port authorities, the newly arrived branch managers of Eastern department stores, the foremen of aircraft plants, Communists outraged over the plight of the Mexican population ruefully considering the rationing of foods they had never been able to afford – these were only some of the special pleaders united by a telling denominator: an anxiety to boost Los Angeles as something like the capital of Western civilization after the war. What a visitor could sense was a sort of exhibitionist patriotism that seemed to have little root in the actual work or daily life of the city.

I had been told, by Army officials in the East, that I might have to be very patient with Army men in California, because 'they're really on the alert out there'. Technically, this was so. I had seen enough coastline fortifications and gun nests on the way up from San Diego to impress me with the Army's determination to take no chances. This alertness communicated itself to many citizens of Southern California as a happy hysteria, as if the Japs had already landed and been repulsed. Perhaps the worst you can say about the mood of 'opinion' in Los Angeles, if such a vague thing can ever take shape in the words and behavior of a city's inhabitants, is that Los Angeles is a Hearstian suburb. The headlines are bigger, and sloppier, and more clamant, and more resonant with self-pity, than in any other place in the country. A visitor had the nauseating feeling that people enjoyed their peril, wallowed in the Pacific 'crisis', felt somehow that their manhood was touchingly vindicated by the fact that they had chosen to be born on the Pacific Coast, in attacking distance of the obscene Japanese. This feeling is passed on to the stranger, I have no doubt, by the 'professional' Californians, but if civilization in Southern California is degraded by them, one can only say that Southern California does not make any public attempt to renounce them.

Los Angeles was the only place I had visited so far on this pilgrimage whose newspapers seemed to thrust at you its 'feeling' about the war as a precious and heroic commodity. You turn from the newspapers and see the fact – a city transformed in two years into a city of heavy industry. And you can then feel a rising awe more genuine than any the newspapers would bully you into – a pride in the trooping thousands of Californians and newcomers who stream on to the buses and streetcars, and form endless worms of automobiles, wriggling into the darkness, going on to the night shift at Lockheed or Vultee. And a pride in the unexpected resources of America, which can overnight change 'nineteen suburbs in search of a city' into a throbbing airplane hangar. I recalled other nights in Los Angeles years ago, roaming around the Mexican section, watching a parade in the Japanese section, mingling with the crummy denizens of South Main Street in burlesque houses, dingy saloons, flea-trap movie houses. Now I was out at Lockheed, fascinated by the wings of bombers moving evenly along an assembly line, and dried hard as rock in a few seconds by an overhanging tube of ultra-violet light. I was standing in a high tower watching the dark battalions of the night-shift click monotonously through the turnstiles, and once outside break into relaxed joshing, going off for a bite toward the collection of lunch-counters and diners they call Ulcer Gulch.

Driving back to the hotel in Pasadena in the very early morning, I got lost in the weaving boulevards, but this was not entirely accidental. For I noticed how magically soothing was the scent of the trees, the black foliage that looms all around you in that dreamlike town, and the occasional trailing of the leaves of pepper trees over the roof of the car. Reckless of my retreaded tires, I let myself be lost for a time and drove aimlessly round the silent boulevards, threading the night foliage like a contented field-snake sliding through undergrowth. The thoughts I was happy to shut out came back to me when I eventually checked into the hotel: watching the regular motions of the robot humans in the airplane factories, and recognizing in occasional dialogue they tossed at each other the accents of Georgia, of Kansas, and of New England, I wondered what these people had expected to find in California and how they lived. Every decade except one in the last seventy years, Los Angeles has doubled its population, and still they come. There came a point, during the invasion of the Okies in the late 1930s, when firm-minded guards stood armed at the state border to keep out the in-pouring human liabilities from the Dust Bowl. But now the doors were wide open and the population of California was soaring beyond the reach of anybody's plans to house it. What I had seen through the South, and on the Gulf Coast, and most lately in San Diego convinced me that to keep your patriotism bright, and your comfort undented, it is as well not to follow the war workers home, not to go beyond the bright façade of B-19s and P-38s and seek the source of the energy that builds them, in the thousand medieval shacks and trailers and single rooms, drab with unwashed dishes and puling, unfed kids.

Of course, there were 'projects' – orderly rows of trailers, impressive as a pattern of rectangles shining in the hot sun, not so impressive when you examined the single unit of one trailer, one family. But their inhabitants had cause to be grateful, if they ever went downtown north of the Plaza and wandered through the unimaginable squalor of the slums where 100,000 Mexican-Americans live.

In the morning, I decided to go and note the sufferings of Hollywood under total war. My appetite to get out there was whetted when I read in the morning newspapers several columns professing outrage at the new order that no American should henceforth be allowed to keep more than $25,000 after his federal and state taxes were paid. Because the American Communist Party had mooted the idea in its platform of 1928, and Mrs Roosevelt and the CIO had been hot for it in 1941, many columnists warned that the death knell of private enterprise had already sounded over the land. Out in Hollywood, the stars were discussing it much more realistically. They thought naturally of the upkeep of their mansions. In the commissary of a famous studio you could hear conversations between male and female stars oddly like the lamentations that sounded through the more exclusive London clubs in the 1920s, after the Socialist government had stepped up death duties and estate taxes. Some of them did not see 'how they were going to live', but with undaunted energy, agents were already beginning to figure out ways of including the palaces and entourage of their clients as essential props of their popularity and, as one studio executive said, 'hence essential to war morale'. The people who were really left high, dry, and panicky were the actors' agents, who saw their best providers going voluntarily into the services or slowly but surely being picked off by the draft. Ten percent of fifty dollars a month was a ghastly dole for men who normally bask very handsomely in the percentage due from 100,000-dollar salaries.

However, most of the people who work in the movies are not producers, stars, feature players, or even agents. In the construction shops, the men who build the sets were working to drastic new restraints. Henceforth they may use no more ironwork. Walls must be made of cotton or muslin. And every time a battleship or a lifeboat sinks in a studio wreck, it must be salvaged and used again. They were told to use nails as sparingly as possible. The government had an official to check on ravenous Hollywood consumption of synthetics and of such oddities as glycerine for tears and breakfast foods for snow. There will be fewer snow scenes till the war is over. The story editors, reacting no more optimistically to the Pacific losses than anybody else, had already prepared a schedule of Pacific war movies reaching well into 1945. On the basis of official war photographs and newsreels, the camera crews concluded that the Salton Sea and its surrounding flora and fauna were astonishingly like that of Wake Island. To make the shores of the Salton Sea as realistic as possible, and also to comply with Navy regulations about the security of equipment, the interested studio built an air base out there and then donated it to the Navy. They were then given permission to go ahead and play all they wanted. The studios hit a difficult snag in the making of these war pictures. They naturally would want to feign a good deal of actual combat, but Hollywood, and the several-thousand-square surrounding miles that have commonly obliged as background for Spanish Loyalists, Yugoslav guerrillas, Foreign Legion sorties, and run-of-the-mill sheik pursuits, is part of the First War Area. The protection of this vast area was sufficiently arduous without having to send reconnaissance units off to distinguish between a detachment of live Japs destroying Bakersfield and Alan Ladd and William Bendix shooting it out for the Academy Award. So the Army decreed that actual combat, and especially aerial combat, must be done in the state of Utah. Accordingly, the first studio to film an epic of the Air Corps had to soften up civilian tension by placing prominent advertisements in the Salt Lake City and Ogden newspapers assuring the residents that a fleet of Jap bombers being destroyed by American fighters would be no cause for celebration. The war would still be on. Which, in an inoffensive way, will be a relief to Hollywood for some time to come. For it is proper to say that Hollywood was reveling in the romantic challenge of the war.

I suppose that the farther you go from the actual battle line the more you have to compensate in imagination for not being part of the real thing. Romanticism may be only the illusion of distance. And the West has always had for Americans the enchantment of a paradise away from the nagging realism of the familiar. In the last century, the California real-estate men worked up a brisk religion out of this appeal, and certainly for many back-broken farmers from the Midwest, a retirement in Southern California has in reality proved as near to Heaven on earth as they ever hoped to come. But the religion is maintained even by Californians who seem to have little here below. It was a poetic event when the motion picture industry, attracted by the notorious sunshine, and the variety of natural scenery, chose Southern California as its spiritual home. It was inevitable that Hollywood should become the temple of this never-never land. So as I walked around the studios, observed the clarion signs pointing to air-raid shelters, and talked with executives who from desks of cypress, and armchairs of white leather, announced in ringing tones their dedication to ultimate victory, there did not seem to me anything tasteless or embarrassing in their attitude. Their professional attitude to life has to be thoroughly romantic and highly stylized. They showed me with engaging pride a set representing an English street complete with tavern. Technical directors – that is to say, expatriate Englishmen of twenty years' standing chronically homesick for a social plane of English life they never in fact attained to – showed me the loving accuracy they had bestowed on the hanging inn sign, the pewter beer mugs, the churchwarden pipes, the low-hanging beams. To say that this inn was unlike any English inn known to our day or Dickens's is irrelevant. Hollywood is the world's assembly-line of the romantic myth. And watching the conscientious tempo of the work going forward on war movies, you would have felt that the writers and executives and producers were honestly giving their all to the nation's war effort, even if that all produces a distortion of human behavior even more sentimental than usual.

There is a curious disparity between the work of the writers and producers and that of the technical crew. The writers brace themselves to picture conceptions grander than usual, but the cameramen and prop men and research departments leave no labor unturned to re-produce the smallest detail of uniforms, terrain, and equipment. Their diligence and calmness reminded me vividly of the air cadets at Randolph Field working in a hangar, or on a test flight, or in the Link trainer. And it would not be surprising if, when the war is over, it is these men – the unpoetic underlings – whose work on war films will rescue for us whatever honesty our war films will later seem to have.

As I drove around the sprawling suburbs of Los Angeles, it became impossible to avoid or forget the Angelenos' resentment of their own Japanese. The Santa Anita Racetrack had been made the reception center for thousands of American-Japanese suddenly confronted with the status of prisoners of war. Along the highways, and along placid streets, you would constantly see signs, 'Truck farm for immediate sale'. 'Nursery garden, 20 years old, must sell'. Enterprising whites were moving into farms they had bought for a song. A Japanese family, faced with their compulsory deportation into the High Sierras before the end of the week, offered me a 1942 Buick De Luxe for five, maybe 400 dollars. They were the last Japanese I saw anywhere on the coast. In contrast to the newspapers' fear of them as a 'menace', and the ominous pronouncements of Lt General De Witt, who was in com-mand of this war area, I heard some interestingly mixed comment about them. Whenever the speaker felt he might be speaking for publication, or as a typical resident of his community, he would invariably assume what he took to be a forthright, no-nonsense American stand and declare with slightly shrill vigor that 'they are mean people. Sure, some of 'em made fortunes out there while good Americans went on relief. We always was too soft with 'em. Well, I guess they got what was comin' to 'em. De Witt's right. They ain't to be trusted.'

In some unlikely people, this attitude had cooled into a frozen prejudice: said a tanned working man in a bus – 'I don't give a damn whether they were born here or not. A Jap's a Jap.' And an oilman dismissed them with the damning remark, 'Japs never did learn to drill oil.' But there were others I talked to, cab-drivers, the last, best standby of correspondents in search of 'the people', personal friends, businessmen talking off the record, who were embarrassed, or skeptical, or strangely without passion: 'Personally, I thought they were nice people, clean, industrious, and they could teach most of us a thing or two when it comes to farming marginal land. Well, it had to be, I reckon. They had a bad break though.'

Whether or not it had to be is a decision that can be left, perhaps too comfortably, to the historians. What a traveler saw was the undeniable fact that a group of American citizens had been treated as a special kind of American, whose liberties under the law could be allowed to function only inside a camp posted with armed guards. It was not a pleasant thought, but dwelling on it might also easily stimulate unwarranted sentimentality. It seemed a good idea to go and see what had happened to the Japanese-Americans and know what their new home was like, whether a 'relocation center' could also be a concentration camp.

The drive out to Manzanar from Los Angeles is, under the right conditions, as beautiful and dramatic as any in the state. These conditions would be a spring day, a pleasant companion, plenty of time, and the obvious freedom to return. None of these conditions existed for the thousands of Japanese-Americans who at the beginning of March 1942 took two blankets and a few personal belongings specified by the Army, and drove out at dawn in a long file of automobiles, northeast of US 6 toward the dry valley floor of the High Sierras. They went through the dark violet shadows of the Tehachapi Mountains, through Red Rock Canyon, up over a sagey plateau of creosote bushes and the spiky crucifix of Joshua trees, across barren flats where the afternoon sun makes the streaks of salt shine as painfully as turned swords, and at last through Lone Pine to Manzanar. Above them was the glistening cold fact of Mount Whitney. And if their spirits were raised by the thought that this austere mountain would be their morning sentinel, they had only to drive on past abandoned ranchhouses to Manzanar and see that their home was to be a valley dry as old chocolate and swirling with dust.

Cooks and clerks were the first people out, and they came to windowless, heatless shacks. In time the construction men built what were to be the evacuees' permanent homes – large, drab tar-paper dormitories each divided into four apartments with movable partitions for big and small families. At the end of each block were a community laundry and a recreation hall.

The idea of most Southern Californians was that all the refugees were poor laborers or nursery gardeners who had amassed great wealth. But they were all sorts of people. Only 15 percent of them were farm workers, the rest housewives, clerks, lawyers, nurses, draftsmen, college boys and girls, seamstresses, cannery workers, midwives, waiters, cabinetmakers, houseboys, dressmakers, bartenders, mechanics, two or three fine scholars and first-rate plant physiologists. They had very little time to get a fair deal for their life's work. Speculators made quick buys on home equipment, took over leases, bought irrigation equipment at pitiful prices. But the Federal Reserve Bank whipped its agents out to the coast and did a fine job of freezing property that the Japanese wanted freezing. This halted the impulsive profiteering of the speculators, who were faced with having property on their hands they had no right to sell.

The awful human problem was what to do with their time. They had, like the first colonists, to start a society, but theirs was the hollow knowledge that it would be a toy society, a sham community barred from matching its skill and resource against the real society outside the barbed-wire fence. The three groups there reacted characteristically.

The old folks, the Issei (born in Japan and reared there), sat around bitter at the frustration of the American adventure to which they had given the sweat of their lives. Their only revenge was to try and draw the family unit closer into a traditional Japanese pattern – to revive domestic customs, games, religious rituals, even to hope that they could at last air old costumes they had sentimentally kept.

But against them stood their thoroughly Americanized children, the biggest group, the Nisei, the first-generation Americans, born, bred, and schooled here. You could hardly find a more typical bunch of easy, irreverent American high-school children – chewing gum, mimicking their favorite radio comedians, reading the comics, arranging block parties, wanting to start a social service bureau, a magazine, a dance, anything to pretend that life was normal. An older girl, wearing a sweater, loafers and bobby socks, her hair neatly ribboned to match her lipstick, sat in the editorial room of the daily paper they had started. She had been about to go to college. She looked at the clattering energy around her and felt unhappy about the pay-off. 'The pay-off,' she said, 'comes when you leave college. You go through high school and, sure, you are Americans playing and working together in the land of the free. Then you go to college and think maybe you'll be a teacher, or a lawyer, or a doctor. But I know what happened to my sister. She was clever and hardworking, but she kidded herself all through college that she was like the other girls. Then you get out and bam – you're a Jap. You're an ignorant minority and there's a special place for you in American life. You can sew, or be a housemaid, or stay with your own kind. These kids are just fooling themselves. They're gonna build a community here and be bigshots in it. Then when the war's over, if we're lucky, they'll go back. To what?'

The only smile that greeted this shrewd speech was from a Kibei, the young minority of American-Japanese born in this country but educated in Japan, proud of their trouble with the English language, unusually brighter and more alone and more purposive than the same generation of Nisei, whom they tolerate and secretly despise.

I went for a walk with a Kibei. He was slender and precise and wore glasses. He might have been eighteen or thirty-eight. With the nicest courtesy he made no bones about where he stood on the war. He frankly hoped the Japanese would win. He considered democracy, gravely and contemptuously, like a fifteen-year-old schoolboy I had once known in Silesia. He had the same disdain of the mob, the same solemn hope for a Fascist aristocracy of government. I offered him some gum, as a bait. He looked at me as at a corrupted soul and took a slightly more hectoring tone. He began to talk about the young Nisei of the camp as arrogantly as a classically trained Frenchman might discuss American state universities.

'Those Nisei,' he said, 'they use all the slogans. They talk about enterprise and the war for democracy. They think they are so American. And,' he added bleakly, 'so they are. They are flabby and talkative. They talk eagerly and get excited, and they are always telling you they are for General MacArthur. But their excitement only hides the doubts they have deep down – maybe like other Americans. They are only half-educated. Democracy is really a talking point, a show. They don't really know what it means, even when they are for it.' We had come to the end of our stroll.

'One good Kibei,' he said magisterially, his arm raised, 'could convert 100 Nisei overnight. So – what is it?' He fumbled affectedly for the idiom he loathed. '*We* should worry! Goodbye.'

No American who searches his soul need come up feeling entirely outraged by this speech. But at least the record of what the Nisei *did* went against some of the cynicism.

In a week the Army helped the camp organize its own police force and works projects. Within a month, one of these brown tar-paper sheds was a hospital, with a tiny operating theater, a minute sterilizing room, and a patient, skilled staff. They took out an appendix. They prepared babies' formulas. A child was born.

The Nisei organized their recreation centers. They held elections for block leaders. Then for assistants. They meant, in their naïve way, to draw up a constitution and a charter of their new society. They started a newspaper, and its editor was a young fellow, half-Japanese, half-Irish. He had one brother in a concentration camp near Tokyo. And another brother in the American Army. He looked more Japanese than Hirohito. His name was Joe Blamey.

Within a month, working under the plant physiologists, they had built lath houses and planted 25,000 cuttings of guayule rubber – rubber, one reflected, for the armies of MacArthur fighting their cousins.

In the spring of 1942, they had launched a poor, brave, pitiful model of the kind of American community they would choose to work and live in. All around them was the scratching, puffing dust. 'They told us,' said one pretty girl, adjusting her tinted glasses to sally off down the block, 'that the wind would be over at the end of March.' She squinted into the brown roller ahead of her, looked at me, gave a trilling laugh, and went off without further comment. Some idealist, a twenty-one-year-old girl, wrote the first editorial in the paper, the *Manzanar Free Press*. This is how it read:

Truth must be the keystone of this community. So we have called this the *Free Press*. We'll buttonhole that parasite rumor and give it the old bounce ... The tradition of mutual help is essential to the American system. Whenever a new settler came to set up his stake in the wilderness, his neighbors from miles around gathered to lend a hand. We must be ever grateful to those boys who carried our blankets and mattresses ... And in other ways too democracy will be tested by its mettle right here.

By our actions, and attitudes, while we live here, we shall be responsible to this and future generations of free men.

Perhaps this is high-school writing, and childish thoughts. But it was not written overlooking the private lawn of an Eastern women's college, nor by a city editor just off for a round of golf and drinks at the country club. Written against the dust of Manzanar, and the beautiful, hopeless ramparts of the Sierras, it is not unworthy of some of those early diaries of the first New Englanders, who landed on a rock, saw before them a prospect of thick forest, and gave thanks to God for his bounty in providing them with wood to make shingles and cranberries to eat.

I drove away from Manzanar none too proud of the showing we had made in running the first compulsory migration of American citizens in American history – not counting the Indians. How slippery seemed the solid abstractions we preach when you journey 6,000 miles and find democracy in a concentration camp.

There was, however, one sad consolation. The valley the Japanese were moved to is of course Owens Valley. By now all the West knows about the shameless rape of its fine farms forty years ago, when Los Angeles, determined to make good its lavish promise of water to a continental railroad system, and sharply recognizing that with enough water it could persuade communities far from Los Angeles to become paying suburbs, 'annexed' the valley farms to use as watershed adjuncts to the 230-mile aqueduct it built to tap the waters of the Owens River. For thirty years the valley farmers kept dynamiting the aqueduct until state guards were posted along the length of it. To this day you can see signs printed long ago by farmers after the dust had entered into their souls. They are signs displayed in public toilets, saying, 'Don't flush the toilet. Los Angeles needs the water'.

When the evacuees arrived in the Valley, they obviously needed water, to drink, to farm with, for the guayule project. The Army ordered Los Angeles to build a line out from its aqueduct to run water back into the valley Los Angeles had once drained dry. Los Angeles did this, for the Japs. There will probably not be a prettier irony in the whole record of the United States at war.

It was late afternoon when I started the long drive north, from Pasadena to San Francisco. I went up to San Fernando and turned west on 118, through the sweeping valley of Santa Susana. Deep-green barley fields poured softly to the horizon, where dotted palms lined the foot of the mountains. And from the crest of the mountains the sun glowed through rain clouds. This is one of the most beautifully composed valleys in the country.

There was not a sign or sound of war. The road was lined with delicate, erect eucalyptuses, their slender trunks burnished by the soft evening sun. On either side the green fields poured out, starting from the wheel of the car as recognizable barley and smears of mustard, but merging slowly into a visionary haze of blue-green before they touched the mountains and the ethereal light above them. I was baffled to know just how this harmless barley could so lose its identity and appear far off as a magic carpet of unearthly color, until I noticed that between me and the horizon, noble battalions of cedars guarded the middle distance, that haunting area between the familiar and the sublime that is the true challenge to all great landscape painting.

I was faraway in my own land of feeling, wondering why there are no great landscape painters of the West, when the highway curved round a smooth buttock of brown soil and there was a Good Humor ice-cream truck. There was nobody in the whole valley but a boy in a white smock, myself, and our two automobiles. We sat on the running board of his truck, and I asked him what the war had done to Good Humors. I expected a smile at best, but he looked hard at his malted stick and said, 'It's plenty tough. I guess you've noticed the way these things have started to drop in quality?' I said that in the East chocolate syrup wasn't what it used to be and ice cream was getting to taste like the European original – something between ice cream and frozen custard.

He said, 'Yes, and it's gonna be worse before it's better. The Good Humor boys bought 10,000 dollars' worth of honey from Colorado, right after the war started. They weren't smart enough, though. The Army froze it on 'em. Now they're using sugar syrup instead of glucose. And we shall lose a lot of flavors. The Army wants the fruit, so no more fresh fruit. And no more coconut.'

We looked out over the sweeping barley and the glowing mountains. He wondered when he'd see this place again. He was cordial and sensitive in his manners, exquisitely grateful for even a casual friendship, modest – the epitome of that best phase of American college boys long before it spreads, in some of them, into a fatty degeneration of feeling. I had been wondering how this taut, decent face, and this gentleness could be so indifferent to the war as to lose itself in problems of Good Humor flavors. But this was one of those self-righteous presumptions we so often make when we assume that a stranger belongs in the place we first met him.

He was doing this job on a nine-day furlough from the Army, while he waited to go to a reception center as an Air Corps cadet. He said, 'I was scared I'd fail the physical.'

'What would you have done then?' I asked him.

'I'd have gone up into Canada to get into the RCAF. Sure thing.'

He was from Madison, Wisconsin, and while he pondered his future he talked of his father 'putting in beef cattle and hybrid corn up there while I'm away'.

The twilight dropped slowly and I got back into my car. The boy stood up and embarrassed me by shaking my hand and saying, 'It sure was a real pleasure to meet you.' I tried to say the same and drove off, as he waved after me. In a year's time I would probably still be banging a typewriter in New York. He might well be roaring over Europe, or lost in the Pacific.

The rest of the evening was escapism pure and simple – the light going from the eucalyptuses, leaving their trunks starchy white in the blue twilight; the long valley turning to a deeper green; at Ventura, the sharp tang of a breeze from the Pacific. On the way up to Santa Barbara a small khaki figure waved at the path of my headlights and a soldier climbed in. He seemed old for the service. He was a cheerful man, still apparently in a daze from the novelty of Army life. He thought the instruction on how to avoid venereal disease was only the most surprising sign of the way the Army looked out for your safety.

'Yes, sir, they do it right. Give you pamphlets, motion pictures, then the doctor talks to you. And a parson. I guess the parson's all right for some of the men. But the doctor's the guy you listen to. You get a dose of anything and it goes on your discharge. That's serious.'

He mentioned he was an Army cook, and I started asking him about food and especially about the prodigious waste of everything from half-eaten beef to fresh fruit that anybody visiting Army camps is bound to notice. He had, however, an oddly unprofessional interest in the subject. And it turned out he had found himself confronted by an officer asking him what specialization he chose. He didn't understand. 'Cook, medical service, what's your job?' He said, 'Cook' right away.

'It's easier on my feet,' he remarked. And then he announced in an offhand way that he had crushed some toes in an accident a few years ago, 'and consequently I don't walk too good.' He got out in Santa Barbara, and I sat and watched him in mild amazement as he hobbled off. The draft boards were certainly getting tough.

On State Street there was a lunch-counter for soldiers. On a street corner a painted sign saying, 'Blackout switch'. A used-car dealer was bravely bucking the rubber conservation program with a guileful ad in his window: 'America Can't Bicycle to Victory. Patriotism does not demand that you lay up your car. On the contrary . . .'

Santa Barbara's patio elegance seemed pretty completely undisturbed by the war. There had been a minor confusion of patriotism, hush-hush secrecy, and eager curiosity when a Japanese pocket submarine came up in the early spring and harmlessly lobbed a few shells over US 101 into a bean field. But most people had been listening to a 'fireside chat' by President Roosevelt and had to invent their 'reaction' to being in the battle zone after it was all over. For the rest, this handsome resort town noticed most the disorganization of its domestic help. The society people normally have Chinese cooks, always men, and Japanese housemaids, always women. The women had gone off to the internment camps. It was interesting to note that Chinatown in Santa Barbara had been a colony of mixed Chinese and Japanese who, though they never intermarried, had mixed very pleasantly together, in barefaced defiance of what our current ideology insists is an impossible proposition.

The journey from Santa Barbara to San Francisco could be told by the men who drive the trucks day and night as an inventory of all the foods that are packed and refrigerated and sent flying east on the fruit expresses: hundreds of fertile miles of beans, sugar beets, potatoes, barley, lettuce, olives, and walnuts, and valleys of lettuce again and broccoli.

It could be told by the Mexicans and other stoop laborers as an uneasy chapter in West Coast labor relations, disfigured in the mid-30s by a tear-gas riot and airplanes nervously reconnoitering for the rumored Communist advance on California.

But when peace restores the automobile to the family man and honeymooning couple, they will know it again as most travelers have known it, as 360 of the loveliest miles of the American landscape. You follow the ocean to Gaviota, and high away on your right are the violet Santa Ynez Mountains trenched with deep purple shadows. On your left are fine bean and walnut farms carpeting down to the edge of the cliffs over the sea. And the highway runs between poplars. Then you go north through a high pass and climbing up the mountains watch the afternoon light break up the smooth green contours of the morning, till the mountains break and fold into all the violent shapes, the fierce blue valleys they have made every afternoon for thousands of years. Occasionally, you see something glisten from the brushwood like the snout of a puppy. It is anti-aircraft guns again.

On a narrow plateau with your back against the hard mountains and your face toward the silver Pacific, you can see islands like mirages floating above low clouds. Up here is La Cumbre Lookout, and tourists are no longer welcome. Here the forest rangers protect thousands of unaware lives by moving fine strings over a map, plotting latitudes, marking with a pencil the first curling whiff of smoke from a canyon 100 miles away. A dropped match, 1,000 miles away in the Cascade Mountains, is flashed to all the lookouts. Today, the rangers keep a tenser vigil than usual. All the way up the coast, as the climate turns cooler and the mountains grow thick with forest, people are certain the Japs will sneak a try to set the biggest bonfire in history. There is certainly beautiful raw material. A couple of suicide planes, dropping incendiaries from Washington to middle California might be able to do it.

Through the Santa Maria Valley, flaming yellow mustard sweeps across soil of a wonderful chocolate brown. You forget all about the marketing of the beans and sugar beets and lettuce that are all around you in the grace and color of their profusion.

You dip out to the ocean at San Luis Obispo, curl round sweeping sand dunes, climb again through wooded hills, roll through almond orchards and cattle ranges, and then funnel out into the splendid vistas of the Salinas Valley. Toward the north, vast fields of alfalfa pour like billiard tables from the highway. Near Salinas the highway is a white arrow barbed with long, glittering channels irrigating the lettuce fields that shoot straight between wide breaks of eucalyptuses all the way into the haze of the blue mountains. A European may read in a Chamber of Commerce folder that the Salinas Valley is 'the Salad Bowl of America' and smile at the naïve grandeur of such a phrase. And few Americans from cozier landscapes would feel much of an itch to see fields of lettuce. But the Salinas Valley is an incurably American conception. It is a sort of natural assembly-line for the growing of lettuce and broccoli, thousands of lettuce, millions maybe. And the production is disciplined with the severe and magnificent functionalism that Americans always show when they are making something – like a bathroom or an airplane engine – that is meant above all to work. So the valley is not merely a small field of lettuce magnified 1,000 times. It is a precise and breathtaking spectacle and from the air looks like the skeleton of a great fish dropped between mountains. Its spine is the white highway. Its bones are the irrigation channels.

In the last stretch, I could have walked into Salinas on lettuces that lay over the highway. There was no doubt what the town's troubles were. And when I began by asking a big grower if he was having labor trouble, he snorted, threw his head back in mock martyrdom, and began to chant the figures that told their own story.

'Twenty-seven thousand cases of lettuces come from this valley. Fifty thousand acres. Four thousand of carrots. Nine thousand of mixed vegetables. The government asks us to grow a third more of everything. All right, so normally we have 6,000 Filipinos who do the gathering, the stoop labor. Two thousand have gone off to, to' – he hesitated for a sufficiently despicable phrase, and taking his hands out of well-lined pockets continued – 'to line their pockets in war factories. Just up and went. Another 1,600 of them are registered in the draft. So far, we're 2,000 short. And they're indispensable. All the government says is, "find replacements." Well, Mexicans – used to be two for a dime. Now you have to go down on your knees to hire 'em. And nowadays, they've gotten ideas, from Mr Roosevelt, I guess. They want showers. Showers! Jesus!'

I mentioned Japs and his face colored with instant wrath.

'Japs? They don't work for us. They work for themselves. They're grower owners. If I had my way, they'd have been shut up in the rodeo grounds the day after Pearl Harbor.'

He looked me in the eye with wary calculation and sermonized furiously about the character of the American-Japanese. At the end his hands were trembling and he closed the subject with the words, spat out in anger and self-pity – 'they're mean, sneaky, selfish people. Isn't anything you can do with 'em.' Then he looked suddenly at a picture in a leather frame on his desk, presumably of his wife, and said bitterly, 'We had 115 boys on Bataan.'

I said something about there being lots of upstanding young boys around the streets of Salinas. But I had missed the point. When he said the labor shortage was desperate, he didn't mean labor. He meant stoop labor. There is a world of difference between available Americans and available Mexicans and Filipinos. Available for what? That is the question. And the sorry answer is, available to do the grueling picking of beets and lettuce at a daily wage no white would work for.

It wasn't till later in the evening that I learned why he had so miserably overreacted against the American-Japanese. His son was one of the 115 lost on Bataan.

There was also in Salinas a curious dislike of the people who had left the Dustbowl in the mid-30s and come to be known as lowly Okies, who picked lettuces and did other similar lowly chores in the Golden State where they had come to build a new way of life. The grudge against them seemed to be that they hadn't lived up to the character that had been conveniently attributed to them. Instead of providing a scummy pool of bums and pickup labor, they had worked hard, saved, and in fact made a new home. They now constitute a comfortable community in Salinas, with clean homes, curtains, family pride, and everything. Just for the record, the natives call their section Little Oklahoma.

It was baking hot in Salinas, and I went west past Del Monte, where the mist hangs, to Pacific Grove, and from there drove the exquisite seventeen miles to Carmel. There was special reason to expect a war aspect to what is a tourist paradise. But when you are driving near Monterey on retreaded tires, and the war seems to stretch out into a dark future, you seize – if you have any sense – a last chance to look again on this narrow and unique coastline, with its blue coves and its gnarled, sun-dappled cypresses on green lawns.

When I paid my fee at the entrance to the scenic drive, the woman looked at me half in awe and suspicion. There had been one other car through there in two days.

At the first bend, I saw some soldiers down on the beach learning Commando tactics in flat-bottomed boats, while the green-blue surf pounded the rocks and a few curious pelicans mocked the men in barges with skittish glides over them. But at Cypress Point, there was nothing but silence, the questioning surf, a few cormorants waddling by. The only sign of a live American was a crushed gardenia on the grass and an unlit stogie. It seemed as if all Americans had gone off to war. And the flower and the cigar were the testimony to a lost tryst. A couple of mild-eyed deer crossed the road. It was so relaxed and pastoral that I roused myself to recall that I was meaning to report on America at war. And north of me was the port and ringing shipyards of San Francisco. So I got back into the car and drove to Carmel.

It is conceivable that Carmel has given much to the war. And no patriotic native should take it badly if I say that its face was exactly as before. It still looked like the American mecca of artsy-craftsyness, like a Rockefeller restoration of a 'refined' English seaside resort of the 1920s; with its little booke shoppes and needlework centers, its earnest men striding importantly in flannels and pipes, its tweedy, dogged women.

Soon I was headed back to Salinas, where, in a drugstore, there was an interesting local variation on the Western folk legend that a teeming domestic production of rubber, and a plethora of new tires, is merely a matter of letting American ingenuity play around for a month or two with the problem of the ordinary automobile owner's desperate need. Salinas is proud of its lettuces, but prouder, for the duration, of its guayule rubber, which is bouncing from its small government-owned mill at the modest rate of forty tons a week. The man sitting at the counter with me sneered at the marvels of synthetic. 'Sure, they can produce barrels of it from grain alcohol. But it falls into shreds if you run it over thirty miles a year. The Germans have been plugging away for decades, but the only place they can use it is on supply trucks. Give us a year or two, and you're gonna hear plenty about this town. The whole Southwest'll be growin' guayule. And why? Because Salinas showed 'em how.'

Through all the towns north to Oakland, I began to notice that the word 'food locker' had passed into the daily vocabulary of the ordinary housewife. Literally hundreds of thousands of Western wives pay not much more than a dollar a month for a key to a locker in a refrigerator plant, where they keep the vegetables, fish, and even sides of beef they bought in season, and when the price was low. Farming families in the West have had this habit for years, but the war has attracted thousands of urban families to do the same. This is not merely family thrift. It is the sharp foresight of people who live close enough to the Army's great dehydration program, and to the freighting of fruit, to know that California could suffer from a serious shortage of the crops it grows in abundance. Just less than one-half of the all-year farm labor was headed for the draft or war plants. And somehow, the work of 150,000 migratory workers who mightn't show up had to be done by anybody who would help. In the first summer of the American war, it was the most rousing thing to see, especially in the north of the state, the intelligence and energy of townships that to a metropolitan Easterner would rate as part of the pitied hinterland that is traditionally unable to grasp the realities of foreign affairs. As it turned out, the crops were gathered – 15 million crates of lettuce, 3 million boxes of grapefruit, 5 million crates of carrots – by schoolboys, housewives, weekending workers from the coast cities, and by every sort of businessman. As I drove through the rich exuberance of the Santa Clara Valley, there was not much to show of the promised famine. But all the pungent loot of this delicious valley – the peaches, cherries, pears, prunes, apples, apricots – would go to the Army for canning. The civilian in California had the odd feeling of living in an orchard that was laid out for his aesthetic pleasure and not for his hunger. Two state Senators, after taking a four-month look at the gorgeous resources of their state, came to the conclusion that before the war was over, California might easily go short of fresh fruit and vegetables.

There seemed to California farmers no way of bringing the war home to Washington, DC, of making the immediacy of their plight vivid to the manpower officials in the capital, who conscientiously demanded 'equal sacrifice' but seemed to interpret this on the glib patriotic level that one man is as good as another. As a man, and in the eyes of God, so he is. But fifty willing drugstore clerks could cheerfully be sacrificed against the worth, in his own job, of a farmer who knew how to plant, irrigate, prune, and trim. The farmers were promised that once war-plant labor had been 'stabilized', then farmhands would be returned to the farmers. But as you came nearer to San Francisco, the injustice to the farmer was obvious from a cursory glance at the shipyards and from every snatch of gossip: the workers in the shipyards, and in the bomber factories up north, were not to be stabilized by decree. They trained for one job and moved into another, or quit when the family payroll went high enough. In other words, the farmers were being asked to wait until the war worker decided to let himself be stabilized, until there was no turnover in the labor supply. There was not then, or later, any such moment of stabilization, in spite of local ordinances freezing workers on their jobs.

Any approach to San Francisco, by air or water or train or, best, driving in through the taffy mist and emerging in the sunlight streaming over the Bay, is an invitation into the past. It is as hard for a visitor to find out what San Francisco does, and what it lives by, as to learn anything sensible about New York or Baghdad. The tourist moons through his stay in an emotive mist of literary associations. It seems a pity to bother about the modern problems of this city when books of memoirs and the movies, and quaint chronicles of the early missionary priests, have built in the mind's eye a romantic unity that is so much easier to enjoy than the unpromising complexity of its reality. San Francisco is the town that miners made, where the smart Yankees came, skimming two oceans in their Clipper ships and getting there as fast as the others, as the Germans and French and English and Swiss, who hurried by land, for gold. A town where, they say, the world moved in and bedded down on straw and spittle for ten dollars a night. It is the town where the Chinese came to mine and stayed to cook and wash clothes (and be lynched and railroaded out of the state). Where the Italians came to fish. And the Scots to build ships. And the Japanese to raise flowers and vegetables. San Francisco, you may insist, is the gaudy town of the vicious Barbary Coast, but they lead you to a mission and recall that it is also the town of Saint Francis. But even when you feel superior to this drugging fantasy, you cannot escape the core of truth that San Francisco is by now a sober blend of many disparate peoples of the earth. Even as you lie in the Berkeley hills and think of anything but sociology, you hear Chinese doves moan through Australian eucalyptus trees, at the foot of mountains with Spanish names.

A statistical 'sample' might discover some unsuspected type of San Franciscan. But a reporter can note only that there is no recognizable type, that you can flavor what the war did to the San Franciscans by considering the fate of three or four families, who might exist separately in any other Western city but who together form an image or microcosm of the city and its ways of life.

There was a railroad transport executive, Ralston by name, whose family went West after the Central Pacific railroad was built. His grandfather had a mansion on Nob Hill that burned down after the earthquake. The family moved out to San Rafael. Ralston was comfortably off, sailed around the Bay in summer, took his wife and an unmarried daughter to the symphony concerts in winter, and never dreamed of living anywhere else. The war made him live mostly in hotels in Cheyenne, in Kansas City and Chicago. He was a liaison chief helping the Army freight its food East. His wife moved into San Francisco. His daughter joined what became the Waves.

There was a Neapolitan fisherman, bred on North Beach, who for thirty-five years had sailed his boats out of the wharf. After Pearl Harbor he became a highly valuable member of the Harbor Patrol. He had a son in the Navy assigned to an aircraft carrier in the Coral Sea.

There was a Chinese switchboard operator, Nellie How, who took calls in Chinese and American. Since the Chinese do not call by number but by name, she had to memorize 2,300 numbers. After Pearl Harbor, she was put on a Navy switchboard and memorized 1,000 more.

There was a Russian, Constantin Rostow, a jeweler, who lived with his wife in the Potrero District. He had a son graduated from Stanford as an engineer and a daughter in her junior year at Berkeley, taking history and home economics. By the spring of 1942, the father, an experienced cutter, had a machine-tool precision job. The son was in the Army engineers. The daughter supervised a class of housewives over at Berkeley, teaching them how to dry the vegetables and fruits from their Victory Gardens in homemade evaporation units.

There was an artist who described himself as 'half Armenian – my father likes to think he's German in a vague sort of way. I wouldn't care to live any place but San Francisco. There are three types o' guys need never go hungry here – writers, sailors, painters. There's Izzy Gomez, for example. When my belly's empty and my pride's running low, he's always good for a steak and a stein of beer.' He became Private Schindler of the Camouflage Corps.

Obviously, then, San Franciscans do not as individuals live in the memory of their old energies. But collectively, like Bostonians, they have come to be sharply aware of the discrepancy between the grand myth of their past and the hedging facts of their present. So if they do not encourage the visitor to recall their past, they don't protest against the habit. They are aware of two present shortcomings that have denied San Francisco a modern destiny: water is hard and expensive to get, and there is no iron and coal to develop a modern industry. So San Francisco looks down with envious contempt on Los Angeles, whose population and manufactures began to pass its own during the 1930s.

Till the war came, San Franciscans had to be content with boasts of their fine natural harbor, their good food, and confess that their chief business was the making of tin cans and the packing of fruit and vegetables into them.

But after the first flash about Pearl Harbor, no city on the continent resumed so grandly its ancient power. San Francisco might still be the town of Saint Francis, but it was now more than anything else the headquarters of the Twelfth Naval District, the shield of the West Coast, the supply base for the Pacific fleets, the chief service station for all Navy planes ranging from San Diego to Seattle. In the middle of town San Francisco looked much the same as ever. But in a single day with the Navy, you could hear a string of dialogue that echoed the strong dependence on San Francisco of hundreds of thousands of men in the Philippines, riding the ocean, flying in the Cascades or in the Coast Range. At the Naval Air Station, you could watch a panel of quiet, attentive operators monitoring air traffic, and on an island that didn't exist in 1940, the huge office of the Naval Supply Base chattered with hundreds of typewriters processing orders.

Commuters crossing the Oakland Bay Bridge sometimes wondered why the exposition buildings on Treasure Island all looked as if the World's Fair were still on. But here was a swarming training station. The California Building was the dispensary. The Fine Arts Building the gas mask shop. The Museum of Art was marked 'anchors and rigging'. The American Indian Building was a barbershop. Over the extended arms, and other things, of the Fair's standing statuary stretched the drying laundry of bluejackets.

But this is underground power, the San Francisco the Navy knows, about which the civilian catches only impressive rumors. What the civilian knows of his city at war is the pride of the shipyards and the full-grown legend of Henry Kaiser.

I was warned that it would be nothing short of bad taste to mention the name Kaiser in the old shipyards of San Francisco. I mentioned it for the effect, and a sixty-year-old shipbuilder rolled his eyes to the ceiling, coughed, and shared a reproving sneer with his manager. The fact that Kaiser had once graveled roads in Cuba was chalked up against his damnation as automatically as a Cockney accent would – before 1939 – have excused an Englishman from any hope of a commission in the Coldstream Guards. However, since reality is no respecter of respectability, both these gaucheries had to be accepted as part of the high price of Hitler.

The professional prejudice against Kaiser is easily understood. A shipyard is a shipyard the world over, but not at Kaiser's Liberty Ship yard in Richmond. By this time, Mr Kaiser has undoubtedly heard of the bow of a ship. But it's almost a point of principle that he should go on calling it the 'front end'. It stresses his deliberate scorn of professionalism. He turned to building ships as an expanding drugstore owner might add fishing rods to his stock of hairnets and magazines. His key men had never seen a ship launched. Before 1939, Kaiser had never built a ship, or an airplane, or handled steel. He merely heard that it took five months to build a freighter. And he decided that if you knew nothing about shipbuilding, and approached the art as a construction job, you might easily 'make' a ship in a month. This is what he did.

The Kaiser yards look like something out of Disney. They are absurdly clean and neat. The elements of a ship are divided into separate piles all the way from the administration building down to the ways. Innumerable cranes swing through the air and clutch precisely at the piles, deposit them at the plate shop, heave them down to the ways, where small armies of Disney characters rush forth with welding guns and weld the parts into a ship as innocently as a child fits A into B on a nursery floor and confronts a destroyer made with his very own hands.

Mr Kaiser's secret is a simple compound of three elements: the pile-up, the cranes, the Assembly Bay. Between the various piles of materials and the finished ships are fifty unvarying automatic processes. Sheets of steel are marked with shameless crudity, because it doesn't matter to Mr Kaiser that the workers have never built a ship before. The sheets are marked VK2 and MQ3, to indicate to a moron where they fit on a ship; a crane swings over, picks up a huge sheet of steel. It is moved down fifty yards, laid on the yard floor. Then a plywood template descends, and thirty men move into place and trace the template on to the steel. Another crane moves in, lifts the sheet down to another place where drills and files break it up into the traced parts.

More cranes whisk the parts off to the plate shop where the parts are welded together.

This is the precision work, and to Mr Kaiser it is a niggling but necessary evil. Way off in lofts, the real solid work begins – whole forepeaks and sterns are prefabricated. Down at the Assembly Bay, you will see a whole bulkhead go in one piece, and so out on to the launching skids.

Mr Kaiser had pat answers for the traditional objections. He uses riveters only for the ribs, where the extra pressure is felt. And as for the old difficulty of taking the precision parts back to the machine shop, he disposed of that by putting a machine tool on every ship, the moment the bottom was laid. It is typical of Kaiser's stubborn originality that he has introduced comic refinements into the hard labor of bending the heavy metal. Instead of fitting one iron to one ship, he wants to see thirty irons made ready for thirty ships. So down at the bending slab, where the channel irons are made for the base of the ships, you see the glowing metal slide from the furnace on to the yard, and instantly two strapping heavyweights run forward and start pounding it with 24-pound sledges. The process is quickened by choosing one left-handed man, and one right.

'It shouldn't be difficult, with a little practice, to turn out a ship a day.' The world's newspapers were greatly amused at that one and generously agreed to think kindly of the crass arrogance typical of the best American stories. In time, however, Mr Kaiser turned out one a day. America, prompted admittedly by some very capable Kaiser press agents, learned to worship, and the world to admire, this heavy man with the bald head and the expression of an amiable bullfrog.

When asked what was the most important part of shipbuilding, he answered at once, 'Keeping the books.' He went on to explain that he meant the purchasing of materials, the transportation of it, the speedy auditing of accounts. He is not interested in airplanes or ships for their own sakes. He got interested in the Liberty Ship only when the U-boats seemed to be imperiling every Allied freighter. At the same time, he got the idea for air freighters. The moment a problem is beaten, he looks around for another problem. Even in 1942, he had only a retrospective pride in Liberty Ships. His theory that everything is a construction problem had made him recognize that the main hitch to fulfilling his boast on ship production would be the assembling of the raw materials, especially steel. Pittsburgh and Gary, Indiana, are a long way from San Francisco. And though he had never tapped a blast furnace in his life, he decided to have for himself a big steel-rolling mill in his own backyard. Naturally, he doesn't take risks on feeding the mill – he has his own mine. This brought him automatically to consider the future of heavy metals. Characteristically, he decided they had none. He fell in love with magnesium, and because we don't yet know too much about it, appointed an army of research men. When the war is over, he figures his plant will turn out 40 million pounds of magnesium. He now dreams of California as the capital of an American empire of light metals. He has plans for battleships built almost entirely of aluminum. He talks of 'a civilization based on light metals, with the West Coast as the fount of it'.

When you come from an interview with Henry Kaiser and drive through the patchwork housing projects where the shipyard workers live, such irritations as one-room homes for a family of four, and fierce restrictions on incoming Negroes, seem as impertinent as a paycheck to an Old Testament prophet. But pending Mr Kaiser's civilization of sweetness and light metals, there is some humble work to be done on such things as the human conditions under which the shipyard workers argue, load, quit, and try to house their families with minimum decency. One man in ten was missing from work for unexplained reasons. The newspapers sermonized about 'absenteeism'. It could mean a sick baby, a shopping tour, a game of poker, the grippe, or the need to come to rest sometime in twenty-four hours and file an income tax return. What you heard around San Francisco was an incredible saga of rumors, many of them well substantiated, about well-organized loafing in the shipyards, about the nepotism of family men appointing shiftless relatives to good jobs that entailed no work except when government inspectors came along. 'What can you do about it?' protested one foreman. 'All right, so the guys play crap on the graveyard shift. Once a bottom's laid, there's no way of checking on 'em. You'd have to go in under there with a blowtorch.' Allowing even for the raging enmity that is now traditional between the long-established white-collar class of a city and the invading 'goons', there is no doubt that the San Francisco shipyards during this war have provided a glimpse of Heaven for caustic newspaper columnists like Westbrook Pegler.

When you leave San Francisco and head inland to the Sacramento Valley, you feel – as a rambling tourist – that you are leaving behind the great workshop of the war. Through the ring of suburbs around the Bay you pass powder plants, and the sweating summer haze is heavy with the smell of oil. At Vallejo, you hear on one side the ordered roar of the Navy yards, and feel better about the people who work there when you pass a well-planned trailer camp with community halls, groceries, schools, and a thousand pants and shirts drying in the community drying pens. But once you leave the balloon barrage there, and ride northeast on US 40, you feel you can forget the war awhile and roll serenely along wide roads shaded by handsome black walnut trees. But you are not escaping from anything so easily. You are leaving behind the invigorating industrial present of the coast cities only to approach the ready cradle for the immense industrial future of the whole West. This future is not precisely the same as Mr Kaiser's vision. It is something long prepared and known about by Westerners, and very much this side of Heaven.

From San Diego to San Francisco, you hear about the great immigration into California. Californians hail this proudly as a demonstration of what their state has to offer in a crisis. But this is the pat Chamber of Commerce stand, a defensive view of what you already have. More thoughtful natives, wondering what the state will have to offer to the 'immigrants' when the war is over, are afraid that these million and a half outlanders will stubbornly cling to the Coast cities in the peace. If they do, California might well face an employment conflict as grating, and twice as bloody, as anything it knew in the days of the Okies. The solution is ready to hand, if the Administration then in office knows enough to believe in it. The solution lies in the unplumbed resources of the great Central Valley – the even distribution of water for which the good soil of the Sacramento and San Joaquin valleys cries aloud. It is astonishing how little one hears, in the East, about what constitutes the greatest irrigation project in history. When Westerners talk of the West's great future, they are apt to be forgiven on the grounds of incurable chauvinism. But many of them are thinking concretely of the conversion of the Central Valley into the single most fertile region of the United States. Many of them hope nervously that Washington too believes in this future and that Congress will have enough foresight about it to see that the project goes through at any cost. As long as Harold Ickes is Secretary of the Interior, a lot of people know that it will go through.

I knew that the best source of this story would be up at Redding, near Shasta Dam, at the very apex of the Central Valley. And I was impatient to cover the 200 miles of the Sacramento Valley, north from Woodland, and looked for signs and omens of the Valley's absorbing interest in its own dramatic future

I went past great, flat barley fields and then past flooded rice fields. These endless fields are flooded to the horizon and sown by airplanes, which is perilous work. The planes roar high over the fields, dive down to within ten or twenty yards of the ground, shower the seed evenly, rise again, turn and roar into another dive. It is obvious that by now there is a shortage of flyers – men who will tease mortality to sow rice are not slow to want the excitement of combat flying.

The road goes on past more rice fields, small ranches that once were unbroken grain fields, past olive groves, at Corning, then into plains of grain fields, so up past the bluffs of the Sacramento River, and by twilight into Redding. The unbuttoned, shambling air of Redding at night gives no clue to its importance as the powerhouse of the Central Valley project. It is an old mining town that never got over it, and all night long the sidewalks murmur with a dribble of customers from small saloons and liquor stores. The 'line', however, has been closed down at the Army's request.

Most people here work either in gold mining (there is about 2 million dollars' worth a year) or on the nearby Shasta Dam. Shasta is the key unit of the whole Valley project. It is the second largest concrete dam in the United States and second in mass only to Grand Coulee. It has five 75,000 kilowatt generators.

The Central Valley Project is a massive attempt to correct the massive stupidity of Nature in providing much rainfall in the winter and none in the summer when it is most needed; in allowing the San Joaquin River to rise in the Sierras and flow *north*, when the needs of the San Joaquin Valley are that it should flow south. The Central Valley has its apex at Redding and ends in a wide base at Bakersfield, a 750-mile stretch of possible abundance. At Redding there is an average of thirty-five inches of rain a year (in 1941 it was sixty-two inches); at Bakersfield there is sometimes eight inches, sometimes ten. So the farmers of the San Joaquin Valley have to use streams from the Sierras for their irrigation. They have come to depend too much on them and have by this time put much more land in cultivation than they can possibly get water for. Great tracts of this land are now going back on them. The whole point of the Central Valley Project is to take the surplus water, stored in the reservoir at the apex, and feed it down to the broad base.

Between the two valleys that compose the Central Valley (the Sacramento and the San Joaquin) is a delta, between San Francisco and San Joaquin. Here in the late winter and spring saltwater from the Bay backs up and ruins a vast area of crops. So the idea is to keep the flow of the Sacramento in summer up above normal, to keep the Delta flushed with water. Down in the Delta, at Antioch, is to be a powerful pumping station to do this and to provide power for San Francisco. Most of the San Joaquin Valley will take enough water from the Sacramento and pump it from dam to dam to back the river upstream. At the very lower end of the Central Valley, at Friant, there is a dam that will take the water from the Upper San Joaquin River (flowing north) and divert it south to irrigate the barren lower reaches of the San Joaquin Valley. Thus the job is to reverse the San Joaquin and replace this deprivation with Sacramento water pumped from Antioch.

It is an ambitious plan, and took twelve years and 2 million dollars to study. But it is the best promise of a wholly changed balance of farming and industry in the West. The realizable prospect is blurred now by the fact that the great dams from Grand Coulee to Friant have for the duration forgone the purpose they were built for – to irrigate the arid West. Their huge power has made possible the dazzling development of shipyards and airplane factories on the coast. But when the war is over, the Central Valley Project will get under way. There will be a valley over 700 miles long waiting for new settlers to use its fertility. There will be, after the inspiration of Henry Kaiser, enough hydroelectric power to vitalize new metal industries.

The East thinks it long ago deflated the myth of the Golden West.

But we have hardly yet begun to hear from the Californians and from the Westerners to the north who live ready to convert the impulse of their great dams. There will be immediate postwar wrangles (very important to San Francisco) over the crippling discrimination of freight rates. If the Central Valley is to produce what it's capable of, there will have to be smooth, cheap transportation into the American market. But once this is settled, nobody can predict what the modern West may be, except to say that if the Orient is industrially reborn and stabilized, and Russia, whose dominion extends to the Pacific, assumes its emerging place as the greatest European land power, then California and Oregon will be at the focal center of the brave new world. The fulcrum of the new balance of power.

8

The Pacific Northwest

California begins in Mexico and ends in the Pacific Northwest. Going north from Redding, you start a slow but continuous climb into mountains. There would be nothing strange in this anywhere south. But when you get into them and watch the Sacramento River dropping away from you and foaming through deep gorges whose peaks are granite, you realize that these mountains are different. You look out the car window and see spruce and Western hemlock everywhere. Quite suddenly you know you have parted from a whole climate system and the many ways of working and worrying united by it. Technically, you are in California, but you have climbed away from what, back East, you most persistently recall as California – the sparkling orange groves, the sweeping valleys of grapes, the dusty eucalyptuses on sun-baked roads, the missions and the open-shirted men, the neon drive-ins and the super-duper hot dogs, the flat beaches overhung with the smell of oil, the tawny hills and the snakes squashed on the turn of a cement road. Above you no more is a cloudless haze but sooty smears of cloud against a gray sky.

After the contrast of green orchards and flat valleys you have lived through, the sight of Mount Shasta, very close and out of scale, is so unexpected that it looks like a quick construction job by Henry Kaiser, topped off with fake Hollywood snow. It stands out quite alone from a comparative plain, an immense artificial pile, whose snow in summer is draped as rhythmically as icing, and having the yellowish cast of a production on a bad Christmas card. This view of it in no way detracts from its grandeur, and I imagine that coming on it from the north it would appear more awesome and less odd. 'Lonely as God and white as a winter moon' was the tribute of Californian poet Joaquin Miller.

The river canyon winds through solid walls of pine, and at Duns-muir and Shasta Springs you come on small mountain resorts that might be in the Colorado Rockies. This sort of country is ideally excit-ing and restful for a correspondent to drive through; his senses are stimulated but there appears to be no price to pay, for over the canyon's edge is inaccessible forest, with no sign of life, in peace or war, to be reported on. It is absolutely innocent of news value.

The holiday is short-lived. Weed is a lumber town whose nearby slopes are graveyards of black stumps. And from here north there is no more guessing about what the mountains have done for the war. After a rest from climbing across the grazing land of the Shasta Val-ley, you come to Yreka City, and wherever there is a clearing by the narrowing forest road there are great piles of stripped wood and, over the treetops, the whistle and rattle of lumber trucks. Several times through the narrow gorges of the Siskiyou Mountains I had to crawl, on steep grades, behind trucks loaded with lengths of pine and fir. On the long, twisting road north to Medford, you hardly consider the loss of them, for you can see little sky or light through the rising luxury of green cedar and yellow pine, hemlock and oaks, and the shaggy green Douglas firs. Between Ashland and Medford it was less difficult to see the wood for the trees; there were signs all over the place advertising, 'Sawwood, body fir, furniture and livestocks, brickettes, slabs'.

Even at a time when this part of the country was not rationed for gasoline, you could never be sure of getting gas anytime after lunch. The stations used up their supply before noon. Out of Medford a mechanic told me that through the Northwest, 'y'oughta drive on top of your tank.'

Still far from any war but Nature's, I went through green mountain valleys black with rain, the car's hood ornament bouncing through the storm like the bow of a ship. The driving was so slow that I climbed out and rested at an old drugstore at Myrtle Creek. There was no sound but the rattle of rain on the store roof and the roaring echo it made outside in the mountains. Inside, a salesman leaned across the soda fountain and talked in ominous low tones with the owner. It was a perfect setting for high crime, and I moved closer, hoping to become a party to some Alfred Hitchcock mischief. The salesman was saying, in a tense whisper, 'I tell you, there ain't gonna be any more. There'll be less and less of it – lavender especially. The soap makers who don't have their own glycerine plants'll just be sunk, that's all. They're rationing the stuff already.'

The owner was very impressed. He stopped wiping a metal shaker and said, 'By golly, and we used to think of glycerine as a by-product of soap. Now soap'll be a by-product of glycerine. What a war!'

'Right,' said the salesman.

When the rain eased I started north again, following the rushing Umpqua River, past the dancing leaves of Oregon myrtle, glossier than ever in the rain. Up past the rose gardens of Roseburg, the green hills were punctuated all the way with lumber clearings and humming sawmills. The road curves slowly down and the fields widen through turkey farms until you start climbing again through the last pass before the Willamette Valley. At Cottage Grove, there was a lumberjack lounging in a general store. He too had the air of having discovered a secret that might lose the war. But it was only the ever-present fear of a Jap raid. He was thanking God for rain and wishing they could have some 'south of here through the High Sierras. All it takes is a couple Japs with a load of incendiaries. They could set the whole goddam coast on fire.'

The hills rolled away to the East, and ahead was the southern end of the green, green Willamette Valley, in which live five-sixths of the Oregon population. Bounded on the west by the Coast Range, and on the east by the Cascades, it stretches for 150 miles north and south, between twenty-five and fifty miles wide. It is what most people mean by Oregon, though there are jungles on the coast, and a desert in the east as sagey as Texas that can greatly surprise visitors from the south.

The Northwest is near enough to the conditions of its settling to want to tell you about it. And most families are proud of the great-grandfather or whoever that came from Montreal across the Rockies, or took the wagon train from St Louis. Yet the Oregonians who talked about these things to me had mellowed their pride with a little gentle cynicism. 'The adventurers,' said Bill Tugman, an editor from Eugene, 'went to California, and the God-fearing people came into Oregon, and skinned the Hudson Bay company of its holdings.' There is much folksy joshing about the legend that Oregon was settled by Missourians who didn't care to work. But the good humor with which the people repeat this pleasantry is a striking sign of security, a symptom of knowing and living fairly sober ideals. It is too bad to report simply that the million residents of the Willamette Valley grow everything from wheat to orchids, are satisfied with small tract holdings (which during the three-month summer drought are irrigated); that they raise sheep, turkeys, and Chinese pheasants; that they can vegetables, and grow more green beans than anywhere else on earth; that their chief payroll is in lumbering and wood fabrication. What you note about them, in striking contrast to the brash and vigorous people of Southern California, is an almost English, or Yankee, strain of complacent competence. Complacency is a deteriorated word and suggests more self-satisfaction than it means. A steady self-respect in the achievement of modest middle-class ideas is better.

I do not know how much scientific proof has been found for the slippery theories of climate and character. But in the Willamette Valley, where the weather is much like England, you would encounter for the first time north of the Mexican border an unassuming acceptance of the chores of wartime that was very close to the English capacity for regarding a blitz as a nuisance. Like the English too, the people, even in time of war, seem to talk mostly about family matters. They grumble about the weather and go forth in a wealth of raincoats. It was accordingly all the harder for a transient reporter to notice dramatic or boasted changes. You heard, almost as offhand detail, that a desperate need for the piling of lumber, which in a unionized industry can hardly be met by the depleted labor force, was met by families going out and doing the piling. This seemed the sensible, foolproof way of evading the Wages and Hours Act.

Sons and grandsons of respectable Midwesterners who came to settle here and brought their libraries and grand pianos, the residents of the Valley, especially of the upper Valley, were locally conservative but nationally for Roosevelt. The President's neutrality proclamation in the fall of 1939 was accepted as a first step that would lead logically to an American participation in the war, and there was reportedly little objection to the sequence of events. Doubtless there are rock-ribbed burghers of the Willamette Valley who, if they should ever read these words, would howl that this is a dastardly half-truth germinated by a White House press agent. All I know is what I heard and checked on. Occasionally I advanced the report and waited for an explosion. But head-shaking resignation was the most violent dissent I ever witnessed.

On a gray day in Eugene, Oregon, I ran into a nice variation on the prevailing English scale of idealism, a touch of craftsman's snobbery that would have done credit to a waiter in an Oxford or Cambridge college. A pleasant Irishman came to the Willamette Valley some years ago and, perhaps in unconscious protest against the gray sobriety of the natives, decided to grow orchids. He did so on a grand and scientific scale. The farm was left to his sons. One of them took me over the farm, which is now a million-dollar business. He scratched the back of his neck and admitted without any enthusiasm that yes there was a boom. I saw thousands of the most exquisite flowers growing in files as ordered as a Guards regiment on parade. He went over to one, cupped his hand to fondle it as tenderly as if it were an ailing Pekinese. Then he said, indifferently, 'You want it? It's no use to me.'

It was a spray orchid, and I thought it time to probe this strange melancholia of a man whose income had doubled since Pearl Harbor. Then he let off his blast, which was a well-modulated sigh, dripping disgust:

'Normal times this is what we like to do. Spray orchids for people who know about orchids. We fly them out of here every day to rich people in the East and South. But now we lost their business. They write letters, saying they're sorry but higher income taxes, War Bonds, one thing and another . . . So there's no fun anymore growing orchids. We just concentrate on the regular common or garden variety, the flossier the better.'

I asked him who the customers were for the orchid as it is known to debs and the presidents of women's clubs. He fell into deeper gloom and replied, 'Who would you think? The defense workers up in Portland and Seattle. Maybe they have a place to sleep, maybe not. But they're crazy for orchids. All they know is if they drape their wives in orchids, the wives begin to rate. I'm talking about shipyard workers, on their night off. But the lumbermen are just as bad these days.' It is an interesting comment on the Roosevelt era of equal rights that to the people Europeans call the poor and Americans the underprivileged, the more abundant life should still be signified by champagne and orchids. But the correct Oregon folk note was sounded by this farmer, swollen with contempt for the undiscriminating hordes that had recently made his fortune.

Up through the Valley you come frequently upon other touches that show a practical belief in scientific farming firmly wedded to an essential respectability. I went over a dairy constructed with the elegant functionalism of the best modern design. Opposite stood the farmer's house, a solid bungalow with the old Missourians' long hangover eaves for the rain to roll off (a practical note eighty years ago, since the pioneers had no gutter material). Inside were wicker chairs and a horsehair sofa, and at the windows curtains of prim lace. Near Albany, another man crystallized the idealism of the Valley people by saying 'the ambition around here is to get me a nut orchard and retire. Walnuts, filberts. This part of the world is intensive culti-vation of limited good land. In other words, it puts a premium on intelligence. The lazy people can go back in the hills and push a pipe into the ground – there's water at fifteen feet – and hunt deer and catch a fish and take it easy. Which they do.'

I went up through pear and cherry orchards into low hills before Salem, and celery gardens north of there deserted by the Japanese who cultivated them. All the way along the highway from here to the out-skirts of Portland are advertisements for bulbs and berries, and where you stop to eat there is a casual lavishness of some of the fine American berries that back East one hears about but seldom eats in pie. I stopped at a diner near Oregon City, and as a pie man, gloated awhile over a menu of raspberries, loganberries, youngberries, straw-berries, and blackberries, before finally settling for a caramel sundae. From here to Portland it was berry canneries and sawmills and quiet bungalow suburbs all the way.

Seen at the peak of the American honeymoon with the Second World War, Portland was the archetype of the war cities I had seen. It had 50,000 men and women in direct war work, 40,000 of them in the Kaiser shipyards. It expected to have over 100,000 people busy with ships, or airplanes, aluminum, chemicals, textiles, lumber and lumber products. There was an unhouseable population streaming into the city in trains, buses, jalopies, on foot, hitchhiking, in trailers, and even on horseback. The shipyards had recruited everything from ballet dancers to insurance salesmen and boasted radio singers, circus performers, wrestlers, several parsons, a state treasurer, and the world's former high-jump champion. Industrial trade schools had switched in a few weeks to robotizing these richly various Americans into shipyard workers with a badge and a union card.

Two hundred of the city's 770 service stations had closed. With high money the call for cabs was far above normal, and a third of the city's taxicabs were beginning to creak and stall. There were no more home deliveries of store purchases. The prodigious crops of apples and berries hereabouts would have to be harvested by students and housewives and children. The canneries were vainly trying to lure incoming workers from the shipyards into the canneries to keep up with their Lend-Lease promises. Just as the lumberyards, which in any country are poor competitors against high wages, tried appealing to the patriotism of intending shipyard workers. What the strangers coming into town had heard about were the shipyard wages. No lumber company could match them, though visibly the Pacific Northwest's inevitable contribution is the prodigal wood of the forest primeval, which nuzzles menacingly up to the very backyards of the cities of the Northwest. Here was a legitimate chance to dramatize the woodpile of the Allies: spruce for airplanes, redwood for tanks, and hemlock for pulp. The lumber companies thought and advertised and pleaded with the 'goons' to resist the shipyards. Here was urgently needed wood: wood for cantonments, for crates, for aircraft, for wartime housing near and far from the Northwest. But lumber workers do not get paid what Kaiser paid, especially since the government had put a ceiling price on lumber. So the labor spilled over from the shipyards, while the fruit canneries begged for 4,000 more workers, and the lumberyards for many thousand more. The labor situation in Portland was not helped by the equal demands of Seattle to the north, and the two big cities of the Northwest were harassed by the fear, and the experience of workers trying out jobs in one city and then the other, with an obvious disorganization of production and an appalling turnover in the aircraft plants and shipyards. The problem was relieved at least by a temporary joint agreement to give Portland most of the ship contracts and Seattle most of the aircraft.

Yet to a passing traveler, Portland had an order in its disorder, an unruffled air of riding a necessary crisis. There was plenty of dissatisfaction, and malingering, in the shipyards, but the air of suburban piety that the Oregon climate, or its folkways, inspired had successfully disguised from a visitor the dishevelment of a wartime society. 'Insurgency,' comments one writer, 'is seldom associated with camellias and rose bushes.' And the Portland citizenry seem to have a communal obsession for the tending of gardens. This trait only adds to its appearance of an English provincial town, where most people stay home nights, 'live home,' play cards, shrug their shoulders quietly at the newcomers, and on Sundays burst out in shirtsleeves to look after their gardens. You hear far less protesting about 'democracy' than you would in California or the Midwest, but there is a quieter assumption of it. I suppose there are country clubs in Portland, and a local aristocracy. But the striking social note of the Northwest is the small difference in mores between the top and bottom fringe. It was a significant remark by one resident that there certainly had been a sudden shortage of domestic servants 'for those that use them'. This, was said by a comfortable and distinguished editor, who in the East would certainly have had a maid and possibly a nurse as well. Women here, who in the East would regard a maid as an essential function of the home, do their own work, war or peace. This is true not only of Oregon but of the whole West Coast. They tell you about it in California; they take it for granted in Portland. Or it might be more accurate to say that where there is a girl to cook or help with the children, she becomes a nearly equal member of the home, eating with the family, working with them, vacationing with them. The West indeed is a middle-class matriarchy to a degree not equaled elsewhere in America. You notice that the mother, as elsewhere in the United States, is not merely the keeper of the shrine, the symbol of the family's stability and social poise, and the focus of its 'cultural' pretensions, but is also a sort of lawgiver, establishing the ethics and mores of the brood she tends. This must surely be due to the remarkable authority of sororities in Western colleges. The sorority your mother belonged to is, in a lesser way, a better hallmark than your father's college would be in the East. I may be wrong about this, and don't want to press it, but nowhere in the United States will you see so many women as there are in the West who are bloomingly healthy, competent in a massive way, able to maintain unstrained poise between an active social life and the household chores. The Northwest does not prate about its social democracy, but it has more of the solid humdrum substance of it than more glittering places. Perhaps it is because the Northwest's pioneers are only one generation away and that they had to establish *in fact* what the East by now asserts in principle but practices irregularly. It should be added that this middle-class unpretentiousness is not the final ambition of the Northwest's citizens. They remind you quietly of the ten hydroelectric units of nearby Bonneville Dam, and its capacity of a half-million horsepower. The power had gone to the war plants and shipyards, but Oregon, like California, awaits a certain industrial future.

Once you cross the Columbia River and pull north out of the truck gardens around Vancouver, Washington, you start a daylong drive through the rich parkland of southern Washington, climb over the banks of the Columbia, then flatten out through expansive grazing lands and go all day through rolling valleys of the densest green, bounded always by massive stands of unbroken fir. The broad valleys of Washington are drenched with rain, and the greenness seems to seep from blade to blade of its thick grass. I swung through one canyon and instinctively jammed on the brakes at the sight below me, a gentle plain of emerald green washed with yellow blossom. At the next turn was a valley blotted with Scotch broom. And wherever the highway rises and you go through a gorge, you emerge on sweeping hills that, round the whole arc of the horizon, stand magnificently tipped with the cathedral spires of Douglas firs. If there is a sublimer tree in America, I have not seen it.

To drive from south to north through the state of Washington was, even in the early days of the American war, a tantalizing seesaw between the old West and the new. Swinging through the valleys west of the Cascades, you saw the green and gracious stability the second generation had made. Here is the happy, undramatic, unfretted balance of natural resources that is – or was – the mark of Western agriculture almost any year before the Second World War. The high mountains yielding to the unhurried lumbermen a seemingly infinite stand of vast forest. Abundant low hills for grazing. And millions of acres of valleys for farming the prosperous domestic crops, the berries, the apples, the walnuts, the turkey farms, the flowers. But now when I hit high ground over the Columbia or the Chehalis, the water was black with lumber for the shipyards, for the airplanes, for Army crating. And through the truck-farming towns moved a new population, headed south to Portland, Oregon, north to Seattle, Washington – families fresh from California or the South, college boys wondering about a machine tool job, youths with suitcases by the highway going to an undetermined job in the war cities. Toward Olympia, the highway was lined with these war migrants thumbing a ride north to Tacoma and Seattle. Beyond Tacoma, the highway was lit by sodium-vapor lights that were probably there before the war. But they reminded me of the lights outside Lockheed at San Diego and switched my thought back again to the special mission of the Pacific Coast – the noisy, clanging, breathless job of spanning the yawning Pacific with ships and supplies. I picked up two high-school boys somewhere along this way. We drove past hundreds of lakeside cabins, closed lunch-counters, and wayside invitations to swim or fish. Some other spring they would have had their thoughts on these things. But they sat in raincoats, their belongings packed on their knees, and never gave the signs or cabins more than a rueful glance. We stopped at a diner outside Seattle and drank apple juice and ate fried oyster pancakes. I noticed for the first time a menu that called hamburgers 'liberty steak'.

An Easterner might have read somewhere that Seattle was the supply base for the prospectors of Alaska (which it was) and expect to land in one of those false-front roaring camps the movies love. But Seattle today is as far from prospector days as California Gold Rush catalyst John Sutter is from labor union boss John L. Lewis. Roughly, you could start the modern history of Seattle from the time in the 1890s when the American Federation of Labor appreciated that 60 percent of the state's income was in lumber and lumber products and took over from the Knights of Labor. The Congress of Industrial Organizations also saw the vision of an industrial Seattle and in the 30s moved in and is still trying to take over from the AF of L.

'Seattle,' said a man with a singsong Swedish accent, 'is run by labor leaders. They are calm about it, but firm. The only authority that will count when the war's over is what the labor leaders say. In the 30s there was great unemployment. When the Japs are licked,' he shrugged his shoulders, 'these newcomers have not stopped to consider what it will be like. This whole coast, it will be like the East in the winter of 1931–32.'

I mentioned the Teamsters' Union. In Seattle, it is like making a secret Masonic sign. One man will declare that all law and order is due to the Teamsters' benign influence. Another will act as if you were digging for material about the Ku Klux Klan. The Swede parried the question. He replied, like a man chanting a piece of dogma, that 'you must understand the Swedes have given this part of the country its traditions, its strictness. We have strong political prestige. We are responsible for the alcohol laws.' Other people I talked with said there was no hard liquor sold in Washington because the Teamsters' Union held the brewery business in rigid control and could annihilate any hard liquor lobby that dared cross the border. 'They have their fingers in everything,' said another man, 'laundries, white-collar workers, automobile renters, truckers, delivery men – they even organize the drugstore clerks.'

It may strike the reader as implausible that within the first hour in a big American city at war, one should hear the expression of several local attitudes toward what you could take to be a local union. You might think you'd hear at once that after Pearl Harbor, no more apples could be shipped from Seattle to Holland and Germany. That was a big blow. But without the nod of labor leader Dave Beck and his Teamsters' Union, no apples would be shipped anywhere. The Teamsters are the symbol of a tamed frontier. Beck made it clear in the mid-30s that union organization was not just a New Deal tactic, or a truce struck with powerful shippers, freighters, and California's wine industry. He taught the West Coast that the complete organization of a whole city is to be a routine technique of industrial law and order. If labor relations had been as raw in 1941 as they were in the Northwest in the early 30s, the whole country would have known about Beck and probably loathed him. As it is, he is symbolically the sheriff of Seattle. He is simultaneously respected, feared, hated, worshiped. And the strikes, even in a swollen and bewildered city, were few and far between.

A quick tour of any stretch of the Puget Sound area soon reveals why a jurisdictional fight in a lumber city might cause you to explore fine definitions. Lumbering to an Easterner is a rough-and-ready occupation calling for the stamina of Paul Bunyan, the vocabulary of a Marine, beefsteaks for nourishment, and much crude, heavy labor at the loading ports. But the fierce competition among the West Coast ports (Seattle is two to three days faster sailing to the Orient than San Francisco) has made the shipping of lumber a heavy industry as subtly high-pressured as the steel industry. Logs are rafted in from the mountains or steamed in by train. They are grabbed by whirring chains, sawed to figured thickness by power saws, and fed on an assembly belt of rollers into the waiting mill. Here men flip switches, press buttons, pull levers, and a thousand chattering electrical devices saw and hack and shape the now unrecognizable logs into beams, rafters, boxes, boards, shingles, airplane and ship parts, and a score of special shapes. The man who saws logs into boxes is no strapping hunk of man. He is almost a typist, sitting precisely at a keyboard, hunting and pecking to set in motion a mesh of gears and saws that cut and saw and shave and shape and transport and assemble wood before his tranquil clerk-like gaze. Labor leaders John L. Lewis and Alfred Green could reasonably be expected to stage a classic legal battle for the right to collect his dues.

Out on the streets, and in the jammed restaurants where service was creepingly slow, you could pick up lively evidence that the standard irritation was the discrepancy in pay rates between the shipyards and the airplane plants. The Boeing plant was worried over a steady drain of workers away to the yards.

'All right, Boeing pays sixty-two cents an hour. The yards pay ninety-five cents. It's as simple as that.' There was much resentment against bright high-school boys who signed up for vocational 'defense' school, learned sheet metal work or welding, at the expense of the US Office of Education, then worked a week in a factory and deserted for the shipyards.

Up here, I heard little talk of the Japs – the American Japs. There were between 6,000 and 7,000 in Seattle. They had gone, not especially resented, nor regretted. And many of their holdings had been taken over by Italians, who locally tend to be florists and truck farmers.

Seattle has had lumber mills for ninety-five years. Its growth as a

modern port has been slow, steady, and untidy. The deceptive organization of Seattle today is not that of 'modern design'. It is the
underlying control of the two great labor unions. Seattle expects to go
on shipping fish and grain and lumber from the Inland Empire. Its
citizens remind you, in case you forgot, of the excellent transcontinental rail connections. They will also drop dark, proud hints of a
future Seattle as the West Coast terminal of transpacific airlines. But
somehow it is hard to construct, from the guesses and mild boasts of
its people, any certain blueprint of Seattle's future. Seattle believes in
a modern future but is not quite sure what it is to be. The Navy is
there, and presumably to stay. People still recall with an easily
excitable nostalgia the great promise of the silk trade with Japan. An
unemployed salesman in nylon stockings appreciated the irony of
being a resident of Seattle.

'When this war's over they'll be starving on dreams of silk, and me,
I'll be resting on my estate in Mr Du Pont's Delaware. It was cute
while it lasted, though. Well, I guess there's always lumber.' In an airplane anywhere through the Cascades, I suppose you'd agree with
him. But there are responsible lumber men who are not so sure. Those
who know their American history in lumbering do not underestimate
the ability of their fellow citizens to mow down huge forests in a
matter of a decade or two, like fields of wheat. And the demand made
on the forests of spruce, fir, and hemlock would be unprecedented,
long before the Pacific war was done.

I left Seattle on a gray, drizzling day. At breakfast, and at subsequent gas stations, I had a final reminder of how a dank, temperate
climate breeds a strain of English gloom in the natives of the Northwest. They smear their weather as easily as Californians glorify theirs.

It was a Sunday, and I followed a score of Seattle cars through high
evergreens up a winding grade to Snoqualmie Falls. Beyond there,
there was only an occasional truck chugging slowly up into the
Cascades. Once again I was threading through the gorgeous raw
material of war but there was no other sign. And unless you are an
ornithologist, no sound but the drip of rain and the drag of your
motor as you slide in second down from the top of the pass through
slopes dark with timber.

Over the timbered cabins of general stores in small mountain resorts you see an occasional Slav or Italian name. You might be in the Alps. You emerge from the mountains on a flat plain before Cle Elum, where you must decide whether to go north again at Teanaway through more mountains or take the short scrubland highway to Spokane across the Washington desert. At Teanaway I looked north toward an encircling smear of rain clouds, spreading mist like taffy through the evergreens. I got out, gingerly examined my tires, and since there were several more hours of daylight, decided to drive through the flat Kittitas Valley to Ellensburg and then follow US 10 through the lonely scrubland of the Big Bend.

At Vantage, there is a store and a gasoline station. I stood on a bridge and looked at one of the most gloomily noble prospects of the Columbia River, banked with rust-colored high rocks, and edged with cottonwoods and dense bushes. The sky was clear now and the falling golden light turned the rocks into those slate grays and dun greens and brooding browns from which in imagination the Oregon-born mystical painter Morris Graves carves his fateful birds. The geology of the scene, unless I am worse on geology than I think, could have been Utah or even New Mexico. But New Mexico would look like this only in a million years or so, when the American continent cools into oblivion. It seemed entirely practical to speculate on the possibility of a flat tire somewhere across the lonely plateau that lay ahead. None too cheerfully I climbed into my car. The man at the gas station replaced and relocked the cap of my gas tank.

'All right,' he said, 'you're all set. East is no way to go this time of day. Good luck.'

I might have been entering the Inferno.

Even the pertinacity of the federal guide writers did not reach to this utterly barren trip. I recall only a plateau of dry sage, clumps of berry bushes, a high wind that made the car lurch threateningly across the road, and total, barren loneliness. The twilight seemed like the end of all things, and when darkness fell it circled all around me. The only sure sign I had that I was on this earth was the jet of light from my headlights. I hung on to the taillight of a speeding truck all the way up through monotonous grain country and came at last into Spokane. The railroad yard was villainously dark, but under high lamps a few workmen were lolling. And from a loudspeaker came the solid monosyllables of news commentator Elmer Davis. He was telling of American reverses everywhere in the Pacific. But after the numb dark and barrenness of the scrubland, his voice was the essence of home-coming. I was back again in the land of the living and reasonable men. It was a liverwurst sandwich after an evening with Dante.

Spokane is pretty much of an unknown city, even in the West. To travelers it is known for the Davenport Hotel, a fabulous block-long memorial to the large appetites of pioneers, where you may dance in one of three ballrooms – the Marie Antoinette Room, the Elizabethan Room, or the Hall of the Doges; where you may convene business meetings in one of five rooms according to your architectural taste, in the Gothic Room, the Green Room, the East Banquet Room, the Mandarin Room, and the Arabic Tent Room; where you may eat either in the Isabella Room, 'in the style of the Spanish Renaissance', in the Italian Gardens, in the Coffee Shop, or if you are a stickler for daintiness and aesthetic sandwiches, in the Delicacy Shop or in the Orange Bower and Fountain Room. The kitchens that supply this munificence are in a vast basement done in white-tiled walls and red-tiled floor, with silver closets and a device that automatically sterilizes the china and silverware. An auxiliary item of pride is a rotary silver burnisher, and a mill into which all silver change is instantly cleansed of the foul infections of the customers' pockets. It is the pride of the Davenport Hotel that nobody ever receives a nickel, dime, or quarter from its cash registers that is not burnished as if newly minted. To the transient movie stars and traveling salesmen, London's Savoy Hotel and New York's Waldorf must be by comparison fairly unpretentious cabins. To people who have never seen Spokane, the occasional dis-covery of a shining dime is a reminder of the incomparable Davenport.

Aside from the Davenport Hotel, Spokane is, certainly in the East, an unknown city, and travelers are likely as not to listen with faint condescension to the assurance, common to Western towns great and small, that it is 'the rising city of the West'. This is an old Western custom. It was the convention sixty years ago for a settlement that had barely managed to feed and clothe itself to circularize the Eastern states of its existence the moment it heard a railroad line was coming through, with handbills inviting prospective residents to come and settle in a region of Roman sumptuosity. Spokane was no exception. When it was promised a connection with the Northern Pacific Railroad, unoffending natives of Philadelphia and New York were urged to journey to 'the manufacturing center of the Great Northwest', there to cushion out their days amid 'luxuries of limitless wealth'.

But Spokane may be the one town that is right in its hopes of becoming a great metropolis of the Northwest. It is the capital of the great eastern plateau known as the Inland Empire, a name that might well have been a brave whistle in the dark, the mere grand echo of a huge plateau of sagebrush that was veined with low-grade gold and better silver. But now the majesty of the name has been matched by the awesome presence of the greatest of man-made powerhouses. Today, the Inland Empire means Grand Coulee, the largest concrete dam on earth. Tomorrow, when the power is switched from the war plants of the coast to the plain it is built on, it will mean a million and a quarter acres of scrubland irrigated into prosperous crops. At first Coulee was to be built as a low dam for power. Then the plan was changed to make it a high dam for irrigating the Columbia Basin. It may be worth noting, as a comment on the doubtful capacity of people to anticipate their own good, that Coulee was at first stubbornly fought. Spokane had its own little Columbia River project, and the state made a survey that produced a majority report in favor of an irrigation canal, a minority report in favor of Coulee. For the duration of the war, irrigation could be no more than a promise, as it is with California's Central Valley. But after the war, the Tennessee Valley Authority will quite likely be equaled by the Central Valley Project, the Columbia Valley Project, and perhaps the Missouri Valley Project. And the greatest of these, say the residents of Spokane, will be the Columbia Authority. For here not only will the pallid face of the scrubland come to prosperous health, the Inland Empire will have prodigious power, and it is a country rich in basic metals. Since the whole area has been raped of lumber – what it does have left is sustained by grace of Theodore Roosevelt's 'perpetual yield' theory – Spokane will probably concentrate on becoming a capital city of the light metals industry. If this is a fair prediction – a region suddenly equipped with great power for light metals, and water to ripen over a million acres – Spokane could easily be the stage for one of the classic conflicts of our time, the battle for public water between the government and the utilities, ending most probably in that curious self-governing compromise, a public corporation, of which at present the Tennessee Valley Authority and the British Broadcasting Corporation are the two most fascinating examples.

Many men in Spokane, flour millers, power contractors, manufacturers, farmers, and especially newspapermen, were keenly aware of this coming struggle, and the daily record of the war made for pretty humble reporting by contrast. But here, such as it could be glimpsed by a visitor, is the brief story.

As long as the Inland Empire remains a scrubland tempered by farming areas sparse and far apart, the residents of the state of Washington spend normally one-third of their income traveling by automobile. I mention this as a staggering fact to explain the air most people have of going about quite humdrum, small-town pursuits. I found people willing to declare that 'we're a frontier people still, with a Colonial viewpoint,' in the youngest section of the country. The natives are 80 percent Anglo-Saxon. The Negroes go to school with the whites, and so do the few Indians around (Indian blood is a proud thing to have, provided you are not too close to the original sire). Here, on a smaller scale, I noticed more sharply the typical mores of the Northwest; a loose social structure, a country club but few people who can afford the dues; a theoretical superiority of Episcopalians, an actual dictatorship of school and college sororities.

They describe their basic trades as being in soil, timber, and ore. The farmers felt that the flight to war industries on the coast had hit them harder than the draft. They were offering $75 a month with keep to farmhands, an unprecedented wage, and failing to lure them. There was a pressing lack of storage space, especially for grain, and it was going into anything with four walls – playgrounds, schools, garages. The Pacific Coast had 45 million bags of grain, and storage room for only 8 million. This is obviously tractor country, and what with the shortage of men, and the difficulty of getting equipment repaired, many of the growers had turned back to horses.

The price of sheep had gone sky high in the year before the war, and since the meat had not been sold by government grades, everybody expected low-grade meat to bring the old high-grade prices. Down in the southwest of the plateau, in the Yakima Valley, the beet growers were enjoying the sarcastic triumph of saying 'I told you so' to the government, which had always met hard resistance in restricting the production of beet sugar to no more than 23 percent of the total consumption of sugar. Now, the government said the sky was the limit, and the growers, begged after Pearl Harbor to grow all they could, were angrily pointing to their restricted facilities. Naturally, the Yakima Valley calls up the subject of the Associated Farmers organization, which some people see as a benevolent protector of the American way of life on the West Coast, and others as a reactionary specter haunting free trade and free speech. For it was in the Yakima Valley that the Associated Farmers put up their last-ditch fight against the union-organizing of field labor, after the unions had managed to organize the California fruit-canners. I heard much casual praise and abuse of the Associated Farmers, and it is clearly too complex a topic for a traveler's tale. But a remark late at night, from a small-town state editor, might illumine this casualness as only a wartime truce. 'Labor problems and feuds,' he said, 'like anti-Semitism and anti-British feeling, are under wraps, but only for the duration.'

It was drizzling heavy rain as I pulled out of Spokane into small-farming country and then across the Idaho border and through young pine and fir up into the Alpine quiet of the Coeur d'Alene country. The rain was spraying the fine needles and the heavy cones and misting up the soft beards of land that taper out into the lake. Either I was wonderfully relaxed, or I fell asleep at the wheel, which is quite possible on these beautiful highways, so rhythmically banked. At any rate, I was unnaturally startled by the stab of American memory that flashed from the roadside in a running sequence of signs that bore the names Terror Gulch, Gold Rush Gulch. Before I knew it I was going over brown sandy cutover flats, saw a flicker of new painted houses, saw the new wing of a yellow-bricked school, and a dog licking a piece of cellophane. And I stopped for lunch at Wallace, Idaho. It was a timeless, silent town (little wonder that the hipbone and molar of a mammoth have been found here), and in a rather frowzy hash-house, an uncommunicative waiter served me macaroni and tomato soup, a fine steak with asparagus and diced potatoes, a banana cream pie, and gallons of milk. A very old lady in an old blue coat and box shoes stood against the cashier's desk pushing nickels into a bell-fruit slot machine with such a timed monotony that she is probably there still.

Then I was on my way up to Lookout Pass, in the heart of the great Bitterroots.

There is a special disadvantage that weighs on anyone living in America who would try to describe what the Greeks coolly labeled 'the sublime'. Our addiction to grandiose adjectives makes grandeur ultimately indescribable. In reading most pieces of American writing on the war, whether it is a statistical summary of airplane production or a color piece on migrant labor, the reader's admiration is staked out for him by the recurrent adjectives: vast, huge, enormous, tremendous, magnificent, immense, and the like. If you have already pinned the word 'magnificent' on the mountain country of the East, on the Green Mountains, say, or the Appalachians, what words are left to describe the Rockies, the High Sierras, the Coast Range, the Cascades, and the Bitterroots? There is a more elemental difficulty over nouns that we share with England, the nouns that describe the simple configuration of the earth at our doorstep. A 'big tree' in England could be a copper beech, in Texas it might be a healthy cottonwood. What simple noun and adjective shall we use, then, to celebrate Sequoia *sempervirens*? Something Miltonic is demanded, but even if the supply of Miltons were not strictly limited, Milton used his epic vocabulary on the hills and lakes of pretty Italy and on fantasies he would have been shocked to see as the actualities of the Carlsbad Caverns (the natural setting for the Inferno), the Grand Canyon, Zion, Bryce, the Great American Desert, and the shaggy forests of the Northwest.

The Bitterroots are, then, not to be described, at least not by me. I can merely say that once again the innumerable spires of great firs, and the solemn hush of entering a high world of impenetrable evergreens, gave me the sense of coming out of a pressing world of little facts into a cathedral. If I was thinking of the war through these ecstasies, it is because the war is relevant to them. I had noticed before that surpassingly beautiful landscape belittles one's immediate interest in the brawling statistics of wartime towns. I do not think this is a reaction anything like so simple as 'escape'. Those who escape into nature, invariably get more than they bargained for. Here in the

Bitterroots, I might seek to belittle the war by observing the grand indifference of nature. But this grandeur, and this unchanging beauty, only threw the war back in my lap, insisted by the automatism of its own laws that it could not help, that it would perform these virtuoso marvels as obligingly for troops of American Fascists, if they should come to power. The bluebirds of purest ultramarine that balanced on the telephone wires and made astonishing trajectories of light across my windshield would be as charming, or as illusive, to a Jap. Indeed, outside Missoula, Montana, there was a prison camp for Italians, and a few Germans, sailors from ships seized in the Panama Canal, who were delighted at their wartime home, the Italians renaming the spot Bella Vista.

On account of this camp, Missoula enjoyed early in the war the unholy pleasure of living with a high-priority secret, and most of its citizens that I talked to were almost religiously cryptic. For a couple of days I felt myself very much like a spy, and a man sketching the plight of the sugar beet industry would watch me uncertainly, half his mind wondering what use the neighboring Italians and Nazis might make of the sugar information I would sell to them. I couldn't get near the railroad shops. But it was possible to gather that what Missoula missed most were the Mexican beet workers, who are accustomed to come in the late spring to tend and weed the beet crop and stay through for the harvesting in the fall. The Mexicans were staying home in large numbers. There had been a rush to enlist right after Pearl Harbor, and now the sugar refining plant, which normally goes at full steam in the fall, was short of young men and having to split its labor for field work. Even up here, there were block wardens and first-aid courses, but no black-outs.

I left Missoula on US 10, went up through Hell Gate Canyon (the French fur-trappers knew it as a favorite Indian ambush and named it *La Porte de l'Enfer*), where a sign says, 'If you're depressed Paradise is only 73 miles away', which it is, to the northwest. This stretch is really the rocky Rockies, with jutting outcrops of hard rock and shale. The roads too were in disrepair; at one place a bulldozer, cranes, and leveler stood untended, frozen with rust, as if the crew had left at a moment's notice, to stem the actual Japanese invasion. In an hour's drive I passed a man and a horse and miles of abandoned badlands. It seems profitless country, until the tiny town of Goldcreek, on the Clark Fork River, reminds you that off to hereabouts was the first Montana Gold Rush, and that off to the horizon on the right, in the Sapphire Mountains, are silver, phosphate, and sapphire. I turned off at Drummond on to US 10 Alternate and climbed up about 1,200 feet through raw badlands relieved by a lake or two and saw ahead the enormous smokestack of the Washoe Smelter at Copperopolis, or – as it is now called – Anaconda.

9

The Great Plains

The visitor coming upon this desolate smelting city from the west will confront just outside the town a tablet inscribed with the boast that although Anaconda has grown 'from a tent town to a modern city . . . it has retained the aggressive spirit' of pioneer days. Anyone who has glanced over records of the Anaconda Company's battles with state tax commissions will hardly need this reassurance. But the sign is only the Westerner's chronic desire to claim the rude virtues and bountiful resources he believes, or thinks, his grandfather had. It is also an unconscious protest against absentee landlords, against the recognition that a Montanan cannot call his state his own, nor his home, nor his farms, nor the precious ores that lie beneath his high hills. Not so much as one-fifth of the land is owned by the men who work it. The unceasing need of water for farms and power would seem to be easily satisfied in a state whose rivers could irrigate 10 million acres, but irrigate only 2 million: the water sites were grabbed up long ago by corporations, who could sit pretty in New Jersey or Chicago while the farms adjacent to these sites dried up from 'drouth'. The load of hydroelectric power sold to resident Montanans in 1940 by the Montana Power Company was 4.5 percent. To the Anaconda Copper Company, and the Milwaukee Railroad, it sold over 75 percent. One should add that the full title of the power company is the Montana Power Company of New Jersey and that it is a subsidiary of Electric Bond and Share of New York.

Is this then no more than a sentimental plea for the Montana cattleman and wheat farmer? After all, you will say, Anaconda is in Montana, and if the Company is such a productive giant it surely gives back to the state the power it takes out. But Montana is not an economic unit. The utilities of Butte are privately owned. The city limits gyrate all over town to insure that the mines shall pay no city taxes. And the Company does not pay anything comparatively similar to the rancher's or the wheat farmer's taxes. In the early 20s the oil industry paid taxes on its gross proceeds of about 1 percent. Coal was paying about 1.5 percent. Copper, producing twice the worth of coal, and six times the worth of oil, was paying six hundredths of 1 percent. In 1942, after taxation battles that had torn the state, it was about 0.8 percent.

You would be deducing no less than the truth from this if you said that no newspaper, school, hotel-keeper, banker, businessman, real-estate office, city official, or university professor throughout the state could last very long if it bucked 'the Company'. And you would then understand what an aura of dread power, of mixed frustration and envy, the name 'Anaconda' calls forth all across the Great Plains. I was soon better able to appreciate the expression, at once wistful and aggrieved, on the face of a farmer looking at the New Jersey license plate of a parked car.

But Anaconda, this bare, gray, unlovely town whose sheds and smelting plants spread over a sloping hill and look as if a railroad had moved into the crude geometry of a forgotten tribe of cliff-dwellers, is only the servant of the city south and east. It is the smelter, as Great Falls is the refiner, of the ore that lies twenty-two miles away, in Butte, the monstrous hill, a mile above sea level, that lies like a prostrate dinosaur, gray and claylike with decay, in whose sides a hundred shafts stab down 4,000 feet, linking at the base nearly 3,000 miles of tunnels that have probed the petrified intestines and spewed up, through the labor and feuds and sweat of miners, 2.5 billion dollars' worth of copper in fifty years.

There is not a sign outside Butte warning travelers to abandon hope. But the drive from Wallace to Missoula seemed already the distance between paradise and the special circle of Hell that one prays is reserved for the men who battened and fattened on the profits of technology. Nature expired three years ago under the unceasing blast of sulfur fumes, from the great charcoal fires that first smelted the ore. The trees gave up and the grass was blighted. Today there are seedlings and strips of 'park' here and there, frail tributes to the New

Deal's work projects. But it is a feeble protest. Butte must be the only city in the country where Roosevelt-haters could never accuse him of financing 'leaf-raking' jobs. They would never want to praise him so highly.

Much has been written about Butte by the traveler, who after one gloomy day or one disorderly night, is only too glad to be a 'transient'. Butte has attracted thousands of spry tourists, drawn there by the promise of the adjectives that have tagged it – Butte the 'boisterous', the sinful, the virile, the uncorseted, the lusty, the Rabelaisian, the 'island of easy money surrounded by whiskey'. Hollywood has slobbered over its romantic stridency and streamlined and sterilized the drab girls of 'the line'. Not even Hollywood has been able to picture a humble miner and make him over into a mine owner. The owners live in other towns and other states, far from the ravined gray hills, the vomit dumps of yellow ore, the tumbling irregular rows of dingy brick houses, the dust, the rotted shrubs and trees, far from this great cluttered hill between barren mountains, this Augean archetype of the English mill town, where every natural blossom or human grace is frozen into shame by a single belch from the mines.

Before the 'recession' of 1937, there were nearly 8,000 men in the mines. After it, there were 800. By the summer of 1942, there were 9,000. They were turning out 73 million pounds of metal (copper, zinc, manganese) a month, two and a half times the First World War's production. But they could easily have used 5,000 more men. Montana, with a little more than a half million population, had lost 25,000 mechanics to war industries. The Army had drafted from the mines – as from other types of industry and farming it knew too little about – many special and irreplaceable skills. There must be accurate blasters, ore shovelers, men who know how to 'timber' the drift, drillers, and the electricians who supervise the hauling. After many draft-board wrangles, some of these men were released, came back, took one look at Butte, and went back to the comparative Elysium of Army camps in Louisiana swamps and Florida mosquito patches. Nobody will know what the production of the mines might have been if the supply of men had been adequate. It's not how much ore there lies in the bowels of the hill but how much can be brought to the surface. The hoisting capacity of a shaft is the only measure of

production. And there are laborious essential processes. Said one foreman, 'They hoist more tons of water than they've ever hoisted ore.'

The men were getting then an average wage of $8.50 a day. This is
boom money. But the banks and retail stores complained of few
deposits, and no sales. The miner, like the farmer, is traditionally
suspicious of a promise of long-time security – the 'ever-normal gran-
ary' or a 'regular guaranteed minimum'. He prefers a contract with
the employer for every cubic foot of ore mined. When the need is
pressing, the wage is high, and he banks it in his own home and takes
the periodic rest all miners crave when he chooses, a last relic of his
'independence' he is loath to sacrifice working month in, month out
on a union guaranteed wage. A public relations man for one of the
mines did his best to make me, as a stranger, feel relieved about the
miners' lot.

'Easy come, easy go. They're tough and tricky to handle. But goodness, they don't have any worries that a coupla drinks won't cure.
They don't want to be tied to a year's contract, good times and bad.'
He looked at me as if he had decided to make a daring statement and
take the rap for it. He threw his head back and said, 'They like their
independence, same as you and me. And frankly, do you blame them?'

I said I didn't.

'You betcha,' he breathed, much relieved that I shared his risky
liberalism. 'If they can make money fast and lay off and spend it when
they choose, *how* they choose – see what I mean?'

I asked him about insurance against silicosis (I didn't know then
that in the 20s not less than 40 percent of the miners had it). It was as
if I had asked him where the twenty-five-yard line was on a baseball
diamond. He looked incredulous and laughed in roguish forgiveness.

'Say,' he said, 'you've been reading Joseph Kinsey Howard. Am
I right?'

I had never heard of Howard at the time and said so. But with
kindly patience he told me about the wet drill and what amounted to
something almost like air-conditioning in the mines of today. I had
been made, he imagined, to feel better, and he saw me out, his arm
around my shoulder, like a school principal who has relieved the
absurd fears of a small body concerned about some such crime as
coming late to class.

It was no trouble at all to climb in the car again and be on my way. Honking a truck ahead of me, as the light changed, I was horrified to notice that my horn had jammed. I drove out of Butte with my horn screaming, feeling that if I was too uninformed to have a solid argument with the public relations man, my car had taken over and was disposing of the mine owners, or their native henchmen, with a noble and sustained Bronx cheer.

Butte is soon forgotten (except by a Montanan) in the grades of the Pipestone Pass and enclosing evergreens as you pass over the Continental Divide. Going down the eastern slopes, you seem to be pulling out of mountains into sage country, but a sign saying 'Avoid Vapor Lock' reminds you you are still 5,000 feet up, and the road winds around steep canyons. Where there are mountain plateaus, you see roaming sheep and stretches of wheat. But often you see granite buttes sticking straight up out of these wheat fields, for not far below the sometimes deceiving soft mold of this surface soil is always the hard layer of rock. In the evening I was moving down into the Gallatin Valley, where the breeze had fallen, and where wheat and cattle abounded. Through Bozeman, you look on your right and see in the distance the high peak of Mount Blackmore, named after – of all people – one Lady Blackmore, wife of an English peer who died here in the 70s as she and her husband were on their way to geologize in Yellowstone. The temperature drops sharply as you slice through the edge of a forest of spruce and Douglas fir and come into the relic town of gingerbread 'mansions' and decayed saloons: Livingston. It is a modest ghost town, content to rest its claims on history in a few Western paintings, an annual Wild West parade, and the honest admission that Calamity Jane was in her boozy decline when she lived here. It is now a railroad terminal for the Northern Pacific railroad, and the maintenance workers for the Rocky Mountain area go out from here. It had little to add to what I had heard a score of times: the young people gone, the skilled maintenance men taken unfairly with the rest, the merchants hard hit, and a crying need of stoop labor in the beet fields. From here to Billings, the guides say, is rough high-mountain country through tortuous canyons. In such country, in Mexico, say, or many places in Europe, you would be too busy steering your car over gravel and through swirling dust to notice much else. But since this is the United States, your journey is about as different as possible from the experience of the white men and women who first walked the land and planted elm and maple in godforsaken valleys. The cement road is smooth and curving, and my chief memory of the drive is the prospect of fine mountain valleys, and much green irrigated land on either side of the undisturbing highway.

One particular scene grows very familiar, though it would be an odd sight in any mountain valley back East. It is the apparent freakish combination of granite buttes looming over haystacks, up-thrusts of intractable rock that appear to mock and threaten the farmer's determination to rear healthy livestock. They say that in the middle of the last century Englishmen came through and dismissed the possibility of farming in this fractious granite land where the Great Plains open out from the eastern slopes of the Rockies. There is a significant scene just near Park City that provides its own silent comments on this judgement. From bare sheep country you suddenly come on a high valley where prosperous farming has a precise geometry. From the highway running half-way up a slow sloping hill is a dense, square beet field. A narrow irrigation canal divides it from a cattle pasture, in the middle of which is a golden haystack neatly fenced around against the depredations of coyotes. On the hill rising slowly beyond the beets and the cattle are sheep peppering the more barren ground. And the sky meets this sheep pasture at a flat-topped granite butte. The signature on this masterpiece of judicious farming unfortunately cannot be enclosed in the picture. It lies a half-mile to the right, where an arrow points down a dirt road and a wooden sign bears the explanation, 'Lutheran Church two miles south. Service in English 8 a.m., in German 6 a.m.' The Germans came through here, got up with the sun, and put the granite in its place.

As the mountains recede behind you, there are many such happy valleys, the exceptions that later prove the rule of the bare, anxious life of the Great Plains, where you need forty acres to keep one cow, where 900 acres is a minimum stake in health and security, where a spring snow leaves no trace but a few more thousand eyeless skulls of cattle that were never designed to walk fifty miles for pasture, and where the good advice of the federal government has often been to get about a quarter-million people out of the Plains and keep them out.

Along the last half of the way toward Billings, the sign 'Stock Crossing – 600 feet' is as monotonous as milestones. The only human interruption of the scene was lonely figures, sometimes of boys, sometimes of old men, standing by the highway, their bags packed at their feet, thumbing a ride West, to the coast and the factories and the prosperity that by now was legendary in any hard-farming country. In the late afternoon near Billings, I also noticed a rare un-American sight – a mother in a floppy hat plowing a cornfield, and two daughters bent over low in the beet fields. When mother and daughter take to the heavy farming, there was no need to be assured – as I was in Billings – that Montana had lost much more than its share of able-bodied youth. 'Where are the peasants?' once asked a puzzled Frenchman in a Maryland valley. He was told that it was an impossible word to translate into American, because the thing it stood for didn't exist. In the first year of the American war, and at harvest time thereafter, across many different landscapes, the American woman became a peasant – a peasant I noticed elsewhere with a tan and a high hairdo, and often with scarlet nails, ready for an evening of jitterbugging with the resident soldiery.

I pushed on through a long afternoon east and south from Billings toward the Wyoming line. It is a bare plateau of cottonwood and sage and illimitable unfenced distances made friendly enough by the pleasant rolling hills that break them and the high shimmer of snow atop the Big Horn Mountains, way to the south. Driving across it in the 1940s, it seems fresh, honest, keen-winded, even dramatic country. But it is not of the stuff that National Parks are made. Is this too the result of our jaded subjection to the age of Publicity, whose cunning pimps stimulate and stimulate the senses until nothing will attract us but what is glamorous, dramatic, highly colored, barbaric, even a landscape that is spellbinding, and scenes that try to achieve the fulsome distortions of Technicolor?

The tourist will find little to give him pause here but gladness at the high dome of sky and the soft wind across the billowing land. And yet here, across a stretch of range a few miles square, by the Little Big Horn River, is a cemetery of frightful history, leaving open to easy access the memorials of young Civil War veterans and redskins, of railroad Irish, of indomitable priests, and, near to the surface, the bones of animals never seen by man. You can go through Hardin, Montana, and on to Crow Agency and feel no apprehension, or know no sign, that you are in the middle of the reservation of the harmless Crow Indians, who today raise barley and wheat and name their children Rides Pretty, and Franklin D. Roosevelt He-Does-It. Farther on is Garryowen, named for an Irish marching tune favored by George Armstrong Custer's unlucky Seventh Cavalry. Along the way you run by eroded trenches whose tumbled rock cover prehistoric fossils. And directly west, sixteen miles across open county is St Xavier, where in the 80s a Jesuit priest and two men built a tent in which they cooked, slept, stored supplies, read, prayed, baptized the Indian, and which they called a mission.

Just off the road to the left is an enclosed area of high, flat ground, and between it and the open sky nothing but a couple of hundred slabs of whitest marble. They are markers of the approximate graves of Custer's men, who fell here in the last pitched battle between the Indian and the white man. In the middle of a global war, it was humbling to walk over this ground and meditate how well-remembered are the American dead. Yet I believe that our ethics about burying the battle dead is a later ritual than we normally assume. For over a year after the massacre at the Little Big Horn, the dead were left here buried in only the most perfunctory way, the enlisted men lying where they fell, barely covered with a few shovels-full of soil. A year later, after the winds had blown, the rotted corpses lay exposed, half eaten by the coyotes and wolves from the mountains that had come to regard the battlefield as a banqueting place. It was only ten years after the battle that the bones were buried deep together and later still when the federal government eventually set up these markers.

The little Rosebud and Wolf mountains lie close to your left and the Little Big Horn River runs beside the highway for a while as you start to climb again through narrow valleys of the encroaching Big Horns. You cross into Wyoming and roll over hills behind which you see curling smoke from coal mines. Then the highway turns abruptly away from the mountains and you are on high ranching plains of grass and sage and cottonwoods. The highway would be spotted occasionally by dead beavers and gophers.

Through the windless, leafy streets of Sheridan, Wyoming, I saw a few Polish families, an occasional Indian in a black hat; cattlemen in high-heeled boots complaining about the shortage of riders, farmers bemoaning the slow delivery of farm equipment, and both groups suspicious of a United States Employment Service man suggesting they use a more centralized labor bureau than the 'call-boards' that stand in saloons, on which ranchers have long been accustomed to chalk up their labor needs.

South of Sheridan there was rich dairy land, the dense greenness of alfalfa fields, and fat Jerseys nuzzling near lines of willows. As I started to climb away from the peacefulness, a hard-driving rain came on and I settled into a monotonous hum through the green hills ahead. Sheltering pines came up, but as I launched on to wide mountain meadows and saw the aspens quivering under the beating rain, I spontaneously ran the window up and turned on the heater. Whatever secret guilt I felt, about basking in the land for which many other men were dying across oceans, was soothed by the thought that this long assignment had its rough moments. A childish comfort, maybe, but it is the kind that most civilians seek, however complacent they may appear on the surface. Just then, on my left, I saw Lake De Smet, yet another reminder of an indomitable priest, who had come from Belgium to walk and wagon hundreds of miles in dry heat and mountain snows, so long before highway restaurants and automobile heaters that in order to eat he had to plant his own oats and potatoes – the first that Montana ever had. And all this to baptize a few Flathead Indians into the Church.

I barely articulated these thoughts. All I was conscious of was first the rich cattle-land, then the rising hills, the uncomfortable rain, the nestling into the warm car, the quick bell of memory as the name of 'De Smet' went by. Without thinking I turned off the heater.

Far enough away from Father De Smet, the car grew unaccountably warm again. I rubbed my palm against the steamed windshield and peered all around at rolling, sage-drenched hills. It was cheerless land, but not so cheerless as the echoes of an earlier century that roadside signs provided: Crazy Woman Creek, Invasion Gulch, the North Fork and the Middle Fork of the Powder River. For more than 100 miles I had seen only a few human beings, and I was struck by the stoic dignity of an old sheepherder who, against a red rock on a desolate alkaline flat, and surrounded by baaing sheep, stood in an overcoat, his head bent over against the rain. As I went by, nothing more than his eyes moved under rimy white eyebrows, and one eye crinkled into a friendly recognition. It amounted to a conversation.

I passed a few trucks and soon, under gray skies, was going by dingy oilfields, past the dusty warehouses, company shacks, a few working pumps, old storage tanks. South of here was the high, gnarled sandstone rock known as Teapot, which will be forever a suspicious landmark since it gave its name to the nearby gusher successively known as Teapot Dome, the US Navy Petroleum Reserve No. 3, and for a brief time as the Waterloo of the ineffable Interior Secretary Albert B. Fall, who oversaw, for a consideration, a cozy lease for oil company cronies. From here I tumbled down to the tanks and refinery stacks of Casper.

Most of its non-merchant population was employed in some capacity or other in the oil refinery. Before the war it had refined gasoline and crude oil and now felt bad that it had lost its chief market, France. An editor expressed a perhaps unconscious objection to the war by saying that the market was lost 'when France and Germany got into the war'! Although he could boast that Wyoming oil was now at an all-time high, there was an active local resentment against the terrific Texas output: 'We are not even producing up to quota, and in Texas they're running more than 132,000 barrels a day above their quota.' They were obviously jealous of the Texas high-octane plants. Wyoming had none and consequently didn't approve of the temporary abolition of the quota system. There was, however, the prospect of a chrome mine near Casper, 'which'll give us the chance, maybe, to open up something impossible in peacetime.' He brightened when I asked him about coal – 'over to Rock Springs, there's the heaviest production since 1929, and they can't mine enough for the Union Pacific traffic that runs through here these days.' The tourist agencies were feeling even unhappier than the oilmen. Gasoline rationing, in force all over the East, would soon be extended to the whole country. Yellowstone, the first and biggest of the National Parks, would again revert to the bears, the deer, the elk, and the eagles. A few wealthy Eastern families, the agents thought, might be able to acquire an illegal pile of ration coupons to get them there, 'but that's a pretty poor substitute for a tourist season.'

Only the sheep ranchers seemed free from envy and immune from the shame and other artificial proprieties with which the newspapers and publicists were just then injecting the city populations of the country. The price of sheep was 50 percent above normal and there was no ceiling on wool. The Army went into an unlimited market and bought what it wanted. The sheep ranchers were paying off their debts from the 30s and feeling fine.

Out of Casper, I picked up a cowhand, a square, heavy-shouldered man with spindly legs and a face like faded copper. He stood by the highway in jeans and a battered black six-gallon hat and was too diffident to thumb me as I went by. When I swerved into the side of the road, he came trotting after me and climbed in. To me, he was just another cowboy hitching a ride into Cheyenne. But to him this was the end of a life. He had come to Wyoming after the last war, in which he'd been wounded four times, once severely disabled by mustard gas (and if he had any teeth, they never showed in conversation). He had worked on ranches for twenty-two years and he was finished with the Plains. He had heard they wanted men in Denver, skilled men for construction work.

We slid through small, smelly oil towns and out over the infinite brown plains. As we swung into Platte County, there was an almost instantaneous change into beet farms and rich, swaying fields of irrigated wheat. My companion marveled: 'Look at that cow. Up to his belly in feed.' At Chugwater, he asked me to stop. He wanted, he said, just one thing. He came out of a gas station chewing on a candy bar. We crossed the river and drove most of the afternoon through alternate stretches of alfalfa fields, valley farms, and grazing plains again. About thirty miles before Cheyenne, the blue sky turned a grayish-yellow, an eerie gold light lined the long fences, and straight ahead we saw gathering a thunderous cumulus cloud. A quick, untimely twilight came on, a sort of dusty violet haze, not night so much as darkness visible. Ahead, a wide, smoky spout poured from the base of the great cloud and obliterated the town beneath it. I stopped and listened for the long sigh of distant rain. I supposed the heavens were unloosed on Cheyenne. But my friend was bland about the whole thing.

'It's a line-storm all right, but it's forty miles the other side of Cheyenne.'

We moved through a haze in which the black silhouettes of horses floated by, and the small white cross on a cattle pony's grave glared like a dagger. The sage and thistle were a smear of darkest purple. Then the sky lightened, the diffused golden light focused on to the smooth dome of the capitol building; and we came into Cheyenne on a perfect evening.

I don't know if it was the serenity of an evening that had threatened a flood, or the actual prosperity of Cheyenne, that made the men I talked to so calmly proud of their town. It may have been the mood imposed on weaker associates by a Scot of strong character, who told me about the railroads and the retail business. With a state payroll as high as ever (Cheyenne is the state capital), and the railroad shops paying out the highest wages in their history, the merchants' only objection was against the freezing of luxury commodities – radios, refrigerators, and automobiles – that the town's money was itching to buy.

Cheyenne's airport had been the largest civilian maintenance depot. 'So now they bring in unfinished bombers and put on RAF insignia here.'

The train traffic was about 60 percent higher than normal, and freight traffic, which rumbled through at record speeds continuously from midnight to dawn, was two or three times as heavy as any they had known. One of the words I had sickened of long before this was the word 'bottleneck'. It became the wartime synonym for obstacle, interruption, hindrance, difficulty. But here it accurately described the enforced narrowing of a wide band of freight through Sherman Pass, the only place for a couple of hundred miles where trains can cross the Rockies. 'A single tunnel on Sherman Hill,' declared the Scot, uttering each syllable like a general ordering the attack, 'is the real bottleneck of continental traffic.' It was the sort of information you did not bandy around press clubs, or trouble to submit to the Censor. Nobody seemed much scared of the Japs around here, but the railroad men gave me to understand that they would feel a whole lot happier, in another war, if Army freight moved some other way than over railroad tracks.

At night, I stood beside a cattle-rancher who was merely garrulous until he noticed a couple of husky youths blowing a trumpet and a clarinet in a dance orchestra. Then he was choleric. 'We're crying for ranch hands and selling off our breeding stock because there's nobody to care for 'em. I come into Cheyenne and watch a couple of six-footers blowing their lungs out in a dance band.'

He watched the even tapping of their feet and had to leave. Under persuasion, he admitted that Wyoming livestock men were making more money than they'd seen in a generation. But he seemed roused to chronic abuse by the ration boards and the Office of Price Administration. I asked him a favorite question, about the ranching skills that could be strictly defined as irreplaceable. He turned his red, veined face toward me.

'You can put it down in black-and-white, the help you can spare and the men you must have. They don't give a damn what the job is, they think that you're tryin' to shield some goddam mother's son or other. Take the sheep ranchers. Branding, shearing, lambing, and fall round-up – you gotta have men that have done it a hundred times. But they sit there like a lot of edgy old spinsters and say, this lad's under twenty-six, and what a fine leatherneck Dan McGoldrick's son'd make.'

As he rose from the table he tossed his hat on his head and, tugging down the brim, said, 'Don't you forget it, son, folks around here are more dubious about Washington than the outcome of the war.' He spoke, of course, for himself. But I was assured that the big cattle and sheep farmers felt the same way.

The next day I continued on US 87 over highland ranges, through irrigated valleys thick with cattle, through hilly cherry orchards, coal-mining settlements, and then joined the heavy trucking traffic from these mines, and the orchards, into Denver.

Denver, Colorado, was the largest city I had been in since Seattle. What you could learn there was not so much the local problems of Denver, which have been specific enough in their time, but the type of war problems that affected a whole region. Denver is not an easy city to know. Tourists from the Eastern or West Coast cities often express an obviously affected disappointment in it: that is, they pretend to be surprised that a city of a quarter million, the biggest American City across the half-continent between Kansas City and Los Angeles, should not flaunt the usual metropolitan appointments. I say this disappointment is pretended because in fact they rarely expect anything else. They dismiss it as an overgrown mining town. So it is. But it is many other things besides.

It is a railroad center, a state capital, the fruit packer for thousands of square miles of irrigated orchards, a labor pool for gold-, silver-, and coal-miners, a winter hangout for all sorts of itinerant farm work. Above all, it is the trading mart of the whole Rocky Mountain region and the Great Plains' central market for 3 million sheep, a half million hogs, a half million cattle, and 15,000 horses and mules, a year.

It was unlike any other city I had seen, because there was an air of surface normality. Unlike San Diego or Portland, it didn't seem to magnify any single headache of the cities at war – housing, delinquency, an outlander population. But below the surface it presented a whole series of different problems, problems of prairie, of cities, of factory labor and stoop labor, seen almost in their naked manifestation as pure cultures of diseases epidemic in greatly different regions of the country.

The 'immigrant' labor: Denver had not been an industrial town and resented each succeeding construction crew. They had had a rubber company that employed about 2,000. Now they had 10,000 more working at a Remington arms plant, another 10,000 at a Boeing heavy bomber assembly plant, and there was to be a new ordnance factory to employ 14,000. 'The only folks on relief are diehard unemployables. The Works Progress Administration had to shut down.' There appeared to be little local pride in these particular industries, but everybody was quick to tell you about the prefabrication of ship parts at the Wright shipyard (a shipyard a mile above sea-level!), which had more to do than Californians knew with some of Mr Kaiser's astonishing ship construction records.

In the trades they knew something about, there were quite new problems. There was a mining problem, a sugar beet problem, a Negro problem, a labor problem.

The Mining Commission of the War Production Board had ruled that mines that did not produce more than 70 percent of basic war materials would lose priorities in mining machinery. This order would have put Colorado's mines out of business. Many mines, Cripple Creek is a good example, have to introduce base metals to smelt their gold and silver. There was naturally an uproar. Washington, however forwent the bureaucratic luxury of maintaining its principles at all costs, even at the cost of efficiency the principles were designed in the first place to ensure. The WPB – at whose sensible prompting I couldn't find out – admitted the real problem and told the Colorado mines that it would not rescind this principle in writing but promised it would not be enforced in practise. It was one of the few instances I was able to gather out West of Washington's willingness to solve a regional war problem with sympathetic realism. So the Colorado mines were working to capacity.

The sugar beet has long been Colorado's pet bone of contention with the Department of Agriculture. Colorado beet production has been forcibly restricted by the government in deference to Cuba and Hawaii, victims of a vast single crop they must export or starve. The two catastrophic depressions of Cuba are too well known to be enlarged on here. But it is surprising to talk to Colorado beet growers and discover an active enmity toward the Hawaiians and Cubans, whom they tend to regard as prospering favorite children of the Department of Agriculture. To point out the heavy American invest-ment in Cuban sugar, the bare need of export that Cuba must satisfy in order to buy any manufactured goods at all, the direct relation of the Colorado beet price to sugar prices in Cuba, the experience of Cuba in seeing its entire economy founder in an ocean of unshipped sugar (so that in 1922 it had to borrow 50 million dollars to keep its government running), to mention all this is to be suspected of being a fifth-columnist. There were 135,000 acres of sugar beets in Colorado in 1941. When the war came, the government had to tell the growers to forget the quota and grow everything they could. It was 220,000 acres in 1942. But this order was not regarded by Colorado's beet farmers as a desperate and temporary expedient. It was a blundering confession from Washington that it had been wrong. The growers might have been expected to jeer with pride and then turn to making the most avid use of their new freedom. But their dilemma was to be told that they could grow all they liked just when they were losing the labor that would guarantee even a minimum crop. At best the sugar beet worker is a slippery commodity. He is a summer worker and a winter dependant. Some of the more comfortable Denver citizens call him a winter parasite on the city. When the Works Progress Administration said it couldn't provide relief for summer labor, 'the sugar companies raised hell, and the WPA had to back down.'

The draft and the war industries soon converted these valued 'parasites' into soldiers or factory workers in better money than any that had ever come their way. They had been thought of as contemptible, necessary drones – Mexicans, Filipinos, Negroes. Busy elsewhere, they were now beyond price. The whites don't like the work, and if they did would demand wages far above the stoop labor rates. The Governor of Idaho had suggested closing the State House and asking all government employees to go to work in the beet fields. Also, the prevailing ethical codes about child-labor were a nagging strain on the conscience, and in some places the conscience yielded. Some growers thought longingly of the thousands of Japanese-Americans who had been 'removed' from the coast. Weren't the Japs beet workers? In Colorado they were, and it is not hard to appreciate the special handicap under which they came into the state.

The War Relocation Board asked the Governors of all the Rocky Mountain states how they felt about receiving large numbers of Japanese-Americans. Eight Governors were absolutely against it. However, Governor Carr of Colorado said that if the government would agree to give protection to the incoming Japanese-Americans he would be willing to accept them. The attitude of Colorado, he said, was that these people are American citizens with equal rights. In 1942, anywhere out West, this simple opinion amounted to a heroic, almost revolutionary stand.

Seventeen hundred of them came in from California under protection of the federal government, and under various degrees of restriction. Denver absorbed most of them. And the sugar growers were in the main disgusted to see that these Japanese were not only *not* a consignment of peasants, but a highly skilled, well-mannered group of Americans, equally as educated and equally indisposed to stoop labor. Many of them did go into the beet fields, but the mere sight of them was enough to titillate the righteous indignation, the vague pride of 'race', and the guilty resentment of their equality before the law, that were just then in the West (and indeed most other places) the dominant and most easily enjoyed of the popular emotions. The citizens of Fort Morgan, the center of the beet farming area, held a public meeting 'to do something about the Japs'.

In Denver, it was gloomily admitted, it might be necessary to fetch Negroes from Oklahoma, and Navajos from New Mexico.

'And that's bad,' said a grower, 'real bad. There's an Army camp right out of Colorado Springs. And there are going to be Negro troops.'

Apparently the labor relations in the new factories were fairly calm, too calm for a disgruntled organizer I talked to. He lamented the failure of a drive to organize the new workers. He found them skeptical and apathetic toward strong unions. The old-timers, he said, had been softened by the wartime largesse of the employers. Under the stress of war contracts, and in the guise of patriotism, an employer could make a better offer to the workers than anything they had ever fought for, in prewar wage drives. 'They can fight niggardliness,' said the organizer, 'but they can't fight generosity.'

He began to generalize from his experience of factories, and mines, in Colorado and was not averse to making pronouncements about the fate of union labor that he intended to cover the whole country. He thought that the rising membership of the CIO was a wartime phenomenon and was due to workers who were new to a good thing and thought the power of the union would be able to freeze it, to convert high wages into a postwar minimum. He thought it was no sort of a trend.

On my way out of Denver next morning, I knew that I was leaving the Great Plains, and that I should soon be out of the West. And again I had the sense that I was leaving behind not a region, which in a European language would mean a county or province, but a country. Another American country.

At such times the whole experience of that country shrinks to a précis, to a few symbols that perhaps have no objective fairness. But to every man these associations will say more about the land and the people he has observed than all his efforts to telescope the industries and crops and statistical resources the guide books list. My mind flipped over with the speed of memory (so much faster than the speed of light) an irrational kaleidoscope of images: the drenched majesty of the Douglas firs in Washington, and through the Bitterroots, the slow service in a restaurant in Seattle, the grimy wounds of Butte and Anaconda, the old sheepherder with his head down, the rancher reddening at a saxophone player in Cheyenne, the walking-beams of oil wells, the granite buttes above fenced haystacks, the dog eating cellophane in Wallace, Montana; the steady clean wind over the heaving plains, the whiteness of the marble slabs marking the Battle of the Little Big Horn, the potlike ultramarine of bluebirds on telephone wires, the white crucifix on a cow pony's grave.

I had come in two weeks through great alternations of mountains and bare plains. The human clearings made in these natural empires do not seem today to be there chiefly to establish temples to God. They were compact settlements of cement and steel and lumber where men poured their energies into the cold, fierce discipline of armament manufacture. There is an almost tragic discrepancy between the disciplines that nature invites, and which in such lovely idealizations as the Tennessee Valley Authority it receives, and the merciless discipline it is able to achieve only when its purpose is the waging of systematic destruction. Suddenly, on breaks in the forests, on high plateaus of the Plains, are small tablets commemorating a priest and a companion, two priests perhaps, who walked 500 miles of plain and mountain to save the souls of a few Indians. Who planted grain, built gristmills, and set up a community of a few families under the priest. These were the servants of the same Church that now appears, to the outsider, to be so secure and urban and enervated in this country. A Church whose servants round the enormous arc from San Diego, California, to St Xavier, Montana, staked out the fundamental communities of half of America. They did not shun desert thirst, mountain snows, arid plains, nor did they make clearings to exert the false disciplines of 'successful' industry. They used nature as the raw material to face and tame if possible, and where it could not be tamed, they admitted defeat with grace. They organized courage and tenderness to make a society, as if society could be made no other way. Here, indeed, in the West, the Far West, and the Northwest, and the Great Plains, Catholicism was a revolutionary religion, moving with the spiritual blitheness of its Founder. Yet it is in America, the country founded on the promise of continuing revolution, that Catholicism has ceased to be revolutionary and become authoritarian, dependent for its unquestioning power on discreet conformity, on old city holdings, firm links with urban politics, enforcing its will by the guilty force of negative taboos. And, as a continuing force in American life, it condones and exploits everywhere the one active discipline of the Western world – the brotherhood men most secretly hate but most publicly fear – the brotherhood of respectability.

The congealing of the first pure, missionary flame into the crust of wealth, authority, and respectability, may, for all I know, be the fate of the Church in many other countries. But in the American West, it is most grand and shocking.

IO

From Wheat to Steel

If the Pecos River is the West's beginning, Denver is, by the same scale of land and living, its last city leaving. It may be an Easterner's view of the West that when there are no mountains there is no West. But as you drive east from Denver, on US 40-287, and the skyline of the Rockies at your back recedes into memory, you have the sense not so much of exploring new country as of being launched on an intervening ocean or plane between West and East. You are driving along the last wide shelf of the Great Plains. There are sheep and cattle and sage, but soon the signs flick by pointing east to the massive layer of black soil that is Western and Central Kansas and the boundless grain country. One of the signs reads, '24,000 acres for family size farms, wheat, corn, beans'.

I left Denver in the early morning with the sun striking horizontally into the windshield. But before noon mile after mile of treeless land offered the same signature of the winter wheat country: the one-story farm buildings, the windmills on the horizon like fishing smacks. And as the sun rose and left shadowless the wide arc of green wheat, far, far ahead you would see grain elevators like smokestacks that never sailed any nearer. As the last slow undulations of the Great Plains flattened into Kansas, the wind came up and tumbleweed scurried across the highway, clung hesitantly to the fences, and then blew away and went bounding out of sight. Hour after hour I drove across a land the length of England, and in every direction was the lazy, waving ocean of green wheat. Not being Milton, I find it impossible to describe the sense of massive and sober reassurance you get from a landscape where there is nothing but luscious wheat. All you can do is say the word 'vast' and strain your imagination to encompass it.

Every single object in this landscape, whether it is a house, a tree, a billboard, or an oncoming automobile is endowed by the surrounding plain with a naked sort of courage. I saw black specks hovering ahead ten minutes before they resolved themselves into six black horses standing against the wind, their manes waving slightly, and as I went by I wanted to pack them into the car and whisk them away to a farm or city or some other place that man has made for human warmth and security. Merely to pass them by is like leaving a wounded man to the oncoming night.

But this level and lonely land is the American factory of winter wheat. A mild winter with regular gentle rain, a warm spring, a long dry summer – these are the natural blessings that, fortified by the magic machine known as a combine, made possible the growing of wheat by assembly-line methods. A hundred years ago it took a Hercules to harvest five acres a day. During the last war the steam thresher, and the horse-drawn reaper, gave Kansas its famous opportunity to pinch-hit for Russia's Black Sea harvest, cut off from the hungry importers of Western Europe. After the last war came the combine, which cuts and threshes the wheat, disposes of the straw as it goes, and pours wheat like oil into waiting trucks. It harvests sixty acres a day. And in 1942, it took only ten men to take care of from 5–10,000 acres. In China it's said to take 243 man-hours of labor to grow an acre of wheat. In Kansas it takes from one to two man-hours. So all through Western and Central Kansas, I did not hear about any invading hordes of Southerners or other 'foreigners'. Nor was there much complaint about a shortage of labor. The combines are the essential workers, and the chief threat to the wheat crop is a shortage of gasoline or a broken tread or stripped gear.

This huge area, which was once nothing but buffalo range, was settled by mixed American stock, including many Germans and Russians. During the last war they changed over to wheat and prospered as the price went up to the dizzy high of $1.75 a bushel. In the early 30s it fell to 38 cents and below. Some of these farmers gave up and moved West. Down in the southwest corner of Kansas, where the topsoil had blown away and the drought of the mid-30s turned the land into a howling Dust Bowl, hungry and heartbroken families scrambled out of their half-buried farmhouses (where even as late as

1939 I saw sand shoaled level with the bedroom windows) and drove off west to California. At one time, the situation was bad enough to convince the economist Rexford Tugwell that all the families living down there should be pulled out and Eastern Colorado and Western Kansas should be allowed to go back to desert. But some farmers stayed on, meaning to keep firm to the insane faith that ruined crops and prolonged drought are the bad accidents of Nature. The Department of Agriculture, marvelously ridiculed at the time for its crusade to put the Dust Bowl back to grass, eventually persuaded some of these farmers that the Dust Bowl was a man-made tragedy. Once the government crusade was accepted by the very people it was primarily directed at, it ceased to be news in the nation's newspapers. 'That man' in the White House had been proved a visionary again. And the columnists and editorial writers turned to the jealous defense of the Supreme Court and other issues. It is hard today to convince even the casual traveler that Eastern Colorado and Western Kansas were only a few years ago barren flats dark at noonday with whirling dust. It may be worth setting down here, for the American record as well as Roosevelt's, that today they have a new name for the Dust Bowl. It is called the Beef Bowl. They put it back to grass – and cattle! Now, in this once stricken area, the farmer pays out 25 percent of his crop and the government takes care of his overhead. His cash return is figured by the government on a twenty-year history of the cash value of the farm. In lean years it pays him accordingly, hoping to smooth out the risks of the 'peaks and valleys' of growing one crop and trusting to God for rain and the regular buyer for a market. In this way, the government calculates, the farmer will be able to be sure of paying for the butcher, the doctor, the school. The gratitude of these Western wheat-farmers is a private sense of security they have rarely known. It is all too little known to the country that attributed the Dust Bowl and the farming depression to the academic mischief of 'professors' and other incompetents in Washington.

After Ogallah, Kansas, the landscape noticeably contracts. And this is reassuring but detracts from the lonely beauty of the wheat-lands. Near Ellis a little creek appears, and trees with picnic tables clinging gratefully to them. At Ellis a roadside sign announces, 'Boyhood home of Walter P. Chrysler'. It was as unexpected as a lighthouse, a startling

assurance that civilization is looming near and all is well. You rumin-
ate over this sign and do not wonder that a young boy should have
fantasies of luxurious automobiles that would whisk him with an
arrow's directness away from yawning Kansas.

Before and after Russell, oil derricks reared up like skeleton lighthouses. Then as the sun went down the welcome smell of hay and
clover floated on the wind. Huge, round-bellied grain elevators
plunged by like battleships. Shade trees broke the long vista, and the
ocean divided up into fields of diversified crops. In the evening twilight
near Salina, soldiers strolled along tree-lined roads. The railroad yard
came into view and ranks of huge grain elevators with parked automobiles at the foot of them. As the lights twinkled and I pulled up near the
busy hotel, I saw a cavalry officer climb into the back seat of a car with
a merry-looking girl. It was a warming sight, like getting your land-legs
again after a long ocean voyage. We were back to civilization, and the
norm of life. I went into a drugstore and celebrated with a double
chocolate milk shake, thick enough to lean in.

In Salina, you learn again that 'war' means all things to all men, but
mostly it means the day-by-day effect on their own job or crop. The
big problem around here is what to do with all the stored wheat that
in peacetime is normally exported. The farmers do not like to be asked
whether the storage of wheat wouldn't have become a Kansas problem anyway, since France and Italy and little Austria started growing
most of the wheat they used to take from the United States and
Canada. The war has made it plausible for the farmers to attribute the
wheat surplus to Adolf Hitler and to the incompetence of 'the men in
Washington' who cannot provide enough boxcars to get the wheat
away from Kansas. They are storing it in schoolrooms and empty
stores, in churches, in railroad shops, and in garages closed down for
lack of gasoline and customers. There is an inevitable grumble brewing among the farmers of Western Kansas over the Department of
Agriculture's proposal to take the subsidy off wheat and use it to
encourage the growing of soybean and other crops that can be
adapted to special military needs. The farmers of the Western part of
the state are the ones who fear this idea most, because theirs is a single crop. For better or worse, they staked their future on wheat. And,
they point out, the government encouraged them.

Every mile east of Salina is a visible move nearer the type of farming the Western farmers complain that the Corn Belt-trained boys in the Department of Agriculture think of when they describe 'a farm' – namely, prosperous, diversified-crop farming. After Salina the horizon seemed to draw closer and fill up with happy cattle. The impressive monotony of wheat is far behind. From here to Kansas City you go through a climate only slightly changed, but changed in the direction of dependability. There is more rain. And so you go past cow pasture and alternating fields of alfalfa and wheat sorghum, barley, and rye. The cattlemen confirm the remarks of the rancher in West Texas. They are rubbing their hands in glee over the enormous demand for cattle. They are not thinking of tomorrow, for that is not in the nature of cattlemen, who are inveterate gamblers, buying on a high market, often being forced to sell when the ceiling price has tumbled down, and losing everything with philosophical blasphemy. Lest, however, you get the idea that the war means nothing to them but fat beef at fancy prices, they suddenly remember their 'patriotism'. The cattlemen then look hard-put-upon and tell you that the cost of labor has gone up by about one-third.

So for a half-day's driving through dairy country, wheat-land, sorghum, and rye, through a landscape cozy with bellowing cattle, I came to the potato belt, then to garden suburbs, and by night threaded my way through the treacherous outskirts of Kansas City (with well-concealed factories glowing at sudden intervals through trees that you supposed harbored nothing but alfalfa).

Going through the black suburbs of the city, I almost ran down a sixteen-year-old boy from a small town in Western Kansas. He hopped aboard and pretty soon we picked up a soldier, and for the next half-hour slid around in the city's dark outskirts like an eel in mud. The boy was eager to see the big city, and the soldier, who was an Easterner, chuckled and kidded him about the implied provincialism of any city west of the Eastern Seaboard. But the boy's enthusiasm was well founded. There is no better archetype of the All-American city than Kansas City. In a sense, it is the only 'typical' American city, which sounds a ridiculous definition until you consider that 'normal' eyesight is the lucky possession of one person in 20,000. For Kansas City is uniquely *of* several regions though not in them. Its daily bread and its politics have their source in the western wheat-lands of Kansas, in the lumber and commercial traffic of the Missouri River, in the dairy interests of the Great Lakes states, in the industrial capitals of the Midwest, Chicago, Detroit, Toledo, Cleveland. The sober front page of the *Kansas City Times* looks like a careful synopsis of the newspapers of the nation. The political news from Washington very rarely hogs the front page. It is a necessary balance to news from four other great regions, in which the people of Kansas City have too realistic an interest to slight. So Kansas City is in this way a genuine American capital city. Rolling into it come trains carrying 2,000 bushels of wheat per car, one-third to a half of all the winter wheat grown in the United States, over an area extending from Southern Nebraska down to the Texas Panhandle and Northern Oklahoma. It is the capital feeder steer market of North America, and its largest pay-roll is in livestock. It handles the luscious strawberry crop of Southwest Missouri. According to the direction from which they come, trains entering Kansas City may also be carrying daylong loads of corn from Missouri, or hogs from Iowa, cotton or bauxite from Arkansas, steers from Texas, dairy cattle from Wisconsin, mules from Missouri. And the trains going out may carry anything from cheese and seed and flour to flat silver and corncob pipes.

The war came and the effects were swift and sure. The price of cattle rose at once. With a ceiling on fed steers, there was an instant fear that the buyers wouldn't be able to pay the old prices for thin steers from the Southwest. They cannot wait for fat cattle and are killing them under two years old. Farm wages went up by ten dollars a month to hold the farmhands away from the factories east. The Missouri strawberry crop declined because the reliable itinerant labor is no longer itinerant. 'Suitcase' farms were being merged or sold, for, as one war-worker said, newly settled in the city, 'I don't have enough rubber on my tires to come from seven miles, bale hay, and go home again.'

But the change that alarmed the oldsters was the gradual but un-preventable threat of Kansas City's turning into a major manufacturing city. An ordnance plant had gone up nearby, a bomber plant, and small arms factories. The buses and automobiles rattled out at dawn to a powder plant at De Soto. Even Mexicans from the packing plants and rail yards had the nerve to leave town for a better job or apply at the neighboring factories. The comfort of the city's calm and leafy residential suburb was being disturbed by the whimsical refusal of hired help, even Negroes, to mow lawns. Domestics who for years had cherished and planned for their night off had gone into the factories and machine shops and now could spend all their evenings off mingling heedlessly with the fine American swarm of accents on Twelfth Street. In darktown, there was high and happy laughter in half-lit bedrooms, and in backyards much clapping and shrill chatter over barbecues. For at the beginning, there were no Negroes in the factories, so they took the place of white domestics and were hired by people who had never had 'help' before in their lives. The Negroes in service, however, contrasted the new prosperity of their homes with the unyielding Jim Crow line down at the railroad station, where there were showers for white soldiers and none for their boys. 'We're all right to shoot at,' was one terse comment, 'but not so good to keep clean.'

Nighttime in Kansas City has its own inimitable pattern of sights and sounds. The running dialogue of Italians and Mexicans shouting across the smoking rail yards, the black bellies of grain elevators on the river bottom, were merely the necessary industrial junk-heap you expect to find leading up to the shopping district. Even a long drive along the boulevards ringing the city, dipping through Negro neighborhoods and swinging through the night into sunken gardens, was nothing to surprise the Easterner who exercised that wonderful selective memory of nostalgia and thought only of what his town had that this town didn't. He sighed for the Wrigley's sign in Times Square and the vaudeville show at Loew's State.

But at last the tour that my passengers tolerated so courteously was over, and when we hit Main and Twelfth, the boy saw hotcakes browning on a well-lit griddle and was seized with sudden hunger. The soldier got out too. It struck me as characteristically American that the country boy from Kansas and the Eastern city boy should both expect the same things from the big city. Their tolerant impatience of the things that make Kansas City unlike any other town on earth only sharpened the oddity of the image they desired in common – the nightlife of a metropolis. In another land, the country boy might have shown some shyness at the approach to a norm of life far from that of his farm kitchen. But most Americans, except perhaps in parts of New England and the South, are at home with city habits to a degree that would awe and terrorize a Normandy peasant or even a city-bred Yorkshire boy on a visit to London. In most cities outside New York, it would be risky to dogmatize about the similarities of people in nightclubs. What you notice about the patrons of a Kansas City nightclub is the general ease and conformity of manners. But this is one of those misleading standardizations that merely makes farmers, lumbermen, steelworkers, furniture salesmen, lawyers, and store clerks come together without friction.

Even in the Terrace Grill of the Hotel Muehlbach, which is the night-blooming cereus of the sprawling workaday city, a city-born European might assume he was at last with his own kind, but he would be failing to recognize one of the minor American achievements – the capacity of people far apart in their social background and origins to clothe themselves in an air of easy elegance. Next morning, the elegance of the Muehlbach's nightlife seemed as far away as Hollywood. In baking heat, early buyers sweated in seersucker suits and bid $13.85 for hogs and $13.35 for packing sows. The wheat market pondered reports from Southwestern Kansas of crop damage due to heat and lack of rain. Through the meat markets, housewives scurried, buying up legs of lamb, chuck roast, chickens, cubed steaks, redfish and kingfish steaks that, just to look upon, would have caused any English housewife to keel over in a dead faint. War-workers' wives, in slacks and halters, dragged bawling children to a furniture sale on Grand Street and put down crisp twenty-dollar bills, and grimy singles, for maple beds, floor lamps, and Hoover Specials ('only one dollar' – with the reservation in almost invisible type, 'if combined with $95 purchase in any department'). There was a war on but you could still buy gas ranges, sterling silver, electric mixers, radios, razor blades, and Lucite combs.

And you could get all the gasoline you wanted. There was no need to feel bad about this because in Chicago former Republican presidential candidate Alf Landon (who lost to Roosevelt in a landslide) was telling a meeting of businessmen that there was no need for rationing of gasoline anywhere, even in the East. He also made a complaint that was applaudingly echoed in Kansas City wherever men wondered about the growing surplus of grain. This was the time when the ordinary American, made to feel foolish by the nation's lack of natural rubber, expected that by Christmas American ingenuity would have discovered some laughably simple substitute, as good or better than the original. In Kansas City they naturally had heard about rubber from grain alcohol, and in the summer of 1942, it would have been a disloyal Missourian who suspected there might be a better method. On this subject, Missourians would have been the last to say 'Show me.' And Mr Landon was speaking as a patriotic Kansan when he urged the government to convert distillers for mass production of alcohol and build new grain alcohol plants 'close to the source of raw materials'. Every farmer in Kansas and Missouri knew where that was. And they could easily forgive the reversal of Republican doctrine implied in Mr Landon's apology, 'I think we should do everything to cut the cost of government, but not in a situation of this kind.'

Leaving Kansas City northeast on US 69, you can have few doubts that you are entering into the country's most prosperous farming area. In another country the road would wind round the high banks of hayfields, and you would have to stop every hour or so and creep courteously past droves of geese and plodding horses. But US 69 starts out as a divided highway and narrows into a cement road so smooth that in Europe it would be known as the Via Germanica or the Great Northeaster, and would be lovingly shown to visiting Americans, who would nod politely and wonder what the excitement was about, since it is merely the old American standby, the nerve system of American travel – the divided cement highway. On each side of it up through Missouri were fields of blackberries and plums, and alternating with the now monotonous patriotic billboards ('Oil is Ammunition, Use It Wisely', 'Pay Your Taxes 'n Beat The Axis', 'Buy Blowproof Tires – Remember More Care Means Less Wear') were local advertisements for 'Saddle Horses Show Prospects', 'Foundation Stock, Prize Stallions for Public Service'. Turning left at Excelsior Springs, you go due north to Winston, whose undying fame is due to the summer night sixty-odd years ago when the Rock Island night train was relieved of $9,000 by, allegedly, the dashing James Brothers. I say 'allegedly' because Frank was acquitted.

This rolling, highly cultivated country goes up hill and down dale, and it is hard to remind yourself that it was once known as the north-western plains. Here it was good to meet men who were not embarrassed to tell you that the war had relieved them of most of their anxieties. They were insuring their crops for three years instead of one. I noticed again, as with wheat farmers, that a man will adopt one of two perfectly sincere attitudes according to how you approach him. Begin by talking about the battlefronts, the depressing Japanese sweep across the Pacific, the murderous Russian offensive, and you have given him the cue to feel and talk like a right-minded citizen. He will then talk responsibly, with the national interest at heart, about the comforting fact that so far there has been no inflation in land values. But walk right into his cornfield, exchange the time of day, admire a stallion, and ask him how's business and he will grin, wipe his forehead, and say that the last two years have been fine, and if the war keeps on the next two years will be better.

After Bethany, the road winds and has beveled shoulders for drainage. This is the region the government has tried to reclaim since the Depression. The signs read, 'US Dept. of Agriculture. Terracing'. Or 'US Soil Reclamation Service – Contour Plowing'. Just before I crossed the Iowa border, I ran into a powerful, rock-jawed old farmer who would give pause to the believers in a peace rooted in the natural bonds of Anglo-American friendship. I admired the careful contouring of his land, the well-kept barns, the fine variety of his crops. 'Yeah,' he said, 'just like the old country.' He had come north from Southern Missouri. He was born in Westphalia.

Des Moines, Iowa, at war is typical of any small Midwestern retail center for a wide farming area. If the farmer is prosperous, the town is prosperous, and there wasn't a retail store I went into that had any complaints to offer. It is the retail and distributing center of the state. Here the farmers buy their washing machines and their farm tools. The small manufacturers of farm tools had switched over to war work. A company that made plows was now making tank treads. Aside from retail prosperity, the main fact, the town did not have to invent good causes to be proud of. The Women's Army Auxiliary Corps had just established its headquarters there, and already the square appearance their uniforms give them was a new source of town pride to high-minded citizens, and the occasion for unprintable ribaldry from store clerks and small fry. It was not the fault of Des Moines that there was, too, a startling circulation of mischievous rumors about the manners and morals of the WAACS that soon traveled around the nation. It would have happened in any town, in any state. But what could not happen in many other states outside the Midwest was the remarkably high enlistment in the Navy. For it is an odd fact that the American Navy recruits more sailors from Iowa, farm boys who have never seen the sea, than from any other state in the country.

The Office of Civilian Defense was having hard-sledding in Des Moines. To most of its citizens there was such a preposterous unreality about the idea of the Nazis bombing a small town in the middle of a corn patch, 1,500 miles from the East Coast, that the recruiting of air-raid wardens had been left, hilariously, to the Junior League. In view of this good irony, it seemed unnecessary to defend Des Moines against charges of complacency. But complacency was just then the word that any angry local group hurled at anybody it disliked, in a thousand cities of America. And the word came up heatedly in conversation. Nobody I talked with seriously seemed to believe that Des Moines would be bombed, except the people who make a profession of finding other people complacent.

There are few states where you can land almost anywhere and pick up a war story that is typical of the whole state. But Iowa is one. From the Missouri River to the Minnesota line, an Iowan from any place could be dropped anywhere else and know he was on his home ground. It is a green and cozy landscape, with square fields of purple-y black soil, planted with corn, running over little folding hills, always up to a house and a barn. The barns have gambrel roofs with an overhang and are gray-white and sometimes red. And their tiny wren-towers flick the open sky like gallant pennants, souvenirs of 'the old country', an Englishman might think. But in Iowa, 'the old country' is all things to all men. In the north central part, they are mostly Scandinavians and Germans. In the central part many small towns are of mixed racial origin, and mixed American origin – Flugstad, McCallsburg, Madrid, Van Meter, Stratford, Scranton, and Guthrie Center. In the northwest, some Dutch (there is a Dutch consul at Orange City). And though like any other state it has its oddities – it makes calendars and fountain pens – it is the *World Almanac* and not the average native that tells you so. Most natives proudly reel off the statistic that over no similar area in the world is the soil so consistently fertile, or the crops so diversified. But to the traveler and to the Allies who benefit from Lend-Lease, Iowa means hogs and corn. I drove hours on end along straight roads that follow the section lines, where the turns are always at right angles. And on every side was the rich, deep, purple soil, the rhythmical embroidery of sprouting corn, and through rolling fields of clover the sleek blobs of hogs. A hog *couchant* in a field of clover would be a happy coat of arms for Iowa, though its reckless flaunting would tend to incite the poor farmers of Tennessee to suicide or immediate migration north and west. Such roadside signs as 'Poland Chinas' and 'Farceur Belgians' are as commonplace in Iowa as historical markers in Virginia.

This is the heart of the farming Midwest. And this is the region to which all foreign economists, agricultural writers, special investigators, and newspapermen gravitate to study 'the American farmer'. Why he should be sought here is probably an intriguing study in itself. Perhaps there is no single reason, though if there were I would agree with the Western wheat and livestock farmer that because the Department of Agriculture is staffed by Midwesterners, Washington and the newspapers and their readers unwittingly accept the small Midwestern diversified-crop farm as 'typical' of the country.

But there is no such animal as a 'typical' American farmer, and it is his constant hardship that there isn't. For if there were, he would be organized and have a representative voice in Washington. The urban reader will wonder just who the powerful and much-touted Farm Bloc represents. And the answer need not be evasive. The Farm Bloc is not a bloc, but a paper name that tries to throw a blanket over the jostling, and competing, inmates of a shared bed in Washington. The Farm Bloc describes several powerful lobbies of big farming interests, marketing cooperatives, regional granges, purchasing and selling agents, and hardy opportunists who frankly make a political profession of playing off the grievances of one group against another. The farmers and their wives who belong to the conservative National Grange often deplore the western Farmers Union as the first Bolshevik organization to mar our fair land. Small farmers the country over rise in choler at the mention of Ed O'Neal, President of the Farm Bureau Federation, as they would at the name of Hitler, and without knowing why.

The combined membership of the three big farm unions is about 2.5 million farmers. Add a generous million more members of the regional breeders and dairy associations and the like. And somewhere across America are left another 26 million men and women who live on farms. Nor must you think of this vast peasantry as a solid tribe of outcasts. They read nearly 300 different farm journals, all thundering righteously in behalf of 'the American farmer', all presuming to represent him with arguments and policies as different as they can be, all magnifying a local vision to embrace a continent they have never seen, all speaking for America when they are talking specifically and strictly for themselves. So it is not only the urban newspaper reader who is deceived into imagining a 'typical American farmer' that doesn't exist. A farmer himself, anywhere across the American landscape, will rarely pause to stress that he is speaking only for his own crop or county or region.

The American farmer in short is a thousand types, plowing the earth over a score of climates, concerned with one crop, and his interests are either poles removed from the other types, or they conflict sharply with them. It is always worth remembering this when, as an Easterner or a European, you drive through the Midwest and believe yourself to be crossing the hallowed ground of 'the typical American farmer'.

Soon after you cross the Minnesota line, after Northwood, the land spreads into prairie, then into larger-scale, more spacious dairy farming country. The highway winds round lakes. The farms are beautifully kept and the barns large and majestic. It is no surprise to notice that the names on the letterboxes and above the stores of small towns are Scandinavian: Holmquist, Lelthold, Huldrist. Although it is only 135 miles from the Iowa line to Minneapolis, it seems like a long, slow ride. But this is because the roads wind again and the landscape has broadened. Soon the French names come up and you know that you are in the old fur-trading country – Lamartine and Faribault. Up here, the long fields are green as only fields are green that are sharpened by frequent rain. It is a northern landscape. The sky is smeared with gray clouds. The horizon is faint with a mist that etches the trees like England. And when you stop the car and rest, you hear the surprising signature tune of the wet summer – a mosquito.

For thirty miles north of Faribault, you swing over wonderful dairy pastures where every prospect pleases and the land seems abundantly able to answer any call the Army or the government could make on it. Intermittent stands of maples and oaks are just so much pleasing decoration to sweeping acres that fatten sleek Holsteins for the butter and cream market. In Northfield, Minnesota, you hear from the natives that they are producing something like 70,000 pounds of cream a day. This is mentioned casually as a natural thing to expect from such land. You follow the Cannon River for a while, and at Farmington they are so indisposed to launch into sales talks that you have to wring from a member of the Milk Producer's Cooperative the astounding fact that this small town with a population of about 1,500 souls receives every day a quarter-million pounds of milk.

You curl west again before going north through green truck-farms, small flour mills at the edge of towns. You feel a cool breeze as you ride around the edge of blue lakes. The Swan flour mills, barns, and railroad lines converge, and ahead of you are the towering cavalcades of flour mills, the bridges spanning the river, the grain elevators of Minneapolis.

What was interesting about the Twin Cities (Minneapolis and St Paul) was not so much the peculiar regional problems of the American flour milling center as the lack of anxiety over social problems that had other cities by the ear. I assume that Minneapolis too has its juvenile delinquents and feels as coldly superior to its 'immigrants' as Mobile, Los Angeles, or Portland, Oregon. But through the Great Lakes states you notice at once, if you have driven up from the South or West, the casual sobriety of the people. Huntington Cairns has written persuasively about the effect of climate on character, and certainly the Twin Cities inhabit another world of values from the bright, violent sentiment of Southern California, the stewing bafflement of the workers in the Gulf Coast war towns, the febrile restlessness of New York. It is a northern climate that attracted mostly Yankees, Scandinavians, and Germans. They do not boast of skyscrapers, fine food, dramatic scenery, or exhilarating nightlife. They do not even boast any longer of their superlative technique of pouring and grinding and cleaning and loading the grain from the elevators to the loading trucks, which long ago caused an English novelist to declare that the function of the Midwest was 'to sublimate human intelligence'. They do not boast at all. They mention first, as if it were anybody's chief social ambition, that Minneapolis has more families who own their own homes than any city in the country. You can well believe it. Drive into the city from the south and you go for several miles through the most handsome and solid suburbs anywhere in the country. It is not the frantic, planless suburbia of a thousand towns of the East and West, but miles of imposing houses and well-tended gardens set back from long avenues of old trees. I wondered about juvenile delinquency only when I had left the city, for the Scandinavian appears so quietly rooted in the family virtues, in well-mannered thrift, and an unprotesting contentment of manner, that the neuroses of abandoned children and parents out on a spree simply never occur to you. Only in the hotels are you restored to the America of brisk, whisking elevators, soldiers and their girls, club women and pineapple salad.

Of course, there are the usual troubles of a transportation center. Since Minneapolis is the wholesale center for Montana, Minnesota, and the Dakotas, and it is a center for the marketing of wheat and corn, the elevators are crammed, and shippers have had to fight for priorities to get their wheat away. As a railroad center for the northern lines from Chicago to the coast, there is now a nightly symphony of freight to disturb the natives' rest. There are, too, the familiar housing problems of workers come in to work two big ordnance plants, one for the Army, and one for the Navy. But nobody fusses about these things, only the newspapers seem to dramatize them in a mood far removed from the humdrum acceptance of war by the stolid Northerners who live up here.

The only howl that went up was over a labor feud between Minneapolis and St Paul. While the ordnance plants were going up, the construction workers of St Paul, solidly AF of L, settled for a closed shop and 10 percent higher wages than the workers of Minneapolis. There has always been a friendly sentimental feud between the cities. Fifty years ago it was so brash and unyielding that the government had to employ neutral enumerators to get an accurate census. But the war aggravated this into a reality when St Paul, short of labor for its war plants, preferred to hire transients rather than the unemployed of Minneapolis.

Possibly, too, it is the resigned sobriety of Northern types that reconciles them sooner to the age of organized labor, which Latins and the mixed breeds of hotter climates resist with all the deep anarchy of an earlier American strain. The Twin Cities are capitals of organized labor, and the big crisis of the war to date was the day when three brothers in a truckers' union – the Teamsters – were about to be ousted for some finagling and tried to switch the whole union over to the CIO. To many people, this seemed like a threat of imminent revolution, and the AF of L kept its hold. 'A status quo in labor here,' commented a labor editor, 'would be as conservative a stand as possible.'

When I set off south in the morning into Wisconsin, I had forgotten about some of the drawbacks to northern Anglo-Saxon sobriety. An apathy to sprightly amenities of travel is one. I left Minneapolis without breakfast and assumed I'd pick up some sizzling eggs and hotcakes any convenient place on the road. But I went hungry. Not for the reason I had noticed out west, because the places were abandoned by owners gone off to war or factories. They just didn't seem to have heard of the traditions of the American highway, which in New England are a grudging concession to people who stay out late, but all through the Southwest and West sprout motels, saloons, barbecues, dine-and-dance shacks, and neon-blazing eateries that alarm the Western night with no shame at all. Down from St Paul I drove ten, fifteen, twenty, thirty miles, but no sign of a highway restaurant, a diner, or Joe's place. It was admittedly a Sunday morning. But it was just like Sunday, or any day, driving through England. The landscape was green and rolling and majestic in a well-bred way. But the traveler was given to understand that self-respecting humans ate their meals at home, and the highway was strictly a means of passage between home and home. The landscape was not intended for skylarking. It was meant for dairy farming, and if you thought it handsome, well, no harm was done.

South all day by the chocolate-brown bluffs of the Mississippi, jutting at the water's edge under gray skies, I hardly passed a soul. It was hard to imagine the brawling pack of lumbermen that had once teemed on this shore, and the million log rafts that had floated down the river. Curving around the bluffs, rolling over small swamps, skimming across bottom lands powdery with willows, there was nothing but a few boats and tents on the riverbanks and a man wearing boots up to his thighs out clamming. The road stayed by the river down to La Crescent, then I crossed over to La Crosse and into Wisconsin.

Even the brashest traveler feels a humble moment when he enters a new country. It is striking to see how a customs barrier sobers cocksureness. There is a similar default of the ego as you cross a state line. Behind you are the things you know about, or think you do. Psychologically, the mere sense that you are leaving a state suggests that you choose to do so because you have exhausted its resources. However highly you think of it, there is the feeling, as when being seen to a train by hospitable natives, that you appreciate your hosts but there are for you other and richer worlds to conquer. This arrogance is fed at every state border, so that it is not uncommon to come across people who have traveled through all the forty-eight states and clearly believe themselves to be superior to all of them. But the pride of rejecting something induces a compensating caution at what you are about to receive. And you tend to pay exaggerated respect to any native you meet just after you have entered his state.

So lighting out across the Mississippi plain, I mentally paid tribute to Wisconsin, the dairy of the Allies. Wisconsin, with its lakes and its careful farmers. Wisconsin, with its warblers, its fine cheeses, its independent political tradition. Wisconsin, with its beer, and its Forest Products Laboratory. These were memories or preconceptions, and after a gorgeous meal I sallied out of a restaurant at La Crosse and pulled into a gas station ready to tank up and believe magnificent things about Wisconsin at war. I was whistling, and the operator of the gas station rebuked me. I remembered again I was in the sober North country, into which I had been borne. And I thought of my mother tearing in to the drawing room on Sundays if my piano fingers wandered from 'Sweet and Low' or a Beethoven minuet and slipped into a single chord of jazz. I remembered it was Sunday. And felt oddly ashamed. Nowhere in America have I ever been aware of Sunday as a sacred day, except in Minnesota and Wisconsin. I don't know whether this is a dreadful sentence or not. It is true.

I drove through tobacco country, with the high, brown bluffs overlooking the flat plain, through Westby, where every other store is named Unset, or Iverson, or Gorgen, or Thorson. Another preconception, and a less pleasant one, came back to me: Wisconsin and Isolationism. It was through here that an old man told me of the last war:

'With most everybody around here German and Scandinavian, what would y'expect? Old Senator La Follette, the father you understan', he was a might powerful influence. We were against the First World War. And against the League of Nations, you bet. Europe's a home I left. My sons figure it can take care of itself. But Hitler made his big mistake, far as we're concerned, when he invaded Norway. We were solid isolationist till then. But that was the first crack.'

If this was true, it was consoling news. Right after the recession of 1937, Bob La Follette's National Progressives of America started active recruiting. It is fair to say that it was a homegrown movement hoping to break the seemingly complacent seesawing of the two traditional parties. But it was a Wisconsin man who said, 'You know, much of our home-grown progressivism derives from an admiration, half-conscious maybe, for Fascism in action.'

Through more open dairy and tobacco country, the plain narrows near Richland Center into thin valleys between hills splotched with sandy rocks. At Richland Center the natives will proudly point out to you a wholesale grocery warehouse of bold design, its red brick divided with thin vertical columns of glass. It was designed by Frank Lloyd Wright for this, his native town, and has a cooling system, which was a bold invention in 1918.

From here to Madison, down across the yellow Wisconsin River, up on to a high prairie, and through the hilly country around Black Earth, almost every town you go through can be tabbed with the label 'dairy center'. For all along here, and south to the Iowa line, is the country that a state editor defined as 'the South that keeps the state.' In Madison, they will grudgingly allow that the North is fine for lumber and tourists, that the Fox River Valley has good paper mills, and that on the rather scrubby central plain known contemptuously as 'the sand country' Poles somehow manage to grow potatoes. Only in farming land as luscious as Wisconsin or Iowa or Minnesota would this region be so dismissed, for it is astonishingly like Eastern Long Island, about which nobody around New York feels embarrassed. And there too the principal crop is potatoes grown by Poles. But the dairy farming of Southern Wisconsin overshadows everything. The millions of gallons of milk, the butter piling up for the Army, the Swiss and Limburger cheese of Greene County (made by a Swiss-American colony), the pride of Plymouth, Wisconsin, as the Cheddar center of the country.

It is on this dairy region that the war has made most demands. Before the war, Wisconsin provided just under 12 percent of the nation's milk supply and 50 percent of its cheese. It is now producing one-third of all its evaporated milk, and one-quarter of its powdered milk. Wisconsin has good reason to be proud of fertility, and of the agriculture department of its University, which applied the social intelligence of disinterested research to natural resources in a way that, if it had been done elsewhere, could have saved America from the lighthearted abuse of millions of acres of green prairie, that could have made impossible the shame of one-fifth of the continent's earth. But America is no better, or worse, than all the strains of men that have made it. And against the shiftless and the callous rapers of the Southland and the West, we can stack the hard, decent Yankees and the independent German liberals who came to Wisconsin and respected its land. You cannot roam over the dairy country of Wisconsin and talk to the agricultural staff of the University without feeling the fair mating of intelligence and pride. 'Its Extension Service,' says Russell Smith, 'carried dairy lore to every hamlet and farm; in its laboratories were produced five of the six tests used everywhere in dairying. One of its staff invented in 1890 a machine for testing milk. This machine records the cow's history and her horoscope; the farmer reads that this cow's milk has 3.1 percent butterfat. Away with her to the hot dog factory! She is not worth milking, nor is she fit to become the mother of the next generation of cows. By the simple process of eliminating the unfit and breeding from good sires, the average annual output of a herd of cows can, in a decade or two, be raised from 3,000 to 6,000 or 7,000 pounds of milk per cow.' The impulse to learn in a lab about the possibilities of soil, and feed, and milk is still eager among men whose forerunners taught the world new tricks. Perhaps in no other state did the principle of Lend-Lease cause such a revolution in farming. It caused not merely an expansion of dairy farming but a change of definition, away from the delivery of separated milk and cream to the delivery of whole milk. Away from the end-product of bottled milk and eggs in shells, to powdered eggs, and evaporated and powdered milk for export. Before the war, there were no egg-drying plants here. Now there are a score. Wisconsin produced in the first six months after Pearl Harbor between 90 and 100 million cases of powdered milk, 'but Britain,' said an anxious dairy farmer, 'is only taking about 60 million.' The chief kick of the individual farmer is that 'the British take only the top grade of our dairy products, and the lesser grades are left on our hands.' It was the same story as fruit grades in California. If the domestic market can't have the best grades, then somehow the government has to be persuaded to allow the farmer to mark up the second grade as top grade, to assure him a fair return without hurting the susceptibilities of the customer. In other words, Americans are only too happy to boast that the boys in uniform must have the best of everything, but it is up to the advertising writers to perform the sleight of mind that leaves the customers at home with the impression that 'just the same' there is no loss of quality in any of the things they eat, use, or wear – a feat of persuasion that produced, during the first two years of the war, some very fancy word-juggling but left the ordinary American housewife stoically resigned for the duration to using 'victory model' strainers, measuring cups, and light plugs that buckle and wilt in a week, and to wearing fabrics that were saved from looking like oilcloth or blotting paper only by the American talent for cutting.

As in the Corn Belt, the war strain is not on the processing plants but on the farmer himself. He moans for the extra pair of hands, and the daylong stamina of a young man he probably took for granted before he went off to New Guinea or England. He must now teach his smallest children to milk and depend on his wife for heavy work that in America farmers' wives don't normally do. And for the dairy farmer there is no break in winter, no quick vacation south. Udders do not recognize the Florida season. And when the government keeps begging for more milk, the farmer accepts overwork as his duty and curses the man who invented Eastern War Time, a variant of Daylight Saving Time that, though the cows never heard of it, rouses him in darkness.

Near Madison, I turned off US 14 and drove down to Lake Mendota for a breath of air. By its sparkling blue waters is an area of old willows, and at the end of the walk you face a furrowed field from which rise the gleaming vertical lines of the US Forest Products Laboratory. At any time, it is one of the world's most fascinating workshops, studying all the woods that grow in America, converting them into paper and cellulose and plastics, receiving every year 3,000 wood samples to work on – serving in fact as the testing ground and transmuter for the 600 million acres of raw material provided by American forests. When the war came, the Laboratory closed its doors to tourists and science pilgrims who trooped every day through its rooms on conducted afternoon tours. It became a laboratory for the armed forces, and most of its current chemistry is still a military secret. But some of its marvels are publishable.

I left Madison in heavy rain, and the cornfields might have been fields of rice they were under such deep water. The short highway to Milwaukee is laid through much the same dairy and creamery country. The combination wooden barn and stone silo is the typical architecture rising from undulating fields in which fat cattle sloshed around in drenching alfalfa.

Then at Waukesha you slap suddenly into the industrial Midwest. Here is a factory town, big enough to be making airplane motors, metal castings, aluminum, small enough to be suspicious of strangers who are curious about its war-work. But then you slip again into a sparkling countryside that is different from the previous dairy country in being more streamlined and mechanized. Long yellow-stone barns on hilltops, where cattle are washed in steel stanchions; lunging tractors roaring across the fields; new storage barns; and bobbing in and out of these buildings farm workers in denim, looking more like farm robots in a future world where the cows are washed, tested, milked and put to bed in an assembly line untouched by human hand.

And then the streetcar tracks begin and you are in Milwaukee.

The interest of most Americans visiting Milwaukee these days would be in the wartime attitudes of its German population. Indeed, the first word I heard from a city editor there was a protest against the magazine feature writers who had been through there sniffing for a story, already written in their minds, about Milwaukee's natural anti-war feeling. 'They read some place, in school I guess, that Milwaukee is a German town. They fish up some stories about the anti-German riots here in 1917. They learn that our labor history has been long and occasionally violent – sure, state troops fired on a labor demonstration in 1886. So they come here all set to write about the fighting on the barricades.'

I felt I was hearing a new twist to an old, old story. Every city in the country is on its guard against the outlander's legendary view of it. The New Yorker, whether he has been to Kansas City or not, has a picture, and a faintly laughable one, in his mind's eye. And one of the astonishments that a traveler soon learns to accept is the fact that most regions of the country, passionately knowledgeable about their own characteristics, and patient in helping the stranger refine his knowledge of them, yet show the blandest ignorance of what goes on thirty or 100 miles away.

Milwaukee has a right to protest. It is no longer a German settlement. In 1845, more than half its population was German and Catholic (here was established the first Catholic bishop in the United States). Then came the Protestant German liberals. Then Poles and Italians. Today there are more Poles than Germans. In September 1939 there was an aggressive Bund movement, and a few German families went back to the Fatherland to work in war factories there. The immediate effect of the invasion of Poland was to spring a tension between the Germans and the Poles. And Milwaukee considers itself lucky that this did not break into open clashes. But since then, the war has only accelerated the declining prestige of the Milwaukee German. There used to be six German daily newspapers. There is now one daily and a bi-weekly. The German theater is no more. The bickering that goes on is among different groups of Germans. The Bund, for instance, hated the Wisconsin Federation of German-American Societies and took the obvious propaganda line that it was a Communist front.

'The US,' said one editor, 'takes a World War I view of Milwaukee. But the troublemakers have been immigrants in the 1920s and later. For every native German here, there's one or two generations of American born. And they're as good Americans as any other.' The chief isolationist line seems to be one that is typical of much of the Midwest but is regularly ignored in interpreting it to America or to the Allied countries. It is the instinctive fear of what was a European invention, the effects of which the immigrants experienced personally and came to the United States to shun. 'We ain't goin' back to what we left,' said a suspicious old brewery foreman. It is the American folk-saying among the European families of the Midwest. It springs from poverty and social frustration that they themselves know, or that they learned to fear at their grandfather's knee.

What these American-Germans gave to their new country was a stability that their hothead haters might well copy. They were thrifty, conservative, and homelike. They weathered the Depression stoically enough because they owned their homes and had money put away. It is largely to them that Milwaukee owes its reputation as a town without nightlife ('It's a nine o'clock town'), its distinguished health, safety, and crime prevention record; its boast of having the lowest automobile death rate and the lowest debt of any big American city; and its freedom from party politics in the city council. When the war came, it was not surprising that Milwaukee should be hypersensitive to the type of new citizen who came from the farms in search of war work or was imported from other states to become machinists. Before Milwaukee was in the swim with its own war industry, it offered to employers all over the country graduates of the country's biggest vocational school for machinists. The most highly skilled men in the city's machine shops – which here assembled everything from turbines to microscopic watch parts – were lured away south, east, and west. Hence the anxiety that the 'immigrants', who came to make up for this skilled labor, would either be sober and thrifty or would drop their tools and go back where they came from when the war is over.

From Milwaukee to North Chicago, US 41 drops straight as a pipeline and is about as well oiled. It is a four-lane divided parkway, and its road marks the shortest distance between two points. For a time there are monotonous cornfields – the edge of the Illinois corn belt – then a few old Lutheran graveyards, and just south of the Wisconsin line the low Des Plaines valley. Then you go gently uphill, get a glimpse of wide pastures and green estates, and after that you descend into flat marshy land, into rundown farm lots, cut-over land, auto junk-heaps, billboards advertising hotels, diners, hot dog stands, and all the frowzy rubbish with which the big city in America appropriates the surrounding countryside for its backyard. There is no point at which you can say, 'Chicago! There she stands.' An hour or more before you hit the lakeside, you are groping through the grimy skirts of the city. An occasional golf course and country club comes up restfully like a billiard table in a pawnbroker's window. Then a breeze blows over your steering arm and you turn gratefully on to the lakeshore and wind through the boulevards, only too aware that once you leave this most handsome façade of American cities, you can plunge into solid miles of some of the world's most reeking slums.

In writing about Chicago at war, I feel the same inevitable caution I did in Los Angeles and San Francisco. World capitals do not yield the secret of even their most material facts to transients. And you could live in Chicago or New York a couple of years and acquire only a set of private reactions to some of the city's work, municipal feuds, and obvious flavors. In a book whose scope is as modest as this, all you can do is plunge into a city and hope to come up with a mouthful of flavor.

Poets and travelers and advertising writers have teased the whole vocabulary of aggression to try to put the taste of Chicago on paper. They call it strident, Gargantuan, husky, titanic, and then give up, hoping the reader can somehow fuse the idea of magnificence with the smell of hog-wallow. It is a tribute to the well-knit character of the city that most writers insist on presenting an image rather than a description. Readers all over the world, who may not have the faintest idea what it is that Chicago butchers, packs, or transports, pause, half in wonder and fright, before the mental image of Hercules in overalls and a box-pack coat, giving out with a muscular sneer.

Begin humbly by saying that Chicago is the railroad depot of the United States, built and rebuilt in a hurry, on a marsh that happened to lie near the world's richest reserve of iron ore, and the two largest inland waterway systems of the continent. Whatever sailed down the

Mississippi, whatever was loaded for passage down the Great Lakes, whatever grew near Chicago, whatever mineral the earth could be scratched for, whatever animal fed on the surrounding pastures – was in the end bound to come into Chicago, be packed, refined, slaughtered, put on a train and sent somewhere else. Chicago made its name and money by never sending out anything the way it came in. It became a metropolis by the process of processing. Eighty years ago, a steer could amble into Chicago, bellow a while, and amble out again. But today he comes in chewing on his cud, is clubbed on the head with a mallet, ripped into accurate sections, goes through a process, his parts shipped on different trains and scattered to 60,000 towns in the United States alone, turning up in New Orleans as knitting needles, in Louisville as a tenderloin steak, in Forest Hills as the strings of a tennis racquet. In 1939, every day 1,300 trains came to or went from Chicago. From the enormous mesh of freight yards, trains scream out to every part of America, carrying hogs and wheat, corn and oats, butter and cheese, hides, wool, soap, furniture, plows, tractors, refrigerators, beer, iron, coal, and people. With the war, Chicago added one-third to its sweating population of slaughterers, packers, and railroad men, working now for Lend-Lease and the Army and Navy. The population of Poles, Italians, Yugoslavs, Czechs, Irish, Greeks, Lithuanians, Scandinavians, and natives of most of the Allies, who work on most of the small industries known to man found themselves making airplane parts instead of electric irons, tanks instead of refrigerators, small rifles instead of automobile parts. The hundreds of small factories technically inside the city limits had to move to outlying ordnance plants.

So Chicago has become a frenzied microcosm of the American city at war. Chicagoans boast that there is no known war problem that does not sprout within its borders. Booming retail trade, desperate housing shortages everywhere, a soaring standard of living with undrafted boys in their early twenties making 100 dollars a week and buying a bond or two on the side, and newly married war-workers plumping down ready cash for homes and furniture; lavish juvenile delinquency; rising venereal disease; a Negro population impatient against the ban on color in war factories but moving up into the trucking, janitoring, clerking jobs the whites have left for 'defense' and high money; and with the big money spilling over the middle classes, the all too human itch to relieve the sense of guilt for this honeymoon by blaming it on the Jews. So, a more vocal anti-Semitism. These are a few of the wartime trends in a city that can take any given trend in human nature and absorb the social mischief and the personal tragedies in the roar of energy given to the main job – the armies of freight handlers, the nonchalant women patriotically ripping the bellies out of cattle, the chatter of thousands of machines turning out propellers, tank treads, arms, powder, for all the sons of immigrants with the US insignia on their collars, gone back to fight where their fathers came from. What matter if the Negroes are procreating furiously in their strict confines between Twelfth and Sixtieth Streets. They have their simple opiates: the Thankful Church, their pool-rooms, anti-kink lotions, and parlors that promise to 'Lighten and Gladden Your Skin'. And, if as it seems, a whole generation of fifteen-year-olds sits gaping over Cokes in teeming nightclubs, well, their stabilizing is something somebody will take care of when the war's over. Meanwhile, there's a war on, and only a social worker would crab the Chicago war effort, and the impudent splendor of its prod-uction, by introducing doubts about homes for incoming workers or the emotional fate of a rising, and war-happy, generation.

Between Chicago and Detroit there are 250 miles of what the guide books call 'open country'. But on today's map it is a mere breathing interruption between industrial cities, so that the suburbs and the towns seem like the reality of this region, and the smears of country-side between them mere 'undeveloped' areas. The first breath of natural air comes in the elegant drive round Lake Michigan, past the Coast Guard station and the glittering flock of yachts bobbing on the water. In another part of the country, you would expect to dive then into rolling countryside but almost at once you descend into the belch-ing smoke, the grime, the freight yards, the steel mills of the town built on bare sand dunes: Gary, Indiana. For sixty miles or more you trundle through sand, and railroad tracks, and scrub pine. And then through the afternoon comes a tranquil stretch of Michigan pasture, and flat park-like country dotted with a lake or two, and the symbols of an older Midwest in the fine red Michigan barns, with the Renais-sance arches of their doorways painted in white. The highway is studded with little maxims on boards, like Burma Shave signs, which have been put there puzzlingly by a bread company. You just begin to get used to things like 'Procrastination Is the Thief of Time' when one of them comes up with the disconcerting remark, 'Labor Is Doing Its Part In This War'. You go through brown grass and alfalfa, past bulb farms. And at twilight, the hot dog stands begin, boys and girls on bicycles, obviously enjoying the fad of having no automobiles to lark around in. And soon the industrial pall descends again and you are in Detroit.

There are regions of America that seem forever haunted by the symbol of the product that made them famous. Floridians are always under the spell of their salable weather. Even the bluebirds of Montana seem to fly by the benevolent permission of Anaconda Copper. A native of Michigan must feel different from other men when an automobile passes him. For the automobile made him. And over Detroit broods always the commanding presence of Henry Ford, who put an engine where a horse used to be, so that a town of 20,000 farmers and small craftsmen multiplied to the rhythm of an internal combustion engine into a quarter of a million humans in forty years. The cheap mass production of automobiles killed off the little craftsmen from Poland and Germany and Hungary and Italy and Scotland and Russia, the immigrants who came to practice European skills in a peaceful place – the men who could keep a small town going by making furniture, and watches, and mending gas pipe, and treating leather for saddles. While they taught their sons to carve wood or later to build an adding machine or a vacuum cleaner, Henry Ford's discovery decided that those same sons should grow up to put in bolt No. 39 on an automobile assembly line. And it was their sons who in 1939 were the necessary cogs in the technique of mass production: gauge grinders, cone operators, jig and fixture men, process engineers, drill press maintenance men. And in 1943 these would be the jobs that were being advertised on chalked blackboards outside the unemployment bureaus.

The switch from automobile production to airplanes and jeeps and tanks is not the whole Detroit story, but it is enough of it to make no difference. And even in outline it is one of the most dramatic of the war, and at the same time the one that most reveals the blindness of the 'experts'. Early in 1940, a newspaper reporter asked a famous automobile manufacturer for a statement about the effect of the war on the automotive industry. The wizard promptly replied: 'Effect of the war? All right. Here is my statement. You may quote me as saying, "There will be no effect whatever." There is simply no connection.'

A year later, in the spring of 1941, Walter Reuther, the CIO union leader, made a national nuisance of himself by insisting that there was no technical reason why the entire automobile industry shouldn't turn over and start producing airplanes. The manufacturers kicked and screamed and ridiculed. A national newspaper editorialized, 'The Reuther plan is a chimerical vision dreamed up to take the problems of production and administration out of the hands of the men whose enterprise has built up our proudest industrial empire. Moreover, every responsible engineer has agreed that the plan is technically impracticable.' Much of the manufacturers' resistance to the plan probably sprang from the mystical fear that to accept it would be to invite war.

Mr Reuther offered to draw up blueprints precisely specifying which airplane parts could be made with which machinery in which factories. At the end of 1941, the same paper ruminated again: 'There is no doubt that the time is rapidly approaching when the automobile industry will have to give the most serious consideration to the conversion plan proposed by Mr Walter Reuther.'

One week later, it was no longer an idea for the men at the top to 'give serious consideration to'. The War Production Board simply ordered, 'No more automobiles'. And by the summer of 1942, the reporter went back to the same manufacturer who had professed to see no connection between war and the making of automobiles. Said the manufacturer, 'Don't ask me about automobile designs when the war's over. I don't care if I never make another passenger car. Right now, I'd rather not think beyond the week after next. I'm concentrating on shooting irons.'

Suddenly about 200,000 automobile workers were out of work, yet the conversion plan, once accepted, would be operating so quickly that by the fall they expected a labor shortage. The United Automobile Workers Union had enunciated the slogan, 'Victory Through Equality of Sacrifice', and agreed to give up Saturdays and double-time for Sundays and holidays. Shortly after Donald Nelson, head of the War Production Board, made his pleas for overtime in war plants, the first Labor-management Production Committees were set up. There was much suspicion of this idea that employers and their workers should meet regularly round a table and discuss their difficulties. The owners were afraid labor would begin to have a hand in production. The workers suspected the paternalism of a set-up in which owners and workers had an equal voice but the owners had the power. Some unions hoped that these committees would speed up production and insure corresponding wage increases. Some workers felt they were being offered a little charity for ingenious ideas from the application of which management stood to make a handsome profit. But the main thing was that a procedure was established unique in American labor relations. And it is unlikely that, once labor has earned its right to sit in on production problems, it will yield this right when peace tests the whole future of American industrial relations.

It was not possible to see even the skeleton of Detroit's war effort, and there is probably no man who has seen enough of it to say where the heart lies and the brain. But one could look at a nerve center here, a bulging bicep there, and wonder what the whole swinging man would do to the Axis.

You would expect a bomber to be the product of a single company. But Hudson Motor Company built the bomber sections, wheeled them off to Chrysler, which finished the fuselages and sent them on to Glenn Martin, which assembled the whole thing, putting in Pratt and Whitney engines from Ford and wings from Goodyear.

Wandering around these factories, I could not help recalling the old discomfiture of other natives of England at the first sight of the mass-production techniques that were to threaten their craftsmanship. Between the wars, the argument settled into an axiom in Europe that a machine that produces a hundred motors, or tools, or fans an hour must, by a law of nature that presumably protected the English and the Swiss, fail to show the fineness and delicacy of a motor, tool, or fan produced in a week by two conscientious men. This was true as long as the careful work of the best craftsmen was pitted against the average product of early mass-production techniques. But it is now doubtful whether there is any such law of nature.

In all the roaring energy and the multitudinous interlocking detail, you could see the bubbling inventiveness, the audacity, the wit even, that mass production could in a crisis stimulate. The old complaint is now, I suspect, a spinsterish protest, a wish uttered by dying small industries against the accomplished fact of a war of vast supply fed from a thousand assembly lines. In Detroit you could examine two-ton drills that would move to the touch, horsepower-measuring instruments, as poised as a Swiss watch, made on the assembly line; cutting tools like fine jewelry; mass-produced airplane engines that once were proud of the 30,000 parts lovingly fixed by hand. Chrysler hit a typical impasse over case-hardening the fingers (sprockets) of tank treads. The heating of a single finger normally takes a day. The sprocket moves around cog by cog and a flame slowly heats each side of a cog. Then somebody said why not heat all the cogs with a series of separate flames. The solution suggested itself: why not treat a sprocket like on a phonograph record-changer, move it into place, attack it with twenty-five flames, then drop the sprocket into a cooling bath. They did this, and the whole process took one minute.

There were of course hundreds of processes that nobody, least of all the Army, wanted to advertise. Americans heard nothing about them. But what you couldn't help hearing about in Detroit in 1942 was the project that soon became famous to the nation and, unfortunately to the Allies, as the master exemplar of American technological genius. I mean Willow Run.

The technical problem was the unquestionably daring job of fitting the biggest assembly line in Ford's history to the wholesale manufacture of bombers. But the real, the historic challenge to industrial courage was the task of providing the minimum conditions of a decent life for the great army of families that were to realize this immense ambition. I say it was the historic challenge because unless there is a deliberate revolution in the pattern of our emerging industrial democracy, Willow Run will inevitably be the prototype of the modern industrial plant. It will be doomed to frightful decay if in enlarging and intensifying the techniques of mass production, we only enlarge and intensify the mass poverty of the nineteenth-century factory town.

In the summer of 1942 it was too early to judge the sincerity of the attempt to house the incoming population that was to work on Willow Run and make 'a bomber every hour'. A naïve traveler might have asked why the plant had to be built thirty miles away from the city, when there was a rubber shortage and a gasoline shortage. He might have wondered why Mr Ford should refuse to build Bomber City, the accompanying housing project, close to the plant. The naïve traveler would then have been informed (perhaps scurrilously) that Mr Ford wanted Washtenaw County to stay Republican and not submit to a Democratic conquest by the invading Kentuckians and Tennesseeans.

However true this may be, what the traveler saw was the sordid formula of total failure in housing. Trailers, shacks, shanties, slums – as long as these were present the solid mass of citizenry, that stable middle class that is the nation's backbone, felt its conscience soothed and attended to its own cares. There were plans for official projects – a trailer city for married couples who would be welcome if they were childless, a tiny lodge for unmarried Negroes.

By this time in the traveler's long journey he could say again, long after Lord Bryce wrote it, that the shame of America was still the shame of its cities. Why it should be, in a technologically imaginative people, and an energetic people, that there is such a premium on shabby improvisation, and a high premium on impotence and asceticism – was an idiot question whose answer is worth seeking. I think it's worth, at this point, reviewing the history of the plans for housing the workers of the fabulous Willow Run.

The government had first wanted to have Ford's factories make aircraft parts, and sub-assemblies, and for bombers to be assembled down South. In January 1941, Ford turned down this offer. He clearly stuck to his ambition 'to erect and construct airplanes on a mass-production scale'.

If he were to be allowed to do this, the government wanted to know where the workers for such a grandiose project would find masses of houses to live in. Ford's counsel demurred and quite properly mentioned the first anxiety of a manufacturer going to work on mass-produced armaments: when the war was over, the plant might be closed down completely. What, then, was to happen to the mass-produced houses?

The general method of financing the great war plants was as follows. Through the Defense Plant Corporation, the owner built his own plant at his own cost. The government agreed to buy it back in installments over a five-year period. If he chose, the owner could then buy it back at a 'fair' (that would be, a deflated) value. The owner thus took the initial responsibility but was freed of it at the war's end.

In the spring of 1941, Ford poured 60 million dollars into the project and broke the ground of sixty-seven acres.

The unions began to be nervous over the lack of a comprehensive housing plan. The United Automobile Workers accordingly proposed that a worker-owned defense city be built close to the plant, a city of 20,000 units with its own recreation halls, laundries, and schools. President Roosevelt, the federal housing authorities, and Donald Nelson of the WPB thought it an admirable plan.

Then the opposition started. It came, not – as was sentimentally reported – from Mr Ford's reputed hatred of labor, from sinister lobbies in Washington, or from anything so simple as the doctrinaire resistance of a great industrial corporation to Mr Roosevelt's federal government. It came at first from the taxpayers' associations, from the property owners of Greater Detroit, and from the chambers of commerce.

The technical issue was a battle over the number of housing units that could be constructed. At this point, it is necessary, if this account is to be at all lucid, to continue the history through 1943.

For more than a year, the fight over 'units' went on, and inevitably engaged not only Mr Ford and his counsels, and the Federal Housing Authorities, but the War Production Board, the labor unions, the health services, the aforementioned property owners and taxpayers, and the water commissions.

The eventual decision was to build a city, Bomber City, of 24,000 units, only 6,000 of which were to be permanent. Everybody with a plausible stake in land or bricks, in transportation or water, joined the fray. The farmers objected to the surveyors. Ford by this time was clearly embittered at the whole brawl. He had conceived an American project worthy of his initial conquest of the American highway. Now he found himself the target of liberal and radical abuse as a monster reactionary. He undoubtedly seized excuses to justify his opposition to a great workers' city near Detroit and near the plant. He bemoaned the lack of water, in places where water lay deep in wells. He patriotically deplored the 'waste' of essential war materials entailed in housing the men who were to add a shine to his fame. He even made public his humanitarian sympathy for the squirrels that the workers' homes would render homeless (*Detroit Free Press*, June 22, 1942). He was investigated by Senator Harry Truman's committee on government waste in defense programs.

Ford then announced that he would require only a little more than half his original estimate of workers. After another battle with the government, the health authorities, and the innumerable interested parties, the plan lowered its sights. It would now try for 8,500 units, only 2,500 to be permanent.

October 12, 1942 is something of a landmark in American industrial history and a red-letter day in the calendar of Ford's battles with Washington. On that day, the plans for any permanent units were abandoned. The government was consoled with the thought that nearby Ann Arbor, with a population of 30,000 and Ypsilanti with 12,000, might be expected to absorb 90–100,000 workers. It was, of course, irksome that the rural areas surrounding these towns, where the workers would move in, had no zoning laws and no garbage disposal, and a septic-tank toilet system. After all, though, many if not most of the invaders would be from the South, where such things are considered no hardship.

The original plan called for 31,000 workers to move into government houses by January of 1943. Of course, the workers came. But by April of 1943, less than 7,000 temporary units had gone up. There were some trailers and dormitories and no family units. During this long and wretched feud, nature itself had not suspended its creative urge. It had helped spawn some fine slums in Washtenaw and Wayne counties.

There were still only 40,000 people at the factory, thousands of them complaining of a lack of continuous or productive work. Mostly, they lived in trailers, garages, chicken coops, tar-paper shacks, or shared outrageously expensive 'hot beds'. The county health authorities confessed their helplessness. In Ypsilanti, whose population had risen from 10,000 to 40,000, there was but a forty-bed hospital. The children enjoyed the privilege of three hours of school a day.

That this bedraggled and embittered multitude of men and their women should somehow manage to exist in undrained fields was the ultimate insult to the property owners of Detroit. They campaigned to have the workers housed in Detroit, where of course the rents could go up. In the summer of '42, a Washington lobby was active to abolish OPA ceilings on rents in Detroit. When the winter came, the absenteeism at Willow Run was three times the national average.

Many a property owner, and many a Congressman, who felt that Ford had been unduly slandered, argued that all this was the inevitable human price to pay for the grand, and proudly American, conception of 'a bomber every hour'. The British had been skeptical of the boast when it was first proclaimed by Ford, but they had had enough intimations of what the United States could do in the mass production of military supplies to lie low and wait. Alas, it would be hard to find a more disquieting example of the American gift for overlooking actual results in the general glow of self-righteousness in which a 'project' is conceived and a promise elaborated.

Americans are less aware than other peoples that they are not taken everywhere at their own valuation. When the British heard of the grandeur of American production plans, their skepticism would have outraged Americans, and it certainly puzzled the Americans in Britain who noticed it. But the British had heard all this before. In the First World War, Americans had regarded the manufacture of warplanes as a challenge they were peculiarly privileged to meet. Americans now hardly credit, what the British of two generations well remember, that no American airplanes were ever delivered to Europe before the Armistice and that the British and French were forced to provide the planes for the American Air Service to fly.

By July 1943, more than two years after the ground was broken at Willow Run, and eight months after the Allied invasion of North Africa, the Truman Committee made the bleak report: 'Until recent months the Ford Motor Company had not produced at Willow Run a plane which was capable of use at the front. The planes produced were used for training.'

It is only fair to add that the last sentence is hardly the stricture my quotation would imply. Through 1942, at least one-third of all American planes were trainer planes for the United States and Canada.

Willow Run will be cited at grandfather's knee as the very type of majesty before which other nations bow their heads in envy. But I have told its melancholy story because it symbolizes the grandiosity that is to other nations the most unpleasant of all American traits – the unbridled promise, the wild freedom of untested assertion, the invitation to share the cornucopia that is stuffed with the peculiar American riches: such unique things, the native honestly believes, as devilish ingenuity wedded to unequaled material and spiritual resources. What exacerbates the foreigner's annoyance is his secret awareness that there is an uncomfortable measure of truth in the boast.

It will not do to judge Henry Ford wholly on Willow Run's performance. He did wonderfully with the humble Jeep even though by the end of 1942 he was behind schedule in everything he made – making forty of every hundred airplane engines estimated, and only 15 percent of a full production of tanks – yet he was making a prodigious number of them. It was true that his war production was declining through the cheerless summer of 1942 and by the fall was 10 percent less than in the previous June. The so-called 'liberal' press made much of this, feeling reluctantly compelled to add the *post hoc propter hoc* item that Ford was at the same time producing great quantities of automobile parts, months after the last automobile had been made. However, at this period, and throughout the following winter, the Detroit plants often confounded the Army by turning out such embarrassing amounts of a needed gun or tank, that when the assembly line was in full swing, a new type of armament would be called for and the assembly line would stop. Plants actually had to shut down until new specifications could be blueprinted into new assembly lines. This happened, I believe, to Ford. It certainly happened to the Fisher Body plant, at Pontiac, whose 90mm guns poured out at such a rate that the Army begged the plant to slow down. Another company tore so recklessly into the production of M-3 tanks that within the space of months they had delivered their full Army order and were dismantling the assembly line and gasping for another assignment.

All this, in its proper exciting detail, was either too technical or too secret for the American people to hear about. What they did hear about, to the unhappy discredit of Detroit, was a befuddled crisis in race relations.

The first explosion of racial feeling in Detroit happened when a

Negro housing project was put in a white neighborhood. The whites protested. Then the Negroes protested. Then the Federal Housing Authority called out the State Guard to protect Negroes being installed. At the Dodge plant whites protested against Negro employment as long as white men were out of work. The company explained that the colored men they retained had seniority in their jobs. (If a man has had six years at Packard and is offered a job at General Motors, he retains his six years' status in the new job but he must agree to be liable to recall. But if he has been trained for a war job, say on airplane engines, he may be making such good money that when General Motors wants him back he may decide to forfeit seniority and keep his lucrative job. This was the kind of complication that the Negro baiters preferred to forget.) Not many official people in Detroit were willing to talk much about the threat of an open break between the Negroes and whites. One lifelong resident said, 'It's something new. And it comes out of fusing these Southern whites with something you may be surprised to hear about: a strong subterranean Ku Klux Klan movement.' Conceivably there was deliberate agitation and organized hate groups, but in casual talk between Negroes and whites, what you noticed was the persistence of lazy clichés among the whites and a delusion of grandeur among the Negroes. When the Negroes started moving up in the scale of peacetime jobs, and making money, they did not seem to want an exclusive smart district of their own (though Heaven knows how they would go about getting it, if they did). Their ambition was to demonstrate their superiority to their fellow Negroes by living in a white neighborhood and seeming to be 'accepted'. The whites for their part resented the invasion of their racial privacy, however poor that privacy might be. And what the white middle-class said, looking on regretfully, was 'well, many times before we have gotten along together, and we must get along together now.'

'The word "together",' commented one Negro, 'covers a multitude of sins.' So it did, until June 1943, when the sins blew the lid off.

I took the night boat from Detroit to Cleveland. As we slid away into the dark waters of Lake Erie, I had the new feeling that I was now riding the real element that has made the Midwest. I had expected it would be a restful interval between one industrial city and another.

But to lean over the rail and watch the lights of freighters far up the lake dipping by all night reminded me that to describe the separate contribution of the cities that ring the Great Lakes is as misleading as testing the drinking water of a dozen houses that draw from a single reservoir. I listened to the regular throb of the ship's engines and heard an echo of the heartbeat of the Industrial Midwest. The beat of this theme song starts with the steam shovels scooping iron ore from the hills around Duluth; washes down the Lakes with the sound of the side-wheelers fully loaded with ore, swishing down Lake Huron to Detroit and Cleveland. It is in the daily roar of the trains into Chicago, the 1,500 passenger, the 2,500 freight; it is the noise of a blast furnace at Toledo, Ohio, or Gary, Indiana. It is the dynamo in a powder plant a few miles from many towns.

It is the sound of taking in what the earth can give and making it over and sending it back as everything a continent can use. This is the daily music of the Industrial Midwest, to which 15 million Americans synchronize the movement of their work. It starts faintly up at the loading ports of the Great Lakes – at Duluth, Superior, Ashland, Marquette: 'D'y' ever see a Great Lakes freighter?' asked a freighter captain.

'It looks like a great floating pier with a doll's house at each end. It has thirty or forty hatches. It'll take 16,000 tons of iron ore, load it in thirty minutes. Five hundred tons a minute. We have these loading buckets that eat twelve tons of ore at a bite.

'Uncover the hatches and there you have the entire hold of the ship – stacked with wheat – half a million bushels of wheat on a trip, three-quarters of a million bushels of oats, loaded through suction pipes.'

The sound gathers strength and harmony as one process chimes in with another, as they unload the ore into the furnaces, down at the southern edge of the Lakes – at Gary, Detroit, Toledo, Cleveland. Then the pig iron runs molten into the steel mills, at Ashtabula, Cleveland, Lorain, Sandusky, Toledo, Gary. The rhythm grows again and the beat is firmer, as the rolled steel comes out of the mills in many shapes and goes into other factories, at Detroit, Flint, Lansing, at Youngstown, Akron, and Pittsburgh. Until what went into the freighters as ore comes out from a hundred factories with a tune of its own, the even hum of an airplane.

The parent stream of supply is the world's record canal traffic through the Soo Locks between Lake Huron and Lake Superior. Without this traffic of ore, the cities of the Lakes' shores could resign themselves to idleness or a new economy. There had been talk of a canal through the Upper Peninsula in case of enemy damage to the Soo Locks. Cities on the Lakes took the threat of this rupture to campaign for a new place in the indispensable traffic: Milwaukee, for instance, reviving its championing of the St Lawrence Waterway, which would make Milwaukee an important ocean port.

Gliding at night across Lake Erie, you can more easily organize in your mind rebellious details of the factories and see them as the active hands, and feet, and brain of an organism that will atrophy the moment the heart stops pumping blood. To the industrial Midwesterner, iron ore is the flesh and marrow of his bone, molten pig iron his blood stream, hydroelectric power his central nervous system, and steel his muscles.

Our passenger boat came into Cleveland with all the self-consciousness of a lady in evening clothes on the subway at 4 a.m., pressed conspicuously in among the exhausted waiters, homebound cooks, and solid charwomen. For hooting and lumbering on all sides of us was the essential traffic of the Lakes that brings down 90 percent of American ore into the eager maw of the American Ruhr – the huge gray industrial area that reaches from Toledo to Akron and Cleveland, from Lorain through Cleveland and down through the Mohoning Valley to Pittsburgh. Most of the ore comes from Minnesota, and some from Michigan and Wisconsin. It is at all times a majestic trade, but there was nothing like enough freighters to carry the raw material of a world war. The Office of Defense Transportation restricted the movement of coal up the Lakes (a load of coal lengthens the voyage by two days) and limestone down. They refurbished old ships and condemned ships, rusty ships, and ships reconditioned and unused for years. They converted the best ships of a fleet of automobile carriers and sent them to shipyards to carry ore. They amended the shipping laws to allow Canadian ships to load ore from and to American ports. They bought up all the boats that Canada could spare. To accommodate bigger freighters they deepened the locks at Sault Sainte Marie. The government allowed them to ignore the maximum loading laws.

From the dock in Cleveland, as far as you could travel in a day was everything mechanical the war would ever need. It would be impossible, within the scope of this chronicle, to attempt even an impressionist portrait of all the towns I went through between Cleveland and Harrisburg, where at last I had the sense of emerging from an industrial nightmare. Where there is a furnace to receive the ore, there is the irrevocable condition of a twentieth-century factory town. Where there is coal below ground, there is certain doom for country living. So that for the 300 miles round the sickle curve from Toledo to Pittsburgh, a notation about the countryside is almost a cry of reaction against the 'natural' terrain, against the mines, the wells, the furnaces, the mills, the railroad shops, the grisly slums and the reek of rubber and oil. By day, one who loves the American landscape has the feeling of riding over its cut-over grave, and by night he may not even enjoy the deception of darkness, for all around him the hoarse glare of converters and furnaces, the blue lights squinting out from the blackened panes of factory windows, will jeer at his antiquarian regrets. There is hardly a modern industry or trade that is not pounding by night or day through this frenzied area. Bituminous coal lies under it, and through it into West Virginia and Pennsylvania. Steel factories and tinplate. Glass factories at Toledo. Ordnance and TNT and shell-loading plants. Every small supply trade that can use the basic diet of the mines or the mills.

Nobody cared to talk about the years before 1939. The industrial layoff had been the common ordeal of about 15 million Americans. The coal mines working skeleton shifts. The steel mills closed. The relief rolls in Cleveland and Pittsburgh serving as wobbly dikes against a collapse of health and morale that unnerved mild men to recall. The farmers fed the Czechs and the Welsh in their shacks that nose out from the petticoats of city slums into the country. The schools fed the children. There was one generation that had never had a job.

One early morning in 1939, a woman who had lived all her life in the veil of Pittsburgh's grime, got out of bed, went over to her window, and saw smoke pouring from across the hill. She ran to the corner store and phoned the police. She asked to report a fire across the valley. Boomed a voice from the other end of the wire, 'That's no fire, lady. Them's the mills.' The first British and French orders were coming in. The upturn was immediate. The steelworkers went back. The metal trades started to pick up. The retail merchants of Cleveland had to clear the sidewalk of people just standing staring at modest window-displays of push-button radios, new refrigerators, and family payment plans.

With the signing of Lend-Lease, Pittsburgh was out of the red. The Poles, the Czechs, the Italians, the Hungarians, the Americans who produce the wealth of the whole region, came out of their dank homes, like Wellsian subterranean workers come aboveground to sniff the master's daylight. They paid off their debts. They started buying things, furniture and jewelry, new paint, and hardware. There were lines of tieless men outside the barbershops. A man who ran a clothing store told me of a Czech miner, who came into his store with his whole family in tow, a wife, a daughter, two sons. They were all desperately shabby. The miner simply said, 'fit us out with new clothes.'

A jeweler told of a Hungarian who came to buy himself a signet ring, a diamond necklace for his wife, a diamond ring for his daughter. A social worker in Pittsburgh commented, 'The coal mines were comparatively slow to get started, but now the miners spend like water. Only the young men don't buy. They figured America was going to be in the war. But the women and the old folks went on a spending drunk. Nobody I know is putting anything away.'

In the nightclubs, I was by now almost oblivious of the fever-eyed fifteen-year-olds with their first shots of liquor. I was struck by the music, for whether it was good or bad, it too seemed to allow them no surcease from the pulse of the rhythms they worked to. In Pittsburgh, jazz seemed more apt than other places. I remembered William Empson's definition of jazz: 'the hypnotized abandonment of self to the exact rhythms of machinery'.

A stranger may wonder how any social hierarchy can be maintained in an industrial city where there seem to be only workers, merchants, and mill-owners. But there are subtle divisions that do something to sustain the pride of men who appear to be all milling around in the hopeless morass of technical slavery. The 'first families' of Pittsburgh are Scotch-Irish, descendants of the first settlers, and originally Presbyterians. Then came the Germans, the earliest of the

non-British immigrants, a fact that to this day makes a German foreman feel superior to an Italian foreman. After them came the Poles,
Czechs, Italians, and Welsh. It is one of the Proustian laws of this city
that the immigrants are *never* absorbed into the ancestral families.
The University of Pittsburgh may boast of racial variety and claim the
varied qualities of the parts that make the whole. But this is a rhetor-
ical cloak for deep, respected divisions. Like most of the immutable
laws of American social life, this one is due for an early change. In the
beginning, the immigrant groups delighted to glorify their differences.
But they did the same work, were up against a general social ex-
clusion. Their quarters overlapped. The children played together, in
and out of school. The Italian hall holds dances, and the Serbs and
Poles are there. Sooner or later they intermarry. Only the Serbs still
stand cautiously apart. To the first generation of Americans, the
homeland is a distant shrine. To the second generation, a family
hobbyhorse. In another generation, the Davidsons and McBrides will
be marrying the Kwiatkowskis. The knell of these folk snobberies was
unmistakably sounded in two sentences of a fifteen-year-old girl, a
bobby-soxer in any language: 'My mother was born in Austria, came
here when she was three, she doesn't know what she is. My father was
born in Carnock. He's Slavish, I guess!'

Off a road through Pittsburgh that winds into the Pennsylvania Turnpike, I saw two miners climbing a hill. They were in old clothes and
wore the Masonic emblem of miners – the folded scarf tucked inside
their coat. They were going hunting and carried beautiful new guns,
shining in shafts of sunshine that carved the mist of steel dust in the
air. It was a pleasant sight that must have considerably soothed the
conscience of the first families.

It must have done something to my own conscience. For I was aware
of a lightening of heart as I came to the toll station of the turnpike that
would take me home. Then the Industrial Midwest was behind me,
shut out from the severe, white, plunging highway ahead, the swift
cement arrow bending through the arch of shining tunnels. The Pennsylvania Turnpike is the most breath-catching of modern highways.
Perhaps because of the place it begins, and the surrounding shambles
of industrial society. For it allies the traveler with mathematics in

motion, makes him all too willing to identify with the non-human purity of its function, and braces his spirit with the tension of style after it has been unstrung in the disorganization of a city of 'organized labor'.

II

The Rise and Fall of New England

New Englanders share with Californians a pride in their countryside so blind, yet so infectious, that a stranger is tempted to look around at once for faults in order to feel that he has some judgment of his own. Yet, there is overwhelming objective proof that the New Englanders and the Californians are both right.

Every state has an autumn peculiar in big and little ways to itself. And every state calls this season the fall. In West Texas it is quite a test of friendship to suggest to a native that the cool, clear nights and the browned sage are not the finest expression of autumn anywhere on the American continent. But the word ought to be reserved for New England. The New England fall is by this time so celebrated that it is in constant danger of being taken for granted, even by New Englanders themselves. However, if God were as poetic as Whistler once wished, and if He had devised a solar system that lighted parts of the globe only at the seasons that showed His best handiwork, the rest of the world would be dark in October while New England enjoyed its hour, just as England would light up for the few magic weeks in late March and early April for its incomparable spring. This is, I admit, a whimsical idea, for spring in the Arizona desert is magical too, and the freshest, greenest spring I ever saw was in Virginia in 1941. Yet the English spring and the New England fall are more than showpieces for connoisseurs of landscape. They are the unique earthly expression of two moods of the human spirit. The English poets have done magnificently by the English spring. They have, too, richly celebrated that 'season of mists and mellow fruitfulness' that is the English autumn, but which bears so little resemblance to the singing color and the stilly warmth of the New England fall.

I started this leg of my continental circuit from New York at the very beginning of October, ambling up through Riverdale through early yellowing maples. The gradualness of fall is one of its early charms. And the modest butternut tree is the groundhog of fall, for its sudden bareness is the irrevocable sign of the glory to be.

As I turned on to the Cross County Parkway, little piles of brown leaves, already dead, lay at the foot of hickory trees. I came on to the Merritt, that most majestic of all parkways, and the countryside scenes to right and left of the sweeping ribbons of cement lay like canvases assembled for the delight of the Merritt's patrons. The ferns were dry. The bracken and blueberry bushes were wine dark, the sumac red. There was everywhere the smell of burning wood, from which violet wisps of smoke smeared the cloudless sky like trickles of milk on sheet glass.

A sudden sign reminded me that this was no vacation. It said, 'Army and Navy traffic keep left'. I turned off the Merritt near New Haven, Connecticut, and passed brick buildings for rent, closed gas stations, and the mockery of an ice-cream parlor with the glaring reminder of the dear, dead days: 'Ice Cream – 32 flavors'. The windows were pasted over with brown paper.

In New Haven's College Toasty, two middle-aged men stood eating pie. Said one, 'It ain't hard to explain. He had two boys helpin' him. Well, Ted, the young one, went into the Army. The other's down in Bridgeport in the factory. So who's going to go to work on 300 bushel of apples? *That's* why there's no cider.' North of New Haven I noticed there was indeed no cider, not a single stand of cider jugs.

I did not recall US 5 to Hartford as an especially thrilling drive in winter or summer, but in the fall even the marsh grass was glinting with color, and the fields of red clay soil near Hartford seemed like a reservoir of pigment for the reddening maples and oaks to draw on.

At gas stations on the outskirts of town there was some headshaking over anyone who meant to sleep in Hartford. At the first two hotels I tried in the city itself, the clerks hardly bothered to say 'No'. At the third, a man said, 'There are no bedrooms. You can have a parlor with running hot and cold water, but you'd be lucky to find one with a bath in this town.' I settled for a cot in a recessed lobby at the end of the corridor. Here the comings and goings of the hotel guests (there was no door on my lobby) and the echoes of enviable ribaldry from the bedroom outside whose door I was legitimately parked, made sleep undesirable for the time being. I indulged for a while the universal pastime of travelers in fantasizing the goings-on next door, but getting little encouragement from the innocent clink of glasses, I pondered over where to begin in Hartford.

The cities of New England presented a new problem. However orderly in appearance, and Hartford is a comparatively orderly town, they are a patchwork of historical crafts and industries, few of which can be regarded as anachronisms. There is a common assumption among Europeans that New Englanders fuss rather naively about the antiquity of their towns. 'What would you do,' is the line of attack, 'if your towns were *six* hundred years old?' The answer is, it would be much easier on everybody. The British comfortably forget the first 300 years of their town's history and date its modern significance from a Corn Riot, or an indignation meeting of early trade unionists, meanwhile paying their respects to the older history in annual holidays, Lord Mayor's parades, and similar folderols. But in New England the tradition is not long enough to forget, and too long to absorb with ease. The old New England stock leaves the impression that they are straining to make their social attitudes conform with their romantic memory of the past. They have, of course, to be more realistic about politics, and a Boston blueblood with political ambitions would not be so rash as even to hope for a city government of his own kind. To retain any active influence, he must blow the horn of the most acceptable Irishman.

But in fact these earliest trades and skills are still the sheet anchor of New England's industries. They exact a high price at home and abroad for the undoubtedly high skill of their craftsmen. And many a strange trade that in 100 years will make interesting reminiscence in the guide books is still an essential ingredient of the Yankee economy. Thus I had that day passed two typical Connecticut towns, one – Wallingford – whose largest firm is the silverware company that started 100 years ago, and the other – Berlin – which 200 years ago beat out the first American pots and pans and whose earliest peddlers tramped out the sales routes for the humble products of other Connecticut towns, whose livelihood today is still based on the manufacture of such single products as needles, cotton threads, suspenders, lacquers, and industrial jewels.

Hartford, this oddly attractive town with wide thoroughfares, a rambling little river, and dikes built against the threat of a flood from the more formidable Connecticut River, is quite possibly known to a rising generation as the place that gave birth to Katharine Hepburn and that onetime housed the authors of *Uncle Tom's Cabin* and *Huckleberry Finn*. But it is the typical New England city. That is to say, an industrial city, whose residential areas divide off squarely into an Italian section, an old line section, a Slav section, a Negro section, and a Jewish section that spills into some of the others. A city famous for an old, highly finished product – a definition that applies as strictly to its insurance policies as to the Colt revolver that appeared sixty-six years after the first fire insurance was issued. Hartford was responsible for the world's first standard inch and for America's first pneumatic tire. It makes bicycles. And it binds books. But it doesn't like anybody to pass over its reputation for pipe organs, or the fame of its gold-beating industry, which has long supplied dentists with their lucrative deposits and in 1942 was rumored to be under government contract for some precious hush-hush metal.

I reflected with alarm that Hartford called for a book on the fate of its innumerable industries and races at war. But this could only be a part of that book, and I made my choice of its two most famous products: insurance and firearms. When the harassed chambermaids had finished flitting back and forth between the rooms of departing guests and the linen closet I was guarding, I took some sleep and woke to pry into the wartime fortunes of insurance and Colonel Colt.

The self-esteem of the insurance business, in this the insurance capital of the world, is something akin to that of the Bank of England or the parent factory of Wedgwood pottery. No attempt was made to impress me, to demonstrate the smooth organization of a business that, I had to find out for myself, employs about 20,000 citizens of Hartford. The great pseudo-Colonial buildings would in another country house the State Department or be memorable relics of the best period of the national architecture. The Aetna Life Insurance Building is a sort of Zwinger of steel-and-concrete Colonial. But nobody showed it off to me, nobody mentioned Hartford's preeminence, nobody invited admiration. Being whisked in silent elevators, crossing gleaming floors, turning past marble pillars over acres of carpets, and entering at last into the holy precincts of a vice-president's office, I felt like an American at Hampton Court, attentive to the lecturing guide, whose offhand monotone implies but never asserts that the magnificence you are stumbling through is inevitable and unsought, though possibly preordained.

I was greeted as if I were a respected client, come on some business that must be settled with care and leisure. They do not show off the insurance business. If I wanted to write a story about the war and insurance, they would merely want to draw my attention to some facts that would make it reasonably accurate. This entailed a routine quiz into my knowledge of the fundamental concepts of marine insurance. Alas, I had none, and a dapper, white-haired man in rimless glasses crossed one scrupulously pressed trouser leg over the other, smiled indulgently, and cast his mind back to the seventeenth century. It was assumed in those days, and before, that almost any voyage you took on the high seas might involve you in an existing war. 'Wars,' he announced, 'were continuous and uncounted.'

He opened a drawer, took out a document, and closed it silently. He unfolded the document and indicated with a silver pencil the text of an insurance policy issued in London in 1692. It is an accomplished sentence, and the reader may share my assumption that to understand however sketchily the effect of the Luftwaffe on insurance, it is required reading. Here it is:

Touching the adventures and the perils which the Assurers are contended to bear and do take upon us in this voyage they are of the seas, men-of-war, fire, enemies, pirates, rovers, thieves, jettesones, letters of mart and countermarts, surprisals, takings at sea, arrests, restraints and detainments of all kings, princes, and people of what nation, condition or quality whatsoever, barratry of the master and mariners, and of all perils, losses, and misfortunes that have or shall come to the hurt, detriment or damage of the said goods, and merchandize or any part thereof; and in case of any loss or misfortune it shall be lawful to the assured . . . factors servants and assigns to sue labour and travel for in and about the defence safeguard and recovery of the said goods and merchandize or any part thereof without prejudice to this insurance, to the charges whereof we the assurers will contribute each one according to the rate and quantity of his sum herein assured.

My teacher leaned forward as to a sympathetic pupil and said, 'The only way our policies of today differ is in the spelling.' Under pressure, he did however admit some interesting changes.

'In the old days,' he went on, 'journeys were so long and slow and there were so many possibilities of misadventure that the merchants and the ship-owners took these risks for granted. So they just naturally wanted complete protection. Then after a while, the steamship came along, improved communications, and the chances of attack or seizure grew less. The underwriters were very traditional men. They didn't write new policies that deleted the risks of war. They added a new clause, specifying that the voyage should be considered free from those risks. In other words, their policies didn't just cover a new situation. They incorporated the history of marine insurance, and you specified which clauses you wanted leaving out. That added clause was known as the Free of Capture and Seizure Clause, and if you still wanted to take out war risk you had to state that your endorsement would cancel that clause. Broadly speaking, that was the situation right up to the World War.

'But the whole business of declared wars, new weapons, the rights of neutrals, quarantine, customs regulations, made the definition of war risk much more complicated. Cargoes had to be distinguished from hulls. Eventually we evolved a distinct and separate war risk policy, which is standard with all underwriters. But we were very worried over the development of aerial warfare. Munich really scared the whole insurance profession. Congested cargoes bombed in a port might represent a liability no commercial underwriter could bear. Some nations, the British especially, decided this sort of insurance would have to be borne by the government.

'Most nations agreed on a Waterborne Only Agreement, which freed commercial underwriters from insuring property on shore, either fixed property or goods in transit. When this war broke out, the British took the lead in Europe in setting up a government war risk insurance office. The idea was to encourage foreign trade that might be hampered by the high premiums a commercial firm would have to fix. The British government rate was a small fraction of what a commercial rate would have to be. The Dutch, French, Norwegians, Swedes, and Danes followed suit. In this country, all the marine insurance companies joined together to form an American Cargo War Risk Reinsurance Exchange. We can insure the merchandise on a vessel to any amount through shared reinsurance. We fixed premiums at standard rates. Of course, some things we won't insure. Nobody in this country will insure any cargo that the British might consider contraband. The British Navy virtually controls the seas, and we can't insure against British capture.

'You can see from all this that profits are a good deal more incalculable than in peacetime. The risks are enormous and the liabilities hard to figure.'

Not to seem too vulgar in my approach, I then asked about the situation since the United States had been in the war. He was more relaxed, now that the historical background had been covered. It seems that shortly before the Washington talks were exploded by Pearl Harbor, there had been a sudden interruption of shipping facilities from Japan, and a lot of American ships and cargoes were left stranded there. The Reinsurance Exchange extended the Waterborne Only cover. The Exchange was also duly proud of its record in protecting the huge imports of war materials into the country. The marine insurance companies covered the builder's risk in constructing vessels for Lend-Lease and for the Maritime Commission. They provided for loss of life and dismemberment insurance for officers and sailors of the Merchant Marine. They were praised by Washington for agreeing to suppress all information about ships' movements, although marine underwriters thus had to juggle their business in the dark. The decision of the underwriters to go on taking the full responsibility for American cargoes was brave but disastrous. By the time they were considering following the European example, the submarine sinkings off the Atlantic Coast were reaching their peak. In June 1942, the government took over all marine insurance, six months after the marine companies had taken appalling losses.

I was able to pick up, too, some figures about the various types of insurance, and they made Hartford seem like a barometer of regional anxiety. From the Alleghenies to the Rockies there was little apparent concern. 'None at all,' the figures showed, in the South and Deep South. And little through the Great Lakes. It was easy to see which parts of the country thought themselves to be directly threatened by aerial attack. In the South, Deep South, and the Gulf Coast, Hartford insurance firms carried only 2,000 war policies. From California alone, there were 15,000. New York took out fifteen times the number of policies of metropolitan Chicago. These were in fire and accident insurance. The banks and insurance companies didn't want this business, but it came from mortgages under pressure from loan companies. Group insurance soared, because it was the best device new war plants had heard of for keeping their workers away from rival plants. Accident insurance was, of course, an immediate by-product of countrywide construction of factories. The migration of working populations, their ability in some places to earn high and make a visible investment in furniture and houses, caused an unprecedented rise in burglar insurance. There was a decrease in life insurance, what with heavier taxes and the urge to buy war bonds, and with so many men away in the armed forces a decrease in personal accident and health insurance. Automobile insurance was rapidly diving out of sight.

As I left the last insurance building, I received the only encouragement I had had to bear in mind the distinguished tradition of insurance in Hartford. It was as if we had been sniffling around too long in the grubby details of wartime insurance and needed to recall to ourselves the Yankee courage that had established the business here in the first place. On my way out, a graying vice-president opened a history of his company and 'thought you might be interested in this'. It was a passage recounting how one Eliphalet Terry, an insurance man from Hartford, had plunged into the smoke that hovered around 700 ruined buildings, after the New York Fire of 1835, stood on a soap box, and proclaimed to the harassed tenants that they would get every cent of their money. They got it, and there was an automatic rush of insurance to Hartford.

'We paid out 15 million dollars after the San Francisco fire,' the vice-president remarked, as he saw me over to the elevators, 'so I guess we shall see this thing through. Goodbye.'

It had been a model study, the ideal investigation during which the whole history of the business had been projected for me, the present war picture had been arrested for a moment, focused for scrutiny, and then the picture ran on again to its end, with a proper reminder of its timeless scope. I went on briskly to Colonel Colt.

It is far from true to say that Hartford is a treeless town. But unlike many places in the West and Midwest, its factories and workshops appear to be a solid element of the soil. To an Englishman, Colt's was the utterly familiar sight of an old early nineteenth-century factory built for eternity with red brick now mellowed with soot. When I told the officials at Colt's some of the places I had been on my months-long journey, their reaction was exactly that of a cotton-mill owner in Lancashire or a Yorkshire woolen foreman: a polite acknowledgment that it was interesting to see the outlanders and their fly-by-night methods, the assembly lines, the steel and concrete, the modern glass walls, the factories on Illinois prairies, the runways ribboning over deserts and swamps. But here it was made evident from the start that I should see the fundamentals of war, the high skill that was expended on weapons a man could care for like a fishing-rod. A New Englander shares with an Englishman distaste for the unpredictable and the rude impersonal. If there must be wars, he feels that a man can save some of his dignity only if he is called upon to meet his enemy face to face and fire at him, accurately, in vulnerable and respectable places. (I recall the late Mr Justice Holmes's immortal entry in *Who's Who in America*: 'wounded in the neck at Antietam, the chest at the first battle of Manassas, the ankle at Bull Run'.)

So it was the most natural thing for the first of the grave and courteous men who showed me around Colt's to begin at the beginning, to sketch the Colt contribution to the Second World War from its origin in the horse pistol that was bequeathed to young Samuel Colt by 'his maternal grandfather', Major John Caldwell, a veteran of the Revolutionary War. In all the other factories I had been in, except in the South, they would lead you to their pet project, the newest technique, and break down the marvel into the processes of its assembly. Here in Connecticut, what Colt had to offer was a product whose perfection could be understood only in the logic of its growth. Patiently they would lead you to this knowledge. And we started off, not with a .50 caliber machine gun, but with the recollection of Mr Colt in 1826 at the age of twelve, tying four gun barrels together and revolving them in turn in the hope of discharging them separately with the same lock. We admitted this failure and traced his successive experiments in firing gun powder with electricity, exploding it underwater with the aid of a waterproof cable, his alarming explosion of a raft in Ware Pond. What had all this to do with Stalingrad, and the Pacific war of supply, with blitzes and Flying Fortresses? In thinking this, the reader may consider himself as suavely rebuked as the writer was in conveying it with a glance. We are now at the year 1830.

Colt was sixteen and on his way to India on the brig *Corlo*. He observed the action of the steering wheel. He saw that its spokes, turning either way, would align with a clutch and be stopped in place. With that burning singleness of mind that has often marked the best inventors, he was unaware that there were in existence guns with cylinders that were revolved by hand. The steering wheel sent him on to his object, the invention of the first automatic, repeating revolver. He carved it with complete accuracy in wood. We then followed his tenacity in getting enough money by running circus shows, bumming and borrowing, to make a few samples, get to Europe and take out English and French patents, take out an American patent, buy the wing of a silk mill in Paterson, New Jersey, and start to manufacture the Paterson revolving pistol. All this took six years after he had carved his wooden model. We then proceeded to the happy event of the Seminole Indian War and the meeting of Colt with Captain Sam Walker of the Texas Rangers, for whom he designed a pistol.

An hour had gone by, but no hour in a war factory was more satisfyingly spent. My sense of time was as relaxed and spread as a marijuana smoker's. Also, like his, it postponed the recognition of just how close was the war outside the window.

We went on through the Mexican War and its happy conclusion due to the high Texan regard for the Walker six-shooter. Came the Forty-Niners; the rushing of Colts to Russia and Turkey, and to Britain, in time for the Crimean War; the British resistance to Colt's pioneer mass-production, and his establishment of the world's largest private armory at the present site on the Connecticut River; Colt's far-sighted preparations for a long Civil War; his lamented death while the war was on; the Gatling gun, the Browning automatic, the First World War.

All this was told without flourishes and with a modest regard for Samuel Colt's failures and miscalculations. And the account was bright with lucid, homespun definitions: 'A pistol is an arm with one chamber and cartridge,' and 'Colonel Colt invented the six-shot pistol, which was called a revolver because it revolved.' We skipped in decent haste the inglorious period between the two World Wars, when employment at Colt's declined to 2,000 workers, many of whom were making switches, refrigerators, and buttons. A few months after Pearl Harbor, there were about 15,000 employees, most of them from Connecticut. The implication was that these were skilled, home-brewed mechanics or intelligent white-collar workers who could soon be trained in the Colt skills. But other factories, making airplane motors, or machine tools, had heavily attracted Southerners as well as New Englanders. And a city-sponsored housing project of a thousand family units, originally designed to replace slum clearances, had to be used for the newcomers.

From a stockpile of over 3,000 different sizes, shapes, and analyses of ferrous, and some non-ferrous, metals, Colt's normally made 180 different types of firearms. They were now down to four basic war arms. I was started in with the breakup of the steel into usable lengths, saw then the application of such mysteries as the grinders, hacksaws, and alligator shears, went on to the roaring drop-shop, where the parts are forged into the main shapes. From this point, the process looked more like watchmaking than armaments. I watched milling machines refine the shapes, profilers pare and refine still further ('A shaver designed by Colt in the 1870s,' said my guide dourly, 'is still the best'), and ended up with the last stages of square-reaming the barrels and chambering the revolver cylinders. To watch this took the better part of a day, and – my guides now feeling that I had been given an intensive and accurate course in the history and manufacture of Colt firearms – they bade me goodbye and went back to their own work. It was in other places that I learned, casually, about the human squeeze in housing the refugee farmers and invading Southerners.

At night on the streets, glaring with neon, reverberating with the periodical crash of pins on bowling alleys, it was impossible not to notice the number of Negroes and the children in their early teens brightly at large. It appeared that wrapper tobacco was the main crop hereabouts, and a lot of colored help had been recruited from the South. They came in hungry and eager, as only an exhausted Southern farmer can be. White and black. Alone and with four or five children. Some of the white farmers never expected to go back. 'Conditions' where they came from ranged from 'not so good' to 'te'ble'. Fifty cents an hour to work tillable land was a foretaste of paradise.

This influx challenged Hartford to relive its most cherished tradition of Abolitionism. It was now not enough to point to the guardian angel of Harriet Beecher Stowe, who lived and died 'on the Hill'. The Northern Negroes, more used to the tolls of city slums, expected little and adjusted.

'As for the Southern Negroes,' said a faintly despairing young editor, running his fingers through his hair, 'well, we don't patronize them but we don't look out for them either. If you get steamed up about this, the people around here will tell you right away about a colored Baptist preacher from here who went South on a visit. He had his glasses knocked off on a train. They started a fund for him, quite genuinely, sincerely, and contributed 800 dollars. That's about what it comes down to: we want to keep our reputation as abolitionists and humanitarians with a conscience about the Southern Negro, but the new Negroes in town constitute a nuisance.'

There was nothing consciously malign in this. Some comfortable people felt Roosevelt had a habit of pressing these issues, of acting too literally on the idealism of the early American scriptures. Before Pearl Harbor, Hartford had been on the whole Isolationist, its upper-middle class especially so. The popular vote went to Roosevelt, though in recent elections the Democrats were getting smaller majorities. Like many another American city with a past, Hartford liked to preserve a status quo, which included a reputation for certain courageous attitudes that were difficult to relive in modern times.

I drove out of Hartford in the early afternoon northeast through Manchester and Vernon toward the Massachusetts line. Along this pleasant way is the seemingly unruffled New England of the Samuel Chamberlain calendars. Through some tobacco and potato fields, then dipping over open fields and brushing stands of woods, you can be lulled to the lovely monotone of the past: here an inn with four chimneys, a whitewashed brick house, another Colonial inn; there a gambrel roof mottled by the yellowing birches; everywhere the leaves liquid with the first drench of gold and scarlet. You would begin to accept the yellow, red, green palette as the full flower of the fall, and then an undulation in the road would suddenly expose a flaming maple, solid as a sapphire, plum-like in its ripeness, its branches erect and rhythmic as a fan. And the knowledge that this was still the early exception made one faint at the fulfillment that lay to the north. For the time being, there were still green fields. But now over a wide horizon threaded with the white steeples of Colonial churches, it was the small treeless things that were trying to be splendid, the undergrowth that pressed on to achieve its humble, exquisite hour. The briar and bushes and vines were sparkling. I do not know them well enough to single out their separate charm, but it is a yearly surprise to see brush that for most of the year is a mess of wire suddenly disclose a jewel of a flower. Pokeweed and pitchpine cone, and unpretentious underfoot things like partridge berry and jack-in-the-pulpit, all of them have a special shining berry, a bursting husk, a momentary crowning bloom. You are aware first only of stretches and rolling banks of glistening undifferentiated brush. You focus on a color, that is to say a wild flower you know, and soon it is quite isolated, until you recognize another and another, and what had seemed at first to be a stretch of shrub fading and blooming through many gradations, becomes a streaming bouquet of a hundred separate blooms. Heady with this vision I walked back to the car again. At the very rim of the tire the smooth cement of the highway had cracked under the tension of cranberry vines. And through and edging the highway, wild cranberries grew. I looked ahead at the line of the engineered highway, white and consummate into the distance, heedless of the pathos of its defeat by the concentrated violence of a delicate vine.

The towns along the way were small, redbrick irrelevancies to this beauty and in memory have hardly any separate identity. This one makes pearl buttons, that one woolen goods, then the rolling, singing country is all around you again, and near the Massachusetts line you streak through high pines that seem inkier and solider in the surrounding contrast of scarlet and showering gold. Through open woodland I came in the evening to Sturbridge, whose maples burned on the level green. The Publick House, a beautifully proportioned Colonial inn, had been taken over by the Army. So I went on to South-bridge.

I had dinner at a restaurant I took to be Greek and was waited on by a sly-looking, pretty girl with a tawny skin and black eyes. I was wondering about her nationality and heard her name called, 'Maria!' She went to a booth where two couples sat. The men were small and pinched-looking, the women dark and lively, with broad faces and quick gestures. Maria took their order and they resumed their talk, in French. They were French-Canadians. I absurdly found myself wondering what they thought they were doing in this most un-European landscape. But the worst shock was yet to come. My eye fell on the menu and I saw plainly the incredible listing: 'fish and chips'. If the landscape was unlike Italy and France, it was certainly 3,000 miles from Lancashire.

This surrealism was explained to me next morning when I went to the American Optical Company. 'Twenty-five years ago,' my host said, 'this town had a floating population of Albanians, Italians, and Greeks, trying to settle themselves in a community mainly of French-Canadians. It's the usual story. The fathers looked back to the old country, the sons looked forward to a life here with the French-Canadian girls. Some, I guess, went back. But I remember one Italian who had some trouble making his mind up. I asked him what finally decided him to stay. Y'know what he said? "Gas cooker and electric light." Most of 'em sent for the old folks, and the company here ran a night school to teach them English.' A look around the Optical Company began to destroy any notions I might have carried over from Hartford that the skilled craft of New England is an Anglo-Saxon monopoly. Again, the plant officials will tell you in their literature about the beginning of the industry here by the narrow stream of the Quinebaug River which dried in summer, so that the first American grinder of optical lenses used a horse for power. Now in all the tidy workshops of the plant you could see men of several races grinding, polishing, testing to the hundred-thousandth of an inch the finest microscope lenses, bombsights, aerial camera lenses, ship's compasses. But there was something to the older prejudice. 'Call over the names,' said a foreman, 'of the men who do the finishing and testing, the men who have to handle and polish parts under a microscope. You'd be surprised how many of 'em are old Yankee stock, with English names. We've had little trouble with the draft board because the irreplaceable men are too old for this war, most of 'em too old for the last one. The Poles tend to do the heavy work, the Italians the repairing, the rest make aviation goggles and so on. It's the old Yankees who keep our reputation going. The Greeks? The Greeks are traders, not workmen.'

In a small community of such widely scattered origins, it would be logical to suppose that a strong union alone could organize their varied human relations into an effective bargaining agent. But the town had shown the most stubborn resistance to being taken under the wing either of the CIO or the AF of L. Four intensive, competing drives had failed. There was no company union. The workmen kept to their old-fashioned faith in the system known as double savings ('fifty cents for life, fifty cents for death' is the philosophical formula) and deposited in the savings banks. They can get very low-cost insurance, and a disgruntled organizer might say they could afford to be independent because somebody else had gone before and fought for them: it was 'the people's attorney', Supreme Court Justice Louis Brandeis, who won a long battle in the state to establish this low-price insurance. As for loans, the company lent the workmen money when they needed it without interest.

It was a simple and apparently happy set-up. But though the natives professed impatience at the crusades of labor unions, theirs is no model for a large industrial community. They are small enough to bargain in person, and they are lucky in their Company.

All the same, Southbridge was a rude reminder of the true nature of New England. I wished I had talked to more Italians and Slavs in Hartford, where I had been given the new feeling that although the war was our present task, it was only the latest event in the natural history of Yankee craft and character. This feeling, like some of the experiences I had put down in Oregon, stirred an old strain. It is the English view of crisis, as being nothing to get vulgarly dramatic about, just the latest hardship, the test that God decrees at intervals to try one's reserves of patience and asceticism. It is what the stranger even at this date expects from New England. Then I remembered that I had been going around with people whose names were Adams, Phelps, Griswold, Lidstone, Hooker, MacCabe, and that the impression I had received ought to be strictly identified as that of the Anglo-Saxon Yankee, who, since New England has more continental European blood within its boundaries than any other region of the country, is a fast declining power. Wherever the popular vote elects New Englanders to office, the returns cannot help but reflect the fact that the foreign strains are increasing twice as fast as the native Yankee. New England today has twelve times as many sons with a foreign-born parent as the South. It is a region where the city-dweller outnumbers the countryman by better than three to one, which is easily a national record. So the typical New Englander today is a city-bred Italian, Polish or Irish Catholic. But a Catholic. The atypical, or recessive, New Englander is a Protestant with an English name.

Along the eight-odd miles cross-state to the Mohawk Trail, the fall came into its full flower. Everything, the birches, maples, oaks, pouring cascades of scarlet and gold down all the hillsides. As I went north, more and more evergreens came up, darkly male and erect against the glowing passion of the oaks and maples. In the still light, birches slid by like slivers of mercury. This was the peak, the indescribable climax, the universal blitheness of color and light, when it is almost possible to believe that for America was reserved a wholly different autumn, in which one might truly see the godlike wedding of youth and majesty.

Through this intoxication of nature, you could discern at intervals some sober items of small-town life that together make a pattern of rural New England at war. I am thinking of the hundreds of towns throughout the region that are run by twenty or thirty officials, mostly unpaid, who by day are dairy farmers or hardware store owners, and who by night supervised fire drills or airplane spotting, made house-to-house collections for the Red Cross units, took turns on the ration and draft boards, and whose busy wives rolled bandages and baked cakes and chicken pies to raise money for this and that. These tiny towns, each housing a few hundred people, were in the main Republican and were whipped into new frenzies of social services, nurses' aid courses, forest-fire courses, by the thought of the crass bungling of the Administration in Washington. They had rather more than their share of boys in the services, and those who were left found their lives abnormally dislocated by a flat tire, a worn plow, a rotted hose, a plumber gone off to war-work in Springfield or Hartford. They were just then most exercised over the mission of the five New England governors to Washington to bully Interior Secretary Harold Ickes into diverting more tank cars their way. While I was there, the rumor came through that New England would in fact get three-quarters of its quota of fuel oil. The rejoicing that followed was as prayerful as that of the first Pilgrims who found corn to get through the first winter.

West on the Mohawk Trail this kind of life was noisily interrupted by towns humming with sawmills, or textile shops, and, at Orange, by the early evening bustle of war workers leaving machine shops. Their appearance, and their humdrum efficiency, took on a dumb sort of pathos as they jogged past Orange's ill-starred war memorial, the statue of a veteran in the act of lecturing a child on the meaningless-ness of war. Beneath are inscribed the words, 'It Shall Not Happen Again'.

From here on, the highway hugged rising hills that marched up to the distant Berkshires. The raging color had simmered into auburn as the sun went down, and in valleys you could see white steeples, like thermometers keeping count of a declining fever. Lumber crews – some volunteers – were coming home from cutting timber. Massachu-setts had decided to cut 2 million feet of lumber for its own use, to make up for the wartime difficulties of transporting timber east. As the evening came on I saw the unaccustomed sight of a lighted town hall, converted for the duration into the GHQ of ration boards, air-raid wardens, and Red Cross classes. As I drove up Route 78 through thick forest, to the north and west the blue outline of mountains was with me all the way, across the New Hampshire line and up by the Ashuelot River and swinging up and down along the broad Connecti-cut until it seemed I was aiming straight for a big black mountain ahead. Then I crossed the river into Vermont and saw a tumbling array of lights at many levels. This was the rambling, hilly, prosperous town of Brattleboro.

It was a Saturday night, and the throngs of people crowding past the bright store windows looked small and thick in girth. But this was only because I had come from Indian summer into a northern climate. The temperature had dropped thirty-five degrees since noon, and the natives here, in their heavy coats and woolen hats, looked as if they were already 'sewn in' for the winter. It is a center of small manufacturing. It has a small cotton mill but manufactures a score of things from wood brush handles, tennis racquets, furniture, heels, penholders, toys. It had been nationally most famous for the Estey pipe-organ works, which had now switched to making bomb boxes and small organs for cantonments. It had twice as many men living there as at any time in the past twenty years, but only half as many as fifty years ago. Not all of these by a long way were employed in the town. 'Brattleboro,' said a printer, 'is the bedroom for Springfield, Greenfield, and Winchester, New Hampshire.' Since the war, the town had had about 1,000 of these 'overnight resident' men who worked at factories in other towns and drove each night to Brattleboro to sleep. It doesn't take a mean imagination to guess at social problems that were frankly admitted elsewhere – high rents, casual infidelity, Victory Girls. But when I asked about these things, the Vermonters made it clear that I was straining their hospitality, and the dubious conclusion I was given was that, 'This is the town that gets the spending but not the civic problems.' The local dairy farmers (Brattleboro is the national headquarters for the Holstein-Friesian breeders) were indignant over the official reply given to their complaints over the man shortage: a study showed that the draft had taken no more men from farming than industry. The farmers maintained that these figures disguised the hundreds of men who had deserted farms for industry before the draft.

Vermonters are not amenable to investigation or questioning by strangers. I encountered an almost willful determination to admit no special problems. Factories that made small products the Army could use made them for the Army. 'The Army can use boots, don't they?' Politics? 'Whoever gets nominated on the Republican ticket in September is in, that's the rule and there don't seem to be any cause to change it.' Shortages? 'We like to get along on our own two feet. What we make we use, what we don't have, we get along without.' Unions? 'Never heard of 'em. The CIO did get into the textile mills up in Windsor County. But what would be the use here of collective bargaining? We don't need another man to bargain for us, we just go along in person.' Racial problems? 'We've gotten along for years together, and it takes more than a war to break us up. There's a large Swedish population, a few French-Canadians, some Italians, a few Jews – but Yankee Jews. Nobody's threatening anybody that I heard about.'

On the way to dinner, I noticed the names over the store fronts. Simons, Mann, Taylor, Pearson, Hunt. The stores are Yankee.

At breakfast next morning, the restaurant was packed with small men and women dressed in coarse tweeds. Very many of them still looked squat and imperturbable. It was a sunny, crisp morning but they greeted each other laconically or not at all and made hardly any kind of social noise. The men especially struck me as having faces of a remarkably English type – the flat, homely features, the baleful eye of English lower-middle-class city workers. Their silent eating spoke volumes more than intensive questioning. They accepted the food as it came, without enthusiasm or criticism. A mild attempt on my part to perk up the waiter's spirits only made him wonder if something was wrong with my order. I said there was nothing, nothing at all, everything was fine. He looked relieved, and I was aware of a set or two of expressionless eyes swiveled my way. Then they swiveled back to their plates. A quartet came in, three women and a man, and I wondered if the women were French. When their food was served they bowed their heads, and the man said a slow grace. Then they ate their meal in silence.

Only two incidents disturbed the northward drive on US 5 through the Connecticut Valley. At Westminster, a quiet village on a valley plain, I pulled into a gas station and asked for four gallons. On the whole New England trip, the mechanic had normally taken the tank key, held the hose till the bell had rung four times, come back to the driving window with the key, and then casually mentioned something about coupons. This old man of Westminster quietly asked at once for my ration book, looked carefully at the name and license number, padded off to the rear wheel to check the plate number, then sold me the gas. He tore out the coupon, handed me the key, took my money, and said, 'Bye.'

Farther north, where the only sound through rolling apple orchards was the whirr of my motor, I was about to pass the first automobile I had seen in miles. My horn went on the blink again as it had done last in Butte, Montana. Through the lovely valley suddenly the scarlet maples and the empty fields were assaulted by the steady bellow of the horn. It was a shocking sound on a Sunday morning in Vermont, and I jammed on the brakes and stood frantic but inept against the open hood of the car. I was aware of being looked at and turned around to see an old farmer, wearing a soft hat with holes in it, eyeing me in the unquestioning, uncritical way of the Brattleboro diner. We said nothing but I instinctively made way for him. He tinkered a while and the bellowing stopped. I mumbled thanks and wondered if he would resent a tip. I looked at him sideways and put this indecent thought from my mind. I thanked him again and he nodded and went back down the road. Something in his stolid gait suggested to me again the full horror of the momentary notion I had had to tip him. I felt hastily for a cigarette, jumped in the car, and beat it.

From here to White River Junction, the river ran ultramarine under a cloudless sky. The leaves, wine-red in places, drifted down to the road. Green terraces of pasture were bounded by fences of piled stones as the land curved up to little rocky hills and a foaming wave of maples. There would be horses at intervals feeding near a barn of solid red. The occasional signs said, 'Maple Syrup – Squash Cabbage'. Pyramids of pumpkins were piled by roadside stands. Then this pastoral scene was cluttered and palled by smoke from the railroad sheds of White River Junction, where I crossed the river into New Hampshire and went up to Hanover.

Coming into Hanover, the sense that the long tour was nearly over was sharpened by the incomparable grace of Dartmouth College, its classic white buildings, its ordered elms, as if the baroque orgy of America at war were here resolved into the sweet dignity of its origins, that Colonial womb to which so many Americans yearn to return but which, alas, was also a place of writhing labor and only in backward imagination can be thought of as a pretty cradle. Or say that after the frenetic discords of the South and Midwest, it was a strain by Haydn. No wonder the New England urge is strong to remember the beginnings of American life, for not since in American life have the actual needs of community life been architecturally expressed with such felicity. When the church had to be church and town-meeting place, the early builders shunned the Gothic and made them places of gaiety and light, so that Christopher Wren would marvel at the delicate cadenzas that have been played in New England on his original theme, and the Adam brothers might well feel that only here was an aristo-cratic façade purified and warmed into something for all the people to delight in. In New Hampshire especially, many farms have achieved a charming childlike unity in nests of buildings where the house and carriage-house and barns and outhouses are joined by roofed corridors.

Bulfinch and Benjamin, thou shouldst be living at this hour! Then we should see the twentieth-century counterpart of these small New England towns and colleges, then should we have beautiful subways, and everywhere exquisite movie theaters, which are, after all, our modern churches.

Dartmouth, it is still pleasing to think, is a relocated school for poor Indians. I know nothing about the second Earl of Dartmouth except that he was fired by the project and efficiently collected £11,000 for it. And, one thinks, he must have been an upright and imaginative man. It was about the Indians that I asked first. I was told proudly that any Indian who passes the entrance requirements can still attend the College tuition-free. The next sentence fell like lead: 'But other expenses virtually debar them.' There were, I believe, in 1942, a couple of Indian students keeping up the statutory benevolence of the founders.

It looked altogether like a Naval college. And so, almost, it had become. From its normal quota of 2,400 students, recruited deliberately from all over the United States and come here to learn something of the liberal arts – political science, classics, history, and, later, business administration – Dartmouth was now a Navy indoctrination school and training center for the Supply Corps. The student registration was going down, down. The healthy ones left waited for their number to come up, finished the semester, and were off to the Army. The Navy and Marine Corps had Reserve programs that might even see a boy right through college, but there was no guarantee of it. The college year had been tightened into three semesters of fifteen weeks each, with a month off at Christmas to save fuel. The famous Winter Carnival had of course been canceled. Some students told me that there was almost no trouble between the Navy and the students, 'because the Navy men are much older and sort of settled in their ways'. Lest any reader picture a muster of reconditioned admirals, I should add for the objective record that all the Navy men I saw were pink cherubs. However, that's how they impressed the students, who also told me that in the pressing matter of sex Dartmouth hewed doggedly to its monkish tradition ('The location of the college' an old gazette had remarked, 'is peculiarly favorable to study and the preservation of morals').

'Trips to girls' colleges are out,' was the comment of one boy, on account of gasoline rationing. He added without emotion, 'Few of us go out with town girls. Anyway, the Navy competition would be too stiff.'

Next morning, a white mist slid over fields drenched with dew. It was autumn in anybody's land. I retraced the road to the Junction and turned northwest into Vermont on State 14, going up between a rocky gorge and curving with the White River up through Sharon, slicing between rolling hills from which the mist was rising. In no time the mist had vanished, and through East and North Randolph the sun glittered low over a wide and sparkling valley whose forests, though still red, were fading into rust. Through the small villages, the gas stations were closed, but since the highway was rising not more than a couple of hundred feet to Montpelier, I figured there was enough gas in the tank to get me there. I crossed on to State 12 and, though the whole panorama had been broadening all morning into sweeping mountain country, it was only now I realized how changed was the landscape from Southern New England. This was the glacial upland that reaches to the St Lawrence Valley. The gray boulders I saw stacked as fences or jutting near the roots of old trees are the shavings of crunched mountains. It was a bleak thought that the section I was driving through is about the only fertile part. At Northfield is a United States Weather Bureau office, whose warnings of the roaring northeasters were now secret information the farmers had to cadge. Here in not much more than a month the snows might be deeper than the Arctic.

At Northfield Falls there was an open gas station, and the aging man who ran it was the sort of local expert on 'conditions' who chants to every passing stranger the burdens of rural life like the refrain from an old ballad.

'This farmer up the road here,' he pointed, 'they took his two sons. Might as well close up the farm. And I reckon there'll be no maple syrup next spring. Just no help, no help at all.'

The streets and houses seemed suddenly poorer, and through River- ton the wooden houses were unpainted and unkempt. I passed under rocky cliffs hanging over the Dog River and came out on to an open valley. There were series of thick stands of maples, whose leaves were as dark as dried blood. Then the road climbed up before it descended into Montpelier. It was noon, when, according to the federal guide, 'the city fairly swarms with a brief punctual life' and 'the insurance offices turn a flood of humanity into State Street.'

It was a ghost town. State Street was unflooded. There were three parked cars and an empty restaurant. But for the elms and grain elevator, a movie star might have thought he was on location some- where out West waiting to shoot the final scene where the street is cleared and at high noon the gentle hero, who has stuttered through every previous scene, now hitches up his pants and is about to throw the rustler over the false-fronts. On the whole continental trip, from February to October, I had not seen a town anywhere so impressively deserted. It is, or was, an insurance and banking town, and the state capital. There had been prosperous granite at Northfield, but the war contracts had gone to Southern granite towns, and the mills expected to close at the beginning of the New Year. There used to be 8,000 people here. There were now fewer than 6,000, and their numbers were falling fast. Whole families had closed their stores and houses and gone down to Springfield or Hartford. The office girls were deserting to jobs in Washington. Right after Pearl Harbor, a large detachment of the National Guard had gone off into training and taken their families with them. The government employees had been mostly taken by the draft. The newspaper had had a staff of fourteen. After twenty-one changes, there were still fourteen, seven men, seven girls and older women. But the only reporter was doing the make-up, and the janitor ran the printing press. The shoe store had closed. Clothing and grocery stores were thinking of doing the same. So there was almost no adver- tising. Nearby copper mines had been abandoned for hopeless lack of miners. 'Montpelier' indeed had been well named: 'the shorn hill'. The Church of the Messiah bore a sign that unintentionally seemed to accept the leavings of other faiths: 'Unitarians, Universalists, and all other Liberals'. As if the state of the town were not enough to weep over, the church provided for any future optimism with the depressing notice – 'Beware when the great God lets loose a thinker on this planet.'

Barre was also in depression. It is, I imagine, at best a gray and utilitarian town. It is the capital city of 'the Belt', the region around Barre, Montpelier, Waterbury, and Northfield that constitutes the largest granite quarry in the world. It lies in the figurative shadow of Millstone Hill, which has been quarried out of any beauty it may have had in the beginning. Barre lies at the foot of a torn gray-green hill by a river oozing yellow dirt alongside sheds, wooden houses, and railroad yards. Its streets are paved with granite blocks. It has granite statues, one of Robert Burns, to remind you that granite workers came originally from Scotland. Its inhabitants breathe an atmosphere compounded of granite dust and the smell of sour apples. But granite is not copper, and the war story was a sad one.

Almost none of the industry could be switched to war. The skilled men, used to air-pressure tools and handling blasts, 'fit nicely into the Army'. The heavy workers, the riggers and the crane operators, had gone off to better pay in the East Coast shipyards. Some of the granite workers left had offered to help the farmers harvest the rotting apples at weekends. And enthusiastic schoolboys had offered to farm on vacation. But a nearby farmer came in from the fields to find a young boy fast asleep by a mechanical milker, which was pumping away on a dry cow bellowing to high heaven. Said the farmer, 'Just ain't worth the anxiety, risking this equipment with boys and men from the quarries. I'd be scared of comin' home and finding the cows and the tits in two separate places.'

The Mayor of Barre was being roundly abused for having appealed to the War Production Board for a war industry on the truthful grounds that the granite business was 'non-essential to war'. Promptly the Quarriers Cooperative, the United Stone Workers of America, and the Barre Granite Association, Inc., refuted this slander with the ghoulish argument that 'we think you will concede that war usually means higher mortality in human lives than in peace times. What are we going to do with the dead? Mass burials on land or sea? Mass cremations? That is reverting back to paganism, is it not?' Paganism or not, few people could see a thriving industrial future in the mass manufacture of tombstones of good Christian granite. The point was decently evaded. How desperate the morale was of these protesting workers, manufacturers, and editors can be gathered from the fact that at the first promise of a war industry needing granite, the evening paper blazoned the news across the headlines. There was at least printed rejoicing over 'a new, important, possibility-laden field for the utilization of Barre granite'. A local quarry had made a deal with a Georgia firm making insoluble chicken grit. Within the space of four weeks only, it was hinted that prosperity would appear from around the corner. Barre would be manufacturing 'crushed granite for chicken grit'. At the outset, it was reported, the project would employ not fewer than twenty-five men. And Barre would soon be giving vital assistance to the 'tremendous expansion of the poultry business' that the government had requested. Insoluble grit from Barre granite would produce those 'healthier, sturdier, and larger chickens' that are the Chickens for Victory.

East of Barre, an unpaved road joins up with US 2, and thence the highway runs by the Winooski River through a valley, then climbs into high hills stiff with evergreens and higher still with short mountain pine and nibbling sheep. The only civilized signs up here were straggling, unpainted barns and advertisements for maple syrup. The sugar farmers were resigned to despair. The syrup is carried in steel drums. The War Production Board had flatly banned the shipment of the sugar in metal containers, an order that applied to drums already owned. Vermont produces about a third of the nation's 3 million gallons of syrup.

With pathetic restraint, the local paper reported this order under a stoic, single-column headline: 'Complete Collapse For Syrup Trade Seen'. This is the last comment I need to make about maple syrup, because, frighteningly, it was the last any farmer I talked to wanted to make. When I tried to fume with a little decent sympathy, I was regarded with slow, eye-blinking boredom. I was simply not one of the family, and the implication was that every family should be left to bury its own. Evidently Vermont, like Texas, is an ideology as well as a state. And the ironies of fate are the butter on a Vermonter's hard-bought bread.

The highway climbed up to rolling uplands of larger farms, distant hills, and to the left and north the seemingly barren heath of Caledonia County. Then it swung down 600 feet into St Johnsbury. Now the towns had the emotional effect of towns in the Colorado Rockies or the scrubland of Eastern Washington; they were cozy fortresses against the long stretches of loneliness. So that I found myself noticing and approving the simplest signs that meant home to someone – out of St Johnsbury such signs as 'Vermont hardwood chairs', 'J. C. Warren, Cattle, Horses, and Real Estate', 'Cream-Top Dairy Farm', and the simple reminder of the solid life, 'S. Goldberg – Autos'. At Concord after a drive through fertile, sloping pastureland there was a line of three-decker houses, like the ones the French-Canadians lived in at Southbridge, Massachusetts.

Then the land crumpled into jutting, stony country and cutover forests, and accordingly the barns were broken down and many of the farms abandoned, the stony fruit of the earth too much even for the patience of a Vermonter. But after Lunenberg, you are in green mountain valleys again and cattle grazing. I crossed the New Hampshire line at Lancaster, and though a state border always suggests a complete change of scene, this was one of the times when the promise comes true. For twenty-five miles the highway curls round forest, dives down glades, cuts through lovely river valleys and opens up to the south on the finest peaks of the Presidentials. I turned up through thinner forest to follow the Androscoggin River past the great pulp mill at Cascades and up to the belching smokestacks, logging sluices, mountains of lumber, miles of brick mills, cluttered frame houses, and three-deckers of Berlin, New Hampshire.

It was startlingly like Butte, Montana – an isolated one-industry town, with houses and mills tumbling over each other as if there were not a spare acre of habitable land in sight. A poor-man's town with an average of four children to a family, so that in a town of not quite 18,000 there were 4,000 children at school. An unsocial, tense town, hemmed in by the mountains from all spaciousness and easy manners. Its war record was impressive, and it would have to be to make up for the apparent blight of human dignity that such single-industry towns unfailingly carry.

It works by wood and wood pulp; normally by newsprint, towels, cable insulation, and an inconceivable amount of paper (annually enough, they boast, to girdle the globe nineteen times). It makes the highest grade of camera-film base. Its chemical plant made 90 percent of American war chemicals. The paper mill was producing gas mask filters and a nitrate pulp to take the place of guncotton.

It has that absolutely solid, ugly, nineteenth-century bricky permanence about it that only a blitz can destroy. As long as industrial processes are stable, the smoke will pour from the smokestacks. But the plants are old and, everybody knows, cannot be rehabilitated. About 100 families had gone down to Hartford, but the majority stayed in the place they were born, would slave and breed and die there. One large, kindly, exhausted man who had lived in the town since boyhood had little hope for the years after the war. 'A lotta people here,' he said, 'have started worrying about it already. The competition's going to be tough, awful tough, after the war, with the prospect of new plants out West and Swedish pulp coming back.'

He mentioned the tight labor situation. 'Honestly, I hope most of those families aren't coming back. I'm scared of what it's gonna be like here, if there's a depression. I'm going to put my family in the car and go out West.'

Increasingly, from Connecticut north, I had felt, in talking to farmers, that I was visiting New England through its second era of abandoned farms. Here in Berlin, I felt, as in Barre, that it was also the first era of abandoned industries. My friend may have been a constitutional pessimist, but he was convinced that the heyday of single industries in New England had been eclipsed by the technological progress of the war, by modern plants, by the threatened industrial rise of California.

It was not hard to drop south to the intersection and head for the coast on US 2 again. The drug of landscape was easy to take again, and in a long grove of birches near Shelburne, hundreds of them were shining like an arch of drawn swords as far as the eye could see. I crossed into Maine, and at Bethel I turned southeast on State 26, along the low, rolling plateau with wide vistas of mountains from which the memory of the fall had almost completely faded. From the cut-off, on State 11, through Mechanic Falls and Auburn the road swings over sparse pineland showered with boulders and ridged with gravel, past spreading lakes, undistinguished woolen mill and oilcloth towns, paper mill towns, and then round the head of two long lakes into Augusta, by the Kennebec.

It is the kind of town that any Easterner, or provincial Englishman or Frenchman, feels he has been in before. The natives were not as introspective and distant as the men of Vermont. Nor were they warm and forthcoming. The war was a fact that didn't seem to call for celebrations or deep gloom, but something in between, something between indifference and sympathy. There is nothing epic about making shoes and blankets. They have been made and worn the same way for a long time now, and nobody entertained fears or hopes about postwar techniques or any threat by Mr Kaiser of making magnesium shoes on an assembly-line. What produces these abrupt changes in the regional balance of character is a topic that will stimulate everybody's guess till the end of time. But some responses to climate have been jotted down before now in this chronicle. And I will risk pressing the pathetic fallacy so far as to say that it would not be hard to guess which section of the country had once been depressed by an immense, slow continental glacier. Having submitted to this providential cooling for thousands of years of the Ice Age, it would be remarkable if the present inhabitants of Maine blew as hot as Texans or Californians. I had the sense, undoubtedly prejudiced by the awful knowledge of the great glacier, that whatever was mercurial or passionate in the Maine character had been on ice these hundreds of years.

'The main business here,' said a contented editor in pince-nez, his hands folded across his lap, 'is government. We have a home for disabled veterans, and after the war we expect it to expand. Let me see, there's two shoe factories, now making Army shoes. We also make skis, which I imagine are for ski-troops. Winthrop is now making Army blankets. Norway and Paris and Wilton used to make heavy shoes for Arctic explorations. Now they're making aviation shoes.'

I asked him about labor, about the huge potato crop, about the tourist trade. He breathed on his pince-nez, replaced them, and, like a college dean indicating the prescribed courses, went on: 'Well, we have had our little troubles, of course. The shipyard labor at Portland draws the lower-paid groups, especially the farmhands. The farmers have been inconvenienced. The potato crop is, however, in the extreme northeast of the state. It's already harvested. The pulp mills, so far as I know, have had no problems. The woodsmen, of course, have – you might say – deserted to the forces and war industries. That's been rather trying.'

In a mild stupor I said goodbye and went to bed in a quiet hotel, following two old ladies in lace down a long corridor and turning with conscious decorum into the room next to theirs.

Next day I headed for the sea, for Portland, the last port of call before returning to New York, driving down the edge of the glacial plain with its stony country and burnt-over pine to Brunswick. As I turned on to US 1, there was a heavy sea mist east, and to the west a clear blue sky. At Yarmouth my car faced the ocean, and it looked indeed like journey's end. There was no outline of anything round the whole curve of the horizon, only a heaving semi-circle of gray sea vaporizing into an oyster-white mist, into which loomed the brown smears of the islands of Casco Bay. Somewhere above, in a high bank of mist, a Coast Guard plane droned over and around the bay. Out to sea there was a fussier drone of a Coast Guard patrol boat. By noon, the mist had lifted and the sun was warm over a gray-green sea.

Here the humdrum population of fishermen and yachtsmen were disciplined into a routine that brought the war lapping to the edge of the rocks. Fishermen known for a lifetime as 'Ned with the drooling beard' had filled out the secret particulars of their life for the Coast Guard. Every farmer with a gun carried a Coast Guard permit. Every boat for every purpose carried a new license from the Coast Guard. Every boat had to be in before dark. The loading of explosives at the shipyards was supervised – by the Coast Guard. The lonely inhabitants of the numberless islands had been plotted and identified for the first time, and licensed to stay there – by the Coast Guard. The lifeboats and lighthouses were under Coast Guard orders. Every foreign ship that came over the horizon had to have military clearance from the Coast Guard. A fishing boat hoisted its sails. A Coast Guard permit ship was after it.

The Coast Guard personnel were recruited from yachtsmen for officers, fishermen for crews. Consequently, there could hardly have been a more democratic branch of the service. The fishermen knew every inlet and island and freak of tide. They would have laughed at Navy discipline exacted from them by keen young men they had taught to sail. It was the fishermen, the crews, who made possible the most laborious and crafty operation of the US Coast Guard – the safeguarding of the thousand entrances to the ports of Maine by the careful sinking of schooners, building of underwater walls, laying of mine fields, booms, and submarine nets.

For Portland was the end of the safe continent, the beginning of the Atlantic and the real war.

When I returned home to New York, I realized that during 1942 it had been the war's most remarkable ghost town. Usually the city was so busy writing about itself as a showplace, and glamorously defying the war with the glitter of bright baubles in its store windows, that not many New Yorkers could tell you offhand how the padding natives make their living. New York to New Yorkers is where the office and the 'El' are, but ask them what New York does and stands for and they will think of museums and parks, nightclubs and café society, Broadway and Wall Street, books, celebrities, Rockefeller Plaza, and perhaps where to buy a jacket with two pairs of pants. Not many of them offhand think of the town as living mainly by its clothing and printing industries and its declining port. Probably very few New Yorkers were aware, at the end of 1942, that almost one-quarter of the nation's unemployed were there among them – over 400,000 idle. Building-trades workers, immobilized by the government order against constructing private buildings for the duration, gone to Army construction work elsewhere or into new jobs in war plants in New Jersey, Maryland, and New England. A third of the garment workers were threatened by clothes rationing and were making too few uniforms. The city's army of store clerks watched the storeroom stocks dwindle away, but made terrific profits on what was left. While Detroit enjoyed war contracts to the extent of $2,750 per capita of its population, and the national average was $480, New York had scrimped up a mere $200. Land-rents being what they are on this small and vastly over-inhabited island, there was little inducement for war manufacturers, big or small, to come in and build. (Although, through 1943, Mayor La Guardia was to fly like a hornet back and forth between New York and Washington, and small plants eventually went up on Long Island, in crowded Queens, and in Brooklyn.) So that when the wind blew from the northeast, it deposited on office desks of midtown skyscrapers a fine powder of unfamiliar soft-coal dust. But this hardly looked like the gold of Midas. New York's great days, some people thought, were over.

Spring came late to the Eastern Seaboard in 1943. But when it came, with the cherry blossoms glowing in Central Park, and the branches of trees everywhere erect for new leaves, Americans of two generations walked in the sunlight and knew that they were missing something. You would see young office workers sitting out on their lunch hour by the plaza at Radio City, staring up wistfully at the parallelograms of blue sky that Mr Rockefeller's project allows the city worker. They talked of Jones Beach, of cooking steaks on spring evenings down at water's edge across the river in New Jersey, of weekends up the Housatonic, or of surfcasting from the South Shore of Long Island. They had only to recall what they had done any previous year with their spring and summer weekends to know what it was the war made them miss most. It was an automobile. You could look down from any high building on Fifth or Madison and see about as many automobiles as Mrs Astor knew twenty-five years ago. They were mostly yellow and red and green – taxis, with a sprinkle of sober limousines bearing an MD's license plate. A visiting Briton looking down on this sight, his belt uncomfortably tight after three-and-a-half years of war, would often remark that it would do Americans good to learn to walk. This is a sound moral observation, but it is as spiritually satisfying to the ordinary American as telling a bankrupt baker that man does not live by bread alone. For the time being, you can discuss standards of want most fairly by comparing normal standards of comfort. And in the past twenty years the automobile has never been, as it still is to Europeans, a symbol of luxury or even of comfort. It is as necessary to the well-being of Americans as love or a place to keep things cold. And by 1943 it was probably the most irksome American loss.

Other than for this, it was substantially the same city in the spring of 1943 as it was in 1942. The war did not appear to threaten New York's present, but it was holding in reserve body blows to New

York's future. In other places, clothes were being made for the armed forces in modern factories that were not likely to close down afterward in deference to Manhattan's third-of-a-million idle clothing workers. Other great ports, from Portland, Maine, to Jacksonville, Florida, had surprisingly surpassed the city's harbor in war cargoes. New Yorkers still could point to New York as some sort of American cultural capital. 'This,' said one writer, 'is the luminous hope held out for it.' But one wondered whether New York, which in many respects is so remote from the United States, was in a position to realize that hope. It is hardly possible that New York will become the 'Paris of the United States', unless somehow it manages to acquire a little more of the national character.

You might come up the long ramp from the track at Grand Central Station and hear the muted, busy footfalls across the concourse, and see the shafts of crystalline light, the ducking redcapped porters, and feel the unresting vibrations of the city. And these signs are good to come back to, because, to anybody who has for long lived in this city, they are, God help us, the signs of home. But today New York is more than ever the home of the homeless, the capital of American as well as European refugees. There is nothing lamentable in this, except that so many speak for America out of it, and report the news of America in this context. But it is a little clearer today that New York is unique as a great metropolis in that, while it unquestionably has its own characteristic life, this life does not focus the life of the rest of the country, as London is the distillation of all English character and custom. But I had a sense this leg of my journey of returning *from* America and entering an international settlement. One mingled with its people, the smart and the swarthy, went down to the docks, caught the nervous chatter at Fifth and Fifty-ninth of the wealthy refugee French, and, it seemed, the entire unscathed population of the Riviera. This impression is worth mentioning if only because it soon gets blurred. It is not New York's view of itself, nor, it would seem, that of the hinterland.

Through the subsequent fall and early winter of 1943, New York became the market town of anybody on the Eastern Seaboard with a 100-dollar bill to spare. And, by the middle of 1943 there were more of these fellows than New York could bed. As if to disguise its precarious economy, New York clapped a clown's mask on and became Tijuana on the Hudson. The hotels had never known such business. The theaters paraded, to ecstatic audiences, some of the vulgarest comedies and ineptest plays that have ever been done in English. The nightclubs minted fortunes unmatched even in the lunatic 20s. And as the cost of living went higher, more and more girls seemed to have mink and silver fox to wear. A fashionable store that had carried only Swedish glass sold its entire stock in October, refilled the space with gaudy cut-glass, and sold out just the same. Whiskey suddenly vanished from the shelves of all the city's liquor stores and was wafted foxily into the cellars, there to be decked out with straw and ribbons and magically produced at Christmas for an unheard-of seven dollars a bottle. Oceans of corrosive Cuban gin came into New Orleans and Baltimore and, tarted up in Brooklyn with clean corks and tinfoil hot from the press, was marketed to thousands of 'privileged' customers as being the authentic produce of Plymouth, Gordon's, Gilbey's, and a handful of other English firms whose tasters would have dropped dead at the first sip. The decent pretense that evening clothes were tasteless in wartime was healthily abandoned around Christmastime, as the unreality of 'the war' slipped further into memory. And this happy unrestraint was imitated on most levels of New York's white society. New York had collected from every warehouse of the Eastern Seaboard and gave its all at Christmas 1943, for one last dizzy spree. Up in Springfield, Connecticut, the federal bankruptcy court closed down for lack of business.

Epilogue: Four Months in 1945

When you are trying to write the history of the living, there is a pathetic pretense involved in beginning a new chapter. A novelist's material is the kingdom of his own fantasy, and his chapters stake his claims to a dramatic sense of order. But chapters are a convention of writing, not of history. And the material of history is continuous, undifferentiated, and unpredictable. The beginnings and the ends, the 'periods' and 'movements' are not facts but interpretations claimed years later by scholars. Nobody can say when Americans at home first became aware of living through a new tedium that was by now old stuff to Europeans, when they began to know the seasons as an ironic cycle of promise, threats, disappointed hopes, scandals, and again back to new promises. There is no obvious or compelling reason for beginning a new chapter for the spring of 1945, or for choosing to skip earlier seasons. Perhaps to Admiral Chester Nimitz, the first day of April was always a historic day. For then the Central Pacific offensive, that had started so bloodily on Tarawa in November 1943, spanning and conquering 3,000 miles of blue water, had landed at the back door of the Japanese homeland, in the Ryukyu Islands. Nimitz's battlefield was as impressive as any in history, roughly a sea area of 4.25 million square miles. And from the end of 1943, the gigantic conquest had proceeded first to the Gilberts, then the Marshalls in early 1944, the Marianas in the summer, Palau in the fall, and through the winter the Philippines had begun to give way inch by inch to General Douglas MacArthur. And now in the grand climax of all amphibious operations, on April 1st, 1945, Americans had landed on Okinawa.

But in the United States, there was no discoverable break with the chronic complexity of the winter. The blooming of the dogwood in the

Northeastern states would be as real a beginning as any. Or the national curfew, which doused the cocky neon of American nighttime in one-street desert towns as much as it did in all the cities. The curfew may have saved little coal, or eased the burden of few railroads, but it gave to evenings in America some of the unwinking European gloom. It sobered the sprouting hopes of the tabloid midnight editions. By negating the cheerfulness of light, it insisted that the war in Europe, from which so many false promises had sprung, might drag on for months. If this was 'good for morale', it was also bad for it in extending the time at home when people could consider the nagging worries of the nation. In the spring of 1945, these were some of them:

Twelve hundred war casualties a day were arriving in the United States, while 200,000 slaphappy Americans were returning refreshed to their wartime labors from Miami Beach, which featured, in a winter season of gorgeous 'normalcy', such happy symbols of Allied unity as a Russian ermine bathing suit, with matching ermine-tailed umbrella, for $2,500, and a Bolivian chinchilla coat for $40,000. For more homespun tastes, New York could offer gold cigarette lighters for $150.00, and gold lipsticks (with 'the acorn effect') for $200.00.

The black market in meat was now so expertly organized that its profits far outshone the amateur take of the liquor lords of the 20s. There were said to be 80 million healthy cattle available in the country, and the American housewife could be puritanically honest and question her butcher on his sources, or feed the faces of her family and pay fancy prices that shocked nobody but the Office of Price Administration. The black market was no longer a clandestine factory of protein. It was the normal source of supply. Any friendly butcher would tell you that at least 90 percent of the butchers in New York dealt, for their own survival, in the black market.

The American housewife was sore and resigned. The Senate began an investigation to find out where the food and the profits were going, why the OPA was helpless, how the Army justified its huge storages. There were daily lines outside the United States Customs barrier at Detroit, an estimated 2,000 householders a day went over into Ontario and came back with hamburger, lamb, pork, and chickens. There were also lines outside most chain drugstores, throughout the country, every time the word got around that a new supply of cigarettes was in. In New York, every morning, the line outside Benson & Hedges went half-way around the block, and was solicited occasionally by cruising taxi-drivers warily offering cartons of standard brands at four dollars a throw.

Mr James F. Byrnes, the Home Front mobilizer, resigned because he thought 'that V-E day is not far distant', which killed all hope that Congress would pass a mild national service bill, for there was an all too apparent absurdity in writing into law nationwide controls on workers at the moment. Mr Byrnes decided to make way for the man who would relax the controls on industry. This rising optimism in Washington was dashed by a public warning issued from Germany by General Dwight D. Eisenhower not to expect 'a clean-cut military surrender of the forces on the Western Front', implying that for many months it might be necessary to roam the mountains of Germany and weed out fanatic pockets of Nazi resistance. Also from Germany came hideous pictures of American prisoners, from the Battle of the Bulge, found in a prison camp at Limburg. The meat-eaters of the United States, starved for steaks, could look with decent embarrassment at the placid skeletons of men for whom rehabilitation would mean the strength to lift a fork to their faces.

The always rumbling suspicion of Russia, increased by dispatches about the likely establishment of a Communist puppet regime in Rumania and the long delay in laying down the 'broad democratic base' of a new Polish government, resounded angrily throughout the nation's press when it became known that a secret agreement had been reached at the Yalta conference whereby Russia would be assured three votes in the future assembly of the United Nations, two extra for the Ukraine and Byelo-Russia. The tricky job of defending this agreement fell on the Secretary of State, Edward R. Stettinius, since – the newsmen had been confidentially told – President Roosevelt was down in Warm Springs, Georgia, resting from the strain of Yalta. Russia then announced that its representative at the San Francisco conference to found a United Nations Organization would be its young Ambassador to Washington, Andrei Gromyko, and not Mr Vyacheslav Molotov, the old diplomatic equal of Mr Anthony Eden and Mr Stettinius. Affection for Russia was further strained by its imperturbable request that since the new Polish government was as yet unformed, the sponsoring powers should invite to the San Francisco conference the provisional Warsaw government. Britain and the United States promptly and indignantly refused.

Several million Americans in the Southern states were anxiously looking north, where the tributaries of the Mississippi were raging far above flood level. In Missouri and Kentucky, German prisoners of war were called in to help Army engineers pile sandbags on the levees. A new edition of De Tocqueville's *Democracy in America* (1835–40) came out. Shirley Temple, the precocious baby star of the 30s, got engaged. Decca Records issued a history of jazz in albums ranging from Jelly-Roll Morton to the Quintette of the Hot Club of France, while saloons and college campuses echoed with an old cowboy song, revived by Tin Pan Alley, 'Don't Fence Me In'. The patrons of New York's Museum of Modern Art saw a retrospective show of the paintings of Georges Rouault. And movie fans were being charmed by the well-worn pairing of Spencer Tracy and Katharine Hepburn in *Without Love*. A Washington mother, whose husband was serving with the Navy, christened her twin babies Iwo and Jima.

Seven Allied armies were way across the Rhine, the US Ninth at the Elbe, only sixty-three miles from Berlin. The Canadians had cut off all Nazi escape through the Netherlands. The British were almost in Bremen. Russians were crashing through Vienna, and other Russians were nearing the outskirts of Berlin. *Variety* reported that the best-selling song of the day was 'My Dreams Are Getting Better All The Time'.

This was the America one was musing over at twelve minutes to six on Thursday, April 12th, when the United Press ticker, tapping out a dispatch from Rome about the British Eighth Army's crossing of the Santerno River, paused after the 'r' in river and waited. Then the bell rang, once, twice – a bulletin maybe. It went on to five times, which is the signal for a flash. But it rang on ceaselessly. There was a moment's silence, a misspelled word appeared, a second's pause, and the paper roller chattered up for another line. Then it tapped out this brief, astounding sentence: WASHINGTON – PRESIDENT ROOSEVELT DIED THIS AFTERNOON.

Many people I have since spoken to are surprised that they cannot recall what they did immediately after they heard the news. Because I was a newsman and at once had to plan to say something about it to a foreign audience, I remember the physical chill and the feeling of having your senses go slightly out of focus. A few minutes later I was out on the streets of New York. I went across town to Broadway and exchanged glances with hundreds of people. Some looked stonily back, some were preoccupied, most of them were curiously suspicious of a direct glance. Down a long midtown street of early evening crowds going to the movies or home from work, I noticed only one couple, young girls, talking and kidding together in a normal way that was now alarming. I asked them if they had heard the news. They had not. When I told them, one of them grabbed the other's forearm and said, 'Oh my God!' with such a full cry of emotion that any other day it would have drawn a crowd. In a drugstore, the manager stood in shirtsleeves, his arms folded, slowly picking his teeth while a band played music over the radio. A girl at the cashier's desk said, 'You gonna leave that music on?' The manager came to with a start and switched it off. Outside Radio City a long line of moviegoers stood restlessly, graver than any American queue could ever be. One family seemed to be in a rising argument about whether to stay. It was the father who broke away, and to the wife and grown daughter following him in embarrassment he made an impatient, deprecatory gesture with his hand and said, 'It wouldn't mean a thing.'

By now the radio networks, which had sent the news to factories and desert ranches, to every crowded and silent part of the land, were deciding to abandon for the time being all entertainment. As you twirled the knob round the dial and back again, the orchestras were fading, the evening serials were cut, there was the unreal surcease of advertising. Suddenly, all over America, nobody was selling anything. The unfailing sales talk, which is to American radio the systole and diastole of a fevered pulse, was flagging; the unceasing signal of the molassic to the moronic had weakened and given out.

Now instead the twirling knob spanned all the cadences that an American voice can sound. Everybody who had ever known Roosevelt, or written about him, or hated him, was called upon to sound historic. Then were the ears of the nation bathed with floods of sentimental and unctuous talk that would have been said of a mediocre man and that were to flow for two whole days and nights and overwhelm the small voice of genuine sorrow. But before this happened, before 'homage' was paid, or 'tributes' planned, when people were thrown off balance by the shock itself, the official plans were being announced over the radio and spoken into a vacuum of national emotion.

It had been a cerebral hemorrhage. He had been going to attend a barbecue, and the fiddlers were already rehearsing his favorite jigs. He had been ill for three weeks. Vice-President Truman had been on call for so long. Mrs Roosevelt had sent a message to her five sons in the forces. The Vice-President was being escorted by Secret Service men to the White House. The Cabinet was in emergency meeting. There would be a service Saturday afternoon in the White House and the funeral up the Hudson, at Hyde Park, on Sunday.

As America went to bed that astounding night, words came in from all over the globe: of men momentarily disheartened on Okinawa, of Chinese in Chungking offering their hands to American soldiers, of lawyers and cleaning women, pool players and ranchers, and hash-slingers and college boys stopped dead in their tracks; of the sad streets of London and the shaking heads in the Moscow subways, while the black flags swirled up over the Kremlin; of the Ninth and First armies pausing in shock at the brink of the Elbe; of suspended gaiety in Belgrade, and the toneless billboards of Paris, 'Roosevelt est mort'; and of those most miserable and outcast in the world, a few raddled survivors of a Nazi concentration camp, ennobling this universal shudder with a gesture typical of its poignancy and helplessness, raising up a torn black rag over Buchenwald.

By the next night all the most splendid words in the language had been milked dry by the radio. If goodness and courage were so cheap, it seemed impossible they could go on moving anybody. But beneath the wealth of protestation, an emotional convulsion had happened to the American people that was most chilling to feel and disturbing to look back on. In those who had liked and admired him, there was a bewildered sense of loss; in those who hated him a moment's irritation that he had failed them. These feelings are the same feeling, or better a positive and a negative reaction to the same unconscious dependency. Either of them is the exact reaction of a child to the loss of a father: one admits the dependence, the other – equally bound – resents it. A Republican I knew, a generous and impulsive man, who had loathed Roosevelt with careful intensity since 1934, remarked in a mutter, 'I could have forgiven him everything but dying on us right now.' Dying *on us*! As if he had performed an actual dereliction of duty.

Through the Friday night, the President's train went up from Georgia to Washington, and to those who accompanied it, or saw it pass, no journey they knew of had been so somber. The coincidence of Lincoln's lonesome train was so pressing that spontaneously, without benefit of a press association cue, newspapers many hundreds of miles apart remembered or reprinted Walt Whitman's poem of 1865. In thus identifying with a single great voice of unashamed expressiveness and power, there was the rare revelation of a country reaching for its essential style. Other nations have at such times the art of irony or decorum. And the citizens of those nations have always to restrain the ache to see America conform to their own notions of taste and propriety. But in echoing Whitman, Americans were for once true to a power that is uniquely theirs, the full-volumed resonance of an emotion that is untidy, unabashed, violent, and grievous. Every sort of Southerner walked or scrambled to the small stations, many tenant farmers dressing their children in all they had, hundreds of families standing in the warm night in freight-yards, at stations, and in the fields standing by the 'lilac blooming perennial and drooping star in the west' to watch the black train slide north. In Washington, in a dreary light, six white horses drew the casket through the streets. The newsreels of these watching crowds are among the most direct expressions I have seen of human beings with their defenses down. There was general weeping, in the many ways that many characters can do it. There was, especially, one tense colored woman who will last as long as the film does, who craned to wave goodbye as the caisson passed, showing almost a panic that he might not turn to make a last recognition. At precisely four in the afternoon, when the service started, and as if he had some typical, dramatic pact with the Almighty, a great fork of lightning struck and a roll of thunder sounded in New York.

At night again the train turned north to New York, and on the Sunday went up along the green valley of the Hudson River, shining with forsythia and cherry on a cloudless day. At the family home in Hyde Park, they buried him in a rose garden bounded by a magnificent hedge of hemlock about twenty feet high. Although the whole hedge was lined with soldiers, sailors, Marines, and on all sides of the grave but one there stood the Cabinet, the Chiefs of Staff, the Supreme Court and, it seemed, all the faces one had ever seen on the covers of national magazines, yet it was a simple affair and a decent burial, that is literally becoming to one who was neither an awe-inspiring nor a solemn man.

When it was all over, an officer took the flag, which had been held continuously over the open grave, and walked over to Mrs Roosevelt and gave it to her. Then the family, and the Generals, and the great men, moved away. The ordinary natives and the tenants at Hyde Park stood a while, a man and a boy bent down and pocketed the cartridge blanks the firing party had left. The sense was strong then that what had to be done with an era and a reputation had been done, and that these children would grow up and have to be told about an incon-sequent festival they had attended. Soon there was nobody left but the high trees and the birds singing in them. We were back to normal life again, where Roosevelt came in long ago.

Nothing could have contributed more to the inevitability of this norm than the presence against the hedge during the service of a small, homely looking man in steel-rimmed glasses and a light felt hat. He was a spare-built Midwestern farmer in a business suit, a face and form you see everywhere on Sundays throughout Kansas and Iowa and Missouri. He had been a railroad porter, a drugstore clerk, an unsuccessful haberdasher, a county judge, and the chore man for a city political machine. He was the new President of the United States. Wrote the *New Yorker*, 'President Roosevelt was for the people, but Harry Truman *is* the people.'

In the following weeks, the President gave to Americans the most satisfying reassurance, the new reassurance of being like themselves. One did not need to memorize his face. It rode on buses at your elbow, nodded to greet you in barbershops, its owner handed money to you at the teller's window, measured you dexterously for a tropical worsted suit. It was inspiring to feel again that any man can be Pres-ident. What we learned about him from the newsreels and the columns was to the good, confirmation of this proverb. His wife cooked his meals and washed the dishes. He was a family man who occasionally played poker with the boys. He enjoyed county fairs and a sociable snort of bourbon. His first proclamation was to set the date for Mother's Day. If he struck panic into any breasts, they must have belonged to members of the Republican National Committee, who for so long had mourned the passing of 'the American way of life'. Truman was it, and by so being was undoubtedly guilty of John Fischer's charge that he had 'infringed the Republican copyright'.

Yet he pacified all comers. Standing trimly before Congress in his first presidential appearance in the House, he promised that the war should go on 'unhampered and unchanged'. He raised both hands and asked only that he might be 'a good and faithful servant of my Lord'. He successfully appealed to Stalin to send Molotov to San Francisco as the chief Russian delegate. He endorsed Lend-Lease, the reciprocal trade program, the Export-Import Bank, the Bretton Woods agreements. He promised that the United States would stay close with its Allies and try 'to serve and not to dominate the world'. The newspapers humanized this accommodating man. His mother had said he plowed the straightest furrow in Jackson County, Missouri. Conservatives disturbed by his blanket endorsement of the Roosevelt policies reminded us that those who learn the facts of life on a farm are rarely visionaries. Old Isolationists who feared for Mr Truman's end of the deal when he came to sit in with Churchill and Stalin were comforted with the folk-legend that Missourians have to be shown.

As the delegates of forty-six nations were landing on American soil and making their way to San Francisco for the United Nations conference, the war indeed was going on unhampered and unchanged. Leipzig was falling. Ernie Pyle, the combat sidekick of every ordinary American, was killed in the Pacific. Berlin was a shambles, and the Russians were talking to the approaching Americans on their field radio sets.

On April 25th, American and Russian patrols met in the late afternoon on a bridge across the Elbe. That same day the United Nations Conference on International Organization opened in San Francisco. The task of these forty-six nations was to consider the Dumbarton Oaks proposals, and the supplementary agreements at Yalta, as a first draft of a United Nations Charter and to write that charter in San Francisco, embodying the framework of a new League of Nations, comprising a General Assembly, in which all the United Nations should be members; an International Court of Justice; an international Secretariat, probably a joint General Staff; above all a Security Council, consisting of the Big Five and six others that would have the chief power to settle quarrels, investigate threats to the peace, devise punishments and enforce them; and an Economic and Social Council, whose vast ambition would be to study a fair share of food and raw materials for the peoples of the earth, to raise the universal standards of health and education, in a word to anachronize war by learning its preventive medicine, its causes and symptoms in economic geography. This, in simplest précis, was the awful job to which these hundreds of urbane and famous statesmen addressed themselves as they sat down under the brilliant milky spotlights in San Francisco's Opera House, in a dramatic blue setting designed by the New York Theater Guild's Jo Mielziner.

Throughout the contentious nine weeks of sessions, only the Big Three could demand a public showdown whenever the wording of a principle suggested a threatening application to their own economic and strategic interests. The small nations and the 'middle powers' could seem to be more idealistic, because their own interests were more local, unlike Russia, Britain, and the United States, whose interests were affected by almost any generalization you might care to formulate about the rights of man. Yet these smaller powers, too, always had a pet grievance in mind, even when the public argument appeared to be a matter of pure linguistics. Toward the end of the conference, the small nations seemed anxious to go on record as making their own interested interpretations of the abstract legal language in which the Charter was written.

One looked down on the house from a box and wondered that a world so varied and unbridled in its passions could here achieve so genteel, so amiable a microcosm: the jutting, elegant profile of Mr Eden, the pink carnation and the occasional dozing head of Lord Halifax. The bald head of Mr Attlee bent low over a paper on which at intervals he drew intricate doodles with a red pencil. Across the aisle, the sleek, broad face and the dazzling white hair of Mr Stettinius, bandying profiles with Mr Eden. The attentive eyes of Senator Arthur Vandenberg, the pince-nez of Representative Sol

Bloom, the grave boyish attention of Commander Harold Stassen. A few rows in front the gleaming white robes of the Arabs, and their well-mannered whispers. A few rows behind, the moon face of Mr Molotov, firmly seated between his delegates, who had the uniform appearance of London School of Economics students but were in reality revolutionary Georgians and Ukrainians tamed and tailored in Sears, Roebuck suits. Far off across the serried rows of business suits, 'unmarred' as one San Francisco paper said 'by a single cutaway' there would be such vivid interruptions as the shaved bullet head of a Chinese admiral, compact in black and gold, the erect torso of South African Field Marshal Jan Smuts, his face newly tanned from dawn excursions up Mount Tamalpais or down to Muir Woods for rare additions to his botany specimens. The only disturbance of this decorum was the rhythm of the news photographers, padding up and down the aisles like housebroken bloodhounds. It required a rousing effort to recall that this suave body of men included Foreign Secretaries who had been known to jail their political opponents; Ministers who not so many months before had been hunted half-way across Europe in the disguise of farmers and old women; Presidents and diplomats who had weathered in their career several assassination attempts; fathers of sons dead or maimed or lost with the underground; and some Chinese who had no notion where or how their families lived.

On the Saturday afternoon of the first week, the rumor got around that the Nazis had surrendered. Mr Molotov was presiding over a plenary session when a Latin-American delegate in a front row suddenly opened an edition of the *Call-Bulletin* and waved its four-inch headline, printed in scarlet, 'Nazis Quit'. An expectant rustle ran around the galleries, and there was a spatter of applause, which the Foreign Minister of Ecuador, then holding forth, took to be approval for a sentiment he had just delivered. He paused, blushed in happy surprise, and Mr Molotov rose, smiled approvingly at the audience, and motioned the speaker to continue. He continued. The photographers alacritously took up strategic positions near to the Russians, the British, the Americans for the moment when the news would be announced from the stage. A French photographer came running into the box I was sitting in, begged the best position, and reloaded his camera for posterity. News service photographers beseeched him to share his vantage point. But the sweat rolled down his face and he refused. Then the speech was over. The photographer focused on Mr Molotov and swore when a translator appeared. Twenty minutes later, however, this chore was done and Mr Molotov arose. You looked quickly over the expanse of upturned faces for some human oddity to preserve to your deathbed. Mr Molotov looked intently at the delegations. He spoke a few intense, decisive sentences in dramatic, strangulated Russian while the bulbs flashed and the shutters clicked. Then to his side came his translator, a stooping, earnest youth with sandy hair and thick glittering glasses. He gripped the lectern, looked straight ahead, and in his eager treble translated Mr Molotov's historic pronouncement. He said, 'The fifth plenary session is now closed. The next plenary session will be held on Monday at 3 p.m.' The French photographer slumped in total disgust. Everybody got up quietly and left to read the newspapers, nobody pointing a finger at Senator Tom Connally, who it turned out had rashly broken the rumor to the luckless Associated Press. Nor did anybody embarrass the Senator in the slightest way, when he appeared again next time to take his seat at this well-bred assembly, which was then the calm dead center of the world's surrounding fury.

And so it continued for two months while tyrants were butchered and wars ended. The delegates of Europe rose to points of order while disorder lunged across the whole of Europe. They spoke with the correct accompanying gestures of peace and honor, arbitration and justice, while an American Army was forcing the population of Wiesbaden to file through the obscenities of 'extermination camps', while Goebbels was poisoning himself and his children in a cellar in Berlin, while Hitler's own body was burning to ashes, while Marines dazed from the slaughter of Iwo Jima were machine-gunning stubborn Japanese from every foot of soil on Okinawa.

On May 1st, which was a Sunday, I stood again on the same spot at Cypress Point where three years before I had seen a stogie and a fallen gardenia. Then the war was on another planet, to which the gallant cigar-smoker had evidently gone, leaving his bride presumably to the waves. Now the writhing cypresses and the pulverized rocks seemed a part of the universal insanity, a beautiful, normal line of coast twisted with the signature of war. I stood watching the sea thrash against the rocks, and from behind me, from inside a parked car, rose an excited voice. It was radio newscaster Walter Winchell telling of Mussolini and his mistress seized in flight and their corpses being strung up from the beams of a gas station.

Although the Conference had to compete, during its first two weeks, with the collapse of the Nazi armies, it was the great American event. Indeed, at a time when life in Europe and Asia was unpredictable in its violence, San Francisco was an oasis of social comfort and international style. The city had spread itself handsomely. Although it was conspicuously the Twelfth Naval District, the provider of more than 65 percent of the men and supplies for the Pacific, it enjoyed returning to the grandeur of its old hospitality, and the hotels went into a flutter unmatched since Ulysses S. Grant bore down on the Palace with his false teeth missing. Delegates and newsmen received weekly baskets of fruit and nuts and wine culled from the neighboring valleys. They were invited to attend innumerable organized tours of the surrounding magnificence of redwood forests, wine valleys, and mountain parks. The elite of Hollywood and West Coast society descended on the city and swelled the army of accredited press men, which at the beginning was bigger than the number of delegates. The typical elevator load at the bigger hotels in those gala days would find Jan Masaryk, Gracie Allen, Lord Halifax, and Lana Turner rubbing shoulders with General de Gaulle's secretary and the editor of the *New Republic*, without any of them being aware of any other's identity. One night I was going up to my room with a radio commentator, an eccentric French correspondent who always carried a toy lamb, key politician James Aloysius Farley, an Australian sheep-rancher, and the *New York Post*'s saloon editor. It occurred to me that all that was missing was Groucho Marx. But at the seventh floor a small swarthy man with a bald head and wicked glasses stepped out and went off down a corridor with an unmistakable lope. It was, of course, Groucho himself. This circus atmosphere was a strain at best, because ever since Senator Connally's boner, correspondents waited for the imminent victory in Europe like the sleepless neighbor waiting for the other shoe to fall. There was one more trial of nerves before the end came. From Reims on May 7th came a dispatch from the AP's

Edward Kennedy reporting that Germany had on the previous evening signed terms of unconditional surrender at General Eisenhower's headquarters in a little schoolhouse. For twenty-four hours, San Francisco was, like every other capital in the world, harried with rumor that the report was false. It turned out to be true, but by the time – nine o'clock in the morning of May 8th – that President Truman and Prime Minister Churchill had officially proclaimed V-E Day, most people were too frustrated to express wholeheartedly the emotion they had dribbled away through the leaks of rumor. Correspondent Kennedy was then congratulated on a scoop, blamed for a boner, and suspended by Eisenhower when it became known that all fifty-five of the accredited correspondents with Supreme Headquarters Allied Expeditionary Force had the story in their notebooks at the same time as Kennedy but had pledged not to file it until the official word was given. The other fifty-four thereupon wrote Kennedy's journalistic obituary by signing a letter of protest to Eisenhower, in which they described themselves as the honorable victims of 'the most disgraceful, deliberate and unethical double cross in the history of journalism'.

Now that San Francisco was not the only breathing space on the map, and since the Conference was settling down in earnest to the tedious and vital work of amending the Dumbarton Oaks proposals, the 'correspondents' deserted it in hundreds, the celebrities returned to Hollywood and their summer homes.

The War Mobilization Director, Fred M. Vinson, immediately lifted the midnight curfew and the ban on horse-racing, and promised that the housewife would as soon as possible be restored to a refrigerator and vacuum cleaner, and the motorist to more gasoline by the fall at latest. The families of men overseas took up an anxious new game, that of calculating the number of 'points' their boy had scored, which would, according to a new system the Army announced, qualify him to return home quickly. America had now to make the practical distinction between re-conversion to peace and conversion to the Pacific War.

In the West, there could be no doubt which was the more pressing problem. For this was the way the new armies would come, the veterans from Europe, and the arms and oil with them. And the essential problem of reversing the direction of the American supply system fell, of course, into the lap of the railroads. There was a natural American difficulty in that when the railroads were first laid across the continent, the West was conceived as the source of the raw materials the trains would carry east. The West would breed the cattle and the sheep and goats and grow the grain and lumber – for the East. If the industrial East would ship a Western farmer a single combine, he would reciprocate with sixty acres of wheat a day. So the heavy freight would go east, and the railroad tracks were laid accordingly, with the stresses fortified mainly on the western slopes of the mountains, for the strenuous climb east. Now, after V-E Day, the inexhaustible supply of heavy freight had to go west, the ammunition, and the oil trains, as well as the troops and food. The railroads pressed for the release of skilled railroad engineers as the high priority civilians of the Pacific War. So it was that in May and June, hundreds of crews went out building new branch lines and strengthening the tracks on the eastern slopes of the Sierras and the Rockies.

In the East and Midwest, there was an impatience to get back to what the business analysts call 'long-range competition', and impatience tempered by the decent requirements of patriotism and the new slogan, 'On to the Pacific'. Chester Bowles, the head of the Office of Price Administration (OPA), began an unpopular campaign to retain price controls, to remind Americans of the sagging prices after the First World War and then the rush into inflation. But manufacturers, thoroughly jittery before the prospective release into a starved consumer market of 100 billion dollars' worth of surplus war property, were itching to chalk up high prices before the flood came. The War Production Board offered them a few crumbs of comfort by announcing that small firms would be given special access to raw materials, and that after July 1st business would have unrestricted right to all but war priority steel, copper, and aluminum.

In Washington, the President was buckling down with what seemed like elaborate foresight to the inevitable problems of mass unemployment, but the air was sweet with applause for victory and the homecoming Eisenhower. And as one Southern Congressman put it, 'Truman's wearing the Roosevelt mantle a little too literally; there'll be time for social security headaches and unemployment legislation when the next term begins.' The popular impression that the news-papers presented was that the President was being an obedient and genial servant of his Congress and that the honeymoon between them would continue serenely through the summer. In fact, the President made earnest recommendations to Congress several times a week, but his diligence was put down to a lively Executive conscience, and neither the Congress nor the public was disposed to fuss over the issues they ignored. Rarely can a bridegroom have been so constantly rebuffed in his wooing and yet manage to convey the notion that the honeymoon was proceeding in unruffled bliss. Before the end of July, the President wrote to Congressional committees on every issue that was later to divide the country. He asked to have state unemployment benefits boosted with federal supplements. He asked to have sixty-five cents declared the basic wage rate. He asked for a permanent Fair Employment Practices Commission to fight racial discrimination when the scramble for jobs began. He pleaded for a full-employment program. He asked for $75 million to start state and city public works projects.

But Congress was evidently not going to commit itself to any fund-amental peacetime legislation without knowing better how much longer the United States would be at war. As it appeared later, the President had in July a shockingly accurate idea of how long that would be, but he could not advertise to Congress the urgency of his reasons. As it was, the heat was steaming up over the District of Columbia swamp and Congress was impatient to capitulate to the mosquitoes and head for home. Accordingly, it did nothing about these requests, except cut the appropriation for state- and local-sponsored public works to less than a quarter of the amount he had asked. Congress waited for Mr Truman to fly back from San Fran-cisco with the Charter of the United Nations in his pocket, and to offer it as the best that could be done. ('The choice is not between this charter and something else. It is between this charter and no charter at all.') The deceptive harmony of San Francisco, which had been that of a conference of doctors pledging themselves to keep the world in permanent health but agreeing not to mention any of the specific diseases that wracked the security of millions, now passed over to the Senate. While the Senate Foreign Relations Committee was favorably studying the Charter, the first troopships were coming home from Europe, the railroads forbade overnight reservations for civilians traveling less than 450 miles, and – with Okinawa conquered, though at prodigious cost – an armada of 2,000 planes attacked Japan, 1,000 of them flying from the carriers of a fleet moving off the Japanese mainland. The Navy had the audacity to publish lists of the fighting ships engaged in this action. With these good tidings moderating the dripping heat of midsummer, the Senate made only a token effort to oppose the Charter. The last masterstroke of Franklin Roosevelt, in appointing a powerful old Republican Isolationist to the American delegation at San Francisco, paid off more handsomely than the Administration dared hope, for Senator Vandenberg arose in the Senate like the prodigal son, repenting of his old ways and confessing his new belief that 'we cannot live unto ourselves alone.' From Michigan rang out the baritone of defeated Republican presidential candidate Thomas Dewey singing, 'Ratify!' and at once the voices of forty-one Governors rose in close harmony. The angel of peace, hovering over Washington in the dog days, must have been a forlorn maiden crying, 'Woe unto me when all men praise me.' What followed in the Senate can hardly be given the name of debate. Only Senator J. W. Fulbright struck some unsporting discords, suggesting that the speeches did not express the actual conflict that the Senate would expose when it became clear, sometime in the future, that peace could not be bought with such easy, fair words. From a sickbed in California and across the twenty-five years that separated Woodrow Wilson's denouement from this debate, Senator Hiram Johnson raised a feeble 'No!' On the last Saturday in July, the Senate ratified the charter 89 to 2 and received the cabled blessing of the President from a meeting at Potsdam with Marshal Stalin and the new British Premier Clement Attlee. But that afternoon, a B-25 bomber flying from Bedford, Massachusetts, to Newark, and unheeding the advice of the control tower operator at La Guardia Field, flew through a high mist straight into the Empire State Building. This crash, the grotesque fulfillment of every child's naïve fear, stole the headlines from the Senate's passing of the Charter.

Then Congress went home to enjoy like other men the promise of more rayon, more rubber, more wood, more cotton goods, more refrigerators, more 'beverage alcohol'; to ponder the reintroduction of 'socialism by free choice' as the new slogan of the revived American Communist Party; to weigh the stock issue of Henry Kaiser who announced the formation of a new corporation to produce two modern automobiles, the lightweight Kaiser and the heavyweight Frazer; and to feel out the sentiment of 'the grass roots' about the re-conversion program it would get down to in the fall. At this point, at the very end of July, a snub was administered to the government so damning and so all-inclusive that it would have aroused the liberal press to orgies of recrimination if it had been uttered by a Republican. It was, however, contained in an official government report, and consequently attracted only passing popular attention. The old Truman Committee, whose wartime chore had been the energetic biting of the hand that fed it, issued its fourth annual report under the chairmanship of Senator Mead of New York. It was a study of re-conversion, and in it the government clearly took sides in the bristling controversy that had up to then been kept alive by two opposing schools of thought.

One school of economists said that for at least five years after the war's end, American industry would comfortably take up the slack of war-plant unemployment by making the automobiles, the refrigerators, the washing machines that were the profitable feed-line of American mass production. It pointed to the great backlog of demand for these things, and when asked where was the money to buy them triumphantly referred to the 140 billion dollars' worth of savings in American pockets.

The other school foresaw a slow, tough time immediately ahead when the returning soldiers would be hunting for regular jobs and maintained that hungry men do not buy refrigerators or automobiles. It predicted the likelihood of mass unemployment and inflation in the coincidence of two facts: in the inability of private industry to float the huge amounts of capital necessary to run the factories the government had built for war production, and in the existence of that same 140 billion dollars' worth of private savings. The unprecedented reserve of money in private pockets it regarded not as a boon to the manufacturer dangling his new gadgets for sale, but as the fertile seed of inflation. This school said that luxury prices would be forced on to scarce commodities that to Americans are bare necessities.

The Mead Report on the whole took the depressing view of the second school. It roundly blamed the Office of War Mobilization, and by implication Secretary of State Byrnes and Secretary Vinson, for failing to give quick help to reconverting private business. It blamed the War Manpower Commission for 'wholly inadequate handling of America's labor supply'. It blamed the War Department for setting up great reserves of troops in the Pacific that 'it cannot hope to use . . . except in the event of an almost disastrous military setback'. It blamed both management and labor for a deep friction of which numerous wildcat strikes were only a surface sign. It blamed the War Surpluses Board for making ineffective plans to absorb into a stable economy the Army and Navy surpluses. It saw a genuine peril of runaway inflation in the lavish money being laid out for 'the small amount of goods you can buy'. It concluded that if the war in the Pacific were to end soon, 'the United States would find itself largely unprepared to overcome unemployment on a large scale.'

But this sounded like a conscientious end-of-term report, and although the Twentieth Air Force announced a complete blockade of shipping to and from the Japanese home islands, the main campaign of the remaining war seemed only just under way, and the battlefield still extended across thousands of miles of land and ocean, from Luzon to Kwangsi Province, from Lower Burma to Honshu Island. Some of the bolder Washington strategists suggested the spring of 1946 as the date of deliverance; some radio smart alecks believed, for mystical reasons known only to their hunches, that it might be all over by Christmas.

Then on Monday, August 6th, the President and the War Department announced that the American air force had dropped an 'atomic bomb' on Hiroshima, Japan. It is fair to say that to the overwhelming mass of Americans the bald statement alone, coming over the radio, did not suggest any other appropriate reaction than the vague feeling that, as with the first news of the bombing of the vaguely located Pearl Harbor, one ought to be impressed. But by nightfall the radio was playing up the new word 'atomic' with all the esoteric fervor of a Second Adventist. Next morning, the newspaper presses again pulled out their banner headlines, and one Broadway character emitted from a vacuum of stupefied ignorance the general suspicion: 'It's dynamite.' The War Department confirmed this hope by adding that the new bomb had more power than 20,000 tons of TNT, was 2,000 times as powerful as the most monstrous British blockbuster. Then did the newspapers begin a terrified and exhilarated campaign of education the like of which had not been seen in the American press since it had had to rewrite the history of British constitutional monarchy as the sub-plot to the romantic demarche of Edward VIII.

The more exhaustively the story was explained, the more cryptic did it become. In some infinitely intricate way, Lord Rutherford tinkering in his laboratory in Manchester, England, decades ago, was experimenting with the dissolution of Hirohito's divinity. The expulsion from Germany of a non-Aryan woman, a Dr Lise Meitner, had assured the Allies the inhuman victory. A group of scientists meeting on the sagebrush desert of New Mexico three weeks before had blown into invisible air the experimental tower they had assembled with infinite care and thus apparently proved that a half-tumbler of water would be able, in the foreseeable future, to drive the *Queen Elizabeth* five times around the world. Scientifically minded amateurs were instantly at home with this challenge of paper propositions, and in no time at all a reader was writing to the *New York Times* questioning the statement 'that on energy released from a cup of water, a 100,000-kilowatt capacity station could operate for one year . . . I find the station could operate for 6.78 years.'

What the ordinary reader could appreciate and tremble at was the War Department story of the industrial organization that for three years had preceded this historic blast: the keeping of the knowledge from all but about 200 of the 300,000 workers engaged in it, the virtual internment of these workers in two secret factories, one in Tennessee, the other in Washington, and at a secret physics research laboratory in New Mexico. The identification tags of the Army and civilian scientists bestowed on them such titles as Wolf, Lone Ranger, and Big Chief. ('Sorry,' one imagined a Nobel prizewinner saying over the telephone in his wife's hearing, 'the Lone Ranger has gone to Chicago.') In the contemplative moments that followed this manic absorption, it was not difficult to be moved in a human way by the account of the New Mexico test, in which when the bomb went off 'the whole country was lighted by a searing light with an intensity many times that of the midday sun.' A blind girl ninety miles away looked up and said the most dramatic sentence of the war: 'What was that?' Thirty seconds after the flash of light came a 'strong sustained awesome roar which warned of doomsday', and in this moment celebrated scientists embraced each other. Man had now attained the knowledge for his own split-second destruction.

After this, there was hardly any 'event' worth the name. On the Wednesday, 40,000 feet below the mushroom cloud where nineteenth-century man lived, the Russians had jumped into the war, advancing across the Manchurian border. On the Thursday, a second atomic bomb was dropped on the naval base of Nagasaki. On the Friday, the Swiss government transmitted to the State Department an offer to surrender, if the Emperor might stay in power. The President accepted the offer, and then for one last weekend millions of the Allied peoples, the armies still in Europe, the flyers still taking off from carriers of the Pacific Fleet were put on the rack of the enemy's hesitation. At last, at seven o'clock in the evening of Tuesday, August 14th, the President called the correspondents to the White House and read aloud a reply that 'I deem full acceptance of the Potsdam Declaration, which specifies the unconditional surrender of Japan.' The country, with what nervous energy was still on tap, blew its top in thousands of tons of ticker-tape, millions of tooting automobile horns, oceans of liquor, the bending of many knees, the tense, uninhibited embrace of countless girls and sailors in public squares, main streets, the tops of trucks and buses.

In the exultant, uncertain calm between August 14th and the surrender ceremonies aboard the battleship *Missouri,* normalcy flashed back on the United States with all the condensed brilliance of a drowning man's memory. The tabloids returned to headlines about strikes, divorces, and hurricanes, and the newsreels to pictures of train wrecks, beauty contests, and footballers in training. The President of the United States was photographed in a Shriner's fez.

Already the wounding memory of the war was blurring into convalescence, and we found ourselves graveled to recall the name of the disease itself. Editors and publishers debated whether it should be 'the late War' or 'World War II' or 'the recent war'. Through some natural impulse toward health and survival, most minds wrote *finis* to the sufferings that knew no end. Now the 22 million homeless of China, drifting back in search of a hearth, were a statistic for a history class. Now the intense agony of the Jews, the putrescence of Europe's courage and mind and body, the London Blitz and Stalingrad, Rudolph Hess and Mussolini, Midway and the Bridge at Remagen, the *Renown* and the *Athenia*, the blight of Rotterdam and the opulence of Lisbon, Mr Kurusu and Lord Haw-Haw, waited only for the official word to be filed away as business completed.

But what was behind was also ahead – the necessary food for Europe; the need to re-educate the adolescents of Germany, to float a loan to Britain, to plan the modern history of Japan; to re-house the one-half and one-third and two-thirds of the winning and the losing nations; above all, in America, the need to synchronize the American fact of an average wage of $1,100 a year with the American myth that all Americans can make a million bucks.

All the undefeatable human aggressions would push on, the search for power disguised as justice, the doctrine of self-determination, the cyclical re-juggling of economics, the practise of diplomacy, the pride of sovereignty, all the vital distractions that permit most men to postpone for a lifetime the business of living.

And there lay ahead a profound new doubt, which among some poetic souls was the vague perception that we had baited the gods and earned the restless anxiety of Prometheus. Politicians knew they would now be dependent on bland little scientists whom they secretly distrusted, as a loud and vivacious youth must obey a neat mother.

We knew this and hoped it wasn't so, and drowned our doubts in the parades, the welcoming home of the brash troopships sailing lustily into ports, the visible signs that the complexity of life was behind us. Wistfully, on September 2nd, we turned to look across the Pacific to our shining battlewagon in Tokyo Bay and yearned to say 'amen' to General MacArthur as he faced the meek overlords of Japan and barked around the world, 'These proceedings – are closed.'

Envoi

During the 1940s Alistair Cooke became a regular contributor to the established BBC radio programme *American Commentary*. His contributions intensified as events unfolded once the United States entered the war. Such was the success of these broadcasts that the BBC commissioned Cooke's own weekly talks as *American Letter*, which in 1950 became the legendary *Letter from America*. In his broadcasts Cooke would occasionally refer back to the key experiences during his journey across America. Reprinted here is his broadcast for *American Commentary* on July 2, 1943 – an eve of Independence Day letter that powerfully conveyed what the Americans were doing for the war.

American Commentary: On Circuit
Alistair Cooke   July 2nd, 1943

For Home and Empire Services

  A couple of weeks ago I stepped off a train in
New York. I had gone 'round and across the
American continent, and I was back where I
started. If you had met me then, and said to me,
'It must have been exciting, what was it like?' –
well, I will try in a few minutes to tell you
some of the things it was like.
  You have heard a lot about America in the past
three years, and perhaps rather too much of
Washington and New York. Since 1939 it has been

hard, and at times embarrassing, to say what America was doing for the war. To you, who had lost your homes and the people you loved, it was hard to talk of American sacrifice. It must have seemed as if we were asking you to take out your handkerchief and weep for a very rich man who had mislaid a favorite diamond ring. Even very early last year, it was the same America, the same landscape; the automobile highways were getting emptier every day; the boy next door went into the army; you heard about small farming towns here and there turning into smokeless powder factories. But last year, however much people felt about the war, or didn't, there <u>was</u> one big and obvious fact. Industry and agriculture were <u>committed</u> to the war and all their brains and investment were going into it. This was something the civilian didn't quite see, until suddenly this year the war took him by the scruff of the neck and moved him across this continent wherever the Army, or war industry or farming needed him. Now this year you <u>can</u> talk about American sacrifice and really mean all sorts of strange and inspiring things that have a special American twist, that are different from the sacrifices of countries which have, for instance, only one climate.

For example, you have known for a long time the minor hardships of traveling by train in wartime. But at least you have the consolation that not many railway journeys in England take two or three or four days, or even an overnight trip. I would pack my bags to leave Tucson, Arizona and get to the station at midnight - the train was meant to leave at eleven o'clock. At one-thirty the great monster came roaring into the station. There were hundreds of people on the platform,

sailors, wives and soldiers, a few Mexicans, a
Chinese or two, long-legged Western girls dressed
in gay colors, shuffling negro porters,
government service men. They all surged forward
to board the train. Then a voice booms out –
'Attention. Train No. 5, the Thunderbolt, now
arriving on track two for Phoenix, Yuma, Los
Angeles and points west. All civilian
accommodation cancelled on this train. Will the
two hundred Selective Service men line up
opposite the subway enclosure. The Californian
will arrive in one hour.' The Thunderbolt shot
into the west. So we waited for another hour,
then sat up all night, then waited until all the
soldiers were fed before we could eat. It's good
to treat civilians like that. In America it's
new, and very cheering.

Then you have heard that Americans haven't got
the petrol they used to have, and maybe you think
this means that the poor things will have to do
without a picnic. But consider that everywhere
west of the Mississippi, cities were built on the
assumption that the only way a human moved was by
motor car. A rancher in West Texas said he was
going to have to work on horseback, for the first
time in fifteen years. Then out on the Great
Plains I stood with a sheep rancher in Wyoming
and he looked over his workshop – it was all the
sweeping, rolling shortgrassed earth between him
and the horizon. He had a rationing form from
Washington in his hand. He looked at it
forlornly. He said, 'It says here, to share your
car with your neighbor. My neighbor lives 97
miles away'.

You may have heard too that the workers in
shipyards and aircraft factories are producing
thousands of torpedo boats and Liberty ships and

four-motored bombers. And so they are. You may
also have heard that they're all living the life
of Riley. Well, a month ago I spoke with a
family, one of hundreds of families living and
working on the damp, hot Gulf Coast of
Mississippi. This family of four was making over
forty pounds a week. But they are in a town that
simply can't house ten times its normal
population. So what does this family's money buy
for it? Well it buys them a tent with a dirt floor
and no lighting and no heat. If they'd gone back
home, to Dallas, Texas, they would have earned a
fifth of what they earn now. But they'd have had
comforts they'll never know till the war's over.
Well, they aren't going home. They'll stick it
out and bring up their children in a tent or
trailer. That, too, is sacrifice.

Or let your mind fly four thousand miles north
and west to the beautiful Cascade and Bitterroot
mountains, and all the drenching green valleys
of Oregon and Washington, where noble Douglas
firs stand across the tops of mountains almost
like avenues of cathedrals. Here is the greatest
congregation of trees in the Western hemisphere.
You'd think that one thing these people wouldn't
lack is wood. You can't buy a stick of wood to
make a toy for your child. When I was there, the
Navy had just gratefully received eleven million
tons of lumber. In the golden Sacramento Valley,
in California, last year, I saw vast fields
flooded and rice being sown - by airplane -
pretty tricky work. You have to skim parallel to
the land not much more than a few yards above
it. They used to lose good flyers. This year I
went back . . . the man I knew who sowed rice
there, and who had never been outside
California, this year used the same low-flying

technique to fly wounded over the barren hills
of North Africa.

There is today no part of America where you can
expect the landscape to look the way it looked
last year. I drove last year through an orchard
in Georgia - a pecan nut orchard, five miles long.
Today, the earth has been ravished by tractors
and bulldozers, and planes sit out there in the
sun, wings touching, like battalions of
bluebottles.

Maybe you have heard some of these things. But
too often the news that's cabled across the ocean
is the people's outcry against a new regulation
from Washington. This is because Americans
temperamentally don't like much government . . .
they think of it as a healthy man thinks of a
surgeon's knife. And when somebody tries to
ration their life, their liberty, and their
pursuit of happiness, they feel that they're
being forcibly plumped on an operating table. You
in Britain have the fine habit of grumbling.
Americans howl. They are as convinced as you are
that the operation is essential to their future
health. But they howl for the record.
Unfortunately, a howl travels across the Atlantic
louder and clearer than a deep conviction of a
hundred and thirty million people. Dr Goebbels
says Americans are mad at the war. Dr Goebbels is
right. But he left out an essential word.
Americans are fighting mad.

They transform a farm the size of Surrey into a
tank training ground. They tear up the sagebrush
from a desert the size of Yorkshire to make an
air base. And if you ask them how many planes
will fly out of here, the number is enough to make
you fall in a dead faint; enough to make Hitler
speed up his plans to abdicate. And when you ask

why they need yet another airfield in a region of the country that breeds airplanes like flies, they say – 'This is one of the air bases we'll use in 1945 or 6.'

They have changed the look of their vast and beautiful landscape; they have set in motion a migration of working populations unequalled since the pioneers walked across the West. They have nine million men tanned, and tough and confident, ready to bounce into action against the anxious armies of the Axis.

They are doing this because they cherish fiercely the things that their nation stood for when it was created a hundred and sixty-seven years ago, and that it stands for now. The boys in the Pacific, one of them said, are fighting for blueberry pie. That's a little thing they don't intend to lose. There are some big things, the right to vote into power any man or government they want. The right to live in their own house and bring their children up as they please, and go fishing on Sunday, and pitch horseshoes, and say what's on their mind whether Washington agrees or not.

And on the eve of Independence Day, this is what the New World, with its blood, its humor, and its roaring energy, is fighting for.

Children in a Japanese-American relocation camp in
Owens Valley, California, 1942

Alistair Cooke fishing in Montana

Alistair Cooke at work in his
Manhattan apartment, 1942

Harry Truman addressing the United Nations organizing conference
in San Francisco on its closing day, June 26, 1945.

Index

abolitionism, 261
accommodation, shortage of, 45
Adolphus, 50
advertising
    Florida tourist, 66
    highway signs, 30, 36–7, 49, 65,
        70, 96, 132–3, 216
    religious, 37, 68
    'Remember Pearl Harbor', 57
Aetna Life Insurance, 253–8
African Americans. *See* Negroes
agriculture
    cattle, 104–5, 106, 210, 212, 213
    citrus fruit, 77–80
    cotton cultivation, 65, 96–7,
        108–9, 120
    dairy, 226–8
    date growing, 126–7, 136
    effect of war on, 134–6, 156–7,
        213, 227
    fruit, 133–7
    irrigation farming, 119–20
    labor problems, 184–5
    lettuce crop, 153–4
    peanut production, 58–60
    quotas, 56
    sheep farming, 199, 200
    sorghum, 50
    soybeans, 59
    subsidies, 210
    sugar crop, 50, 92, 94, 136, 187,
        203
    tenant farmers, 36–7
    tobacco cultivation, 39
    unions, 219–20
    wheat, 209, 211, 213
Agriculture, Commissioner of, 50
Agriculture, Department of, 19, 22,
    36, 56, 58, 79, 105, 203,
    210
Air Corps Officer Candidate School,
    70, 73
Air Corps Replacement and Train-
    ing Center, 70, 73
Air Corps Technical Training
    School, Biloxi, 88
air-raid wardens, 34–5, 97, 218
air raids, 55, 61–2, 83
aircraft production, 128, 131–2,
    234–9, 307–8
Ajo copper mine, 116–17
Akron, Ohio, 245
Albany, Oregon, 173
All-American Canal, 123
Alpine, Texas, 106–8
ambulance drivers, 90
American Cargo War Risk
    Reinsurance Exchange, 256
American Civil War, 29, 51–2, 104,
    258

Farm Bureau Federation, 220
Farm Security Administration,
    58–9, 84
Farmers Union, 219
Farmington, Minnesota, 221
federal administration, suspicion of,
    83
federal benefits, 56
Federal Housing Authority, 97, 243
fire, risk of, 153, 170
first-aid training, 90
First World War, 68, 69, 191, 241
fishing, commercial, 133
Florida
    Army takes over Miami hotels,
        70–74
    cattle, 104
    citrus country, 77–81
    civil defense, 83
    climate, 70
    the Everglades, 75–6
    Gulf Coast, 85–7
    hotel room prices, 74
    military population, 67–8, 85
    Negro population, 83–4, 87
    peninsula, 68–70
    prostitution, 67–8
    sponge-fishing fleet, 81–2
    tourism, 66, 71–2, 284
    turpentine production, 67
    West Coast, 73
Florida barge canal, 91–2
food
    black market, 284
    canning, 134–5
    cheese, 226
    chess pie, 38
    crayfish bisque, 95
    crop, 1942, 19
    dehydration, 135
    fruit grading, 135–6

hot and spicy, 86
    meat consumption, 105
    rationing, 36
    US Army waste, 151
food lockers, 156
food-production loans, 59
Ford, Henry, 234, 238–40, 242
foreign correspondents, 52–3, 54–5
Forest Products Laboratory, 224,
    228
forest rangers, 152–3
Forever Ulysses (Rodocanachi),
    81–2
Fort Barrancas, Florida, 86
Fort Morgan, Colorado, 205
Fox, Captain, 24–5
Friant Dam, 166
Fulbright, Senator J. W., 299
Fullerton, Calif., 133–4

Gallatin Valley, Montana, 193
Garces, Father Francisco, 124
Gary, Indiana, 162, 233, 244
gasoline, 97–8, 169, 198, 215, 268
Georgia
    Coastal Plain, 65–6
    economic occupation of, 61
    landscape, 58, 60, 308
    peanut production, 58–60
    Piedmont, 63–5
    state politics, 62–3
Georgia Experimental Station, 63
German-Americans, 99, 229–30
Germany, 51, 117, 285
Gila-Salt River, 119–20
Glasgow, Kentucky, 49
Glass, Carter, 12
goats, 106–7
gold mining, 165
Gomez, Izzy, 159
Good Humor ice cream, 149–50

Tennessee
American Civil War in, 51–2
attitudes to the war, 53–8
backcountry, 50–51
Tennessee Valley Authority, 56, 183, 184, 206
terpenes, 80
Terry, Eliphalet, 257
Texas
cattle, 104–5, 106
cotton, 96–7, 108–9
fall, 250
feel of, 96
German population, 99
goats, 106–7
Mexican population, 107–8, 109–10
military population, 101–2
Negro population, 98–9
oil production, 97–8, 198
prostitution, 102
shipping, 96–7
Texan identity, 100
western, 103–13, 307
Time, on the US Navy, 5, 7
tin, shortage of, 135
tobacco cultivation, 39
Tobacco Road (play), 50
Tocqueville, Alexis de, 52–3
Toledo, Ohio, 244, 245, 246
trains, artificiality of picture produced, 124
Truman, Harry, 240, 288, 290–91, 297, 298, 303
Tucson, Arizona, 113–16
Tugman, Bill, 170
Tugwell, Rexford, 210
turpentine production, 67

Umpqua River, 170
unemployment, 301

unions, 56, 84, 97, 109, 177–8, 219–20, 223, 235–6, 239, 264, 267
United Automobile Workers Union, 235–6, 239
United Nations, 285, 291–2, 298–9
US Army
accommodation rates, 74
discipline, 64
enlistments, 89
fruit demands, 135–6, 150
Negro troops, 205
occupation of Palm Springs hotels, 125–6
takes over Miami hotels, 70–74
waste food, 151
US Coast Guard, 278–9
US Navy
and the attack on Pearl Harbor, 7
confidence in, 5
and Dartmouth College, 270–71
landing barges, 93
recruits, 105–6, 218
Twelfth Naval District, 160
Utah, 116, 142

Valentine, 108
Vallejo, Calif., 164
Vandenberg, Arthur, 293, 299
Vantage, Washington, 181
venereal disease, 68
Vermont, 266–9, 271–5
Vinson, Fred M., 296, 301
Virginia Military Institute, 29–30

wages, 57, 109, 121, 141, 174, 179, 184, 192, 200, 205, 213, 298, 304, 307–8
Wages and Hours Act, 171
Walker, Captain Sam, 258
Wallace, Idaho, 185–6